POINTERS ON C

KENNETH A. REEK

ROCHESTER INSTITUTE OF TECHNOLOGY

ADDISON-WESLEY

An imprint of Addison Wesley Longman, Inc.

Reading, Massachusetts • Harlow, England • Menlo Park, California
Berkeley, California • Don Mills, Ontario • Sydney • Bonn • Amsterdam
Tokyo • Mexico City

Associate Editor: Deborah Lafferty
Production Editor: Amy Willcutt
Marketing: Amy Cronin
Copyeditor: Karen Jolie
Proofreader: Lorraine Ferrier
Cover Designer: Diana Coe

Library of Congress Cataloging-in-Publication Data
Reek, Kenneth A.
    Pointers on C / Kenneth A. Reek.
      p.   cm.
    Includes bibliographical references and index.
    ISBN 0-673-99986-6
     1. C (Computer program language)
I. Title   97-10744
QA76.73.C15R44   1998   CIP
005.13'3—DC21

Reproduced by Addison-Wesley from camera-ready copy supplied by the author.

Cover image © Gregory Voth /SIS

Access the latest information about Addison-Wesley titles from our World Wide Web site:
http://www.awl.com/cseng

Reprinted with corrections, July 1998.

To my wife, Margaret

Preface

Why Another C Book?

There are many good C books on the market; why do we need another one? In my ten years of teaching a college-level course on C programming, I have yet to find a book that covers pointers the way I would like. Many books cover pointers in a single chapter dedicated to the topic, often late in the book. It is not enough to describe the syntax of pointers and show only simple examples of their use. I discuss pointers early and often. I describe their effective use in various contexts and show programming idioms in which they appear. I discuss related issues of program efficiency versus maintainability. Pointers are a thread that is woven throughout this book.

Why are pointers so important? My belief is that pointers are what gives C its power. Pointers allow the C programmer to implement many tasks more efficiently than is possible in other languages, and to perform some tasks, such as accessing the hardware directly, that are impossible in other languages. A thorough knowledge of pointers, then, is a prerequisite to becoming a good C programmer.

However, the power of pointers comes with a price. You can cut wood faster with a chain saw than with a nail file, but the chain saw can injure you a lot more seriously, and more quickly. Pointers are like the chain saw. Used correctly, they can simplify the implementation of an algorithm as well as make it more efficient. Used incorrectly, they can be the cause of errors that exhibit subtle and confusing symptoms and are thus extremely difficult to find. An incomplete understanding of pointers is dangerous because it invariably leads to pain rather than pleasure. This book gives you the depth of knowledge in pointers that you need to avoid the pain.

Why Learn C?

Why is the C language still so popular? Historically, industry has embraced C for a number of reasons. Among these are its efficiency; good C programs can be nearly as efficient as assembly language programs, but they are considerably easier to develop. C gives programmers more control over where data is stored and how it is initialized than many languages do. C's lack of "safety net" features also contributes to its efficiency, but increases the likelihood of errors. For example, subscripts to arrays and accesses through pointers are not checked for validity, which saves time but makes it much more important that these features be used correctly. If the language is used with discipline, the potential problems can be avoided.

The rich collection of operators provided in C give the programmer power to efficiently perform low-level computations, such as shifting and masking, without resorting to assembly language. This ability has prompted many to characterize C as being a "high-level" assembly language. However, when needed, C programs can interface easily with assembly language. These characteristics make C a good choice for implementing operating systems and software for embedded controllers.

Another reason for its popularity is its ubiquity. C compilers are widely available for a great number of machines. In addition, the ANSI Standard improves the portability of C programs among different machines.

Finally, C is the foundation upon which C++ is built. C++ provides a different view of program design and implementation than C. Nevertheless, a thorough knowledge of C skills and techniques, such as using pointers and the standard library, will also be useful for the C++ programmer.

Who Should Use this Book?

This book is not an introductory text on programming. It is intended for people who already have some programming experience and wish to learn C without being held back by discussions of why loops are important or when to use an `if` statement.

On the other hand, I assume that the reader has no prior knowledge of C. I cover all of its many aspects. This broad coverage makes the book useful for both students and professionals, that is, for programmers first learning C and more experienced users wishing to improve their command of the language.

The better C++ textbooks concentrate on issues relating to the Object-Oriented (OO) paradigm, such as class design, rather than fundamental C techniques, and rightly so. But C++ is built upon C—the fundamental skills are still important, particularly for those implementing reusable classes. While

C++ programmers using this book will be able to skip some familiar material, they will also find a wealth of useful C tools and techniques.

Organization of the Book

The book is organized as a tutorial for people with prior programming experience. It is written in the style of a mentor looking over your shoulder and giving you tips and advice. My goal is to pass along the kind of knowledge and insight that ordinarily takes years of experience with the language to attain. This organization influences the ordering of the material—topics are generally introduced and explained completely in one place. Thus, the book is also useful as a reference.

There are two notable exceptions to this organization. The first is pointers, which are discussed in many different contexts throughout the book. The second is Chapter 1, which gives a quick introduction to the basics of the language. The introduction helps get you started writing simple programs quickly. The topics it presents are covered more thoroughly in subsequent chapters.

The book is more verbose in many areas than other texts, usually to provide the depth in a topic that you would otherwise get only from experience. In addition, I use a few examples that are not often seen in real programs. Though they may be obscure, these examples shed light on interesting aspects of the language.

ANSI C

This text describes ANSI C, as defined by ANSI/ISO 9899–1990 [ANSI 90] and described by [KERN 89]. I choose this dialect of C for two reasons: it is the successor to and has essentially replaced the older C (sometimes referred to as Kernighan and Ritchie [KERN 78] or K&R C), and it is the foundation upon which C++ is built. All of the examples in this book are written in ANSI C. I will often refer to the ANSI C standards document as simply "the Standard."

Typography

Syntax descriptions, such as the following example, and function prototypes are shown on a light gray background to help make them easy to find when you need them later.

```
if( expression )
        statement
else
        statement
```

Four typefaces are used in the syntax descriptions. Code that must be written exactly as shown (such as the keyword `if` in this example) is set in `Courier`. Abstract descriptions of required code (such as `expression` above) appear in `Courier Italic`. Some statements also have optional parts. Code that you must write exactly as shown if you decide to use the optional part (for example, the `else` keyword) is shown in **`Courier Bold`**, and abstract descriptions of optional parts (the second **`statement`** above) appear in ***`Courier Bold-Italic`***. New terms are introduced with *Helvetica Italic*.

Complete programs are numbered and displayed in the format shown in Program 0.1. The caption gives the title of the program. The filename in which the source code can be found appears beneath the right-hand corner—these files are available from the Addison Wesley Longman web site.

 This margin symbol indicates a programming tip. Many of these tips are discussions of good programming techniques—ways to make programs easier to write and easier to read and understand later. Often a little extra effort when a program is first written can yield large time savings later when the program must be modified. Other tips will help you write code that is more compact or efficient.

Other tips deal with software engineering issues. C was designed long before modern principles of software engineering evolved. Thus, some language features and common techniques are now discouraged by these principles. The issue is often the tradeoffs between the efficiency of a certain construct and its effect on the readability and maintainability of the code. The

```
/*
** Comment describing what the function or program does.
*/

void
function(){
        /* something or other */
}
```

Program 0.1   Sample program listing   filename.c

discussions will give you the background you need to help you decide whether the gain in efficiency justifies the loss of these other qualities.

Pay close attention when you see this symbol: I am pointing out one of the mistakes that beginning (and sometimes experienced) C programmers often make or something that does not work as you might expect it to. The caution sign makes these hints hard to miss and easy to find later.

This symbol indicates a discussion of an important difference between ANSI C and K&R C. Although most programs written in K&R C should run with only minor modification in ANSI C environments, you might some day run into a pre-ANSI compiler or encounter an older program written for one. The differences will then be important.

Finally, I typeset the book myself using lwroff, a troff clone that I wrote, and I uploaded the resulting PostScript files to the publisher. Thus, the final responsibility for any errors in the book is mine. I would appreciate receiving mail about errors or other correspondence at kar@cs.rit.edu.

Chapter Questions and Programming Exercises

Each chapter ends with a selection of questions and programming exercises. The questions range from simple syntax problems to discussions of more complex issues such as tradeoffs between efficiency and maintainability. The programming exercises have been rated for their difficulty: ★ is easiest and ★★★★★ is most difficult. Many of these exercises have been class tested for many years. The symbol ⬧ before the number of a question or exercise means that a solution for it appears in the Appendix. The remaining solutions are found in the *Instructor's Guide*.

Supplementary Materials

Addison Wesley Longman maintains a World Wide Web site for this book. Its URL is http://www.awl.com/cseng/titles/0-673-99986-6/. The site includes copies of the numbered programs in the book, organized by chapter. The latest errata list is also available. Contact your Addison Wesley Longman representative to get the *Instructor's Guide*, which contains the answers to the remaining questions and programming exercises.

Software for automated submission and testing of student programs on UNIX systems [REEK 89, REEK 96] is available free for educational users via anonymous ftp from ftp.cs.rit.edu in the directory pub/kar/try.

Acknowledgments

I cannot possibly list all the people who contributed to this book, yet I would like to acknowledge and thank all of them. My wife Margaret provided abundant encouragement and moral support, and she patiently put up with the disruptions to our lives that resulted from this work.

I would like to thank Professor Warren Carithers, one of my colleagues at RIT, for proofreading the first draft. His careful critique helped me produce a clear, coherent manuscript from a binder full of lecture notes and examples.

Many thanks to the students in my C Programming Seminar for their assistance in finding typos and suggesting improvements and for putting up with a textbook in draft form. You were my guinea pigs, and your reactions to what I wrote provided valuable feedback that helped me improve the text.

I am indebted to Steve Allan, Bill Appelbe, Richard C. Detmer, Roger Eggen, Joanne Goldenberg, Dan Hinton, Dan Hirschberg, Keith E. Jolly, Joseph F. Kent, Masoud Milani, Steve Summit, and Kanupriya Tewary, who reviewed the book before publication. Their suggestions and insights were a great help in refining my presentation.

Finally, I'd like to express my gratitude to my Editor at Addison-Wesley, Ms. Deborah Lafferty, and my Production Editor, Ms. Amy Willcutt. It is because of these people that this text is a *book* rather than a computer manual. They both gave me many valuable suggestions and encouraged me to change a lot of typography that I thought was fine. Now that I have seen the result, I realize that they were right.

Now it is time to begin. Above all, I hope you have fun learning C!

Churchville, NY

Kenneth A. Reek
`kar@cs.rit.edu`

References

[ANSI 90] 1990. *American National Standard for Programming Languages—
     C.* ANSI/ISO 9899–1990. New York, NY: American National Standards Institute.

[KERN 89] Kernighan, Brian and Dennis Ritchie. 1989. *The C Programming Language, Second Edition.* Englewood Cliffs, NJ: Prentice Hall.

[KERN 78] Kernighan, Brian and Dennis Ritchie. 1978. *The C Programming*

Language. Englewood Cliffs, NJ: Prentice Hall.

[REEK 89] Reek, Kenneth A. 1989. "The TRY System—or—How to Avoid Testing Student Programs." *Proceedings of the Twentieth SIGCSE Technical Symposium on Computer Science Education* Volume 21: 112–116.

[REEK 96] Reek, Kenneth A. 1996. "A Software Infrastructure to Support Introductory Computer Science Courses." *Proceedings of the Twenty Seventh SIGCSE Technical Symposium on Computer Science Education* Volume 28: 125–129.

Table of Contents

Chapter 17: *Classic Abstract Data Types* 493

1

A Quick Start

1.1 Introduction

It is always difficult to start describing a programming language because little details do not make much sense until one knows enough to understand the "big picture." In this chapter, I try to give you a glimpse of the big picture by looking at a sample program and explaining its workings line by line. This sample program also shows you how familiar procedures are accomplished in C. This information plus the other topics discussed in the chapter introduce you to the basics of the C language so that you can begin writing useful programs.

The program we dissect reads text from the standard input, modifies it, and writes it to the standard output. Program 1.1 first reads a list of column numbers. These numbers are pairs and indicate ranges of columns in the input line. The list is terminated with a negative number. The remaining input lines are read and printed, then the selected columns from the input lines are extracted and printed. Note that the first column in a line is number zero. For example, if the input is

```
4 9 12 20 -1
abcdefghijklmnopqrstuvwxyz
Hello there, how are you?
I am fine, thanks.
See you!
Bye
```

then the program would produce:

```
Original input : abcdefghijklmnopqrstuvwxyz
Rearranged line: efghijmnopqrstu
```

1

```
Original input : Hello there, how are you?
Rearranged line: o ther how are
Original input : I am fine, thanks.
Rearranged line:  fine,hanks.
Original input : See you!
Rearranged line: you!
Original input : Bye
Rearranged line:
```

The important point about this program is that it illustrates most of the basic techniques you need to know to begin writing C programs.

```c
/*
** This program reads input lines from the standard input and prints
** each input line, followed by just some portions of the lines, to
** the standard output.
**
** The first input is a list of column numbers, which ends with a
** negative number.  The column numbers are paired and specify
** ranges of columns from the input line that are to be printed.
** For example, 0 3 10 12 -1 indicates that only columns 0 through 3
** and columns 10 through 12 will be printed.
*/

#include <stdio.h>
#include <stdlib.h>
#include <string.h>
#define MAX_COLS        20      /* max # of columns to process */
#define MAX_INPUT       1000    /* max len of input & output lines */

int     read_column_numbers( int columns[], int max );
void    rearrange( char *output, char const *input,
            int n_columns, int const columns[] );

int
main( void )
{
        int     n_columns;              /* # of columns to process */
        int     columns[MAX_COLS];      /* the columns to process */
        char    input[MAX_INPUT];       /* array for input line */
        char    output[MAX_INPUT];      /* array for output line */
```

Program 1.1 Rearrange characters   *continued . . .*

```
        /*
        ** Read the list of column numbers
        */
        n_columns = read_column_numbers( columns, MAX_COLS );

        /*
        ** Read, process and print the remaining lines of input.
        */
        while( gets( input ) != NULL ){
                printf( "Original input : %s\n", input );
                rearrange( output, input, n_columns, columns );
                printf( "Rearranged line: %s\n", output );
        }

        return EXIT_SUCCESS;
}

/*
** Read the list of column numbers, ignoring any beyond the specified
** maximum.
*/
int
read_column_numbers( int columns[], int max )
{
        int     num = 0;
        int     ch;

        /*
        ** Get the numbers, stopping at eof or when a number is < 0.
        */
        while( num < max && scanf( "%d", &columns[num] ) == 1
            && columns[num] >= 0 )
                num += 1;

        /*
        ** Make sure we have an even number of inputs, as they are
        ** supposed to be paired.
        */
        if( num % 2 != 0 ){
                puts( "Last column number is not paired." );
                exit( EXIT_FAILURE );
        }

        /*
        ** Discard the rest of the line that contained the final
```

Program 1.1   Rearrange characters   *continued . . .*

```
        ** number.
        */
        while( (ch = getchar()) != EOF && ch != '\n' )
                ;

        return num;
}


/*
** Process a line of input by concatenating the characters from
** the indicated columns.  The output line is then NUL terminated.
*/
void
rearrange( char *output, char const *input,
    int n_columns, int const columns[] )
{
        int     col;            /* subscript for columns array */
        int     output_col;     /* output column counter */
        int     len;            /* length of input line */

        len = strlen( input );
        output_col = 0;

        /*
        ** Process each pair of column numbers.
        */
        for( col = 0; col < n_columns; col += 2 ){
                int     nchars = columns[col + 1] - columns[col] + 1;

                /*
                ** If the input line isn't this long or the output
                ** array is full, we're done.
                */
                if( columns[col] >= len ||
                    output_col == MAX_INPUT - 1 )
                        break;

                /*
                ** If there isn't room in the output array, only copy
                ** what will fit.
                */
                if( output_col + nchars > MAX_INPUT - 1 )
                        nchars = MAX_INPUT - output_col - 1;

                /*
```

Program 1.1 Rearrange characters   continued . . .

```
                    ** Copy the relevant data.
                    */
                    strncpy( output + output_col, input + columns[col],
                        nchars );
                    output_col += nchars;
            }

        output[output_col] = '\0';
    }
```

Program 1.1   Rearrange characters   rearrang.c

1.1.1 Spacing and Comments

Now, let's take a closer look at this program. The first point to notice is the spacing of the program: the blank lines that separate different parts from one another, the use of tabs to indent statements to display the program structure, and so forth. C is a free-form language, so there are no rules as to how you must write statements. However, a little discipline when writing the program pays off later by making it easier to read and modify. More on this issue in a bit.

While it is important to display the structure of the program clearly, it is even more important to tell the reader what the program does and how it works. Comments fulfill this role.

```
/*
** This program reads input lines from the standard input and prints
** each input line, followed by just some portions of the lines, to
** the standard output.
**
** The first input is a list of column numbers, which ends with a
** negative number. The column numbers are paired and specify
** ranges of columns from the input line that are to be printed.
** For example, 0 3 10 12 -1 indicates that only columns 0 through 3
** and columns 10 through 12 will be printed.
*/
```

This block of text is a *comment*. Comments begin with the /* characters and end with the */characters. They may appear anywhere in a C program in which white space may appear. However, comments cannot contain other comments, that is, the first */ terminates the comment no matter how many /*'s have appeared earlier.

Comments are sometimes used in other languages to "comment out" code, thus removing the code from the program without physically deleting it from the source file. This practice is a bad idea in C, because it won't work if the code you're trying to get rid of has any comments in it. A better way to logically delete code in a C program is the **#if** directive. When used like this:

```
#if 0
            statements
#endif
```

the program statements between the #if and the #endif are effectively removed from the program. Comments contained in the statements have no effect on this construct, thus it is a much safer way to accomplish the objective. There is much more that you can do with this directive, which I explain fully in Chapter 14.

1.1.2 Preprocessor Directives

```
#include <stdio.h>
#include <stdlib.h>
#include <string.h>
#define MAX_COLS        20       /* max # of columns to process */
#define MAX_INPUT       1000     /* max len of input & output lines */
```

These five lines are called *preprocessor directives*, or just *directives*, because they are interpreted by the *preprocessor*. The preprocessor reads the source code, modifies it as indicated by any preprocessor directives, and then passes the modified code to the compiler.

In our sample program, the preprocessor replaces the first **#include** statement with the contents of the library header named stdio.h; the result is the same as if the contents of stdio.h had been written verbatim at this point in the source file. The second and third directives do the same with stdlib.h and string.h.

The stdio.h header gives us access to functions from the *Standard I/O Library*, a collection of functions that perform input and output. stdlib.h defines the EXIT_SUCCESS and EXIT_FAILURE symbols. We need string.h to use the string manipulation functions.

This technique is also a handy way to manage your declarations if they are needed in several different source files—you write the declarations in a separate file and then use #include to read them into each relevant source file. Thus there is only one copy of the declarations; they are not duplicated in many different places, which would be more error prone to maintain.

The other directive is **#define**, which defines the name MAX_COLS to be the value 20, and MAX_INPUT to be the value 1000. Wherever either name appears later in the source file, it is replaced by the appropriate value. Because they are defined as literal constants, these names cannot be used in some places where ordinary variables can be used (for example, on the left side of an assignment). Making their names uppercase serves as a reminder that they are not ordinary variables. #define directives are used for the same kinds of things as symbolic constants in other languages and for the same reasons. If we later decide that 20 columns are not enough, we can simply change the definition of MAX_COLS. There is no need to hunt through the program looking for 20's to change and possibly missing one or changing a 20 that had nothing to do with the maximum number of columns.

```
int     read_column_numbers( int columns[], int max );
void    rearrange( char *output, char const *input,
            int n_columns, int const columns[] );
```

These declarations are called *function prototypes*. They tell the compiler about the characteristics of functions that are defined later in the source file. The compiler can then check calls to these functions for accuracy. Each prototype begins with a type name that describes the value that is returned. The type name is followed by the name of the function. The arguments expected by the function are next, so read_column_numbers returns an integer and takes two arguments, an array of integers and an integer scalar. The argument names are not required; I give them here to serve as a reminder of what each argument is supposed to be.

The rearrange function takes four arguments. The first and second are *pointers*. A pointer specifies where a value resides in the computer's memory, much like a house number specifies where a particular family resides on a street. Pointers are what give the C language its power and are covered in great detail starting in Chapter 6. The second and fourth arguments are declared **const**, which means that the function promises not to modify the caller's arguments. The keyword void indicates that the function does not return any value at all; such a function would be called a *procedure* in other languages.

If the source code for this program was contained in several source files, function prototypes would have to be written in each file using the function. Putting the prototypes in header files and using a #include to access them avoids the maintenance problem caused by having multiple copies of the same declarations.

1.1.3 The Main Function

```
int
main( void )
{
```

These lines begin the definition of a function called `main`. Every C program must have a main function, because this is where execution begins. The keyword `int` indicates that the function returns an integer value; the keyword `void` indicates that it expects no arguments. The body of the function includes everything between this opening brace and its matching closing brace. Observe how the indentation clearly shows what is included in the function.

```
int     n_columns;              /* # of columns to process */
int     columns[MAX_COLS];      /* the columns to process */
char    input[MAX_INPUT];       /* array for input line */
char    output[MAX_INPUT];      /* array for output line */
```

These lines declare four variables: an integer scalar, an array of integers, and two arrays of characters. All four of these variables are local to the main function, so they cannot be accessed by name from any other functions. They can, of course, be passed as arguments to other functions.

```
/*
** Read the list of column numbers
*/
n_columns = read_column_numbers( columns, MAX_COLS );
```

This statement calls the function `read_column_numbers`. The array `columns` and the constant represented by `MAX_COLS` (20) are passed as arguments. In C, array arguments behave as though they are passed by *reference*, and scalar variables and constants are passed by *value* (like **var** parameters and value parameters, respectively, in Pascal or Modula). Thus, any changes made by a function to a scalar argument are lost when the function returns; the function cannot change the value of the calling program's argument in this manner. When a function changes the value of an element of an array argument, however, the array in the calling program is actually modified.

The rule about how parameters are passed to C functions actually states:

All arguments to functions are passed by value.

Nevertheless, an array name as an argument produces the call-by-reference

behavior described above. The reason for this apparent contradiction between
the rule and the actual behavior is explained in Chapter 8.

```
/*
** Read, process and print the remaining lines of input.
*/
while( gets( input ) != NULL ){
        printf( "Original input : %s\n", input );
        rearrange( output, input, n_columns, columns );
        printf( "Rearranged line: %s\n", output );
}


return EXIT_SUCCESS;
}
```

The comment describing this piece of code might seem unnecessary.
However, the major expense of software today is not writing it but maintaining
it. The first problem in modifying a piece of code is figuring out what it does,
so anything you can put in your code that makes it easier for someone (perhaps
you!) to understand it later is worth doing. Be sure to write accurate comments, though, and to keep them up-to-date when you change the code. Inac-
curate comments are worse than none at all!

This piece of code consists of a **while** loop. In C, while loops operate
the same as they do in other languages. The expression is tested. If it is false,
the body of the loop is skipped. If the expression is true, the body of the loop
is executed and the whole process begins again.

This loop represents the main logic of the program. In brief, it means:

> *while we were able to read another line of input*
> > *print the input*
> > *rearrange the input, storing it in* output
> > *print the output*

The **gets** function reads one *line* of text from the standard input and stores it
in the array passed as an argument. A line is a sequence of characters terminated by a newline character; gets discards the newline and stores a NUL
byte at the end of the line.[1] (A NUL byte is one whose bits are all 0, written as
a character constant like this: '\0'.) gets then returns a value that is not

---

[1] NUL is the name given in the ASCII character set to the character '\0', whose bits are all zero. NULL refers
to a pointer whose value is zero. Both are integers and have the same value, so they could be used interchangeably. However, it is worth using the appropriate constant because this tells a person reading the program not only
that you are using the value zero, but *what* you are using it for.

NULL to indicate that a line was successfully read.[2] When gets is called but there is no more input, it returns NULL to indicate that it has reached the end of the input (end of file).

Dealing with character strings is a common task in C programs. Although there is no "string" data type, there is a convention for character strings that is observed throughout the language: a string is a sequence of characters terminated by a NUL byte. The NUL is considered a terminator and is not counted as a part of the string. A *string literal* is a sequence of characters enclosed in quotation marks in the source program.[3] For example, the string literal

```
"Hello"
```

occupies six bytes in memory, which contain (in order) H, e, l, l, o, and NUL.

The **printf** function performs formatted output. Modula and Pascal users will be delighted with the simplicity of formatted output in C. printf takes multiple arguments; the first is a character string that describes the format of the output, and the rest are the values to be printed. The format is often given as a string literal.

The format string contains format designators interspersed with ordinary characters. The ordinary characters are printed verbatim, but each format designator causes the next argument value to be printed using the indicated format. A few of the more useful format designators are given in Table 1.1. If

Format	Meaning
%d	Print an integer value in decimal.
%o	Print an integer value in octal.
%x	Print an integer value in hexadecimal.
%g	Print a floating-point value.
%c	Print a character.
%s	Print a character string.
\n	Print a newline.

Table 1.1 Common printf format codes

---

[2] The symbol NULL is defined in the header stdio.h. On the other hand, there is no predefined symbol NUL, so if you wish to use it instead of the character constant '\0' you must define it yourself.

[3] This symbol is a quotation mark: ", and this symbol is an apostrophe: '. The penchant of computer people to call them "single quote" and "double quote" when their existing names are perfectly good seems unnecessary, so I will use their everyday names.

the array input contains the string Hi friends!, then the statement

```
printf( "Original input : %s\n", input );
```

will produce

```
Original input : Hi friends!
```

terminated with a newline.

The next statement in the sample program calls the rearrange function. The last three arguments are values that are passed to the function, and the first is the answer that the function will construct and pass back to the main function. Remember that it is only possible to pass the answer back through this argument because it is an array. The last call to printf displays the result of rearranging the line.

Finally, when the loop has completed, the main function returns the value EXIT_SUCCESS. This value indicates to the operating system that the program was successful. The closing brace marks the end of the body of the main function.

1.1.4 The read_column_numbers *Function*

```
/*
** Read the list of column numbers, ignoring any beyond the specified
** maximum.
*/
int
read_column_numbers( int columns[], int max )
{
```

These lines begin the definition of the read_column_numbers function. Note that this declaration and the function prototype that appeared earlier in the program match in the number and types of arguments and in the type returned by the function. It is an error if they disagree.

There is no indication of the array size in the array parameter declaration to the function. This format is correct, because the function will get whatever size array the calling program passed as an argument. This is a great feature, as it allows a single function to manipulate one-dimensional arrays of any size. The down side of this feature is that there is no way for the function to determine the size of the array. If this information is needed, the value must be passed as a separate argument.

When the `read_column_numbers` function is called, the name of one of the arguments that is passed happens to match the name of the formal parameter given above. However, the name of the other argument does not match its corresponding parameter. As in most other languages, the formal parameter name and the actual argument name have no relationship to one another; you can make them the same if you wish, but it is not required.

```
int     num = 0;
int     ch;
```

Two variables are declared; they will be local to this function. The first one is initialized to zero in the declaration, but the second one is not initialized. More precisely, its initial value will be some unpredictable value, which is probably garbage. The lack of an initial value is not a problem in this function because the first thing done with the variable is to assign it a value.

```
/*
** Get the numbers, stopping at eof or when a number is < 0.
*/
while( num < max && scanf( "%d", &columns[num] ) == 1
        && columns[num] >= 0 )
        num += 1;
```

This second loop reads in the column numbers. The **scanf** function reads characters from the standard input and converts them according to a format string—sort of the reverse of what `printf` does. `scanf` takes several arguments, the first of which is a format string that describes the type of input that is expected. The remaining arguments are variables into which the input is stored. The value returned by `scanf` is the number of values that were successfully converted and stored into the arguments.

You must be careful with this function for two reasons. First, because of the way `scanf` is implemented, all of its scalar arguments must have an ampersand in front of them. For reasons that I make clear in Chapter 8, array arguments do not require an ampersand.[4] However, if a subscript is used to identify a specific array element, then an ampersand *is* required. I explain the need for

---

[4] There is no harm in putting an ampersand in front of an array name here, however, so you may use one if you wish.

the ampersands on the scalar arguments in Chapter 15. For now, just be sure to put them in, because the program will surely fail without them.

The second pitfall is the format codes, which are not identical to those in `printf` but similar enough to be confusing. Table 1.2 informally describes a few of the format designators that you may use with `scanf`. Note that the first five read scalar values, so the variable given as the argument must be preceded with an ampersand. With all of these format codes (*except* `%c`), white space (spaces, tabs, newlines, etc.) in the input is skipped until the value is encountered, and subsequent white space terminates the value. Therefore, a character string read with `%s` cannot contain white space. There are many other format designators, but these will be enough for our current needs.

We can now explain the expression

```
scanf( "%d", &columns[num] )
```

The format code `%d` indicates that an integer value is desired. Characters are read from the standard input, any leading white space found is skipped. Then digits are converted into an integer, and the result is stored in the specified array element. An ampersand is required in front of the argument because the subscript selects a single array element, which is a scalar.

The test in the `while` loop consists of three parts.

```
num < max
```

makes sure that we do not get too many numbers and overflow the array. `scanf` returns the value one if it converted an integer. Finally,

```
columns[num] >= 0
```

checks that the value entered was positive. If any of these tests are false, the loop stops.

Format	Meaning	Type of Variable
%d	Read an integer value.	int
%ld	Read a long integer value.	long
%f	Read a real value.	float
%lf	Read a double precision real value.	double
%c	Read a character.	char
%s	Read a character string from the input.	array of char

Table 1.2 Common `scanf` format codes

The Standard does not require that C compilers check the validity of array subscripts, and the vast majority of compilers don't. Thus, if you need subscript validity checking, you must write it yourself. If the test for num < max were not here and the program read a file containing more than 20 column numbers, the excess values would be stored in the memory locations that follow the array, thus destroying whatever data was formerly in those locations, which might be other variables or the function's return address. There are other possibilities too, but the result is that the program will probably not perform as you had intended.

The && is the "logical and" operator. For this expression to be true, the expressions on both sides of the && must evaluate to true. However, if the left side is false, the right side is not evaluated at all, because the result can only be false. In this case, if we find that num has reached the maximum value, the loop breaks and the expression

```
columns[num]
```

is never evaluated.[5]

Be careful not to use the & operator when you really want &&; the former does a bitwise AND, which sometimes gives the same result that && would give but in other cases does not. I describe these operators in Chapter 5.

Each call to scanf reads a decimal integer from the standard input. If the conversion fails, either because end of file was reached or because the next input characters were not valid input for an integer, the value 0 is returned, which breaks the loop. If the characters are legal input for an integer, the value is converted to binary and stored in the array element columns[num]. scanf then returns the value 1.

Beware: The operator that tests two expressions for equality is ==. Using the = operator instead results in a legal expression that almost certainly will *not* do what you want it to do: it does an *assignment* rather than a comparison! It is a legal expression, though, so the compiler won't catch this error for you.[6] Be extremely careful to use the double equal sign operator for comparisons. If your program is not working, check all of your comparisons for this error. Believe me, you *will* make this mistake, probably more than once, as I have.

---

[5] The phrase "the loop breaks" means that it terminates, not that it is has suddenly become defective. This phrase comes from the break statement, which is discussed in Chapter 4.

[6] Some newer compilers will print a warning about assignments in if and while statements on the theory that it is much more likely that you wanted a comparison than an assignment in this context.

The next `&&` makes sure that the number is tested for a negative value only if `scanf` was successful in reading it. The statement

```
num += 1;
```

adds 1 to the variable `num`. It is equivalent to the statement

```
num = num + 1;
```

I discuss later why C provides two different ways to increment a variable.[7]

```
/*
** Make sure we have an even number of inputs, as they are
** supposed to be paired.
*/
if( num % 2 != 0 ){
        puts( "Last column number is not paired." );
        exit( EXIT_FAILURE );
}
```

This test checks that an even number of integers were entered, which is required because the numbers are supposed to be in pairs. The `%` operator performs an integer division, but it gives the remainder rather than the quotient. If `num` is not an even number, the remainder of dividing it by two will be nonzero.

The `puts` function is the output version of `gets`; it writes the specified string to the standard output and appends a newline character to it. The program then calls the `exit` function, which terminates its execution. The value `EXIT_FAILURE` is passed back to the operating system to indicate that something was wrong.

```
/*
** Discard the rest of the line that contained the final
** number.
*/
while( (ch = getchar()) != EOF && ch != '\n' )
        ;
```

`scanf` only reads as far as it has to when converting input values. Therefore, the remainder of the line that contained the last value will still be

---

[7] With the prefix and postfix `++` operators, there are actually four ways to increment a variable.

out there, waiting to be read. It may contain just the terminating newline, or it may contain other characters too. Regardless, this `while` loop reads and discards the remaining characters to prevent them from being interpreted as the first line of data.

The expression

```
(ch = getchar()) != EOF && ch != '\n'
```

merits some discussion. First, the function **getchar** reads a single character from the standard input and returns its value. If there are no more characters in the input, the constant EOF (which is defined in `stdio.h`) is returned instead to signal end-of-file.

The value returned by `getchar` is assigned to the variable `ch`, which is then compared to EOF. The parentheses enclosing the assignment ensure that it is done before the comparison. If `ch` is equal to EOF, the expression is false and the loop stops. Otherwise, `ch` is compared to a newline; again, the loop stops if they are found to be equal. Thus, the expression is true (causing the loop to run again) only if end of file was not reached and the character read was not a newline. Thus, the loop discards the remaining characters on the current input line.

Now let's move on to the interesting part. In most other languages, we would have written the loop like this:

```
ch = getchar();
while( ch != EOF && ch != '\n' )
        ch = getchar();
```

Get a character, then if we've not yet reached end of file or gotten a newline, get another character. Note that there are two copies of the statement

```
ch = getchar();
```

The ability to embed the assignment in the `while` statement allows the C programmer to eliminate this redundant statement.

The loop in the sample program has the same functionality as the one shown above, but it contains one fewer statement. It is admittedly harder to read, and one could make a convincing argument that this coding technique should be avoided for just that reason. However, most of the difficulty in reading is due to inexperience with the language and its idioms; experienced C programmers have no trouble reading (and writing) statements such as this one. You should avoid making code harder to read when there is no tangible benefit to be gained from it, but the maintenance advantage in not having multiple copies of code more than justifies this common coding idiom.

A question frequently asked is why ch is declared as an integer when we are using it to read characters? The answer is that EOF is an integer value that requires more bits than are available in a character variable; this fact prevents a character in the input from accidentally being interpreted as EOF. But it also means that ch, which is receiving the characters, must be large enough to hold EOF too, which is why an integer is used. As discussed in Chapter 3, characters are just tiny integers anyway, so using an integer variable to hold character values causes no problems.

One final comment on this fragment of the program: there are no statements in the body of the while statement. It turns out that the work done to evaluate the while expression is all that is needed, so there is nothing left for the body of the loop to do. You will encounter such loops occasionally, and handling them is no problem. The solitary semicolon after the while statement is called the *empty statement*, and it is used in situations like this one where the syntax requires a statement but there is no work to be done. The semicolon is on a line by itself in order to prevent the reader from mistakenly assuming that the next statement is the body of the loop.

```
    return num;
}
```

The return statement is how a function returns a value to the expression from which it was called. In this case, the value of the variable num is returned to the calling program, where it is assigned to the main program's variable n_columns.

1.1.5 The rearrange *Function*

```
/*
** Process a line of input by concatenating the characters from
** the indicated columns.  The output line is then NUL terminated.
*/
void
rearrange( char *output, char const *input,
    int n_columns, int const columns[] )
{
        int     col;            /* subscript for columns array */
        int     output_col;     /* output column counter */
        int     len;            /* length of input line */
```

These statements define the `rearrange` function and declare some local variables for it. The most interesting point here is that the first two parameters are declared as pointers but array names are passed as arguments when the function is called. When an array name is used as an argument, what is passed to the function is a pointer to the beginning of the array, which is actually the address where the array resides in memory. The fact that a pointer is passed rather than a copy of the array is what gives arrays their call by reference semantics. The function can manipulate the argument as a pointer, or it can use a subscript with the argument just as with an array name. These techniques are described in more detail in Chapter 8.

Because of the call by reference semantics, though, if the function modifies elements of the parameter array, it actually modifies the corresponding elements of the argument array. Thus, declaring `columns` to be `const` is useful in two ways. First, it states that the intention of the function's author is that this parameter is not to be modified. Second, it causes the compiler to verify that this intention is not violated. Thus, callers of this function need not worry about the possibility of elements of the array passed as the fourth argument being changed.

```
len = strlen( input );
output_col = 0;

/*
** Process each pair of column numbers.
*/
for( col = 0; col < n_columns; col += 2 ){
```

The real work of the function begins here. We first get the length of the input string, so we can skip column numbers that are beyond the end of the input. The **for** statement in C is not quite like other languages; it is more of a shorthand notation for a commonly used style of `while` statement. The `for` statement contains three expressions (all of which are optional, by the way). The first expression is the *initialization* and is evaluated once before the loop begins. The second is the *test* and is evaluated before each iteration of the loop; if the result is false the loop terminates. The third expression is the *adjustment*, which is evaluated at the end of each iteration just before the test is evaluated. To illustrate, the `for` loop that begins above could be rewritten as a `while` loop:

```
col = 0;
```

```
while( col < n_columns ){
        body of the loop
        col += 2;
}
```

```
int     nchars = columns[col + 1] - columns[col] + 1;

/*
** If the input line isn't this long or the output
** array is full, we're done.
*/
if( columns[col] >= len ||
    output_col == MAX_INPUT - 1 )
        break;

/*
** If there isn't room in the output array, only copy
** what will fit.
*/
if( output_col + nchars > MAX_INPUT - 1 )
        nchars = MAX_INPUT - output_col - 1;

/*
** Copy the relevant data.
*/
strncpy( output + output_col, input + columns[col],
    nchars );
output_col += nchars;
```

Here is the body of the `for` loop, which begins by computing the number of characters in this range of columns. Then it checks whether to continue with the loop. If the input line is shorter than this starting column, or if the output line is already full, there is no more work to be done and the `break` statement exits the loop immediately.

The next test checks whether all of the characters from this range of columns will fit in the output line. If not, `nchars` is adjusted to the number that will fit.

It is common in "throwaway" programs that are used only once to not bother checking things such as array bounds and to simply make the array "big enough" so that it will never overflow. Unfortunately, this practice is sometimes used in production code, too. There, most of the extra space is wasted, but it is still possible to overflow the array, leading to a program failure.[8]

Finally, the `strncpy` function copies the selected characters from the input line to the next available position in the output line. The first two arguments to `strncpy` are the destination and source, respectively, of a string to copy. The destination in this call is the position `output_col` columns past the beginning of the output array. The source is the position `columns[col]` past the beginning of the input array. The third argument specifies the number of characters to be copied.[9] The output column counter is then advanced `nchars` positions.

```
    }

    output[output_col] = '\0';
}
```

After the loop ends, the output string is terminated with a NUL character; note that the body of the loop takes care to ensure that there is space in the array to hold it. Then execution reaches the bottom of the function, so an implicit `return` is executed. With no explicit `return` statement, no value can be passed back to the expression from which the function was called. The missing return value is not a problem here because the function was declared `void` (that is, returning no value) and there is no assignment or testing of the function's return value where it is called.

1.2 Other Capabilities

The sample program illustrated many of the C basics, but there is a little more you should know before you begin writing your own programs. First is the **putchar** function, which is the companion to `getchar`. It takes a single integer argument and prints that character on the standard output.

Also, there are many more library functions for manipulating strings. I'll briefly introduce a few of the most useful ones here. Unless otherwise noted, each argument to these functions may be a string literal, the name of a character array, or a pointer to a character.

---

[8] The astute reader will have noticed that there is nothing to prevent `gets` from overflowing the `input` array if an extremely long input line is encountered. This loophole is really a shortcoming of `gets`, which is one reason why `fgets` (described in Chapter 15) should be used instead.

[9] If the source of the copy contains fewer characters than indicated by the third argument, the destination is padded to the proper length with NUL bytes.

strcpy is similar to strncpy except that there is no specified limit to the number of characters that are copied. It takes two arguments: the string in the second argument is copied into the first, overwriting any string that the first argument might already contain. **strcat** also takes two arguments, but this function appends the string in the second argument to the end of the string already contained in the first. A string literal may not be used as the first argument to either of these last two functions. It is the programmer's responsibility with both functions to ensure that the destination array is large enough to hold the result.

For searching in strings, there is **strchr**, which takes two arguments— the first is a string, and the second is a character. It searches the string for the first occurrence of the character and returns a pointer to the position where it was found. If the first argument does not contain the character, a NULL pointer is returned instead. The **strstr** function is similar. Its second argument is a string, and it searches for the first occurrence of this string in the first argument.

1.3 Compiling

The way you compile and run C programs depends on the kind of system you're using. To compile a program stored in the file testing.c on a UNIX machine, try these commands:

```
cc testing.c
a.out
```

On PC's, you need to know which compiler you are using. For Borland C++, try this command in a MS-DOS window:

```
bcc testing.c
testing
```

1.4 Summary

The goal of this chapter was to describe enough of C to give you an overview of the language. With this context, it will be easier to understand the topics in the next chapters.

The sample program illustrated numerous points. Comments begin with /* and end with */, and are used to include descriptions in the program. The preprocessor directive #include causes the contents of a library header to be processed by the compiler, and the #define directive allows you to give symbolic names to literal constants.

All C programs must have a function called main in which execution begins. Scalar arguments to functions are passed by value, and array arguments have call by reference semantics. Strings are sequences of characters terminated with a NUL byte, and there is a library of functions to manipulate strings in various ways. The printf function performs formatted output, and the scanf function is used for formatted input; getchar and putchar perform unformatted character input and output, respectively. if and while statements work much the same in C as they do in other languages.

Having seen how the sample program works, you may now wish to try writing some C programs of your own. If it seems like there ought to be more to the language, you are right, there is much more, but this sampling should be enough to get you started.

1.5 Summary of Cautions

1. Not putting ampersands in front of scalar arguments to scanf (page 12).
2. Using printf format codes in scanf (page 13).
3. Using & for a logical AND instead of && (page 14).
4. Using = to compare for equality instead of == (page 14).

1.6 Summary of Programming Tips

1. Using #include files for declarations (page 6).
2. Using #define to give names to constant values (page 7).
3. Putting function prototypes in #include files (page 7).
4. Checking subscript values before using them (page 14).
5. Nesting assignments in a while or if expression (page 16).
6. How to write a loop with an empty body (page 17).
7. Always check to be sure that you don't go out of the bounds of an array (page 19).

1.7 Questions

1. C is a free-form language, which means that there are no rules regarding how programs must look.[10] Yet the sample program followed specific spacing rules. Why do you think this is?

✎ 2. What is the advantage of putting declarations, such as function prototypes, in header files and then using #include to bring the declarations into the source files where they are needed?

3. What is the advantage of using #define to give names to literal constants?

4. What format string would you use with printf in order to print a decimal integer, a string, and a floating-point value, in that order? Separate the values from one another with a space, and end the output with a newline character.

✎ 5. Write the scanf statement needed to read two integers, called quantity and price, followed by a string, which should be stored in a character array called department.

6. There are no checks made on the validity of an array subscript in C. Why do you think this obvious safety measure was omitted from the language?

7. The rearrange program described in the chapter contains the statement

```
strncpy( output + output_col,
    input + columns[col], nchars );
```

The strcpy function takes only two arguments, so the number of characters it copies is determined by the string specified by the second argument. What would be the effect of replacing the strncpy function call with a call to strcpy in this program?

✎ 8. The rearrange program contains the statement

```
while( gets( input ) != NULL ){
```

What might go wrong with this code?

1.8 Programming Exercises

★ 1. The "Hello world!" program is often the first C program that a student of C writes. It prints Hello world! followed by a newline on the standard output. This trivial program is a good one to use when figuring out how to run

---

[10] Other than for the preprocessor directives.

the C compiler on your particular system.

⚙ ★★ 2. Write a program that reads lines from the standard input. Each line is printed on the standard output preceded by its line number. Try to write the program so that it has no built-in limit on how long a line it can handle.

★★ 3. Write a program that reads characters from the standard input and writes them to the standard output. It should also compute a *checksum* and write it out after the characters.

The checksum is computed in a `signed char` variable that is initialized to −1. As each character is read from the standard input, it is added to the checksum. Any overflow from the checksum variable is ignored. When all of the characters have been written, the checksum is then written as a decimal integer, which may be negative. Be sure to follow the checksum with a new-line.

On computers that use ASCII, running your program on a file containing the words "Hello world!" followed by a newline should produce the following output:

```
Hello world!
102
```

★★ 4. Write a program that reads input lines one by one until end of file is reached, determines the length of each input line, and then prints out only the longest line that was found. To simplify matters, you may assume that no input line will be longer than 1000 characters.

⚙ ★★★ 5. The statement

```
if( columns[col] >= len ... )
        break;
```

in the rearrange program stops copying ranges of characters as soon as a range is encountered that is past the end of the input line. This statement is correct only if the ranges are entered in increasing order, which may not be the case. Modify the rearrange function so that it will work correctly even if the ranges are not entered in order.

★★★ 6. Modify the rearrange program to remove the restriction that an even number of column values must be read initially. If an odd number of values are read, the last value indicates the start of the final range of characters. Characters from here to the end of the input string are copied to the output string.

2

Basic Concepts

There is no doubt that learning the fundamentals of a programming language is not as much fun as writing programs. However, *not* knowing the fundamentals makes writing programs a lot less fun.

2.1 Environments

In any particular implementation of ANSI C, there are two distinct *environments* that are of interest: the *translation environment*, in which source code is converted into executable machine instructions; and the *execution environment*, in which the code actually runs. The Standard makes it clear that these environments need not be on the same machine. For example, cross-compilers run on one machine but produce executable code that will be run on a different type of machine. Nor is an operating system a requirement; the Standard also discusses *freestanding environments* in which there is no operating system. You might encounter this type of environment in an embedded system such as the controller for a microwave oven.

2.1.1 Translation

The translation phase consists of several steps. First, each of the (potentially many) source files that make up a program are individually converted to *object code* via the compilation process. Then, the various object files are tied together by the *linker* to form a single, complete executable program. The linker also brings in any functions from the standard C libraries that were used in the program, and it can also search personal program libraries as well. Figure 2.1 illustrates this process.

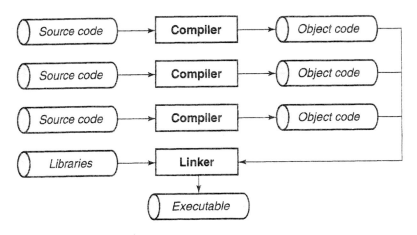

Figure 2.1   The compilation process

The compilation process itself consists of several phases, with the first being the *preprocessor*. This phase performs textual manipulations on the source code, for example, substituting the text of identifiers that have been #define'd and reading the text of files that were #include'd.

The source code is then *parsed* to determine the meanings of its statements. This second stage is where most error and warning messages are produced. Object code is then generated. Object code is a preliminary form of the machine instructions that implement the statements of the program. If called for by a command-line option, an *optimizer* processes the object code in order to make it more efficient. This optimization takes extra time, so it is usually not done until the program has been debugged and is ready to go into production. Whether the object code is produced directly or is in the form of assembly language statements that must then be assembled in a separate phase to form the object file is not important to us.

Filename Conventions

Although the Standard does not have any rules governing the names used for files, most environments have filename conventions that you must follow. C source code is usually put in files whose names end with the .c extension. Files that are #include'd into other C source code are called *header files* and usually have names ending in .h.

Different environments may have different conventions regarding object file names. For example, they end with .o on UNIX systems but with .obj on MS-DOS systems.

Compiling and Linking

The specific commands used to compile and link C programs vary from system, but many work the same as the two systems described here. The C compiler on most UNIX systems is called cc, and it can be invoked in a variety of ways.

1. To compile and link a C program that is contained entirely in one source file:

    ```
    cc program.c
    ```

    This command produces an executable program called a.out. An object file called program.o is produced, but it is deleted after the linking is complete.

2. To compile and link several C source files:

    ```
    cc main.c sort.c lookup.c
    ```

    The object files are not deleted when more than one source file is compiled. This fact allows you to recompile only the file(s) that changed after making modifications, as shown in the next command.

3. To compile one C source file and link it with existing object files:

    ```
    cc main.o lookup.o sort.c
    ```

4. To compile a single C source file and produce an object file (in this case, called program.o) for later linking:

    ```
    cc -c program.c
    ```

5. To compile several C source files and produce an object file for each:

    ```
    cc -c main.c sort.c lookup.c
    ```

6. To link several object files:

    ```
    cc main.o sort.o lookup.o
    ```

The -o *name* option may be added to any of the commands above that produce an executable program; it causes the linker to store the executable program in a file called *name* rather than a.out. By default, the linker searches the standard C library. The -l*name* flag tells the linker to also search the library called *name*; this option should appear last on the command line. There are other options as well; consult your system's documentation.

Borland C/C++ 5.0 for MS-DOS/Windows has two interfaces that you can use. The Windows Integrated Development Environment is a complete self-contained programming tool that contains a source-code editor, debuggers, and compilers. Its use is beyond the scope of this book. The MS-DOS command line interface, though, works much the same as the UNIX compilers, with the following exceptions:

1. its name is bcc;

2. the object files are named `file.obj`;

3. the compiler does not delete the object file when only a single source file is compiled and linked; and

4. by default, the executable file is named after the first source or object file named on the command line, though the `-ename` option may be used to put the executable program in `name.exe`.

2.1.2 Execution

The execution of a program also goes through several phases. First, the program must be loaded into memory. In *hosted* environments (those with an operating system), this task is handled by the operating system. It is at this point that preinitialized variables that are not stored on the stack are given their initial values. Program loading must be arranged manually in freestanding environments, perhaps by placing the executable code in read-only-memory (ROM).

Execution of the program now begins. In hosted environments, a small startup routine is usually linked with the program. It performs various housekeeping chores, such as gathering the command line arguments so that the program can access them. The main function is then called.

Your code is now executed. On most machines, your program will use a runtime *stack*, where variables local to functions and function return addresses are stored. The program can also use *static* memory; variables stored in static memory retain their values throughout the program's execution.

The final phase is the termination of the program, which can result from several different causes. "Normal" termination is when the main function returns.[11] Some execution environments allow the program to return a code that indicates why the program stopped executing. In hosted environments, the

---

[11] Or when some function calls `exit`, described in Chapter 16.

startup routine receives control again and may perform various housekeeping tasks, such as closing any files that the program may have used but did not explicitly close. The program might also have been interrupted, perhaps due to the user pressing the break key or hanging up a telephone connection, or it might have interrupted itself due to an error that occurred during execution.

2.2 Lexical Rules

The *lexical* rules, like spelling rules in English, govern how you form the individual pieces, called *tokens*, of a source program.

An ANSI C *program* consists of declarations and functions. The functions define the work to be performed, whereas the declarations describe the functions and/or the kind of data (and sometimes the data values themselves) on which the functions will operate. *Comments* may be interspersed throughout the source code.

2.2.1 Characters

The Standard does not require that any specific character set be used in a C environment, but it does specify that the character set must have the English alphabet in both upper and lowercase, the digits 0 through 9, and the following special characters.

```
!   "   #   %   '   (   )   *   +   ,   -   .   /   :
;   <   >   =   ?   [   ]   \   ^   _   {   }   |   ~
```

The newline character is what marks the end of each line of source code and, when character input is read by the executing program, the end of each line of input. If needed by the runtime environment, the "newline" can be a sequence of characters, but they are all treated as if they were a single character. The space, tab, vertical tab, and form feed characters are also required. These characters and the newline are often referred to collectively as *white space* characters, because they cause space to appear rather than making marks on the page when they are printed.

The Standard defines several *trigraphs*—a trigraph is a sequence of characters that represents another character. Trigraphs are provided so that C environments can be implemented with character sets that lack some of the required characters. Here are the trigraphs and the characters that they represent.

??(	[	??<	{	??=	#
??)	]	??>	}	??/	\
??!	|	??'	^	??-	~

There is no special significance to a pair of question marks followed by any other character.

Although trigraphs are vital in a few environments, they are a minor nuisance for nearly everyone else. The sequence ?? was chosen to begin each trigraph because it does not often occur naturally, but therein lies the danger. You never think about trigraphs because they are usually not a problem, so when one is written accidentally, as in

```
printf( "Delete file (are you really sure??): " );
```

the resulting] in the output is sure to surprise you.

There are a few contexts in writing C source code where you would like to use a particular character but cannot because that character has a special meaning in that context. For example, the quotation mark " is used to delimit string literals. How does one include a quotation mark within a string literal? K&R C defined several *escape sequences* or *character escapes* to overcome this difficulty, and ANSI C has added a few new ones to the list. Escape sequences consist of a backslash followed by one or more other characters. Each of the escape sequences in the list below represents the character that follows the backslash but without the special meaning usually attached to the character.

\?   Used when writing multiple question marks to prevent them from being interpreted as trigraphs.
\"   Used to get quotation marks inside of string literals.
\'   Used to write a character literal for the character '.
\\   Used when a backslash is needed to prevent its being interpreted as a character escape.

There are many characters that are not used to express source code but are very useful in formatting program output or manipulating a terminal display screen. Character escapes are also provided to simplify their inclusion in your program. These character escapes were chosen for their mnemonic value.

K&R C

The character escapes marked with † are new to ANSI C and are not implemented in K&R C.

`\a`	† Alert character. This rings the terminal bell or produces some other audible or visual signal.
`\b`	Backspace character.
`\f`	Formfeed character.
`\n`	Newline character.
`\r`	Carriage return character.
`\t`	Horizontal tab character.
`\v`	† Vertical tab character.
`\ddd`	*ddd* represents from one to three octal digits. This escape represents the character whose representation has the given octal value.
`\xddd`	† Like the above, except that the value is specified in hexadecimal.

Note that *any number* of hexadecimal digits may be included in a `\xddd` sequence, but the result is undefined if the resulting value is larger than what will fit in a character.

2.2.2 Comments

C comments begin with the characters `/*`, end with the characters `*/`, and may contain anything except `*/` in between. Whereas comments may span multiple lines in the source code, they may not be nested within one another. Note that these character sequences do not begin or end comments when they appear in string literals.

Each comment is stripped from the source code by the preprocessor and replaced by a single space. Comments may therefore appear anywhere that white space characters may appear.

A comment begins where it begins and ends where it ends, and it includes everything on all the lines in between. This statement may seem obvious, but it wasn't to the student who wrote this innocent looking fragment of code. Can you see why only the first variable is initialized?

```
x1 = 0;        /**********************
x2 = 0;        ** Initialize the     **
x3 = 0;        ** counter variables. **
x4 = 0;        **********************/
```

Take care to terminate comments with `*/` rather than `*?`. The latter can occur if you are typing rapidly or hold the shift key down too long. This mistake looks obvious when pointed out, but it is deceptively hard to find in real programs.

2.2.3 Free Form Source Code

C is a *free form* language, meaning that there are no rules governing where statements can be written, how many statements may appear on a line, where spaces should be put, or how many spaces can occur.[12] The only rule is that one or more white space characters (or a comment) must appear between tokens that would be interpreted as a single long token if they were adjacent. Thus, the following statements are equivalent:

```
y=x+1;

y = x + 1 ;

y = x
+
1;
```

Of the next group of statements, the first three are equivalent, but the last is illegal.

```
int
x;

int     x;

int/*comment*/x;

intx;
```

This freedom is a mixed blessing; you will hear some soapbox philosophy about this issue shortly.

2.2.4 Identifiers

Identifiers are the names used for variables, functions, types, and so forth. They are composed of upper and lowercase letters, digits, and the underscore character, but they may not begin with a digit. C is a *case sensitive* language, so abc, Abc, abC, and ABC are four different identifiers. Identifiers may be any length, though the Standard allows the compiler to ignore characters after the first 31. It also allows an implementation to restrict identifiers for external names (that is, those that the linker manipulates) to six monocase characters.

---

[12] Except for preprocessor directives, described in Chapter 14, which are line oriented.

The following C *keywords* are reserved, meaning that they cannot also be used as identifiers.

```
auto       do        goto       signed     unsigned
break      double    if         sizeof     void
case       else      int        static     volatile
char       enum      long       struct     while
const      extern    register   switch
continue   float     return     typedef
default    for       short      union
```

2.2.5 Form of a Program

A C program may be stored in one or more source files. Although one source file may contain more than one function, every function must be completely contained in a single source file.[13] There are no rules in the Standard governing this issue, but a reasonable organization of a C program is for each source file to contain a group of related functions. This technique has the side benefit of making it possible to implement abstract data types.

2.3 Program Style

A few comments on program style are in order. Freeform languages such as C will accept sloppy programs, which are quick and easy to write but difficult to read and understand later. We humans respond to visual clues so putting them in your source code will aid whoever must read it later. (This might be you!) Program 2.1 is an example that, although admittedly extreme, illustrates the problem. This is a working program that performs a marginally useful function. The question is, what does it do?[14] Worse yet, suppose you had to make a modification to this program! Although experienced C programmers could figure it out given enough time, few would bother. It would be quicker and easier to just toss it out and write a new program from scratch.

---

[13] Technically, a function could begin in one source file and continue in another if the second were `#include`'d into the first. However, this procedure is not a good use of the `#include` directive.

[14] Believe it or not, it prints the lyrics to the song *The Twelve Days of Christmas*. The program is a minor modification of one written by Ian Phillipps of Cambridge Consultants Ltd. for the International Obfuscated C Code Contest (see http://reality.sgi.com/csp/ioccc). Reprinted by permission. Copyright © 1988, Landon Curt Noll & Larry Bassel. All Rights Reserved. Permission for personal, educational or non-profit use is granted provided this copyright and notice is included in its entirety and remains unaltered. All other users must receive prior permission in writing from both Landon Curt Noll and Larry Bassel.

```
#include <stdio.h>
main(t,_,a)
char *a;
{return!0<t?t<3?main(-79,-13,a+main(-87,1-_,
main(-86, 0, a+1 )+a)):1,t<_?main(t+1, _, a ):3,main ( -94, -27+t, a
)&&t == 2 ?_<13 ?main ( 2, _+1, "%s %d %d\n" ):9:16:t<0?t<-72?main(_,
t,"@n'+,#'/*{}w+/w#cdnr/+,{}r/*de}+,/*{*+,/w{%+,/w#q#n+,/#{l,+,/n{n+\
,/+#n+,/#;#q#n+,/+k#;*+,/'r :'d*'3,}{w+K w'K:'+}e#';dq#'l q#'+d'K#!/\
+k#;q#'r}eKK#}w'r}eKK{nl]'/#;#q#n'){)#}w'){){nl]'/+#n';d}rw' i;# ){n\
l]!/n{n#'; r{#w'r nc{nl]'/#{l,+'K {rw' iK{;[{nl]'/w#q#\
n'wk nw' iwk{KK{nl]!/w{%'l##w#' i; :{nl]'/*{q#'ld;r'}{nlwb!/*de}'c \
;;{nl'-{}rw]'/+,}##'*}#nc,',#nw]'/+kd'+e}+;\
#'rdq#w! nr'/ ') }+}{rl#'{n' ')# }'+}##(!!/")
:t<-50?_==*a ?putchar(a[31]):main(-65,_,a+1):main((*a == '/')+t,_,a\
+1 ):0<t?main ( 2, 2 , "%s"):*a=='/'||main(0,main(-61,*a, "!ek;dc \
i@bK'(q)-[w]*%n+r3#l,{}:\nuwloca-O;m .vpbks,fxntdCeghiry"),a+1);}
```

Program 2.1   Mystery program   mystery.c

Poor style and poor documentation are two of the reasons why software is so
expensive to create and maintain. Good programming style goes a long way
toward making your programs easier to read. The direct result of good style is
that the programs are easier to get working. The indirect result is that they are
easier to maintain, which translates to big cost savings.

The examples in this book use a style that emphasizes the structure of the
program through judicious use of white space. Here are some of the characteristics of this style, and why I chose them.

1. A blank line separates statements into logical groups based on their func-
    tionality. The reader can easily skip an entire group without having to
    read each line of code to see where the group logically ends.

2. The parentheses in if and related statements are part of the statement, not
    part of the expression being tested. Thus I use spaces to separate the
    parentheses from the expression so that the expression stands out more
    clearly. The same is true of function prototypes.

3. Spaces are used around most operators in order to make expressions more
    readable. Sometimes I omit spaces in complex expressions to show the
    grouping of the subexpressions.

4. Statements that are nested within other statements are indented to show
    this relationship. It is easier to line up related statements by using tabs to
    indent rather than spaces. It is important to use a large enough indent to

be able to visually locate matching parts of the program over a page of code. Two or three spaces are not enough.

Some people avoid tabs because they think tabs indent statements too much. In complex functions with deeply nested statements, the large tab indent means that there is little space left on the line to write the statements. However if the function is that complex, it would probably benefit from being broken into smaller functions, one of which contains the statements that were formerly nested so deeply.

5. Most comments are written in blocks, which makes them stand out visually from the code. They are easier for the reader to find, and easier to skip.

6. In the definition of a function, the return type appears on a separate line before the function name, which appears at the beginning of the next line. To locate the definition of a function, search for the function name at the beginning of a line.

There are many other characteristics that you will see as you study the code examples. Other programmers have other personal styles that they prefer. Whether you adopt this style or a different one is not nearly as important as consistently using *some* reasonable style. If you are consistent, any competent reader will be able to figure out your code easily enough.

2.4 Summary

The source code of a C program is stored in one or more files, with each function being completely contained in one file. Placing related functions in the same file is a good strategy. Each source file is individually compiled to produce an object file. The object files are then linked to form the executable program. This may or may not be done on the same machine that will eventually run the program.

The program must be loaded into memory before it can be executed. In hosted environments, this task is performed by the operating system; in freestanding environments, the program is often stored permanently in ROM. Static variables that have been initialized are given their values before execution begins. Execution of your code begins in the main function. Most environments use a stack to store local variables and other data.

The character set used by a C implementation must include certain characters. Trigraphs allow you to write characters that are missing from some character sets. Escape sequences allow characters with no printable representation, such as white space characters, to be included in a program.

Comments begin with /* and end with */, and may not be nested. Comments are removed by the preprocessor. Identifiers are composed of letters, digits, and the underscore character, and may not begin with a digit. Uppercase and lowercase characters are distinct from one another in identifiers. Keywords are reserved and may not be used as identifiers. C is a free form language; however, writing programs with a clear style makes them easier to read and maintain.

2.5 Summary of Cautions

1. Characters in string literals being mistakenly interpreted as trigraphs (page 30).

2. Badly written comments can unexpectedly enclose statements (page 31).

3. Improper termination of comments (page 31).

2.6 Summary of Programming Tips

1. Good style and documentation result in programs that are easier to read and maintain (page 34).

2.7 Questions

1. Comments in C do not nest. What would be the result of "commenting out" the code in the example shown below?

```
void
squares( int limit )
{
/* Comment out this entire function
        int     i;      /* loop counter */

        /*
        ** Print table of squares
        */
        for( i = 0; i < limit; i += 1 )
                printf( "%d %d0, i, i * i );
End of commented-out code */
}
```

2. What are the advantages of putting a large program into a single source file? What are the disadvantages?

3. Show the string literal that you would use with `printf` in order to print the following text, including the quotation marks:

   ```
   "Blunder??!??"
   ```

4. What is the value of \40? Of \100? Of \x40? Of \x100? Of \0123? Of \x0123?

5. What is the result of this statement?

   ```
   int     x/*blah blah*/y;
   ```

6. What (if anything) is wrong with the following declaration?

   ```
   int     Case, If, While, Stop, stop;
   ```

7. True or False: Because C (excluding the preprocessor directives) is a free-form language, the only rules that govern how programs are written are the syntax rules, so it doesn't matter how the program actually looks.

8. Is the loop in the following program correct?

   ```
   #include <stdio.h>

   int
   main( void )
   {
   int     x, y;

   x = 0;
   while( x < 10 ){
           y = x * x;
           printf( "%d\t%d\n", x, y );
           x += 1;
   }
   ```

   Is the loop in this program correct?

   ```
   #include <stdio.h>

   int
   main( void )
   {
           int     x, y;
   ```

```
x = 0;
while( x < 10 ){
        y = x * x;
        printf( "%d\t%d\n", x, y );
        x += 1;
}
```

Which program was easier to check?

9. Suppose you have a C program whose main function is in the file main.c and has other functions in the files list.c and report.c. What command(s) would you use on your system to compile and link this program?

10. How would you modify the command for the previous question in order to link a library called parse with the program?

△ 11. Suppose you have a C program composed of several separate files, and they include one another as shown below.

File	Includes Files
main.c	stdio.h, table.h
list.c	list.h
symbol.c	symbol.h
table.c	table.h
table.h	symbol.h, list.h

Which files would have to be recompiled after you make a change to list.c? To list.h? To table.h?

2.8 Programming Exercises

★ 1. Write a program with three functions in three separate source files. The function increment should take a single integer argument and return the value of that argument plus one. This function should be in the file increment.c. The second function is called negate. It also takes a single integer argument and returns the negated value of that argument (for example, if the argument is 25, the function should return -25; if the argument is -612, the function should return 612). The final function is main, in the file main.c, and it should call each of the other functions with the values 10, 0, and -10 and print the results.

△ ★★ 2. Write a program that will read C source code from the standard input and ensure that the braces are paired correctly. Note: you need not worry about braces that appear within comments, string literals, or character constants.

3

Data

Programs operate on data, and this chapter describes data: its various types, its characteristics, and how to declare it. Three properties of variables—their scope, linkage, and storage class—are also described. These three properties determine the "visibility" of a variable (that is, where it can be used) and its "lifetime" (how long its value lasts).

3.1 Basic Data Types

There are only four basic data types in C—integers, floating-point values, pointers, and *aggregate* types such as arrays and structures. All other types are derived from some combination of these four. Let's begin by introducing the integers and floating-point types.

3.1.1 The Integer Family

The integer family contains *characters*, *short integers*, *integers*, and *long integers*. All have both *signed* and *unsigned* versions.

It sounds as though a "long integer" ought to be able to hold larger values than a "short integer," but this assumption is not necessarily true. The rule regarding the relative sizes of integers is simple:

Long integers are as least as large as integers, which themselves are at least as large as short integers.

Type	Minimum Range
char	0 to 127
signed char	−127 to 127
unsigned char	0 to 255
short int	−32,767 to 32,767
unsigned short int	0 to 65,535
int	−32,767 to 32,767
unsigned int	0 to 65,535
long int	−2,147,483,647 to 2,147,483,647
unsigned long int	0 to 4,294,967,295

Table 3.1   Minimum variable ranges

K&R C

Note that there is no requirement that a long integer actually be longer than a short integer, it simply cannot be any shorter. The ANSI Standard adds a specification for the minimum allowable range of values that each different type may represent, as shown in Table 3.1. This specification is a big improvement over K&R C when portability among environments is important, especially when the environments are on machines with wildly different architectures.

A short int must be at least 16 bits, and a long int at least 32 bits. It is up to the implementor to decide whether to make the default int 16 or 32 bits, or something else. Usually the default is chosen to be whatever is most natural (efficient) for the machine. Note that there is still no requirement that the three sizes actually be different. An environment for a machine with 32-bit words and no instructions to deal effectively with shorter integral values could implement them all as 32-bit integers.

The include file limits.h specifies the characteristics of the various integer types. It defines the names shown in Table 3.2. limits.h also defines the following names. CHAR_BIT is the number of bits in a character (at least eight). CHAR_MIN and CHAR_MAX define the range for the default

| Type | Signed | | Unsigned |
	Minimum Value	Maximum Value	Maximum Value
Character	SCHAR_MIN	SCHAR_MAX	UCHAR_MAX
Short integer	SHRT_MIN	SHRT_MAX	USHRT_MAX
Integer	INT_MIN	INT_MAX	UINT_MAX
Long integer	LONG_MIN	LONG_MAX	ULONG_MAX

Table 3.2   Limits of variable ranges

character type; these will be the same as either SCHAR_MIN and SCHAR_MAX or zero and UCHAR_MAX. Finally, MB_LEN_MAX specifies the maximum number of characters in a multibyte character.

Although the intention behind char variables is for them to hold characters, characters are actually tiny integer values. The default char is always either a signed char or an unsigned char, but what you get depends on the compiler. This fact means that a char on different machines might hold different ranges of values, so programs that use char variables are portable only if they restrict these variables to values in the intersection of the signed and unsigned ranges. For example, the characters in the ASCII character set all fall within this range.

The portability of programs that use characters as little integers can be improved by explicitly declaring these variables as either signed or unsigned. This practice ensures that their signed-ness is consistent from machine to machine. On the other hand, dealing with signed characters on a machine that is more comfortable with unsigned characters will be less efficient, so declaring all char variables as either signed or unsigned is probably not a good idea. Also, many library functions dealing with characters declare their arguments as char, which may cause a compatibility problem with arguments that are explicitly declared signed or unsigned.

When portability is an issue, the signed-ness of characters poses a dilemma. The best compromise is to limit the values stored in char variables to the intersection of the signed and unsigned ranges, which maximizes portability without sacrificing efficiency, and perform arithmetic only on char variables that are explicitly signed or unsigned.

Integer Literals

The term *literal* is an abbreviation for *literal constant*—an entity that specifies its own value, and whose value cannot be changed. This distinction is important because ANSI C allows the creation of *named constants* (variables declared to be const), which are very much like ordinary variables except that, once initialized, their values cannot be changed.

When an integer literal is written in a program, which of the nine different types of the integer family does it have? The answer depends on how the literal is written, but the default rules can be overridden for some literals by appending a suffix to the end of the value. The characters L and l (that's an *el*, not the digit one) cause a literal to be interpreted as a long integer value, and the characters U and u specify an unsigned value. A literal may be designated unsigned long by appending one of each to it.

There are many different ways to specify integer literals in source code. The most natural are decimal integer values, such as these:

123   65535   −275[15]

Decimal literals are either `int`, `long`, or `unsigned long`. The shortest type that will contain the value is what is used by default.

Integers can be given in octal by starting with the digit zero, or in hexadecimal by starting with `0x`, as in

```
0173      0177777     000060
0x7b      0xFFFF      0xabcdef00
```

The digits 8 and 9 are illegal in octal literals; the characters `ABCDEF` or `abcdef` may all be used as digits in hexadecimal literals. Octal and hexadecimal literals are `int`, `unsigned int`, `long`, or `unsigned long`: the shortest one that is big enough to hold the value is what is used by default.

And then there are character literals. These always have type `int`; you cannot use the unsigned or long suffixes on them. A character literal is a single character (or character escape or trigraph) enclosed in apostrophies, as in

```
'M'       '\n'       '??('       '\377'
```

Multibyte character literals such as `'abc'` are allowed by the Standard, but their implementation may vary from one environment to the next so their use is discouraged.

Finally, *wide character literals* are written as an `L` followed by a multibyte character literal, as in:

```
L'X'      L'e^'
```

These are used when the runtime environment supports a large character set.

When you need an integer literal, the compiler doesn't care which form you write, although it makes a big difference to a human reader. Which form you choose, then, should be determined by the context in which the literal is used. Most literals are written in decimal form because it is the most natural for people to read. Here are a couple of examples where other types of integer literals are more appropriate.

---

[15] Technically, −275 is not a literal constant but a *constant expression*. The minus sign is interpreted as a unary operator instead of being part of the number. This ambiguity has little practical consequence, though, as the expression is evaluated by the compiler and has the desired effect.

A literal that identifies certain bit positions within a word would be better written as a hexadecimal or octal value, because these forms display more clearly the special nature of the value. For example, the value 983040 has a 1-bit in positions 16–19, but you would never guess it from looking at its decimal value. Written in hexadecimal, though, the value is 0xF0000, which clearly shows those bits as 1 and the remaining bits 0. If this value is being used in a context in which these specific bits are important, for example as a mask to extract the corresponding bits from a variable, then writing the literal in hexadecimal makes the meaning of the operation much clearer to a human reader.

If a value is going to be used as a character, expressing the value as a character literal makes clearer the meaning that is intended for the value. For example, the statements

```
value = value - 48;
value = value - \60;
```

are entirely equivalent in operation to

```
value = value - '0';
```

but it is much easier to see from the latter that the digit stored in value is being converted from a character to a binary value. More importantly, the character constant yields the correct value no matter which character set is used, so it improves portability.

Enumerated Type

An *enumerated* type is one whose values are symbolic constants rather than literal. These are declared in this fashion:

```
enum Jar_Type { CUP, PINT, QUART,
        HALF_GALLON, GALLON };
```

which declares a type called Jar_Type. Variables of this type are declared like this:

```
enum Jar_Type milk_jug, gas_can, medicine_bottle;
```

If there is only one declaration of variables of a particular enumerated type, both statements may be combined like this:

```
enum { CUP, PINT, QUART, HALF_GALLON, GALLON }
    milk_jug, gas_can, medicine_bottle;
```

The variables are in fact stored as integers, and the values used internally to represent the symbolic names are the integer values 0 for CUP, 1 for PINT, etc. Where appropriate, specific integer values may be specified for the symbolic names like this:

```
enum Jar_Type { CUP=8, PINT=16, QUART=32,
            HALF_GALLON=64, GALLON=128 };
```

It is legal for only some of the symbols to be given values this way. Any symbol not given an explicit value gets a value one greater than the symbol before it.

The symbolic names are treated as integer constants, and variables declared with an enumerated type are actually integers. This fact means that you can assign the literal -623 to a variable of type Jar_Type, and you can assign the value HALF_GALLON to any integer variable. Avoid using enumerations in this manner, however, because their value is weakened by mixing them indiscriminately with integers.

3.1.2 Floating-Point Types

Numbers such as 3.14159 and $6.023{\times}10^{23}$ cannot be stored as integers. The first is not a whole number, and the second is far too large. They can, however, be stored as *floating-point* values. These are usually stored as a fraction and an exponent of some assumed base, such as

$$.3243F{\times}16^1 \qquad .110010010000111111{\times}2^2$$

both of which represent the value 3.14159. There are many different methods of representing floating-point values; the Standard does not dictate any specific format.

The floating-point family includes float, double, and long double types. These types usually provide single precision, double precision, and on machines that support it, extended precision values respectively. The ANSI Standard requires only that long doubles be at least as long as doubles, which themselves must be at least as big as floats. It also imposes a minimum range; all floating-point types must be capable of storing values in the range -10^{37} through 10^{37}.

An include file called float.h defines the names FLT_MAX, DBL_MAX, LDBL_MAX to the maximum values that can be stored in a float, double, and long double, respectively; minimum values are given by FLT_MIN,

DBL_MIN, and LDBL_MIN. Additional names that specify certain characteristics of the floating-point implementation, such as the radix being used and the number of significant digits the different lengths have, are also defined here.

Floating point literals are always written in decimal and must contain either a decimal point, an exponent, or both. Here are some examples:

```
3.14159    1E10    25.    .5    6.023e23
```

Floating point literals are double values unless they are followed by a suffix: L or l specify long double, and F or f specify float.

3.1.3 Pointers

Pointers are a major reason why the C language is popular. Pointers allow the efficient implementation of advanced data structures such as trees and lists. Other languages, such as Pascal and Modula-2, implement pointers but do not allow arithmetic or comparisons to be performed on them. Nor do they allow any way of creating pointers to existing data objects. The lack of such restrictions is what allows the C programmer to produce programs that are more efficient and compact than programs in other languages. At the same time, the unrestricted use of pointers in C is the cause of much weeping and gnashing of teeth by both beginning and experienced C programmers.

The values of variables are stored in the computer's memory, each at a particular location. Each memory location is identified and referenced with an *address*, just as the houses on a street can be located by their address. *Pointer* is just another name for an address; a *pointer variable* is a variable whose value is the address of some other memory location. There are operators that allow you to obtain the address of a variable and to follow a pointer variable to the value or data structure to which it points, but we will discuss those in Chapter 5.

The idea of accessing data by its address instead of by its name frequently causes confusion. It shouldn't, because you have been doing this all your life. Locating houses on a street by their address is exactly the same thing. No one ever confuses the address of a house with its contents; no one ever mistakenly writes a letter to "Mr. 428 Elmhurst St." living at "Robert Smith."

A pointer is exactly the same. Imagine the computer's memory as houses along a very long street, each identified by its own unique number. Each location contains a value, which is separate and distinct from its address, even though both are numbers.

Pointer Constants

Pointer constants are fundamentally different from nonpointer constants. Because the compiler takes care of assigning variables to locations in the computer's memory, the programmer usually has no way of knowing in advance where some particular variable will reside. Therefore, you obtain the address of a variable by using an operator rather than writing its address as a literal constant. For example, if we want the address of the variable xyz, we cannot write a literal such as 0xff2044ec because we have no way of knowing whether that is where the compiler will actually put the variable. Indeed, an automatic variable may be allocated at different places each time a function is called. Thus, there is little use for pointer constants expressed as literal numeric values, so there is no notation built into C specifically for them.[16]

String Literals

Many people find it strange that there is no string type in C, yet the language has a *string literal*. There is in fact a notion of a *string*, a sequence of zero or more characters terminated by a NUL byte. Strings are usually stored in character arrays, which is why there is no explicit string type. Because the NUL is used to terminate strings, it is not possible for a string to contain NULs. This restriction is usually not a problem, though; NUL was chosen as a terminator because it has no printable graphic associated with it.

String literals are written as a sequence of characters enclosed in quotation marks, like these:

```
"Hello"    "\aWarning!\a"    "Line 1\nLine2"    ""
```

The last example illustrates that a string literal (unlike a character literal) may be empty; the terminating NUL byte will always be there, though.

K&R C

String literals cause the specified characters and a terminating NUL byte to be stored somewhere in the program. K&R C made no mention as to whether the characters in a string literal could be modified by the program, but it explicitly stated that string literals with identical values were stored separately. Many implementations, therefore, allowed literals to be modified by the program.

ANSI C states that the effect of modifying a string literal is undefined. It also allows the compiler to store a string literal once even if it appears many times in the source code. This fact makes modifying string literals extremely risky, because a change made to one literal may change the value of other

---

[16] There is one exception: the NULL pointer, which can be expressed as the value zero. See Chapter 6 for more information.

string literals in the program. Therefore, many ANSI compilers do not let you modify string literals, or provide compile-time options to let you choose whether or not you want modification of literals to be allowed. Avoid this practice; if you need to modify a string, store it in an array instead.

I discuss string literals along with pointers because using a string literal in a program generates a "constant pointer to character." When a string literal appears in an expression, the value used in the expression is the *address* where its characters were stored, not the characters themselves. Thus, you can assign a string literal to a variable of type "pointer to character," which makes the variable point to where the characters are stored. You cannot assign a string literal to a character array, though, because the immediate value of the literal is a pointer, not the characters themselves.

If not being able to assign or copy strings sounds inconvenient, you should know that the standard C library includes a suite of functions whose purpose is to manipulate strings. The suite includes functions to copy, concatenate, compare, and compute the length of strings and to search strings for specific characters.

3.2 Basic Declarations

Knowing the basic data types is of little use unless you can declare variables. The basic form of a declaration is

```
specifier(s) declaration_expression_list;
```

For simple types, the `declaration_expression_list` is just a list of the identifiers being declared. For more involved types, each of the items in the list is actually an expression that shows how the name being declared might be used. If this idea seems obscure now, don't worry, we explore it in more detail shortly.

The `specifier(s)` includes keywords that describe the base type of the identifiers being declared. Specifiers may also be given to change the default storage class and scope of the identifier. We discuss these topics shortly.

You saw some basic declarations in the sample program in Chapter 1. Here are a couple more.

```
int     i;
char    j, k, l;
```

The first declaration indicates that the variable `i` is an integer. The second declares `j`, `k`, and `l` to be character variables.

The specifiers may include keywords to modify the length and/or signed-ness of the identifier. These include

```
short      long      signed      unsigned
```

Also, the keyword int may be omitted from the declaration of any integral type if at least one other specifier is given in the declaration. Thus, the following two declarations are equivalent:

```
unsigned short int      a;
unsigned short          a;
```

Table 3.3 shows all of the variations on these declarations. The declarations within each box are equivalent. The signed keyword is ordinarily used only for chars because the other integer types are signed by default. It is implementation dependent whether char is signed or unsigned, so char is equivalent to either signed char or unsigned char. Table 3.3 does not include this equivalence.

The situation is simpler with the floating-point types, because none of the specifiers are applicable except for long double.

3.2.1 Initialization

A declaration may specify an initial value for a scalar variable by following the variable name with an equal sign and the desired value. For example,

```
int      j = 15;
```

declares j to be an integer variable and assigns it the value 15. We return to the topic of initialization again later in this chapter.

short short int	signed short signed short int	unsigned short unsigned short int
int	signed int signed	unsigned int unsigned
long long int	signed long signed long int	unsigned long unsigned long int

Table 3.3   Equivalent integer declarations

3.2.2 Declaring Simple Arrays

To declare a one-dimensional array, the array name is followed by a subscript that specifies the number of elements in the array. This is the first example of the `declaration_expression` mentioned earlier. For example, consider the declaration:

```
int     values[20];
```

The obvious interpretation of this declaration is that we are declaring an array of 20 integers. This interpretation is correct, but there is a better way to read the declaration. The name `values`, when followed by a subscript, yields a value of type `int` (and by the way, there are 20 of them). The "declaration expression" shows the identifier used in an expression that results in a value of the base type, integer in this case.

The subscripts of arrays always begin at zero and extend through one less than the declared size of the array. There is no way to change this property, but if you absolutely must have an array whose subscripts begin at ten, it is not difficult to just subtract ten in each of your subscripts.

Another aspect of arrays in C is that the compiler does not check the subscripts to see whether they are in the proper range.[17] The lack of checking is both good and bad. It is good because there is no time lost checking array subscripts that are known to be correct, and it is bad because invalid subscripts are not detected. A good rule of thumb to use is:

If a subscript was computed from values that are already known to be correct, then there is no need to check its value. Any value that is derived in any way from data that the user has entered must be checked before being used as a subscript to ensure that it is in the proper range.

We cover the initialization of arrays in Chapter 8.

3.2.3 Declaring Pointers

Declaration expressions are also used to declare pointers. In Pascal and Modula, a declaration gives a list of identifiers followed by their type. In C, the *base* type is given, followed by a list of identifiers used in the expressions needed to produce that base type. For example,

---

[17] It is technically possible for a compiler to accurately check subscript values but doing so involves a lot of additional overhead. Some later compilers, such as Borland C++ 5.0, implement subscript checking as a debugging tool that can be turned on or off.

```
int      *a;
```

states that the expression *a results in the type int. Knowing that the *
operator performs indirection, we can infer that a must be a pointer to an
integer.[18]

The free form nature of C makes it tempting to write the asterisk near the type,
like this:

```
int*     a;
```

This declaration has the same meaning as the previous one, and it now seems
to more clearly declare that a is of type int *. This technique is not good,
and here is why.

```
int*     b, c, d;
```

People naturally read this statement as declaring all three variables to be
pointers to integers, but it doesn't. We are fooled by how it looks. The asterisk is really part of the expression *b and applies only to that one identifier. b
is a pointer, but the other two variables are ordinary integers. Here is the
correct declaration for three pointers.

```
int      *b, *c, *d;
```

Declarations of pointer variables may also specify initial values for the
variables. Here is an example in which a pointer is declared and initialized to
a string literal.

```
char     *message = "Hello world!";
```

This statement declares message to be a pointer to a character and initializes
the pointer to the address of the first character in the string literal.

One danger with this type of initialization is that it is easy to misinterpret its
meaning. In the previous declaration, it appears that the initial value is
assigned to the expression *message when in fact the value is assigned to
message itself. In other words, the previous declaration is equivalent to:

```
char     *message;
message = "Hello world!";
```

---

[18] Indirection is only legal on a pointer value. The pointer points to the result, and the indirection "follows"
the pointer to obtain the result. See Chapter 6 for more details.

3.2.4 Implicit Declarations

There are a few declarations in which type names may be omitted altogether. Functions, for example, are assumed to return integers unless declared otherwise. When declaring formal parameters to functions in the old style, any parameters whose declarations are omitted are assumed to be integers. Finally, if the compiler can see enough to determine that a statement is in fact a declaration, an omitted type is assumed to be integer.

Consider this program:

```
int     a[10];
int     c;
b[10];
d;

f( x )
{
        return x + 1;
}
```

The first and second lines are not unusual, however the third and fourth lines are illegal in ANSI C. The third line omits the type, but there is enough information left that some K&R compilers can still figure out that the statement is a declaration. Amazingly, a few K&R compilers correctly process the fourth line as a declaration too. The function f is assumed to return an integer, and its argument is assumed to be an integer.

Depending on implicit declarations is a bad idea. An implicit declaration always leaves a question in the reader's mind: Was the omission of the type intended, or did the programmer simply forget the proper declaration? Explicit declarations make your intent clear.

3.3 Typedef

C supports a mechanism called **typedef**, which allows you to define new names for various data types. Typedefs are written exactly the same as ordinary declarations except that the keyword typedef appears at the beginning. For example, the declaration

```
char    *ptr_to_char;
```

declares the variable ptr_to_char to be a pointer to a character. But add the keyword typedef and you get

```
typedef char     *ptr_to_char;
```

which declares the identifier `ptr_to_char` to be a new name for the type pointer to character. You can use the new name in subsequent declarations just like any of the predefined names. For example,

```
ptr_to_char      a;
```

declares a to be a pointer to a character.

Using a `typedef` to declare types, particularly complex ones, reduces the chances of messing up a declaration.[19] Furthermore, if you should decide later to change the type of some kind of data being used in your program, changing one `typedef` is easier than changing all declarations of all variables (and functions) in the program that deal with that data.

 Use `typedef` rather than #define for creating new type names, because the latter is unable to properly handle pointer types. For example,

```
#define d_ptr_to_char    char *
d_ptr_to_char    a, b;
```

declares a properly but declares b to be a character. Definitions of names for more complex types, such as pointers to functions or arrays, are also handled better with `typedef`.

3.4 Constants

ANSI C allows you to declare *constants*, which are exactly like variables except that their values cannot be changed. You use the **const** keyword to declare constants, as shown in the following examples.

```
int      const    a;
const    int      a;
```

Both of these statements declare a to be an integer whose value cannot be changed. Pick whichever form of declaration you find easiest to understand and stick with it.

Of course, if a's value cannot be changed, you can't assign anything to it, so how do you give it a value in the first place? There are two ways. First, you can initialize it in the declaration, like this:

---

[19] `typedef` is particularly useful with structures; see Chapter 10 for some examples.

```
int     const   a = 15;
```

Second, `const` formal parameters of a function are given the values of the actual arguments when a function call is performed.

The situation becomes more interesting with pointer variables, because there are two things that might be constant—the pointer variable and the entity to which it points. Here are some sample declarations:

```
int     *pi;
```

`pi` is an ordinary pointer to an integer. The variable

```
int     const  *pci;
```

`pci` is a pointer to a constant integer. You can change the pointer's value but not the value to which it points. Contrast this example with `cpi`:

```
int     * const cpi;
```

which is a constant pointer to an integer. Here the pointer is the constant; its value cannot change, but you are free to modify the integer to which it points.

```
int     const   * const cpci;
```

Finally, there is `cpci`; in this example both the pointer and the value to which it points are constant.

 Use the `const` keyword when declaring variables whose values will not change. This practice not only makes your intent more clear to others reading the program, but it also lets the compiler catch places where such a value is accidentally modified.

The `#define` directive is another mechanism for creating named constants.[20] For example, both of the following statements create a named constant for the value 50.

```
#define MAX_ELEMENTS    50
int     const   max_elements = 50;
```

The `#define` form is more useful than the `const` variable because you can use the former wherever a literal constant is allowed, such as in declaring the size of arrays. The constant variable can only be used where variables are allowed.

---

[20] See Chapter 14 for a complete description.

Named constants are valuable because they give symbolic names to quantities that would otherwise be written as literals. Defining sizes of arrays or limits on loop counters with named constants rather than literal constants improves the maintainability of the program—should a value have to change, only the declaration need be touched. It is much easier to change one declaration than to search through the entire program changing all instances of a literal constant, especially when the same literal value is used for two or more different purposes.

3.5 Scope

When a variable is declared in one part of a program, it can be accessed only in a certain area of the program. The extent of this area is determined by the identifier's scope. The *scope* of an identifier is the area in the program in which that identifier may be used. For example, the scope of a function's local variables is limited to the body of the function. This rule means two things. First, no other function may access these variables by their names, because the names are not valid outside of their scope. Second, it is legal to declare different variables with the same names so long as they are not declared in the same scope.

The compiler recognizes four different types of scope—file scope, function scope, block scope, and prototype scope. The location where an identifier is declared determines its scope. The program skeleton in Figure 3.1 illustrates all the possible locations.

3.5.1 Block Scope

A list of statements enclosed in braces is called a *block*. Any identifiers declared at the beginning of a block have *block scope*, which means that they are accessible to all statements in the block. The variables in Figure 3.1 labeled six, seven, nine and ten all have block scope. The formal parameters of a function definition (declaration five) also have block scope in the function's body.

When blocks are nested, the scope of identifiers declared in the nested blocks extends only to the end of that block. However, if an identifier in a nested block has the same name as one in any outer block, then the inner definition hides the outer one—the variable in the outer block cannot be referenced by name from within the inner block. The f in declaration nine is a different variable than the f in declaration six, and the latter is not accessible by name from within the inner block.

```
1 ——➤ int a;
2 ——➤ int b ( int c );          3
4 ——➤ int d ( int e )           5
         {
6 ——➤      int f;                    8
7 ——➤      int g ( int h );

           ...

           {
9 ——➤          int f, g, i;

               ...

           }
           {
10 ——➤         int i;

               ...

           }
         }
```

Figure 3.1   Identifier scope example

Duplicate variable names in nested blocks should be avoided. There is no good reason for using them, and they cause confusion during debugging or maintenance of the program.

Blocks that are not nested within one another are a little different. Variables declared in each block are inaccessible from other blocks because their scopes do not overlap. Because it is impossible for variables in both blocks to exist at the same time, the compiler is free to store them in the same memory locations. For example, i in declaration ten could share the same memory location as any of the variables in declaration nine. There is no danger in this sharing, because only one of the non-nested blocks can be active at any time.

In K&R C, the scope of formal parameters to a function began at the declarations of the parameters, which was outside of the body of the function. If there were local variables declared in the function with the same names as the parameters, they hid the parameters, which were then inaccessible anywhere in the function. In other words, if declaration six had included an e, then the body of the function could only access the local variable; the parameter e would be inaccessible. Of course, no one ever hides a parameter intentionally because there is no point in passing an argument if you are not going to use its value in the function. ANSI C prevents this error from happening by giving the formal parameters block scope in the function's outermost block. Local variables declared in the outermost block cannot have the same name as any of the parameters, because they are all declared in the same scope.

3.5.2 File Scope

Any identifier declared outside of all blocks has *file scope*, meaning that the identifier may be accessed anywhere from its declaration to the end of the source file in which it was declared. Declarations one and two in Figure 3.1 are in this category. The names of the functions defined in a file have file scope, because the name itself is not within any blocks (as in declaration four). I should point out that declarations written in a header file that is then #include'd into another file are treated as if they were written directly in the including file; their scope is not limited by the end of the header file.

3.5.3 Prototype Scope

Prototype scope applies only to argument names declared in function prototypes, as in declarations three and eight in Figure 3.1. In a prototype (as opposed to the function definition) the argument names need not appear. If they are given, however, you may choose any names you wish; they need not match either the formal parameter names given in the function definition or the names of the actual arguments used when the function is called. Prototype scope prevents these names from conflicting with any other names in the program. Indeed, the only possible conflict is using the same name more than once in the same prototype.

3.5.4 Function Scope

The final type of scope is *function scope*. It applies only to statement labels, which are used with **goto** statements. Basically, function scope boils down to a simple rule—all statement labels in a function must be unique. I hope that you never use this knowledge.

3.6 Linkage

After the individual source files comprising a program are compiled, the object files are linked together with functions from one or more libraries to form the executable program. However, when the same identifier appears in more than one source file, do they refer to the same entity, as in Pascal, or to different entities? The *linkage* of an identifier determines how multiple occurrences of the identifier are treated. The scope of an identifier is related to its linkage, but the two properties are not the same.

There are three types of linkage—*external, internal,* and *none.* Identifiers that have no linkage are always individuals, that is, multiple declarations of the identifier are always treated as separate and distinct entities. Internal linkage means that all declarations of the identifier within one source file refer to a single entity, but declarations of the same identifier in other source files refer to different entities. Finally, all references to an identifier with external linkage refer to the same entity.

The program skeleton in Figure 3.2 illustrates linkage by showing all of the different ways that names can be declared. By default, the linkage of identifiers b, c, and f is external; and the remaining identifiers have no linkage. Thus, another source file that contains a similar declaration for b and calls the function c will access the entities defined in this source file. f has external linkage because it is a function name. Calls to the function f in this source file will be linked with the function definition that appears in some other source file, or perhaps the function definition might come from a library.

The keywords extern and static are used in declarations to modify the linkage of the identifiers being declared. When used on a declaration of

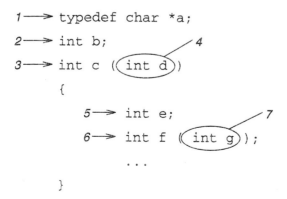

Figure 3.2 Linkage example

something that normally has external linkage, the keyword **static** gives it internal linkage instead. For example, if declaration two were written

```
static   int       b;
```

then the variable b would remain private to this source file; references to the variable b in other source files would be linked to a different variable. Similarly, defining a function to be static, for example,

```
static int c( int d )
```

prevents it from being called from other source files.

static only has this effect in declarations whose default linkage is external. Although it is legal to add static to declaration five, for example, it has an entirely different effect because e does not default to external linkage.

The rules for the **extern** keyword are more complicated. In general, it specifies external linkage for an identifier and is used to get access to an entity that is defined elsewhere. Consider the example in Figure 3.3. Declaration three specifies external linkage for k, which gives this function access to an external variable declared in another source file.

Technically, the keyword is only required in declarations, such as number three in Figure 3.3, whose default linkage is not external. Its use is optional in declarations that have file scope. However, it is easier for a reader to understand your intentions if you define the variable once and use extern in every other declaration that refers to it.

When extern is used on the first declaration in the source file for an

```
1 ──➤ static int i;

    int func()

    {

        2 ──➤ int j;
        3 ──➤ extern int k;
        4 ──➤ extern int i;

            . . .

    }
```

Figure 3.3 Using extern

identifier, it specifies that the identifier has external linkage. When used on the second or subsequent declarations of an identifier, however, the keyword does not change the linkage specified by the first declaration. For example, declaration four in Figure 3.3 does not change the linkage of i established by declaration one.

3.7 Storage Class

The *storage class* of a variable refers to the type of memory in which the variable's value is stored. The storage class of a variable determines when it is created and destroyed and how long it will retain its value. There are three possible places to store variables: in ordinary memory, on the runtime stack, and in hardware registers. Variables stored in these three places will have different characteristics.

The default storage class for a variable depends on where it is declared. Variables declared outside of any blocks are always stored in *static* memory, that is, in memory that is not part of the stack. There is no way to specify any other storage class for these variables. Static variables are created before the program begins to run and exist throughout its entire execution. They retain whatever value they were assigned until a different value is assigned or until the program completes.

The default storage class for variables declared within a block is *automatic*, that is, on the stack. There is a keyword auto, but it is rarely used because it doesn't change the default. Automatic variables are created just before the program execution enters the block in which they were declared, and they are discarded just as execution leaves that block. If the block is executed several times, as in the case of a function that is called repeatedly, new copies of the automatic variables are created each time. These new variables may or may not occupy the same memory locations on the stack as the previous instances of the same variables, and even if they do there is no guarantee that the memory was not used for some other purpose in the meantime. We therefore say that automatic variables disappear at the end of a block; they generally will not have their previous values the next time the block is entered.

On variables declared within a block, the keyword static changes the storage class from automatic to static. Variables with static storage class exist for the entire duration of the program, rather than just the duration of the block in which it is declared. Note that changing the storage class of a variable does not change its scope; it is still accessible by name only from within the block. The formal parameters to a function cannot be declared static, because arguments are always passed on the stack to support recursion.

Finally, the **register** keyword may be used on declarations of automatic variables to indicate that they should be stored in the machine's hardware registers rather than in memory. Usually, such variables can be accessed more efficiently than those stored in memory. However, the compiler is free to ignore the register keyword. If too many variables are designated as register, only the first ones will actually be stored in the registers, and the rest will be automatic. A compiler that does its own register optimization may ignore register altogether on the grounds that the compiler can do a better job deciding which values should be in registers than a human.

Typically, you want to declare the variables that are used most heavily as register variables. On some computers, the program can benefit if we declare pointers as register variables, particularly those pointers on which the most indirection is performed. You may declare the formal parameters of a function as register variables, and the compiler will generate instructions at the beginning of the function to copy the values from the stack to the registers. It is entirely possible, however, that the space and time savings in subsequent accesses to the parameters may not be enough to offset the overhead of this copying.

Register variables are created and destroyed at the same time as automatic variables, but there is some additional work needed. Before a function that has used register variables returns, the previous contents of the registers must be restored in order to ensure that the caller's register variables are not destroyed. Many machines use the runtime stack to accomplish this task. When a function begins, contents of any registers that it will use are saved on the stack. These values are then copied back to the registers just before the function returns.

Many hardware implementations do not assign addresses to the registers. Also, because of the saving and restoring of register values, a particular register may contain many different values at different times. For these reasons, you are not allowed to take the address of a register variable.

3.7.1 Initialization

We now return to the topic of initialization of variables in their declarations. There is an important difference in how initialization works on automatic variables versus static variables. Initialization of variables with static storage class is accomplished by placing the desired value in the executable program file in the location that will be used by the variable when the program is executing. When this executable file is loaded into memory, the location assigned to the variable starts out with the correct value already in it. No extra time is taken to accomplish this task, nor are any instructions executed in the program to do it. The variable just starts out with the right value. Static variables are initialized to zero unless an explicit initialization specifies some other value.

Initialization of automatic variables takes more overhead because the location used to store the variable cannot be determined when the program is linked. Indeed, local variables in a function may occupy different locations each time the function is called. For this reason, there is no default initialization of automatic variables, and explicit initialization is performed with an invisible assignment statement inserted in the beginning of the block.

This technique has four consequences. First, initialization of automatic variables is no more efficient than an assignment statement. Except for variables declared as `const`, initializing the variable in its declaration or using assignment statements is solely a matter of style. Second, the implicit assignment statement causes automatic variables to be reinitialized each time the function (or block) in which they were declared is entered. This behavior is quite different from static variables, which are initialized only once before the program begins to execute. The third consequence is an advantage. Because initialization is performed at run time, you may use any expression as an initializer, for example,

```
int
func( int a )
{
        int     b = a + 3;
```

Finally, unless you initialize them explicitly, automatic variables will contain garbage when they are created.

3.8 The Static Keyword

It is indeed unfortunate that the `static` keyword has different meanings when used in different contexts, because it always causes confusion for beginning C programmers. This summary and the following example should help clarify the issue for you.

When used on function definitions, or declarations of variables that appear outside of blocks, the keyword `static` changes the *linkage* from external to internal—the storage class and scope are not affected. Functions and variables declared in this way are accessible only from within the source file in which they were declared.

When used on variable declarations that appear inside of a block, the keyword `static` changes the *storage class* from automatic to static—the linkage and scope are not affected. Variables declared in this manner are created when the program begins to execute and continue to exist for its entire duration, instead of being created and destroyed every time execution enters and leaves the block.

3.9 Scope, Linkage, and Storage Class Example

Figure 3.4 contains an example which illustrates scope, linkage, and storage class. Declarations with file scope default to external linkage, so a in line 1 is

```
1       int             a = 5;
2       extern  int     b;
3       static  int     c;

4       int d( int e )
5       {
6               int             f = 15;
7               register int    b;
8               static  int     g = 20;
9               extern  int     a;
10              ...
11              {
12                      int             e;
13                      int             a;
14                      extern  int     h;
15                      ...
16              }
17              ...
18              {
19                      int     x;
20                      int     e;
21                      ...
22              }
23      ...
24      }

25      static int i()
26      {
27              ...
28      }

29      ...
```

Figure 3.4   Scope, linkage, and storage class example

external. The `extern` keyword in line 2 is technically not needed but stylistically desired if b is defined elsewhere. The `static` keyword in line 3 overrides the default linkage for c, giving it internal linkage instead. Other source files that declare variables named a or b with external linkage will access the same variables declared here. However, c can only be accessed from within this source file due to its internal linkage.

The storage class of a, b, and c is static, meaning that they are not stored on the stack. Thus, these variables are created when the program begins executing, and they retain their values until it finishes. a will be initialized to five when the program begins.

The scope of these variables extends through the rest of this source file, but local declarations of variables named a and b in lines 7 and 13 hide these variables from those portions of the program. Thus, the scopes of these first three variables are,

a	lines 1–12, 17–29
b	lines 2–6, 25–29
c	lines 3–29

Line 4 declares two identifiers. The scope of d extends from line 4 through the end of this file; the definition of function d serves as its prototype for any functions later in this source file that wish to call d. As a function name, d defaults to external linkage, so functions in other source files can call d as long as they have a prototype.[21] We could change the linkage to internal by declaring the function `static`, but doing so would make it inaccessible from other source files. Storage class is not an issue for functions because code is always stored in static memory.

The argument e has no linkage, so we can access it by name only from within this function. It has automatic storage class, so it comes into existence when the function is called and disappears when the function returns. Its scope is limited to lines 6–11, 17–19, and 23–24 due to conflicting local declarations.

Lines 6–8 declare local variables, thus their scope ends at the end of the function. They have no linkage, so they cannot be accessed by name from anywhere outside of this function (which is why they are called local). The storage class of f is automatic, and it is initialized to 15 by an implicit assignment statement each time the function is called. b has register storage class so its initial value is garbage. The storage class of g is static, so it exists throughout the program's execution. It is initialized to 20 once at the beginning of execution. It is *not* initialized each time the function is called.

---

[21] Actually, the prototype is only required if d returns something other than an integer. Prototyping all functions that you call is recommended because it reduces the chances for undetected errors.

The declaration in line 9 is not needed. This block is within the scope of the declaration in line 1.

Lines 12 and 13 declare local variables for the block. They are automatic, have no linkage, and their scopes extend through line 16. These variables are separate from the a and e declared earlier, and the earlier variables are inaccessible from this block because of the name conflict.

Line 14 makes the global variable h accessible from within the block. It has external linkage and resides in static storage. This is the only declaration where the extern is vital. Without it, h would be another local variable.

Lines 19 and 20 create local variables (automatic, no linkage, scope restricted to this block). This e is a different variable than the argument e, and it is also a different variable from the e declared in line 12. The blocks starting at lines 11 and 18 are not nested, so the compiler can use the same memory to store their local variables. Thus, there is a chance that the same memory location will be used to store the variable e in both blocks. If you need e to be the same variable in both blocks, then it shouldn't be declared as local to them.

Finally, line 25 declares the function i with static linkage. Static linkage prevents it from being called by any functions outside of this source file. Indeed, another source file may declare its own function called i, which will be separate and distinct from this one. The scope of i extends from this declaration to the end of this source file. Function d cannot call function i because no prototype for i appears prior to d.

3.10 Summary

Entities with external linkage are what other languages would term *global* and are accessible to all functions in all source files. External linkage occurs by default with variable declarations that are not in any block and with function definitions. Adding extern to a variable declaration inside of a block causes it to refer to global variables rather than local ones.

Entities with external linkage always have static storage class. Global variables are created before the program begins to execute and exist throughout its execution. The local variables belonging to functions come and go as the functions execute, but the machine instructions in the functions exist for the life of the program.

Local variables, those that are used in a function and not referenced by name from any other function, default to automatic storage for two reasons. First, storage is allocated to these variables only when they are needed, thus reducing the total memory requirement for the program. Second, allocating

Variable Type	*Where Declared*	*Stored on Stack*	*Scope*	*If Declared* `static`
global	outside of all blocks	no [1]	remainder of this source file	prevents access from other source files
local	beginning of a block	yes [2]	throughout the block [3]	variable is not stored on the stack, keeps its value for the entire duration of the program
formal parameters	function header	yes [2]	throughout the function [3]	not allowed

[1] Variables stored on the stack retain their values only while the block to which they are local is active. When execution leaves the block, the values are lost.

[2] Variables *not* stored on the stack are created when the program begins executing and retain their values throughout execution, regardless of whether they are local or global.

[3] Except in nested blocks that declare identical names.

Table 3.4   Scope, linkage, and storage class summary

them on the stack allows recursion to be implemented efficiently. You can change the storage class of local variables to static if it is important that the values of these variables be retained between executions of the function.

This information is summarized in Table 3.4.

3.11 Summary of Cautions

1. Writing misleading declarations for pointer variables (page 50).

2. Misinterpreting the meaning of initializations in pointer declarations (page 50).

3.12 Summary of Programming Tips

1. For the best portability, restrict character variables to values in the intersection of the signed and unsigned character ranges or don't perform arithmetic on them (page 41).

2. Express literals in the form that is most natural for how they are used (page 42).

3. Don't mix integers with enumerated values (page 44).

4. Don't depend on implicit declarations (page 51).

5. Use `typedef` rather than `#define` to define new type names (page 52).

6. Use `const` to declare variables that will not change (page 53).

7. Use named constants rather than literal constants (page 54).

8. Don't use duplicate variable names in nested blocks (page 55).

9. Use `extern` in all declarations for an entity but one (page 58).

3.13 Questions

1. What is the range for characters and the various integer types on your machine?

2. What is the range for each of the floating-point types on your machine?

3. Suppose you are writing a program that must run on two machines whose default integers are different sizes: 16 bits and 32 bits. The size of long integers on these machines is 32 bits and 64 bits, respectively. Some of the values used in this program are small enough to fit in a default integer on either machine, but some values are large enough to require 32 bits. One possible solution is to simply use `long` integers for all values, but this approach wastes time and space on the 16-bit machine for those values that would fit in 16 bits and wastes time and space on the 32-bit machine as well.

   How can you write the declarations for these variables so that they are the right size for both machines? The correct approach avoids the need to modify these declarations when compiling the program on either machine. *Hint:* Try including a header file that contains declarations specific to each particular machine.

4. Suppose you have a program that assigns a `long integer` variable to a `short integer` variable. What happens when you compile this program? What happens when you run it? Do you think that other compilers will give the same results?

5. Suppose you have a program that assigns a `double` variable to a `float`. What happens when you compile this program? What happens when you run it?

6. Write a declaration for an enumeration that defines values for coins, using the symbols PENNY, NICKEL, and so forth.

7. What is printed by this fragment of code?

```
enum Liquid { OUNCE = 1, CUP = 8, PINT = 16,
```

```
        QUART = 32, GALLON = 128 };

enum    Liquid  jar;
...
jar = QUART;
printf( "%s\n", jar );
jar = jar + PINT;
printf( "%s\n", jar );
```

8. Does your C implementation allow string literals to be modified by the program? Are there any compiler options that allow the modification of string literals to be enabled or disabled?

9. If the integer types are normally signed, what is the purpose of the `signed` keyword?

10. Can an unsigned variable hold a larger range of values than a signed variable of the same size?

11. Assuming that they are both 32 bits long, which type of variable can hold more distinct values, an `int` or a `float`?

12. The two fragments of code shown below came from the beginning of a function.

```
int     a = 25;                 int     a;
                                a = 25;
```

How do they differ in what they accomplish?

13. If the declarations in the code fragments in question 12 included the word `const`, how would they differ in what they accomplished?

14. A variable declared in a block may be accessed by name from anywhere in that block. True or false?

15. Suppose function a declares an automatic integer variable called x. You can access the variable x from a different function by using a declaration such as this one.

```
extern int x;
```

True or false?

16. Suppose the variable x in question 15 had been declared `static`. Does this modification change your answer?

17. Suppose the file `a.c` begins with this declaration:

```
int     x;
```

What declaration (if any) would be needed to access this variable from a function found later in the same file?

18. Suppose the declaration in question 17 included the keyword `static`. Would this modification change your answer?

19. Suppose the file `a.c` begins with this declaration:

```
int     x;
```

What declaration (if any) would be needed to access this variable from a function found in a different source file?

20. Suppose the declaration in question 19 included the keyword `static`. Would this modification change your answer?

21. Suppose a function that contains automatic variables is called twice in a row. Is it possible that the variables will have the same values at the beginning of the second call that they had at the end of the first call?

22. What is the difference in the behavior of the declaration

```
int     a = 5;
```

when it appears inside of a function as compared to when it appears outside?

23. Suppose you wanted to write two functions, x and y, in the same source file, that use the following variables:

Name	Type	Storage Class	Linkage	Scope	Initial- ized to
a	int	static	external	accessible to x; not y	1
b	char	static	none	accessible to x and y	2
c	int	automatic	none	local to x	3
d	float	static	none	local to x	4

How and where would you write the declarations for these variables? Note: All initialization must be made in the declarations themselves, not by any executable statements in the functions.

24. Identify any errors contained in the following program. (You may wish to try compiling it to be sure.) After you have removed the errors, determine the storage class, scope, and linkage of every identifier. What will be the initial value of each variable? There are many duplicate identifiers; do they refer to the same variable or to different ones? From where can each of these functions be called?

```
1    static   int       w = 5;
2    extern   int       x;

3    static float
4    func1( int a,  int b,  int c )
5    {
6            int       c, d, e = 1;
7            ...
8            {
9                    int       d, e, w;
10                   ...
11                   {
12                           int       b, c, d;
13                           static   int       y = 2;
14                           ...
15                   }
16           }
17           ...
18           {
19                   register int     a, d, x;
20                   extern   int     y;
21                   ...
22           }
23   }

24   static   int       y;

25   float
26   func2( int a )
27   {
28           extern   int       y;
29           static   int       z;
30           ...
31   }
```

4

Statements

You will find that C implements all of the statements found in other, modern high-level languages, and most of them work the way you would expect. The if statement chooses between alternate sequences of code, and the while, for, and do statements implement different kinds of loops.

There are some differences, though. For example, C does not have an assignment statement; an "expression statement" is used instead. The switch statement performs the same job as other languages' case statements, though in an unusual way.

Before I discuss the details of C statements, though, let's review the different typefaces used in syntax descriptions. Code that must be written exactly as shown is set in Courier, while abstract descriptions of code appear in *Courier Italic*. Some statements also have optional parts. Code that you must write exactly as shown if you decide to use the optional part is shown in **Courier Bold**, and descriptions of optional parts are in ***Courier Bold-Italic***. Also, the statement syntax is illustrated with the same indentation used in the program examples. This spacing is not required by the compiler but is valuable for human readers (such as yourself).

4.1 Empty Statement

The simplest statement in C is the *empty statement*, which consists of a semicolon all by itself. The empty statement doesn't perform any work but is occasionally useful anyway. It is used in situations where the syntax requires a statement, but there isn't any work to be performed. Some of the later examples in this chapter include empty statements.

4.2 Expression Statement

If there is no "assignment statement" in C, how is assignment performed? The answer is that assignment is an *operation* just like addition and subtraction, so assignment is performed by writing an *expression.*

You can turn an expression into a statement simply by putting a semi-colon at the end of it. Thus, statements such as

```
x = y + 3;
ch = getchar();
```

are really expression statements, not assignment statements.

This distinction is important to understand because it is perfectly legal to write statements such as these:

```
y + 3;
getchar();
```

When these statements are executed, the expressions are evaluated, but the results are not saved anywhere because an assignment operator was not used. The first statement, therefore, has no effect whatever, and the second statement gets the next character of input but then ignores it.[22]

If it seems strange that you can write statements that have no effect, consider this one:

```
printf( "Hello world!\n" );
```

printf is a function and functions return values, yet the value returned by printf (the number of characters actually printed) is usually of no concern and therefore ignored. The statement "has no effect" only in the sense that the value of the expression is ignored; the printf function performs useful work. Such work is called a *side effect.*

Here is another example:

```
a++;
```

There is no assignment operator, yet it is a perfectly reasonable expression statement. The ++ operator increments the variable a as a side effect. There are other operators with side effects, and I will discuss them in the next chapter.

---

[22] Actually, it *can* affect the outcome of the program, but how it does so is so subtle that we must wait until Chapter 18 and our discussion of the runtime environment to explain it.

4.3 Statement Blocks

A *block* is a list of declarations and a list of statements, both optional, enclosed in braces. The syntax for a block is straightforward:

```
{
        declarations
        statements
}
```

A block may be used anywhere a statement is required, and it lets you use a list of statements in places where the syntax only calls for one. Blocks also allow you to declare data very close to where it is used.

4.4 If Statement

The **if** statement in C works pretty much the same as those in other languages. The syntax looks like this:

```
if( expression )
        statement
else
        statement
```

The parentheses are part of the if statement, not part of the expression, so they are required even for simple expressions.

 Either of the *statement*s may be a block instead. A common error is to forget to put in the braces when adding a second statement to either clause of an if statement. Many programmers prefer to use the braces all the time precisely to avoid this error.

If the *expression* is true, then the first *statement* is executed; otherwise, it is skipped. If there is an else clause, then its *statement* is executed only when the *expression* is false.

There is one difference between C if statements and if statements in other languages. C doesn't have a boolean type; integers are used for this purpose. Thus, the *expression* can be any expression that results in an integer value—zero means "false" and all nonzero values mean "true."

C has all of the relational operators that you would expect, but they produce the integer values zero and one rather than boolean values "true" and "false." Thus the relational operators end up functioning the same as in other languages.

```
if( x > 3 )
        printf( "Greater\n" );
else
        printf( "Not greater\n" );
```

evaluates the expression x > 3, which yields a value of either zero or one. If
the value is one, Greater is printed; if it is zero, Not greater is printed.
Integer variables can also hold boolean values, as in this example

```
result = x > 3;
...
if( result )
        printf( "Greater\n" );
else
        printf( "Not greater\n" );
```

This code fragment executes exactly the same as the previous one; the only
difference is that the result of the comparison, which is either a zero or a one,
is saved in a variable and tested later. There is a potential trap here. Even
though all nonzero values are considered true, comparing one nonzero value to
a different nonzero value yields false. I discuss this problem in more detail in
the next chapter.

When if statements are nested within one another, the *dangling else*
problem can appear. For example, to which if statement does the else
clause belong in the following fragment?

```
if( i > 1 )
        if( j > 2 )
                printf( "i > 1 and j > 2\n" );
    else
                printf( "no they're not\n" );
```

The else clause is indented strangely to illustrate this question. The answer,
as in most other languages, is that the else clause belongs to the closest if
that is incomplete. If you want it to be associated with an earlier if statement,
you must complete the closer if either by adding an empty else to it or by
enclosing it in a block as in this fragment.

```
if( i > 1 ){
        if( j > 2 )
                printf( "i > 1 and j > 2\n" );
}
else
        printf( "no they're not\n" );
```

4.5 While Statement

The **while** statement is also a lot like its counterpart in other languages. The only real difference is the expression, which works the same as in the if statement. Here is the syntax.

```
while( expression )
        statement
```

The test in this loop is performed before the body is executed, so if the test is initially false, the body will not be executed at all. Again, a block may be used if more than one statement is needed for the body of the loop.

4.5.1 Break and Continue Statements

The **break** statement may be used in a while loop to terminate the loop prematurely. After a break, the next statement to be executed is the one that would have been performed had the loop terminated normally.

The **continue** statement may be used in a while loop to terminate the current iteration of the loop prematurely. After a continue, the expression is evaluated again to determine whether the loop should execute again or end.

If either of these statements is used within nested loops, it applies only to the innermost loop; it is not possible to affect the execution of the outer nested loop with a break or continue.

4.5.2 Execution of the While

We can now illustrate the flow of control through a while loop. For those who have never seen flowcharts before, the diamond represents a decision, the box represents an action to be performed, and the arrows show the flow of control between them. Figure 4.1 shows how the while statement operates. Execution begins at the top, where the *expr* is evaluated. If its value is zero, the loop terminates. Otherwise, the body of the loop (*stmt*) is executed and control returns to the top where the whole thing starts again. For example, the loop below copies characters from the standard input to the standard output until the end of file indication is found.

```
while( (ch = getchar()) != EOF )
        putchar( ch );
```

If a continue statement is executed in the body of the loop, the remaining

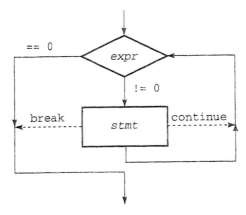

Figure 4.1   Execution of the while statement

statements in the body are skipped and the next iteration begins immediately. continue is useful in situations where the body of the loop only applies to some of the values that are encountered.

```
while( (ch = getchar()) != EOF ){
        if( ch < '0' || ch > '9' )
                continue;
        /* process only the digits */
}
```

The alternative is to invert the test performed in the if and have it control the entire body of the loop. The difference is solely stylistic; there is no difference at execution time.

If a break statement is executed, the loop exits immediately. For example, suppose a list of values to be processed is terminated with a negative number:

```
while( scanf( "%f", &value ) == 1 ){
        if( value < 0 )
                break;
        /* process the nonnegative values */
}
```

An alternative is to include the test in the while expression, like this:

```
while( scanf( "%f", &value ) == 1 && value >= 0 ){
```

This style may be difficult, however, if some computations must be performed before the value can be tested.

Occasionally, a `while` statement does all the work in its expression, and there is no work left for the body. In this case, the empty statement is used for the body. It is good practice to write the empty statement on a line by itself, as illustrated in the loop below, which discards the remainder of the current input line.

```
while( (ch = getchar()) != EOF && ch != '\n' )
        ;
```

This form clearly shows that the body of the loop is empty, making it less likely that the next statement in the program will be misinterpreted by a human reader as the body of the loop.

4.6 For Statement

The C **for** statement is more general than the `for` statements in other languages. In fact, the `for` statement in C is really just a shorthand notation for a very common arrangement of statements in a `while` loop. The syntax of the `for` statement looks like this:

```
for( expression1; expression2; expression3 )
        statement
```

The `statement` is called the *body* of the loop. `expression1` is the *initialization* and is evaluated once before the looping begins. `expression2` is the *condition* and is evaluated before each execution of the body, just as in a `while` loop. `expression3` is called the *adjustment* and is evaluated after the body and just before the condition is evaluated again. All three expressions are optional and may be omitted. A missing condition means "true."

The `break` and `continue` statements also work in a `for` loop. `break` exits the loop immediately, and `continue` goes directly to the adjustment.

4.6.1 Execution of a For

The `for` statement is executed (almost) exactly the same as the following `while` statement:

```
    expression1;
    while( expression2 ){
            statement
            expression3;
    }
```

Figure 4.2 diagrams the execution of the `for` statement. Can you see how it differs from a `while` loop?

The difference between the `for` and the `while` loops is with `continue`. In the `for` statement, a `continue` skips the rest of the body of the loop and goes to the adjustment. In the `while` loop, the adjustment is part of the body, so a `continue` skips it, too.

A stylistic advantage of the `for` loop is that it collects all of the expressions that are responsible for the operation of the loop together in one place so they are easier to find, especially when the body of the loop is large. For example, the following loop initializes the elements of an array to zero.

```
    for( i = 0; i < MAX_SIZE; i += 1 )
            array[i] = 0;
```

The following `while` loop performs the same task, but you must look in three different places to determine how the loop operates.

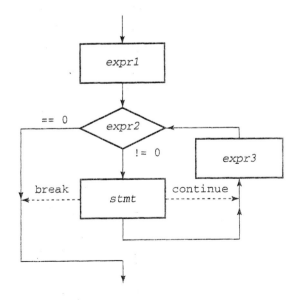

Figure 4.2   Execution of the `for` statement

```
i = 0;
while( i < MAX_SIZE ){
        array[i] = 0;
        i += 1;
}
```

4.7 Do Statement

The C **do** statement is very much like the *repeat* statement found in other languages. It behaves just like a while statement except that the test is made after the body is executed rather than before, so the body of the loop is always executed at least once. Here is its syntax.

```
do
        statement
while( expression);
```

As usual, a block may be used if multiple statements are needed in the body. Figure 4.3 shows how execution flows in a do statement.

How do you choose between a while and a do?

When you need the body of the loop to be executed at least once, use a do.

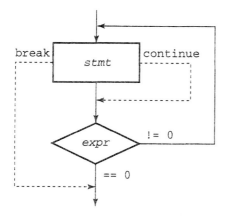

Figure 4.3   Execution of the do statement

The loop below, which prints from one to eight spaces to advance to the next tab stop (set every eight columns), illustrates this.

```
do {
        column += 1;
        putchar( ' ' );
} while( column % 8 != 0 );
```

4.8 Switch Statement

The **switch** statement in C is a little unusual. It serves the same role as the case statement in other languages, but it is different in one very important respect. Let's look at the syntax first. The *expression* must produce an integer value.

```
switch( expression )
        statement
```

Although it is legal to write a switch statement with only a single statement as its body, there is no point in doing so. Practical switch statements look like this one:

```
switch( expression ){
        statement-list
}
```

Sprinkled throughout the statement list are one or more *case labels* of the form

```
case constant-expression:
```

Each case label must have a unique value. A *constant expression* is an expression that is evaluated at compile time; it may not contain any variables. What is unusual is that the case labels do not partition the statement list into separate sections; they identify *entry points* into the list of statements.

Let's follow the execution of this statement. First, the *expression* is evaluated. Then, execution goes to the statement in the list that is identified by the case label whose value matches the expression's value. From here, the statement list is executed all the way to its end, which is at the bottom of the switch statement.

Do you see the difference in the execution of the `switch`? Execution flows *through* case labels rather than stopping at them, which is why case labels identify entry points to the statement list rather than partitioning it. If this behavior doesn't seem right, there is a way to fix it—the `break` statement.

4.8.1 Break in a Switch

If a `break` is encountered in a `switch` statement, execution proceeds immediately to the end of the statement list. Thus, 97% of all `switch` statements in C have `break` statements at the end of each case. The following example, which examines a character entered by the user and invokes the function that it selects, illustrates this usage.

```
switch( command ){
case 'A':
        add_entry();
        break;

case 'D':
        delete_entry();
        break;

case 'P':
        print_entry();
        break;

case 'E':
        edit_entry();
        break;
}
```

In effect, the `break` statements partition the statement list so that the `switch` will work in the more traditional manner.

What is the purpose of the `break` in the last case of the statement? It has no effect at run time, because there aren't any more statements in the `switch`, but it also doesn't hurt anything. This `break` is there for future maintenance. Should someone decide later to add another case to this statement, there is no chance that they will forget to add a `break` at the end of the statements for the previous case.

The `continue` has no effect in a `switch` statement. You may put a `continue` in a `switch` statement only if the `switch` is enclosed by a loop; the `continue` applies to the loop rather than the `switch`.

In order to execute the same group of statements with two or more values, multiple case labels are given, as in this example.

```
switch( expression ){
case 1:
case 2:
case 3:
        statement-list
        break;

case 4:
case 5:
        statement-list
        break;
}
```

This technique works because execution flows through the case labels. C does not have any shorthand notation for specifying ranges of values, so every value in a range must be given as a separate case label. If the range of values is large, you may prefer a series of nested if statements instead.

4.8.2 Defaults

The next question is, what happens if the expression's value does not match any of the case labels? Nothing at all—the statement list is skipped entirely. The program does not abort or give any indication of error because this situation is not considered an error in C.

What if you don't want to ignore expression values that do not match any case labels? You can add a *default* clause to the statement list by writing

```
default:
```

in place of a case label. The default clause is where execution of the statement list begins when the expression value does not match any of the case labels, so there can be only one of them. However, it can go anywhere in the statement list, and execution flows through the default the same as a case label.

It is good practice to use a default clause in every switch statement so that illegal values can be detected. Otherwise the program will continue to run with no indication that an error occurred. The only reasonable exceptions to this rule are when the value being tested has been checked for validity earlier, and when you are only interested in a subset of the possible values.

4.8.3 Execution of the Switch

Why is the `switch` statement implemented in this manner? Many programmers think that it was a mistake, but once in a blue moon it is useful to have control flow from one statement group into the next.

For example, consider a program that counts the number of characters, words, and lines in its input. Each character must be counted, but space and tab characters also terminate whatever word they followed, so for them, both the character count and the word count must be incremented. Then there is the newline; this character terminates a line and a word, so there are three counters to adjust for a newline. Now examine this statement:

```
switch( ch ){
case '\n':
        lines += 1;
        /* FALL THRU */

case ' ':
case '\t':
        words += 1;
        /* FALL THRU */

default:
        chars += 1;
}
```

The logic is simpler than what would appear in a real program, for example, only the first of a sequence of spaces terminates the preceding word. Nevertheless, the example does what we want: newlines cause all three counters to be incremented, spaces and tabs increment only two, and everything else increments only the character counter.

The `FALL THRU` comments make it clear to the reader that execution is supposed to fall through the case labels. Without the comments, a careless maintenance programmer looking for a bug might notice the lack of `break` statements and decide that this omission is the error and not look any further. After all, it is so rare that you actually *want* execution to flow through the case labels that a missing `break` statement is much more likely to be an error than not. But in "fixing" this problem, he would not only have missed the bug he was originally looking for, but he would have introduced a new one as well. The small effort of writing these comments now might pay off in a lot of time saved later.

4.9 Goto Statement

Lastly, there is the **goto** statement, which has this syntax.

```
goto statement-label;
```

To use it, you must put *statement labels* before each statement to which you wish to go. Statement labels are identifiers followed by a colon. goto statements that include these labels may then be placed anywhere in the same function.

The goto is a dangerous statement, because when learning C it is too easy to become dependent on it. Inexperienced programmers sometimes use goto's as a way to avoid thinking about the program's design. The resulting programs are nearly always more difficult to maintain than carefully designed ones. For example, here is a program that uses goto's to perform an exchange sort of the values in an array.

```
            i = 0;
outer_next:
            if( i >= NUM_ELEMENTS - 1 )
                    goto outer_end;
            j = i + 1;
inner_next:
            if( j >= NUM_ELEMENTS )
                    goto inner_end;
            if( value[i] <= value[j] )
                    goto no_swap;
            temp = value[i];
            value[i] = value[j];
            value[j] = temp;
no_swap:
            j += 1;
            goto inner_next;
inner_end:
            i += 1;
            goto outer_next;
outer_end:
            ;
```

This is a tiny program, yet you must spend a considerable amount of time studying it to understand its structure.

Here is the same program without goto's. Its structure is much easier to see.

```
for( i = 0; i < NUM_ELEMENTS - 1; i += 1 ){
        for( j = i + 1; j < NUM_ELEMENTS; j += 1 ){
                if( value[i] > value[j] ){
                        temp = value[i];
                        value[i] = value[j];
                        value[j] = temp;
                }
        }
}
```

However, there is one situation in which many claim that a `goto` might be appropriate in a well structured program—breaking out of nested loops. Because the `break` statement only affects the innermost loop that encloses it, the only way to immediately exit a deeply nested set of loops is with a `goto`, as shown in this example.

```
while( condition1 ){
        while( condition2 ){
                while( condition3 ){
                        if( some disaster )
                                goto quit;
                }
        }
}
quit: ;
```

There are two alternatives to using a `goto`. First, a status flag can be set when you want to exit all of the loops, but the flag must then be tested in every loop:

```
enum { EXIT, OK } status;
...
status = OK;
while( status == OK && condition1 ){
        while( status == OK && condition2 ){
                while( condition3 ){
                        if( some disaster ){
                                status = EXIT;
                                break;
                        }
                }
        }
}
```

This technique does the job but makes the conditions more complex. The second alternative is to put the entire set of loops in a separate function. When disaster strikes in the innermost loop, you can use a `return` statement to leave the function. Chapter 7 discusses `return` statements.

4.10 Summary

Many of the statements in C behave the same as their counterparts in other languages. The `if` statement conditionally executes statements, and the `while` statement repeatedly executes statements. Because C does not have a boolean type, both of these statements test an integer expression instead. The value zero is interpreted as false, and nonzero values are interpreted as true. The `for` statement is a shorthand notation for a `while` loop; it collects the expressions that control the loop in one place so that they are easy to find. The `do` statement is similar to a `while`, but `do` guarantees that the body of the loop is always executed at least once. Finally, the `goto` statement transfers execution from one statement to another. In general, `goto` should be avoided.

C also has some statements that behave a little differently than their counterparts in other languages. Assignment is done with an expression statement rather than an assignment statement. The `switch` statement performs the job of the `case` statement in other languages, but execution in a `switch` passes through the case labels to the end of the `switch`. To prevent this behavior, you must put a `break` statement at the end of the statements for each case. A `default:` clause in a `switch` will catch expressions whose values do not match any of the given case values. In the absence of a `default`, the body of the `switch` is skipped if none of the case labels match the expression's value.

The empty statement is used when a statement is required but there is no work needed. Statement blocks allow you to write many statements in places where the syntax calls for a single statement. When a `break` statement is executed inside of a loop, it terminates the loop. When a `continue` statement is executed inside of a loop, the remainder of the body is skipped and the next iteration of the loop begins immediately. In `while` and `do` loops, the next iteration begins with the test, but in `for` loops, the next iteration begins with the adjustment.

And that's it! C does not have any input/output statements; I/O is performed by calling library functions. Nor does it have any exception handling statements; these are also done with library functions.

4.11 Summary of Cautions

1. Writing expressions that have no result (page 72).

2. Be sure to use braces around statement lists in an `if` statement (page 73).

3. Execution flowing unexpectedly from one `case` of a `switch` statement into the next (page 81).

4.12 Summary of Programming Tips

1. In a loop without a body, put the semicolon for the empty statement on a line by itself (page 77).

2. It is easier to read `for` loops than `while` loops because the expressions that control the loop are all together (page 78).

3. Use a `default:` clause in every `switch` statement (page 82).

4.13 Questions

1. Is the following statement legal? If so, what does it do?

   ```
   3 * x * x - 4 * x + 6;
   ```

2. What is the syntax of the assignment statement?

3. Is it legal to use a block in this manner? If so, why would you ever want to use it?

   ```
   ...
   statement
   {
           statement
           statement
   }
   statement
   ```

4. How would you write an `if` statement that had no statements in the *then* clause but had statements in the `else` clause? How else could an equivalent statement be written?

5. What output is produced from the loop below?

   ```
   int     i;
   ```

```
. . .
for( i = 0; i < 10; i += 1 )
        printf( "%d\n", i );
```

6. When might a while statement be more appropriate than a for statement?

7. The code fragment below is supposed to copy the standard input to the standard output and compute a checksum of the characters. What is wrong with it?

```
while( (ch = getchar()) != EOF )
        checksum += ch;
        putchar( ch );

printf( "Checksum = %d\n", checksum );
```

8. When is the do statement more appropriate than a while or a for statement?

9. What output is produced from this code fragment? *Note:* The % operator divides its left operand by its right operand and gives you the remainder.

```
for( i = 1; i <= 4; i += 1 ){
        switch( i % 2 ){
        case 0:
                printf( "even\n" );

        case 1:
                printf( "odd\n" );
        }
}
```

10. Write statements that read an integer value from the standard input and then print that many blank lines.

11. Write statements to validate and report on some values that have already been read. If x is less than y, print the word WRONG. Also, if a is greater than or equal to b, print WRONG. Otherwise, print the word RIGHT. *Note:* In case you need it, || is the "or" operator.

12. Years that are divisible by four are leap years, except that years that are divisible by 100 are not. However, years that are divisible by 400 *are* leap years. Write statements to determine whether the value in year is a leap year, and set the variable leap_year to one if it is a leap year, and zero if it is not.

13. Newspaper reporters are trained to ask who, what, when, where, and why? Write statements that will print who if the variable which_word is one, what

if the variable is two, and so forth. If the value is not in the range one through five, print `don't know` instead.

14. Pretend that a "program" controls you, and this program contains two functions: `eat_hamburger()` makes you eat a hamburger, and `hungry()` returns a true or false value depending on whether you are hungry. Write the statements that allow you to eat as many hamburgers as you want until you're no longer hungry.

15. Modify your answer to question 14 to satisfy your grandmother—You've got to eat something!—so that you always eat at least one hamburger.

16. Write statements to print a capsule summary of the current weather according to the values of the variables `precipitating` and `temperature`.

If `precipitating` is ...	and `temperature` is ...	then print ...
true	< 32	snowing
	>= 32	raining
false	< 60	cold
	>= 60	warm

4.14 Programming Exercises

1. The square root of a positive number n can be computed as a series of approximations, each more accurate than the last. The first approximation is one; successive approximations are given by the following formula.

$$a_{i+1} = \frac{a_i + \dfrac{n}{a_i}}{2}$$

Write a program to read a value and compute and print its square root. If you print all of the approximations you can see how quickly this method converges on the correct value. In principle, the computation could go on forever, yielding more and more accurate values. In practice, though, the restricted precision of floating-point variables prevents the program from continuing. Have your program stop computing when an approximation is equal to the previous one.

2. An integer is called *prime* if it is not evenly divisible by any integer other than itself and one. Write a program to print those numbers in the range 1–100 that are prime.

3. All three sides of *equilateral* triangles are the same length, but only two of the sides of an *isosceles* triangle are equal. If all of the sides of a triangle are

different lengths it is called *scalene*. Write a program to prompt for and read three numbers that are the lengths of the three sides of a triangle. The program should then determine what type of triangle the numbers represent. *Hint:* What else should the program be looking for?

△ ★★ 4. Write the function `copy_n` whose prototype is shown below.

```
void copy_n( char dst[], char src[], int n );
```

The function is to copy a string from the array `src` to the array `dst` but with the following requirement: exactly n characters must be stored into `dst`; no more, no less. If the length of the string in `src` is less than n, then you must add enough NUL characters after the copied characters to get a total of n characters stored. If the length of the string in `src` is greater than or equal to n, then stop after you have stored the n'th character; in this case `dst` will not be NUL-terminated. Note that a call to `copy_n` should store something into `dst[0]` through `dst[n-1]`, and only those locations, regardless of the length of `src`.

   If you are planning on using the library routine `strncpy` to implement your program, you are congratulated for reading ahead, but the goal here is for you to figure out the logic yourself, so you may not use any of the library string routines.

★★ 5. Write a program that reads the standard input line by line and does the following: for each set of two or more identical, adjacent lines in the file, one line from the set should be printed out; nothing else should be printed out. You may assume that the lines in the file will not exceed 128 characters in length (127 characters plus one for the newline that terminates each line).

   Consider the input file shown below.

```
This is the first line.
Another line.
And another.
And another.
And another.
And another.
Still more.
Almost done now --
Almost done now --
Another line.
Still more.
Finished!
```

Assuming that there are no trailing blanks or tabs on any of the lines (which wouldn't be visible but would make the line different from its neighbors), this program would produce the following output from this input file.

```
And another.
Almost done now --
```

One line from each set of adjacent identical lines is printed. Notice that
"Another line." and "Still more." are not printed because, although there are
two of each in the file, they are not adjacent.

    Hints: Use `gets` to read the input lines, and `strcpy` to copy them.
There is a routine called `strcmp` that takes two strings as arguments and compares them. It returns zero if they are equal and a nonzero value if they are
not.

★★★ 6. Write a function that extracts a substring from a string. The function should
have the following prototype:

```
int substr( char dst[], char src[], int start,
    int len )
```

It should copy the string that begins `start` characters past the beginning of the
string in `src` into the array `dst`. At most `len` non-NUL characters should be
copied from `src`. After copying, `dst` must be NUL-terminated. The function
should return the length of the string stored in `dst`.

    If `start` specifies a position beyond the end of the string in `src`, or
either `start` or `len` are negative, then `dst` should be given the empty string.

★★★ 7. Write a function that removes excess white space from a string of characters.
The function should have this prototype:

```
void deblank( char string[] );
```

Every run of one or more white space characters should be replaced by one
space character. Be sure that the string is terminated with a NUL byte when
you're through with it!

5

Operators and Expressions

C provides all of the operators that you expect in a programming language and many more. In fact, one of the characteristics of C that many people cite as a shortcoming is its vast assortment of operators, because they make the language harder to master. On the other hand, many of the C operators are unavailable in other languages, which is part of what makes C suitable for such a wide variety of applications.

After the explanations of the operators, I discuss the rules for expression evaluation, including operator precedence and arithmetic conversions.

5.1 Operators

For the purposes of explanation, the operators are grouped into categories according to either what they do or how they are used. For reference purposes, it is more convenient to group them by their precedence; Table 5.1, which appears later in this chapter, is organized this way.

5.1.1 Arithmetic

C provides all the usual arithmetic operators:

```
+       -       *       /       %
```

Except for %, these operators work both for floating-point and integer types. The / operator performs a truncating integer division when both of its operands are integers, otherwise it performs a floating-point division.[23] % is the modulo operator; it takes two integer arguments, divides the left operand by the right operand, but returns the remainder rather than the quotient.

5.1.2 Shifting

Assembly language programmers are already familiar with shifting. Here is a brief introduction for well-adjusted people. A *shift* simply slides the bits in a value to the left or the right. On a left shift, bits on the left side of the value are discarded, and zero bits are put into the space created on the right side by the shift. Figure 5.1 is an example of a left shift of three bits on an 8-bit value, shown in binary. The bits in the value all move left by three positions; the ones that fall off the left end are lost, and zeros are put into the positions vacated on the right.

Right shifts include a quirk not found in left shifts: there are two ways that new bits can be shifted in on the left side. The first is called a *logical shift*, in which zeros are shifted in on the left side. The other is called an *arithmetic shift*. A right arithmetic shift puts copies of the sign bit into the left side of the value, thus preserving its sign. If the value 10010110 is shifted right two positions, the result of a logical shift is 00100101, but the result of an arithmetic shift is 11100101. Arithmetic and logical left shifts are identical. Only the right shifts differ, and then only for negative values.

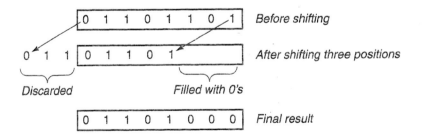

Figure 5.1   Left shift of three bits

---

[23] If either of the operands of an integer division is negative, the result of the division is implementation defined. Refer to the div function in Chapter 16 for details.

The left shift operator is << and the right shift operator is >>. The value given by the left operand is shifted the number of bit positions specified by the right operand. Both operands must have an integral type.

The Standard states that logical shifts are performed on all unsigned values but leaves it up to the implementation whether arithmetic or logical shifts are used for signed values. You can write a simple test program to see how your implementation works, but your test is no guarantee that any other compiler will work the same, thus programs that do right shifts on signed values are inherently nonportable.

Beware of shifts like this one:

```
a << -5
```

What does a left shift of -5 bit positions mean? A right shift of 5 bits? No shift at all? On one machine, this expression actually does a left shift of 27 bits—not exactly intuitive. What about shift counts that are larger than the number of bits in the operand?

The Standard states that the behavior of such shifts is undefined, so it is up to the implementation. However, few implementors address these situations explicitly, so the results are not likely to be meaningful. Thus, you should avoid using these types of shifts because their effects are unpredictable and nonportable.

The function shown in Program 5.1 uses a right shift to count the number of 1 bits in a value. It accepts an unsigned argument to avoid the right shift ambiguity and uses the modulo operator to determine whether the least significant bit is nonzero. We'll improve this function later after the &, <<= and += operators have been described.

5.1.3 Bitwise

The bitwise operators perform the logical operations AND, OR, and XOR (exclusive-OR) on the individual bits of their operands. Again, assembly language programmers are familiar with these operations but here is a brief introduction for everyone else. The AND of two bits produces a one only if both of the bits are one; otherwise the result is zero. The OR of two bits produces a result of zero only if both bits are zero; otherwise the result is one. Finally, the XOR of two bits produces a result of one if both bits are different, and a result of zero if both bits are the same. These operations are summarized in charts below.

```
/*
** This function returns the number of 1-bits that appeared in
** the argument value.
*/
int
count_one_bits( unsigned value )
{
        int     ones;

        /*
        ** While the value still has some 1-bits in it ...
        */
        for( ones = 0; value != 0; value = value >> 1 )
                /*
                ** If the low-order bit is a 1, count it.
                */
                if( value % 2 != 0 )
                        ones = ones + 1;

        return ones;
}
```

Program 5.1   Counting one bits in a value: preliminary version   count_1a.c

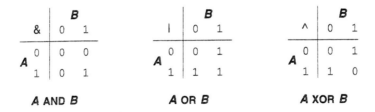

The bitwise operators are:

& | ^

for AND, OR, and XOR respectively. They require integer-type operands, and
they perform the indicated operation on the corresponding bits of their
operands, one pair of bits at a time. To illustrate this, suppose the variable a
has the binary value 00101110, and b has the binary value 01011011. Then a
& b results in the value 00001010, a | b gives the value 01111111, and a ^
b produces 01110101.

Bit Manipulation

The following expressions show how you can use shifting and bitwise operators to manipulate individual bits in an integer value. The expressions assume
that the variable `bit_number` is an integer value in the range zero to one less
than the number of bits in an integer and that the bits in an integer are numbered from right to left. The first example sets the specified bit to one.

```
value = value | 1 << bit_number;
```

The next clears the specified bit to zero.[24]

```
value = value & ~ ( 1 << bit_number );
```

These expressions are often written with the `|=` and `&=` operators, described in
the next section. Finally, this expression tests the specified bit and is nonzero
if the bit is set.

```
value & 1 << bit_number
```

5.1.4 Assignment

Finally we get to the assignment operator, which is the equal sign. Assignment is an expression rather than a type of statement, so an assignment is legal
anywhere an expression is legal. The statement

```
x = y + 3;
```

contains two operators, + and =. The addition is performed first, so the
operands of the = are the variable x and the value of the expression y + 3.
The assignment operator stores the value of the operand on the right into the
location specified by the operand on the left. But an assignment is an expression, and an expression has a value. The value of an assignment expression is
the new value of the left operand, which can be used as an operand of another
operator, as in this statement:

```
a = x = y + 3;
```

The assignment operator associates (is evaluated) from right to left, so this
statement is equivalent to:

---

[24] The unary ~ operator, to be described shortly, computes the one's complement of its operand.

```
a = ( x = y + 3 );
```

and has exactly the same meaning as:

```
x = y + 3;
a = x;
```

Here is a slightly more ambitious example.

```
r = s + ( t = u - v ) / 3;
```

This statement assigns to t the value of the expression u - v, then divides that value by three, adds s, and assigns the result to r. Although this is legal, the following statements are just as good

```
t = u - v;
r = s + t / 3;
```

In fact, they are even better because they are easier to read and easier to debug. It is very easy to go overboard with embedded assignments and write expressions that are difficult to read. Therefore, before you use this "feature," be sure that it is justified by some substantial, tangible benefit.

It is incorrect to say that the same value is assigned to both a and x in the statement:

```
a = x = y + 3;
```

If x were a character, the value y + 3 would be truncated to fit; a would then be assigned this truncated value. Truncation is precisely the problem in this common mistake:

```
char    ch;
...
while( (ch = getchar()) != EOF ) ...
```

The value EOF requires more bits than a character value, which is why getchar returns an integer value, not a character. However, storing it first in ch truncates the returned value. This truncated value is then promoted to an integer and compared with EOF. When this erroneous code is run on machines with signed characters, reading the byte \377 causes the loop to end as if end of file had been reached. When it is run on machines with unsigned characters, the loop never ends!

Compound Assignment

There is a compound assignment form for each of the operators presented so far:

```
+=       -=       *=       /=       %=
<<=      >>=      &=       ^=       |=
```

We discuss only the += operator because the others work the same way with their respective operators. The += operator is used like this:

```
a += expression
```

It reads "add expression to a" and is equivalent to the following expression

```
a = a + ( expression )
```

except that the operand on the left side of the += (a in this case) is only evaluated once. Note the parentheses: they ensure that expression is fully evaluated before the addition, even if it contains an operator whose precedence is lower than addition.

What is the point of having two ways to add something to a variable? The K&R C designers thought that compound assignment operators allowed the programmer to write code more clearly. Plus, the compiler would be able to produce more compact code. Now, the difference between a = a + 5; and a += 5; is not very dramatic, and modern compilers have no trouble producing optimal code for both expressions. But consider these two statements, which are equivalent if the function f has no side effects:

```
a[ 2 * (y - 6*f(x)) ] = a[ 2 * (y - 6*f(x)) ] + 1;
a[ 2 * (y - 6*f(x)) ] += 1;
```

The first form requires that the expression selecting the location to be incremented be written twice, once on the left and once on the right side of the equals sign. Because the compiler has no way of knowing whether f has any side effects, it must evaluate the subscript expression twice. The second form is more efficient because the subscript is evaluated only once.

A much more important advantage to += is that it makes the source code easier to read and write. To figure out what the first statement in the example above is doing, the reader must closely examine both subscript expressions to verify that they are identical and must then examine the function f to see whether it has any side effects. There is no such problem reading the second statement. It is also easier to write than the first, with fewer chances of typing errors. It is because of these advantages that you should use assignment operators.

We can now rewrite Program 5.1 using assignment operators as shown in Program 5.2. The assignment operators also simplify the expressions to set and clear individual bits in a value:

```
value |= 1 << bit_number;
value &= ~ ( 1 << bit_number );
```

5.1.5 Unary

There are a number of *unary* operators, that is, operators that take only one operand. They are

!	++	–	&	sizeof
~	--	+	*	(*type*)

Let's look at these operators one by one.

The ! operator performs a logical negation of its operand; if the operand is true the result is false, and if the operand is false the result is true. Like the

```
/*
** This function returns the number of 1-bits that appeared in
** the argument value.
*/
int
count_one_bits( unsigned value )
{
        int     ones;

        /*
        ** While the value still has some 1-bits in it ...
        */
        for( ones = 0; value != 0; value >>= 1 )
                /*
                ** If the low-order bit is a 1, count it.
                */
                if( ( value & 1 ) != 0 )
                        ones += 1;

        return ones;
}
```

Program 5.2   Counting one bits in a value: final version   count_1b.c

relational operators, this operator actually produces an integer result, either zero or one.

The ~ operator produces the one's complement of an integer-type operand. The one's complement is obtained by changing the value of each of the operand's bits from one to zero or from zero to one.

The – operator produces the negative of its operand.

The + operator yields the value of its operand; in other words, it does nothing. It is provided only for symmetry with –.

& produces the address of its operand. For example, in the following statements an integer variable and a pointer to an integer variable are declared. Then, the address of the variable a is determined with the & operator and is assigned to the pointer variable.

```
int     a, *b;
...
b = &a;
```

This example illustrates how you give a pointer variable the address of an existing variable.

* is the indirection operator and is used with pointers to access the value being pointed to. After the assignment in the previous example is performed, the value of the expression b would be the address of the variable a, but the value of the expression *b would be the value of a.

The sizeof operator determines the size of its operand, measured in bytes. The operand may be either an expression (often it is just a single variable), or a type name enclosed in parentheses. Here are two examples:

```
sizeof( int )    sizeof x
```

The first returns the number of bytes in an integer variable, which of course depends on the environment you are using. The second example returns the number of bytes used by the variable x. Note that the size of a character variable, by definition, is one. When used with the name of an array, sizeof returns the size of the array in bytes. It is legal to surround an expression operand with parentheses, like this:

```
sizeof( x )
```

because parentheses are always legal in expressions. Determining the size of an expression does *not* evaluate the expression, so sizeof(a = b + 1) does not assign anything to a.

The (*type*) operator is called a *cast* and is used to explicitly convert the value of an expression to another type. For example, to get the floating-point equivalent of the integer variable a you would write

```
(float)a
```

The name "cast" is easier to remember if you use the metallurgy metaphor: casting something into a different mold. The cast has a very high precedence, so a cast in front of an expression will only change the type of the first term in the expression. In order to cast the result of the expression, you must enclose it in parentheses.

Finally we come to the increment ++ and decrement -- operators. If there is any one operator that captures the "feel" of C programming, it must be one of these. Each one comes in two variations, called *prefix* and *postfix*. Both versions of both operators require a variable, not an expression, for an operand. Actually, the restriction is somewhat less rigid. What the operators really require is an "L-value," but we haven't covered this topic yet. The gist of the restriction is that ++ and -- may be applied only to expressions that may appear on the left side of an assignment operator.

In the prefix version of ++, the operator appears ahead of the operand. The operand is incremented, and the value of the expression is the incremented value of the variable. In its postfix version, the operator appears after the operand. The operand is still incremented, but the value of the expression is the value the operand had *before* the increment took place. This rule is easy to remember if you consider where the operator is placed—before the operand increments before the value is used in the expression; after the operand increments after its value is used in the surrounding expression. The -- operator works the same way, except that it decrements rather than incrementing.

Here are some examples.

```
int a, b, c, d;
...
a = b = 10;      a and b get the value 10
c = ++a;         a is incremented to 11, and c gets the value 11
d = b++;         b is incremented to 11, but d gets the value 10
```

The remarks above describe the results of these operators but do not state the way in which the result is obtained. Abstractly, both the prefix and postfix versions make a *copy* of the variable's value. It is this copy that is used in the surrounding expression (the "surrounding expression" in the example above is the assignment). The prefix operator increments before making this copy, and the postfix operator increments after making the copy. It is important to realize that the results of these operators are *not* the variable that was modified but a copy of its value. This point is important because it explains why you cannot use the operators in this way:

```
++a = 10;
```

The result of ++a is a copy of the value of a, not the variable itself, and you cannot assign something to a value.

5.1.6 Relational

These operators test various relationships between their operands. All the usual ones are provided, though there is a pitfall in this group. The operators are

```
>        >=      <       <=   ,  !=      ==
```

The first four are self explanatory. The != operator tests for "not equal," and the == operator tests for "is equal to."

Although the relational operators accomplish what you would expect, the way in which they do it is a little different. These operators all produce an integer, not boolean, result. If the indicated relationship holds between the operands, the result is one; otherwise the result is zero. The result is an integer value and can be assigned to integer variables, but what usually happens is that the value is tested in an if or a while statement. Remember how those statements work: an expression that evaluates to zero is considered false and any nonzero value is considered true. The relational operators work the same way, producing zero when the relation does not hold and one when it does. Thus, there is no functional need for a distinct boolean data type.

This use of integers to represent boolean values leads directly to some shortcuts that are commonly used when testing expressions.

```
if( expression != 0 ) ...
if( expression ) ...

if( expression == 0 ) ...
if( !expression ) ...
```

The two statements in each of these pairs are equivalent to one another; the test for "not equal to zero" can be performed with a relational operator or by simply testing the value of the expression. Similarly, the test for "equal to zero" can also be performed by testing the expression's value and then taking the logical NOT of the result. Which of these forms you choose to use is a matter of style. Be careful with the last one, though. The ! operator has high precedence, so if the expression contains any operators, you will probably have to enclose it in parentheses.

If this error is not the most common made by beginning C programmers, it is certainly the most irritating. Most other languages use the = operator to perform a comparison. In C, you *must* use the double equal sign == for comparison; a single equal sign will perform an assignment.

The pitfall is that an assignment is *legal* anywhere it is legal to compare for equality, so it is not a syntax error.[25] This unfortunate property is the disadvantage of not having a distinct boolean type; both expressions are legitimate integer expressions, so they are both legal in this context.

What happens if you use the wrong operator? Consider this example, which looks perfectly good to Pascal and Modula programmers:

```
x = get_some_value();
if( x = 5 )
        do something
```

x gets a value from the function, but instead of comparing it to the literal constant five, we *assign* five to x, thus destroying the value obtained from the function.[26] This result is surely not what the programmer intended. But there is another problem, too. The if statement will *always* be true because the value of the assignment expression is the new value of x, which is nonzero.

Get into the habit of double-checking comparisons for equality when you write them to make sure you used the double equal sign. When you find that a program is not working, take a quick look at your comparisons; you may save yourself a lot of debugging time.

5.1.7 Logical

The logical operators are && and ||. These operators look like the bitwise operators, but their operation is quite different—these evaluate expressions looking for true and false values. Let's look at one of them.

```
expression1 && expression2
```

The result of this expression is true if both *expression1* and *expression2* are true; if either of them is false, the entire expression is false. So far, so good.

---

[25] Some compilers produce a warning message for such suspicious expressions. In the rare occasions when assignment is what you want, try enclosing the assignment in parentheses to get rid of the warning message.

[26] The = operator used in this manner is sometimes jokingly called the "it is now" operator. "Is x equal to five? *It is now!*"

An interesting aspect of this operator is that it controls the order in which the subexpressions are evaluated. For example, look at this expression:

```
a > 5 && a < 10
```

The precedence of `&&` is lower than that of either the `>` or the `<` operator, so the subexpressions are grouped like this:

```
( a > 5 ) && ( a < 10 )
```

However, despite its lower precedence, the `&&` exerts control over the evaluation of the two relationals. Here is how it works: the left operand of a `&&` is always evaluated first. If its value is true, then the right operand is evaluated. If the value of the left operand is false, the right operand is not evaluated because it doesn't matter: the result of the `&&` is already known to be false. `||` has the same property. The left operand is evaluated first; if it is true, the right operand is not evaluated because the value of the overall expression has already been determined. This behavior is often called *short-circuited evaluation.*

This ordering is guaranteed and is quite useful. The example below is illegal in standard Pascal:

```
if( x >= 0 && x < MAX && array[ x ] == 0 ) ...
```

In C, the code first checks whether the value is in the legal range of subscripts for the array. If it is not, the subscript expression is skipped entirely. Because Pascal fully evaluates all expressions, an invalid subscript would cause the program to abort with a subscript error, despite the checking that the programmer tried to do.

The bitwise operators are often confused with the logical operators, but they are *not* interchangeable. The first difference is that `||` and `&&` are short circuited; if the value of the expression can be determined from the left operand alone, the right operand is not evaluated. In contrast, both operands of `|` and `&` are always evaluated.

Second, the logical operators test for zero or nonzero values, whereas the bitwise operators compare the corresponding bits in their operands. Here is an example:

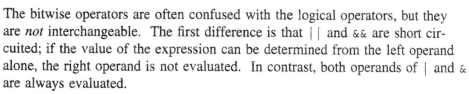

```
if( a < b && c > d ) ...
if( a < b & c > d ) ...
```

Because the relational operators produce either a zero or a one, these two statements will have the same result. But if a is one and b is two, the next pair of statements do not produce the same result.

```
if( a && b ) ...
if( a & b ) ...
```

Both values are nonzero so the first statement is true, but the second is false because there are no bit positions that contain a one in both a and b.

5.1.8 Conditional

The *conditional* operator takes three operands. It also controls the order in which its subexpressions are evaluated. Here is how it is used:

```
expression1 ? expression2 : expression3
```

The conditional operator has a very low precedence, so operands that are expressions will group properly even without parentheses. Nevertheless, many people prefer to parenthesize the subexpressions for the sake of clarity.

expression1 is evaluated first. If it is true (has any nonzero value), then the value of the entire expression is *expression2*, and *expression3* is not evaluated at all. But if *expression1* is false (zero), then the value of the conditional is *expression3*, and *expression2* is not evaluated.

If you have trouble remembering how this operator works, try reading it as a question. For example,

```
a > 5 ? b - 6 : c / 2
```

is read: "a greater than five? Then b - 6, otherwise c / 2." The choice of the question mark character for this operator was no accident.

Where is the conditional operator used? Here are two program fragments:

```
if( a > 5 )                          b = a > 5 ? 3 : -20;
        b = 3;
else
        b = -20;
```

The two sequences of code perform exactly the same function, but the one on the left requires that "b =" be written twice. But so what? There is no advantage to using the conditional here. But, take a look at this statement:

```
if( a > 5 )
        b[ 2 * c + d( e / 5 ) ] = 3;
else
        b[ 2 * c + d( e / 5 ) ] = -20;
```

Here, it is a major nuisance to have to write the subscript twice; the conditional is much cleaner:

```
b[ 2 * c + d( e / 5 ) ] = a > 5 ? 3 : -20;
```

This example is a good place to use a conditional because there is a tangible benefit in doing so: there is less chance for error typing the conditional than in the previous version, and the conditional may result in smaller object code as well. After you become accustomed to reading conditionals, it is nearly as easy to read as the if statement.

5.1.9 Comma

The comma operator will sound trite at first, but there are situations in which it is quite useful. It works like this:

```
expression1, expression2, ... , expressionN
```

The comma operator separates two or more expressions. The expressions are evaluated one by one, left to right, and the value of the entire expression is just the value of the last expression in the list. For example,

```
if( b + 1, c / 2, d > 0 )
```

is true if the value of d is greater than zero. No one ever writes code like this example, of course, because there is no purpose in evaluating the other two expressions; their values are just discarded. However, take a look at this piece of code.

```
a = get_value();
count_value( a );
while( a > 0 ){
        . . .
        a = get_value();
        count_value( a );
}
```

The test in this loop is preceded by two separate statements to obtain the value, so there must be a copy of these statements both before the loop and at the end of the loop's body. However, with the comma operator you can rewrite this loop as:

```
while( a = get_value(), count_value( a ), a > 0 ){
        . . .
}
```

You might also use an embedded assignment, like this:

```
while( count_value( a = get_value() ), a > 0 ){
        . . .
}
```

Now there is only a single copy of the code needed to get the next value for the loop. The comma operator makes the source program easier to maintain; if the way the values are obtained should change in the future, there is only one copy of the code that needs to be fixed.

It is easy to go overboard with this, though, so before using the comma operator, ask yourself whether it would make the program better in some way. If the answer is no, then don't use it. By the way, "better" does not include "trickier," "cooler," or "more impressive."

Here's a technique that you might occasionally see:

```
while( x < 10 )
        b += x,
        x += 1;
```

In this example the comma operator is used to make a single statement out of the two assignments in order to avoid putting braces around them. This practice is a bad idea, because the subtle visual difference between a comma and a semicolon is too easy to miss.

5.1.10 Subscript, Function Call, and Structure Member

I describe the remaining operators in more detail elsewhere in the book but mention them here for completeness. The *subscript* operator is a pair of brackets. A subscript takes two operands: an array name and an index value. Actually, you can use subscripts on more than just array names, but we will discuss this issue in Chapter 6. Subscripts in C work much like subscripts in other languages, although the implementation is somewhat different. C subscript values always begin at zero, and subscripts are not checked for validity. Except for their precedence, subscript operations are equivalent to indirection expressions. Here is the mapping:

```
array[ subscript ]
*( array + ( subscript ) )
```

The fact that subscripting is implemented in this way becomes important when we begin to use pointers more, in Chapter 6.

The *function call* operator takes one or more operands. The first is the name of the function you wish to call, and the remaining ones are the arguments to pass to the function. The fact that function calling is implemented as an operation implies that "expressions" may be used instead of "constants" for the function name, which is indeed the case. The function call operator is covered in Chapter 7.

The . and -> operators are used to access the members of a structure. If s is a structure variable, then s.a accesses the member of that structure named a. The -> operator is used instead of . when you have a pointer to a structure rather than the structure itself. Structures, their members, and these operators are all described in Chapter 10.

5.2 Boolean Values

C does not have an explicit boolean type so integers are used instead. The rule is,

> *Zero is false, and any nonzero value is true.*

However, what the Standard doesn't say is that the value one is "more true" than any other nonzero value. Consider this code fragment:

```
a = 25;
b = 15;
if( a ) ...
if( b ) ...
if( a == b ) ...
```

The first test checks whether a is nonzero, which is true. The second test checks to see if b is not equal to zero, which is also true. But the third test does not check whether a and b are both true, it checks whether they are equal to each other.

The same kind of problem can happen with integer variables tested in boolean contexts.

```
nonzero_a = a != 0;
...
if( nonzero_a == ( b != 0 ) ) ...
```

This test is supposed to be true if a and b are either zero together or are nonzero together. The test works fine as shown but try substituting the "equivalent" expression b for (b != 0).

```
if( nonzero_a == b ) ...
```

The expression is no longer testing for a and b being zero or nonzero together: now it is checking whether b has a specific integer value, namely zero or one.

Although all nonzero values are considered true, you must be careful when comparing true values to one another, because many different values can represent true.

Here is another shortcut that programmers often use with if statements— one in which this same kind of trouble can occur. Assuming that you have made the following #define's, then each of the pairs of statements below seem equivalent.

```
#define FALSE   0
#define TRUE    1
...
if( flag == FALSE ) ...
if( !flag ) ...

if( flag == TRUE ) ...
if( flag ) ...
```

But the second pair of statements is *not* equivalent if flag is set to arbitrary integer values. It is the same only if the flag was set to TRUE, to FALSE, or to the result of a relational or logical expression.

The solution to all of these problems is to avoid mixing integer and boolean values. If a variable contains an arbitrary integer value, test it explicitly:

```
if( value != 0 ) ...
```

Don't use the shortcuts to test the variable for zero or nonzero, because those forms incorrectly imply that the variable is boolean in nature.

If a variable is supposed to contain a boolean value, always set it to either zero or one, for example:

```
positive_cash_flow = cash_balance >= 0;
```

Do not test the variable's truth value by comparing it with any specific value, even TRUE or FALSE. Instead, test the variables as shown here:

```
if( positive_cash_flow ) ...
if( !positive_cash_flow ) ...
```

If you have chosen descriptive names for your boolean variables, this technique will reward you with code that is easy to read: "if positive cash flow, then ..."

5.3 L-values and R-values

To understand the restrictions on some of these operators, you must understand the difference between L-values and R-values. These terms were coined by compiler writers many years ago and have survived to this day even though their definitions do not exactly fit with the C language.

An *L-value* is something that can appear on the left side of an equal sign (L for left). An *R-value* is something that can appear on the right side of an equal sign. Here is an example:

```
a = b + 25;
```

a is an L-value because it identifies a *place* where a result can be stored. b + 25 is an R-value because it designates a *value*.

Can they be interchanged?

```
b + 25 = a;
```

a, which was used as an L-value before, can also be used as an R-value because every place contains a value. However, b + 25 cannot be used as an L-value because it does not identify a specific place. Thus, this assignment is illegal.

Note that when the computer evalutes b + 25 the result must exist *somewhere* in the machine. However, there is no way that the programmer can either predict where the result will be or refer to the same location later. Consequently, this expression is not an L-value. Literal constants are not L-values for the same reason.

It sounds as though variables may be used as L-values but expressions may not, but this statement is not quite accurate. The L-value in the assignment below is an expression.

```
int     a[30];
...
a[ b + 10 ] = 0;
```

Subscripting is in fact an operator so the construct on the left is an expression, yet it is a legitimate L-value because it identifies a specific location that we can refer to later in the program. Here is another example:

```
int     a, *pi;
...
pi = &a;
*pi = 20;
```

The second assignment is where the action is: the value on the left is clearly an expression, yet it is a legal L-value. Why? The value in the pointer pi is the address of a specific location in memory, and the * operator directs the machine to that location. When used as an L-value, this expression specifies the location to be modified. When used as an R-value, it gets the value currently stored at that location.

Some operators, like indirection and subscripting, produce an L-value as a result. Others produce R-values. For reference, this information is included in the precedence table, Table 5.1, later in this chapter.

5.4 Expression Evaluation

The order of expression evaluation is determined partially by the precedence and associativity of the operators it contains. Also, some of the expression's operands may need to be converted to other types during the evaluation.

5.4.1 Implicit Type Conversions

Integer arithmetic in C is always performed with at least the precision of the default integer type. To achieve this precision, character and short integer operands in an expression are converted to integers before being used in the expression. These conversions are called *integral promotions*. For example, in the evaluation of

```
char    a, b, c;
...
a = b + c;
```

the values of b and c are promoted to integers and then added. The result is then truncated to fit into a. The result in this first example is the same as the result if 8-bit arithmetic were used. But the result in this second example, which computes a simple checksum of a series of characters, is not the same.

```
a = ( ~ a ^ b << 1 ) >> 1;
```

Because of the one's complement and the left shift, 8 bits of precision are insufficient. The Standard dictates full integer evaluation, so that there is no ambiguity in the result of expressions such as this one.[27]

---

[27] Actually, the Standard states that the result shall be that obtained by full integer evaluation, which allows the possibility of using 8-bit arithmetic if the compiler can determine that doing so would not affect the result.

5.4.2 Arithmetic Conversions

Operations on values of different types cannot proceed until one of the operands is converted to the type of the other. The following hierarchy is called the *usual arithmetic conversions:*

```
long double
double
float
unsigned long int
long int
unsigned int
int
```

The operand whose type is lower in the list is converted to the other operand's type.

This fragment of code contains a potential problem.

```
int     a = 5000;
int     b = 25;
long    c = a * b;
```

The problem is that the expression a * b is evaluated using integer arithmetic. This code works fine on machines with 32-bit integers, but the multiplication overflows on machines with 16-bit integers, so c is initialized to the wrong value.

The solution is to convert one (or both) of the values to a long before the multiplication.

```
long    c = (long)a * b;
```

It is possible to lose precision when converting an integer to a float. Floating values are only required to have six decimal digits of precision; if an integer that is longer than six digits is assigned to a float, the result may be only an approximation of the integer value.

When a float is converted to an integer, the fractional part is discarded (it is *not* rounded). If the number is too large to fit in an integer, the result is undefined.

5.4.3 Properties of Operators

There are three factors that determine the order in which complicated expressions are evaluated: the *precedence* of the operators, their *associativity,* and whether they control the execution order. The order in which two adjacent

Oper	Description	Sample Usage	Result	Asso-ciativity	Controls Eval
( )	Grouping	(*exp*)	same as *exp*	N/A	
( )	Function call	*rexp*(*rexp*, ... , *rexp*)	*rexp*	L-R	No
[ ]	Subscript	*rexp*[*rexp*]	*lexp*	L-R	No
.	Structure member	*lexp*.*member_name*	*lexp*	L-R	No
->	Structure pointer member	*rexp*->*member_name*	*lexp*	L-R	No
++	Postfix increment	*lexp*++	*rexp*	L-R	No
--	Postfix decrement	*lexp*--	*rexp*	L-R	No
!	Logical negate	!*rexp*	*rexp*	R-L	No
~	One's complement	~*rexp*	*rexp*	R-L	No
+	Unary plus	+*rexp*	*rexp*	R-L	No
-	Unary minus	-*rexp*	*rexp*	R-L	No
++	Prefix increment	++*lexp*	*rexp*	R-L	No
--	Prefix decrement	--*lexp*	*rexp*	R-L	No
*	Indirection	**rexp*	*lexp*	R-L	No
&	Address of	&*lexp*	*rexp*	R-L	No
sizeof	Size in bytes	sizeof *rexp* sizeof(*type*)	*rexp*	R-L	No
(*type*)	Type conversion	(*type*)*rexp*	*rexp*	R-L	No
*	Multiplication	*rexp* * *rexp*	*rexp*	L-R	No
/	Division	*rexp* / *rexp*	*rexp*	L-R	No
%	Integer remainder	*rexp* % *rexp*	*rexp*	L-R	No
+	Addition	*rexp* + *rexp*	*rexp*	L-R	No
-	Subtraction	*rexp* - *rexp*	*rexp*	L-R	No
<<	Left shift	*rexp* << *rexp*	*rexp*	L-R	No
>>	Right shift	*rexp* >> *rexp*	*rexp*	L-R	No

Table 5.1   Operator precedence   *continued . . .*

operators are evaluated is determined by their precedence. If they have the same precedence, the order of evaluation is determined by their associativity. Simply stated, associativity is whether a sequence of operators is evaluated from left to right or from right to left. Finally, there are four operators that exert some control over the order in which the entire expression is evaluated, specifying either that one subexpression is guaranteed to be evaluated before anything in another subexpression is computed, or that a subexpression may be skipped entirely.

All of the properties are listed for each of the operators in the precedence table, Table 5.1. The columns show the operator, a brief description of what it does, an example showing how it is used, what type of result it gives, its

Oper	Description	Sample Usage	Result	Asso-ciativity	Controls Eval
>	Greater than	rexp > rexp	rexp	L-R	No
>=	Greater than or equal	rexp >= rexp	rexp	L-R	No
<	Less than	rexp < rexp	rexp	L-R	No
<=	Less than or equal	rexp <= rexp	rexp	L-R	No
==	Equal to	rexp == rexp	rexp	L-R	No
!=	Not equal to	rexp != rexp	rexp	L-R	No
&	Bitwise AND	rexp & rexp	rexp	L-R	No
^	Bitwise exclusive OR	rexp ^ rexp	rexp	L-R	No
|	Bitwise inclusive OR	rexp | rexp	rexp	L-R	No
&&	Logical AND	rexp && rexp	rexp	L-R	Yes
||	Logical OR	rexp || rexp	rexp	L-R	Yes
?:	Conditional	rexp ? rexp : rexp	rexp	N/A	Yes
=	Assignment	lexp = rexp	rexp	R-L	No
+=	Add to	lexp += rexp	rexp	R-L	No
-=	Subtract from	lexp -= rexp	rexp	R-L	No
*=	Multiply by	lexp *= rexp	rexp	R-L	No
/=	Divide by	lexp /= rexp	rexp	R-L	No
%=	Modulo by	lexp %= rexp	rexp	R-L	No
<<=	Shift left by	lexp <<= rexp	rexp	R-L	No
>>=	Shift right by	lexp >>= rexp	rexp	R-L	No
&=	AND with	lexp &= rexp	rexp	R-L	No
^=	Exclusive OR with	lexp ^= rexp	rexp	R-L	No
|=	Inclusive OR with	lexp |= rexp	rexp	R-L	No
,	Comma	rexp , rexp	rexp	L-R	Yes

Table 5.1   Operator precedence

associativity, and whether it exerts some control over the order of evaluation of the expression in which it appears. The sample usage indicates where L-values are required; the term *lexp* indicates an L-value expression, and *rexp* is an R-value expression. Remember than an L-value denotes a *place* and an R-value denotes a *value*; so an L-value may be used anywhere an R-value is needed, but an R-value cannot be used where an L-value is needed.

5.4.4 Precedence and Order of Evaluation

In an expression with more than one operator, what determines the order in which the operations are performed? Each of the C operators is assigned a precedence, which indicates its relationships to the remaining operators. But precedence alone does not determine the order of evaluation. Here is the rule:

> *The order of evaluation of two adjacent operators is determined by their precedence. If they have the same precedence, the order is determined by their associativity. Otherwise, the compiler is free to evaluate expressions in any order that does not violate the order of evaluation imposed by parentheses or by the comma, &&, ||, or ?: operators.*

In other words, the precedence of the operators in an expression only determines how the components of the expression are grouped together during evaluation.

Here is an example:

```
a + b * c
```

In this expression, the multiplication and addition are adjacent. The multiplication is performed before the addition because the * operator has higher precedence than +. The compiler has no choice here: the multiplication must occur first.

Here is a more interesting expression:

```
a * b + c * d + e * f
```

If precedence alone determined the order of evaluation, all three multiplications would occur before any of the additions. In fact, this ordering is not necessary. All that is required is that the multiplications on either side of each addition be performed before the addition. For example, the expression might be evaluated in the following order. The boldfaced operator is the one being computed in each step.

```
a * b
c * d
(a*b) + (c*d)
e * f
(a*b)+(c*d) + (e*f)
```

Notice that the first addition is performed before the last multiplication. The same result would be obtained if the expression were evaluated in this order:

```
c * d
e * f
a * b
(a*b) + (c*d)
(a*b)+(c*d) + (e*f)
```

The associativity for addition requires the two additions to be done left to right, but the order for the rest of the expression is not constrained. Specifically, there isn't any rule that requires all of the multiplications to be computed first, nor is there a rule that determines the order in which they are done relative to one another. The precedence of the operators is not relevant here. Precedence only controls the order in which adjacent operators are evaluated.

The fact that the order of expression evaluation is not completely determined by the precedence of the operators makes statements like this one dangerous.

```
c + --c
```

The precedence of the operators indicates that the -- should be performed before the +, but there is no way to tell whether the left operand of the + will be evaluated before or after the right operand. It makes a difference with this expression, because -- involves a side effect. The expression produces a different result if --c is evaluated before or after c.

The Standard states that the value of expressions such as these is undefined. Although every implementation will produce *some* value for the expression, there is no *correct* answer. Expressions like this one are therefore not portable and must be avoided. Program 5.3 illustrates this problem rather dramatically. Table 5.2 lists the values produced by this program on each of these implementations. Many implementations give different values depending on whether the program was compiled with or without optimization; for example, using the optimizer with gcc changes the result from -63 to 22. Although each compiler has evaluated the expression in a different order, *none of these answers is wrong!* It is the expression itself that is faulty; its order of evaluation is ambiguous because of the side effects of many of the terms it contains.

```
/*
** A program to demonstrate that the order of expression evaluation
** is only partially determined by operator precedence.
*/
main()
{
        int      i = 10;

        i = i-- - --i * ( i = -3 ) * i++ + ++i;
        printf( "i = %d\n", i );

}
```

Program 5.3   An illegal expression   bad_exp.c

Value	Implementation
-128	Tandy 6000 Xenix 3.2
-95	Think C 5.0.2 (Macintosh)
-86	IBM PowerPC AIX 3.2.5
-85	Sun Sparc cc (a K&R compiler)
-63	gcc, HP-UX 9.0, Power C 2.0.0
4	Sun Sparc acc (an ANSI compiler)
21	Turbo C/C++ 4.5
22	FreeBSD 2.1R
30	Dec Alpha OSF1 2.0
36	Dec VAX/VMS
42	Microsoft C 5.1

Table 5.2   Results of illegal expression program

K&R C

In K&R C, the compiler was free to evaluate the expressions shown below in any order.

```
a + b + c
x * y * z
```

The reasoning behind this decision is that the value of b + c (or of y * z) might still be available from some earlier expression, so it would be more efficient to reuse that value than compute it again. Addition and multiplication are associative, so where is the harm?

Consider the expression below, which uses signed integer variables:

```
x + y + 1
```

If the result of the expression x + y is larger than an integer is capable of storing, an *overflow* has occurred. On some machines, the result of the test

```
if( x + y + 1 > 0 )
```

will depend on whether x + y or y + 1 is evaluated first, because the overflow occurs at different points in each case. The problem is that the programmer could not predict with certainty which way the compiler would evaluate the expression. Experience showed that this practice was a bad idea, so it is not allowed with ANSI C.

The following expression illustrates a related problem.

```
f() + g() + h()
```

Although the left addition must be performed before the right addition, there is no rule constraining the order in which the functions are called. If their execution had side effects, such as doing any I/O or modifying global variables, the result may be different for different orders of evaluation. If the order makes any difference, use temporary variables so that each function is called in a separate statement.

```
temp = f();
temp += g();
temp += h();
```

5.5 Summary

C has a rich collection of operators. The arithmetic operators include + (addition), – (subtraction), * (multiplication), / (division), and % (modulo). All of these except modulo work with both integer and floating-point values.

The << and >> operators perform left and right shifts, respectively. The &, |, and ^ operators perform bitwise AND, OR, and XOR operations, respectively. All of these operators require integral operands.

The = operator performs assignment. Furthermore, there are compound assignment operators for all of the preceding operators:

```
+=        -=        *=        /=        %=
<<=       >>=       &=        ^=        |=
```

The compound assignments perform the indicated operation between the left and right operands, and then assign the result to the left operand.

The unary operators include ! (logical NOT), ~ (one's complement), – (negative), and + (positive). The ++ and –– operators increment and decrement their operand, respectively. Both of these operators have prefix and postfix forms; the prefix form returns the value of the operand after it is modified, while the postfix form returns the value before the operand is modified. The & operator returns a pointer to (the address of) its operand, and the * operator performs indirection on its operand (which must be a pointer). sizeof returns the size of its operand, measured in bytes. Finally, a cast is used to change the type of an expression.

The relational operators are:

```
>        >=        <        <=        !=        ==
```

Each operator returns either true or false depending on whether the operands have the indicated relationship. The logical operators evaluate complex boolean expressions. && is true only if both of its operands are true, and || is false only if both of its operands are false. Both of the logical operators exert control over the evaluation of the expression in which they appear. If the result of the expression can be determined from the left operand, then the right operand is not evaluated.

The conditional operator ?: takes three operands, and also exerts control over expression evaluation. If the first operand is true, the result is the value of the second operand and the third operand is not evaluated. Otherwise, the result is the value of the third operand, and the second is not evaluated. The comma operator joins two or more expressions, which are evaluated from left to right. The result of the entire expression is the result of the rightmost subexpression.

C does not have an explicit boolean type, so integer expressions are used to represent boolean values. However, mixing boolean values with arbitrary integers in expressions can cause errors. To avoid these errors, treat each variable as either a boolean or an integer. Do not use boolean tests on integer variables or vice versa.

An L-value is an expression that can be used on the left side of an assignment; it denotes a place in the computer's memory. An R-value denotes a value, so it can only be used on the right side of an assignment. Every expression that is an L-value is also an R-value, but the reverse is not true.

Operations on values of different types cannot proceed until one of the operands is converted to the type of the other. The usual arithmetic conversions determine which operand is converted. The precedence of operators relative to one another determines the order in which adjacent operators will be evaluated. If their precedence is the same, then the operators' associativity determines the order in which they will be evaluated. However, these rules do not completely determine the order of evaluation, and the compiler is free to evaluate complex expressions in any order that does not violate the precedence or associativity rules. Expressions whose result depends on the order of evaluation are inherently nonportable and should be avoided.

5.6 Summary of Cautions

1. Right shifts on signed values are not portable (page 95).

2. Shifting with negative shift counts (page 95).

3. Chained assignment among variables with different sizes (page 98).

4. Using = rather than == to perform a comparison (page 104).

5. Using | instead of ||, or & instead of && (page 105).

6. Comparing different nonzero values as boolean values (page 110).

7. The location to which an expression is assigned does not determine the precision with which the expression is evaluated (page 113).

8. Writing expressions whose value depends on the order of evaluation (page 117).

5.7 Summary of Programming Tips

1. Using assignment operators makes the program easier to maintain (page 99).

2. Using the conditional operator rather than if to simplify expressions (page 106).

3. Using the comma operator to eliminate duplicate code (page 108).

4. Do not mix integer and boolean values (page 110).

5.8 Questions

1. What is the type and value of the expression?

   ```
   (float)( 25 / 10 )
   ```

2. What is the result of the following program?

   ```
   int
   func( void )
   {
           static   int     counter = 1;

           return ++counter;
   }

   int
   main()
   {
           int     answer;

           answer = func() - func() * func();
           printf( "%d\n", answer );
   ```

```
}
```

3. What uses can you think of for the bitwise and shifting operators?

✎ 4. Is the conditional operator faster or slower at run time than an `if` statement? Specifically, compare these two code fragments:

```
if( a > 3 )                        i = a > 3 ? b + 1 : c * 5;
        i = b + 1;
else
        i = c * 5;
```

5. Years that are divisible by four are leap years with one exception—years that are divisible by 100 are not. However, years that are divisible by 400 *are* leap years. Write a single assignment that sets `leap_year` true if the value in `year` is a leap year, and false if it is not.

✎ 6. Which operators have side effects, and what are they?

7. What is the result of this code fragment?

```
int     a = 20;
. . .
if( 1 <= a <= 10 )
        printf( "In range\n" );
else
        printf( "Out of range\n" );
```

8. Rewrite this fragment of code to eliminate the redundancies.

```
a = f1( x );
b = f2( x + a );
for( c = f3( a, b ); c > 0; c = f3( a, b ) ){
        statements
        a = f1( ++x );
        b = f2( x + a );
}
```

9. Does the following loop accomplish what it is trying to do?

```
non_zero = 0;
for( i = 0; i < ARRAY_SIZE; i += 1 )
        non_zero += array[i];

if( !non_zero )
        printf( "Values are all zero\n" );
```

```
          else
                    printf( "There are nonzero values\n" );
```

10. Given the variable declarations and initialization below, evaluate each of the following expressions. If an expression has side effects (that is, if it changes the value of one or more variables), note them as well. Use the initial values given below for each variable, not the results of the preceding expression, to evaluate each expression.

```
     int      a = 10, b = -25;
     int      c = 0, d = 3;
     int      e = 20;
```

a.   b

b.   b++

c.   --a

d.   a / 6

e.   a % 6

f.   b % 10

g.   a << 2

h.   b >> 3

i.   a > b

j.   b = a

k.   b == a

l.   a & b

m.   a ^ b

n.   a | b

o.   ~b

p.   c && a

q.   c || a

r.   b ? a : c

s.   a += 2

    t.   b &= 20

    u.   b >>= 3

    v.   a %= 6

    w.   d = a > b

    x.   a = b = c = d

    y.   e = d + (c = a + b) + c

    z.   a + b * 3

    aa. b >> a - 4

    bb. a != b != c

    cc. a == b == c

    dd. d < a < e

    ee. e > a > d

    ff. a - 10 > b + 10

    gg. a & 0x1 == b & 0x1

    hh. a | b << a & b

    ii. a > c || ++a > b

    jj. a > c && ++a > b

    kk. ! ~ b++

    ll. b++ & a <= 30

    mm. a - b, c += d, e - c

    nn. a >>= 3 > 0

    oo. a <<= d > 20 ? b && c++ : d--

11. Several expressions are listed below. Determine how each expression is being evaluated by the compiler, and remove as many parentheses as possible without changing the order of evaluation.

    a.   a + (b / c)

    b.   (a + b) / c

    c.   (a * b) % 6

    d.   a * (b % 6)

    e.   (a + b) == 6

f.   ! ((a >= '0') && (a <= '9'))

g.   ((a & 0x2f) == (b | 1)) && ((~ c) > 0)

h.   ((a << b) - 3) < (b << (a + 3))

i.   ~ (a ++)

j.   ((a == 2) || (a == 4)) && ((b == 2) || (b == 4))

k.   (a & b) ^ (a | b)

l.   (a + (b + c))

12. How can you determine whether a right shift of a signed value is performed on your machine as an arithmetic or a logical shift?

5.9 Programming Exercises

✎ ★ 1. Write a program that reads characters from the standard input and writes them to the standard output. All characters should be written exactly as they were read except that uppercase letters should be converted to lowercase.

★★ 2. Write a program that reads characters from the standard input and writes them to the standard output. All characters should be written exactly as they were read except for alphabetic characters, which are encrypted before being written.

The encryption process is straightforward: each letter is changed to whatever letter appears 13 places after (or before) it in the alphabet. For instance, an A is changed to an N, a B is changed to an O, a Z is changed to an M, and so forth. Note that both upper and lowercase letters must be converted. *Hint:* It may help to remember that a character is really just an integer with a small value.

✎ ★★★ 3. Write the function

```
unsigned int reverse_bits( unsigned int value );
```

This function returns the number constructed by reversing the order of the bits in value from left to right. For example, on a 32-bit machine the number 25 contains these bits:

```
00000000000000000000000000011001
```

The function should return 2,550,136,832, which is composed of these bits:

```
10011000000000000000000000000000
```

Try to write your function so that it does not depend on the integer size of your machine.

★★★★ 4. Write a set of functions that implement an array of bits. The functions should have the following prototypes:

```
void set_bit( char bit_array[],
    unsigned bit_number );

void clear_bit( char bit_array[],
    unsigned bit_number );

void assign_bit( char bit_array[],
    unsigned bit_number, int value );

int test_bit( char bit_array[],
    unsigned bit_number );
```

The first argument in each of these functions is a character array in which the bits are actually stored. The second argument identifies the bit to be accessed; it is up to the caller to ensure that this value is not too large for the array being used.

The first function sets the specified bit to one, and the second clears it. The third function sets the bit to zero if the value is zero, otherwise it sets the bit to one. The last function returns true if the specified bit is nonzero, else false.

★★★★ 5. Write a function that will store a given value into specified bit positions of an integer. It should have this prototype:

```
int store_bit_field( int original_value,
    int value_to_store,
    unsigned starting_bit, unsigned ending_bit );
```

Assume that the bits in an integer are numbered from right to left. Thus, the starting bit position may not be less than the ending bit position.

To illustrate, this function should return the following values:

Original Value	Value to Store	Starting Bit	Ending Bit	Returned Value
0x0	0x1	4	4	0x10
0xffff	0x123	15	4	0x123f
0xffff	0x123	13	9	0xc7ff

Hint: There are five steps in storing a value in a field of bits.

1. Construct a *mask*, a value with ones in the bit positions that correspond to the desired field.

2.   Using the one's complement of the mask, clear all of the bits in the field.

3.   Shift the new value left so that it is aligned in the field.

4.   AND the shifted value with the mask to ensure that it has no bits outside of the field.

5.   OR the resulting value into the original integer.

The most difficult of these tasks is constructing the mask. You might begin by casting the value ~0 to an unsigned value and then shifting it.

6

Pointers

It's time we talk in detail about pointers, because we will be using them constantly throughout the rest of the book. You may already be familiar with some or all of the background information discussed in this chapter. If you aren't, study it carefully because your understanding of pointers will rest on this foundation.

6.1 Memory and Addresses

As mentioned earlier, we can view the computer's memory as a row of houses on a long street. Each house is capable of holding data and is identified by a house number.

This analogy is useful but limited. Computer memories are composed of millions of *bits*, each capable of holding either the value 0 or the value 1. This limited range of values is not terribly useful, so bits are usually grouped together and treated as a unit in order to store a wider range of values. Here is a picture of a few memory locations on a real machine.

100	101	102	103	104	105	106	107
□	□	□	□	□	□	□	□

Each of these locations is called a *byte*, and each contains as many bits as necessary to store a single character. On many modern machines, each byte contains eight bits, which can store unsigned integers from 0 to 255 or signed integers from -128 to 127. The previous diagram does not show the contents of the locations, though every location in memory always contains *some* value. Each byte is identified by an address, which is represented in the diagram by the numbers above each box.

To store even larger values, we take two or more bytes and treat them as if they were a single, larger unit of memory. For example, many machines store integers in *words*, each composed of two or four bytes. Here are the same memory locations, this time viewed as four-byte words.

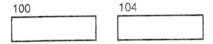

Because they contain more bits, each word is capable of holding unsigned integers from 0 to 4,294,967,295 ($2^{32}-1$) or signed integers from $-2,147,483,648$ (-2^{31}) to 2,147,483,647 ($2^{31}-1$).

Note that even though a word contains four bytes, it has only one address. It is machine-dependent whether the address of a word is the address of the leftmost byte in the word or the rightmost. *Boundary alignment* is another hardware issue. On machines with this requirement, integers can only begin with certain bytes, usually those whose addresses are multiples of two or four. But these issues are the hardware designer's problem, and they rarely affect C programmers. We are interested in only two issues:

1.   Each location in memory is identified by a unique address.

2.   Each location in memory contains a value.

6.1.1 Address Versus Contents

Here is another example, this time showing the contents of five words in memory.

100	104	108	112	116
112	-1	1078523331	100	108

Five integer values are shown, each in its own word. If you remember the address where you stored some value, you can use that address later to retrieve the value.

It is cumbersome to remember all of those addresses, though, so one of the things that high-level languages provide is the ability to refer to memory locations by name rather than by address. Here is the same picture, this time with names substituted for addresses.

a		b	c	d		e	
	112	-1	1078523331		100		108

Of course, these names are what we call *variables*. It is important to remember that this association of names with locations is not provided by the hardware, it is something that the compiler does for us. All variables give us is a more convenient way of remembering the addresses—*the hardware still accesses memory locations using addresses.*

6.2 Values and Their Types

Now let's look at the values stored in these locations. The first two locations appear to contain integer values. The third is a very large integer, and the fourth and fifth are also integers. Or so it seems. Here are the declarations for these variables:

```
int     a = 112, b = -1;
float   c = 3.14;
int     *d = &a;
float   *e = &c;
```

The declarations confirm that the variables a and b do indeed contain integer values, but claim that c ought to contain a floating-point value. But c was shown in the illustration as an integer. Well, which is it, an integer or a floating-point number?

The answer is that the variable contains a sequence of bits, 0's and 1's. They could be interpreted either as an integer or as a floating-point number, depending on the manner in which they are used. If integer arithmetic instructions are used, the value is interpreted as an integer. If floating-point instructions are used, it is a floating-point number.

This fact leads to an important conclusion: *the type of a value cannot be determined simply by examining its bits.* To determine its type (and therefore its value) you must look at the way the value is used in the program. Consider this 32-bit value, shown in binary:

```
01100111011011000110111101100010
```

Here are a few of the many ways that these bits might be interpreted. These values were all obtained from a Motorola 68000-based processor. Another system with different data formats and instructions would interpret the same bits differently.

Type	Value(s)
one 32-bit integer	1,735,159,650
two 16-bit integers	26,476 followed by 28,514
four characters	glob
floating-point	1.116533×10^{24}
machine instructions	beq .+110 followed by ble .+102

Here is a single value that could be interpreted as five different types. Clearly, the type of a value is not something inherent in the value itself but depends on how it is used. Thus to get correct answers, it is important to use the values correctly.

Of course, the compiler helps us avoid these errors. Declaring c to be a float causes the compiler to generate floating-point instructions when accessing it and to complain when we attempt to access it in a way that is not appropriate for a float. It is now obvious that the diagram showing the values was misleading, because it showed the integer representation of c. The floating-point value is really 3.14 .

6.3 Contents of a Pointer Variable

Getting back to pointers, let's look at the declarations for the variables d and e. They are both declared as pointers, and they are initialized with the addresses of other variables. The initialization is done with the & operator, which produces the memory address of its operand (see Chapter 5).

a	b	c	d	e
112	-1	3.14	100	108

The contents of d and e are addresses rather than integers or floating-point numbers. Indeed, it is easy to see from the diagram that the contents of d match the address at which a is stored and the contents of e match the address where c is stored, as we would expect from the initialization. It is important to distinguish between the address of the variable d (112) and its contents (100), and to realize at the same time that this number 100 identifies (is the address of) some other location. At this point the house/street address analogy fails, because the contents of a house are never the address of another house.

Before moving to the next step, let's look at some expressions involving these variables. Consider these declarations once more.

```
int      a = 112, b = -1;
float    c = 3.14;
int      *d = &a;
float    *e = &c;
```

What is the value of each of these expressions?

```
a
b
c
d
e
```

The first three are easy: the value of a is 112, the value of b is -1, and the value of c is 3.14 . The pointer variables are just as easy. The value of d is 100, and the value of e is 108. If you said 112 and 3.14 for d and e, then you've made a very common mistake. The fact that d and e are declared as pointers does not change how these expressions are evaluated: the value of a variable is the number stored in the memory location assigned to the variable. It is a mistake to think that you automatically go to the locations 100 and 108 and get the values there simply because d and e are pointers. The value of a variable is the number stored in the memory location assigned to the variable, even for pointer variables.

6.4 Indirection Operator

The process of following a pointer to the location to which it points is called *indirection* or *dereferencing the pointer*. The operator that performs indirection is the unary *. Here are some examples using the declarations in the previous section.

Expression	R-Value	Type
a	112	int
b	−1	int
c	3.14	float
d	100	int *
e	108	float *
*d	112	int
*e	3.14	float

The value of d is 100. When we apply the indirection operator to d, it means to go to location 100 in memory and look there instead. Thus, the R-value of *d is 112—the contents of location 100. The L-value would be location 100 itself.

Note the types of the expressions in the list above: d is a pointer to an integer and dereferencing it produces an integer. Similarly, applying indirection to a float * produces a float.

Normally, we don't know which location the compiler will choose for each variable, so we cannot predict their addresses in advance. Thus, when drawing pictures of pointers in memory, it is inconvenient to use the actual numbers for addresses, so most books use arrows instead, like this:

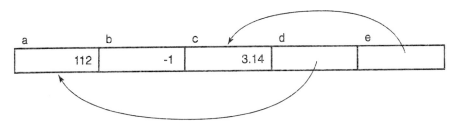

However, this notation can be misleading because the arrows can trick you into doing indirection even when there is no indirection to be done. For example, what is the value of the expression d from the diagram above?

If you answered 112, then you were tricked by the arrow. The correct answer is the address of a, not its contents. The arrow, though, seems to pull our eyes to a. It is hard not to follow the arrow and that is the problem: you must not follow the arrow unless there is an indirection operator.

The modified arrow notation shown below tries to eliminate this problem.

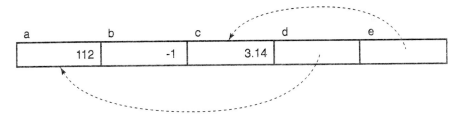

The intent is to show the value of the pointer without the strong visual cue that the arrow is a path that must be followed. Indeed, the value of a pointer variable is simply a collection of bits until an indirection is performed on it. When indirection is performed, a solid arrow is used to show what actually took place.

Note that the arrow originates *inside* of the box because it represents the value stored in that variable. Also, the arrow points to a location, not to the value in the location. This notation implies that following the arrow with indirection produces an L-value. It does, as we shall see later.

Although the arrow notation is useful, in order to be able to use it properly you must remember that the value of a pointer variable is just a number. The arrow shows the value of this number, but the arrow notation does not change the fact that it is just a number. A pointer has no built-in property of indirection, so you must not follow the arrow unless there is an indirection operator that tells you to do so.

6.5 Uninitialized and Illegal Pointers

The code fragment below illustrates a very common error:

```
int     *a;
...
*a = 12;
```

The declaration creates a pointer variable called a, and the assignment stores a 12 in the location to which a points.

But where does a point? We declared the variable but never initialized it, so there is no way to predict where the value 12 is being stored. A pointer variable is no different from any other variable in this respect. If the variable is static, it is initialized to zero; but if the variable is automatic, it is not initialized at all. In neither case does declaring a pointer to an integer "create" any memory for the storage of an integer.

So what happens when this assignment is performed? If you're lucky, the initial value of a will be an illegal address, and the assignment will cause a fault that terminates the program. On UNIX systems, this error is called a "segmentation violation" or a "memory fault." It indicates that you have tried to access a location that is outside of the memory allocated to your program. On a PC running Windows, indirection on an unitialized or illegal pointer is one of the causes of General Protection Exceptions.

On machines that require integers to be at a particular boundary, accessing an address that is on the wrong boundary for its type also causes a fault. This error is reported on UNIX systems as a "bus error."

A much more serious problem is when the pointer accidentally contains a legal address. What happens then is simple: the value at that location is changed, even though you had not intended to change it. Errors like this one are very difficult to find, because the erroneous code may be completely unrelated to the code that is supposed to manipulate the value that changed. Be extremely careful that pointer variables are initialized before applying indirection to them!

6.6 The Null Pointer

The Standard defines a *NULL pointer* as a pointer value that does not point to anything at all. To make a pointer variable NULL you assign it the value zero, and to test whether a pointer variable is NULL you compare it to zero. The choice of the value zero is a source code convention; internally, the value for a NULL pointer might actually be something different. In this case, the compiler takes care of translating between zero and the internal value.

The concept of a NULL pointer is quite useful because it gives you a way to specify that a particular pointer is not currently pointing to anything at all. For example, a function whose job is to search an array for a specific value may return a pointer to the array element that was found. If no element in the array contained the right value, a NULL pointer could be returned instead. This technique allows the return value to convey two different pieces of information. First, was an element found? Second, if an element was found, which one was it?

Although this technique is commonly used in C programs, it violates a software engineering principle. It is risky for a single value to have two different meanings because it is easy to be confused later on as to which meaning is actually intended. This problem is more serious in larger programs because it is impossible to keep the entire design in your head at once. A safer strategy is to have the function return two separate values: the first is a status value indicating the result of the operations, and the second is the pointer, which is used only when the status indicates that a match was found.

Dereferencing a pointer gives you the value to which it points. But the NULL pointer, by definition, points to nothing at all. Therefore, it is illegal to dereference a NULL pointer. Before dereferencing a pointer, you must first make sure that it is not NULL.

What happens if indirection is performed on a NULL pointer? The result is implementation dependent. On some machines, the indirection accesses memory location zero. The compiler ensures that there aren't any variables stored at location zero, but the machine doesn't prevent you from accessing or modifying the location. This behavior is very unfortunate, because the program contains an error but the machine hides its symptoms, thus making the error more difficult to find.

On other machines, indirection on a NULL pointer causes a fault that terminates the program. It is much better to announce that an error was discovered than to hide it, because the programmer can then correct it more easily.

It would be nice if all pointer variables, not just those in static memory, were automatically initialized to NULL, but they are not. No matter how your machine handles dereferencing a NULL pointer, it is a good idea to explicitly initialize all your pointer variables. Use the desired address if it is known, otherwise initialize them to NULL. In well-written programs that check pointers before dereferencing them, this initialization can save you a lot of debugging time.

6.7 Pointers, Indirection, and L-values

Can expressions involving pointers be used as L-values? If so, which ones? A quick check of the precedence chart in Table 5.1 confirms that the operand needed by the indirection operator is an R-value, but the operator produces an L-value.

We'll return to an earlier example. Given these declarations

```
int     a;
int     *d = &a;
```

consider the expressions below:

Expression	L-value	Indicated Location
a	Yes	a
d	Yes	d
*d	Yes	a

Pointer variables may be used as L-values, not because they are pointers but because they are variables. Applying indirection to a pointer variable indicates that we should follow the pointer. The indirection identifies a specific memory location, thus we can use the result of an indirection expression as an L-value. Follow these statements:

```
*d = 10 - *d;
d = 10 - *d;     ← ???
```

The first statement contains two indirections. The expression on the right is being used as an R-value, so it obtains the value in the location to which d points (the value of a). The indirection on the left is being used as an L-value, so the location to which d points (which is a) receives the new value computed by the right side.

The second statement is illegal because it specifies that an integer quantity (10 - *d) be stored in a pointer variable. The compiler helps us out by complaining when we try to use a variable in a context that is inconsistent with its type. These warning and error messages are your *friends*. The compiler is *helping* you by producing them. Although we would all prefer not to have to deal with any such messages, it is a good idea to correct the errors right away, especially with warning messages that do not abort the compilation. It is a lot easier to fix problems when the compiler tells you exactly where they are than it is to debug the program later; the debugger cannot pinpoint such problems nearly as well as the compiler.

K&R C Old C compilers did not complain when pointer and integer values were intermixed. However, we know better these days. It is only rarely useful to convert an integer to a pointer or vice versa. Usually such conversions are unintentional errors.

6.8 Pointers, Indirection, and Variables

If you think you've mastered pointers, take a look at this expression and see if you can figure out what it does.

```
*&a = 25;
```

If you said that it assigns the value 25 to the variable a, congratulations— you're right. Let's unravel the expression. First, the & operator generates the address where the variable a is stored, which is a pointer constant. (Note that it is not necessary to know the actual value of the constant in order to use it.) Then, the * operator goes to the location whose address is given as the operand. In this expression, the operand is the address of a, so the value 25 is stored in a.

How is this statement any different from just saying a = 25;? Functionally, it is identical. It does, however, involve more operations. Unless the compiler (or optimizer) realizes what you're doing and discards the extra operations, the resulting object code will be larger and slower. Worse, the additional operators make the source code harder to read. For these reasons, no one ever (intentionally) uses expressions such as *&a.

6.9 Pointer Constants

Let's examine another expression. Assuming that the variable a is stored at location 100, what does this statement do?

```
*100 = 25;
```

It looks like the statement assigns 25 to a, because a is the variable at location 100. But not so! The statement is actually invalid because the literal 100 is of type integer, and indirection can only be performed on expressions of type pointer. If you really want to store 25 in location 100, you must use a cast.

```
*(int *)100 = 25;
```

The cast converts the value 100 from an "integer" to a "pointer to an integer." It is legal to apply indirection to this expression, so if a is stored in location 100, this statement stores the value 25 in a. *However, you will need this technique rarely, if ever!* Why? As mentioned earlier, you usually cannot predict where in memory the compiler will choose to put any specific variable, so you don't know its address ahead of time. It is easy to obtain the address of a variable with the & operator but the expression won't be evaluated until the program executes, so it is too late to copy the answer into the source code as a literal constant.

The only reason this example is useful is for the few times when you need to access a specific location in memory by its address, which is never done to access a variable but rather to access the hardware itself. For example, an operating system needs to communicate with the input and output device controllers to start I/O operations and to obtain results of prior operations. On some machines, communication with device controllers is accomplished by reading and writing values at specific memory addresses. Instead of accessing memory, however, these operations access the device controller interface. These locations, then, must be accessed via their addresses, which are known in advance.

Chapter 3 mentioned that there is no built-in notation for writing pointer constants. In the rare instances when they are required, they are generally written as integer literals and converted to the proper type with a cast.[28]

6.10 Pointers to Pointers

We will spend only a brief moment here on an example that suggests topics to come. Consider these declarations:

```
int     a = 12;
int     *b = &a;
```

---

[28] Implementations for segmented machines, such as the Intel 80x86, may provide a macro to construct pointer constants. The macro converts a segment and offset pair into the pointer value.

They allocate memory as shown in the following diagram:

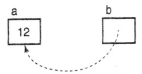

Suppose we had a third variable called c and initialized it with this statement:

```
c = &b;
```

Here is what memory would look like:

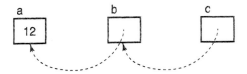

The question is: what is the type of c? Clearly it is a pointer, but what does it point to? The variable b is a "pointer to an integer," so anything that points to b must be a pointer to a "pointer to an integer," or more generally, a pointer to a pointer.

Is this legal? Yes! A pointer variable is like any other variable in that it occupies a specific location in memory, so it makes sense that we can obtain its address with the & operator.[29]

How would this variable be declared? The declaration

```
int     **c;
```

says that the expression **c is of type int. Table 6.1 lists some expressions that may help illustrate this concept; the expressions assume these declarations.

```
int     a = 12;
int     *b = &a;
int     **c = &b;
```

The only new expression in the table is the last one, so let's unravel it. The * operator has right-to-left associativity, so this expression is equivalent to *(*c). We must evaluate it from the inside out. *c takes us to the location to which c points, which we know to be the variable b. The second

---

[29] Except variables declared register.

Expression	Equivalent expression(s)
a	12
b	&a
*b	a, 12
c	&b
*c	b, &a
**c	*b, a, 12

Table 6.1   Double indirection

indirection then takes us to where *this* location points, which is a. The only thing tricky about pointers to pointers is keeping all of the arrows straight and remembering that an arrow is followed only if an indirection operator causes it.

6.11 Pointer Expressions

Now let's take a look at a variety of pointer expressions and see how they are evaluated when used both as R-values and L-values. Some of these expressions are commonly used, but not all. The purpose of this exercise is not to give you a "cookbook" of expressions but rather to build your skill in reading and writing them. First, let's set the stage with some declarations.

```
char    ch = 'a';
char    *cp = &ch;
```

We now have two variables initialized like this:

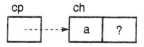

The memory location that follows ch is also shown because some of the expressions that we evaluate will access it, albeit erroneously. Because we don't know what its initial value is, a question mark is shown.

Let's figure out an easy one first to get the ball rolling. The expression is:

```
ch
```

When used as an R-value, this expression has the value 'a' and is illustrated as:

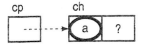

The heavy oval indicates that the value in the variable ch is the value of the expression. But when this expression is used as an L-value, it is the location that counts rather than the value that it contains, so it is illustrated differently:

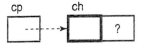

Here the location is marked with a heavy box, indicating that the location is the result. Additionally, its value is not shown because it isn't important; indeed, the value is about to be replaced by some new value. The remaining expressions are shown in a tabular form. Each table is followed by a description of the expression's evaluation.

Expression	R-value	L-value
&ch	cp → ch [a	?] ← ◯	Illegal

As an R-value, this expression's value is the address of the variable ch. Note that this value is the same as the value stored in the variable cp, but the expression doesn't mention cp so that's not where the value comes from. Thus the oval is not around the arrow in cp. The second question is, why is this expression not a legal L-value? The precedence table shows that the & operator produces an R-value as a result, and they cannot be used as L-values. But why? The answer is easy. When the expression &ch is evaluated, where is the result held in the computer? It must be somewhere, but you have no way of knowing where. The expression does not identify any specific location in the machine's memory, and thus it is not a legal L-value.

Expression	R-value		L-value	
cp				

You've seen this expression before. Its R-value is the value in `cp`, as indicated. The L-value is the location `cp`. There is no indirection in this expression, so you do not follow the arrow.

Expression	R-value	L-value
&cp		*Illegal*

This example is similar to `&ch` except that this time we take the address of the pointer variable. The type of this result is pointer to pointer to character. Once again, the value is stored in an unidentifiable location so the expression is not a legal L-value.

Expression	R-value		L-value	
*cp				

Now we have added indirection so the results should come as no surprise. But the next few expressions begin to get more interesting.

Expression	R-value	L-value
*cp + 1	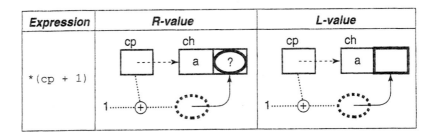	*Illegal*

This diagram is more involved, so let's do it step by step. There are two operators here. `*` has a higher precedence than `+`, so the indirection is performed first (as shown by the solid arrow from `cp` to `ch`), which gets us its value (indicated by the dotted oval). A copy of this value is taken and added to one, giving the character `'b'` as a result. The dotted lines show the movement of data as the expression is evaluated. The final result does not reside in any identifiable location, so this expression is not a legal L-value. The precedence table confirms that the result of `+` is not an L-value.

Expression	R-value	L-value
*(cp + 1)		

In this example, we've added parentheses to the previous expression. The parentheses force the addition to go first, which adds one to a copy of the address in `cp`. The result so far is the pointer in the dotted oval. The indirection follows this arrow to the location just after `ch`, and the R-value of the expression is the value in that location. The L-value, of course, is the location itself.

There is an important point to be learned here. Note that the result of the pointer addition is an R-value because it does not reside in any identifiable location. Without the indirection, this expression would not be a legal L-value. However, the indirection follows the pointer to a specific location. Thus, `*(cp + 1)` may be used as an L-value even though `cp + 1` may not. The indirection operator is one of only a few whose result is an L-value.

But the expression is accessing the location after `ch`; how can we tell what resides there? In general, we can't, so expressions like this one are illegal. I discuss this topic in more depth later in this chapter.

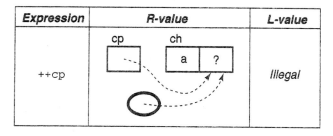

Expression	R-value	L-value
++cp	cp ch a ?	*Illegal*

The ++ and -- operators are frequently used with pointer variables, so it is important to understand them in this context. In this expression, we increment the pointer variable cp. (To unclutter the diagrams, we no longer show the addition.) The result is a copy of the incremented pointer, because the prefix ++ increments before using the value in the surrounding expression. The copy is not stored in any identifiable location, so it is not a legal L-value.

Expression	R-value	L-value
cp++	cp ch a ?	*Illegal*

The postfix ++ produces the same value in cp, but it increments after the copy is made. Thus, the value of the expression is a copy of the original value of cp.

Neither of the previous two expressions are legal L-values. But they would be if we add indirection, as illustrated in the next two expressions.

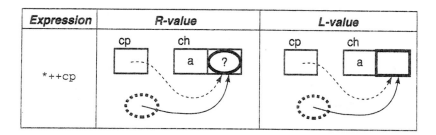

Expression	R-value	L-value
*++cp	cp ch a ?	cp ch a

Here, indirection is applied to the copy of the incremented pointer, so the R-value is the value in the location following ch and the L-value is that location.

Expression	R-value	L-value
*cp++	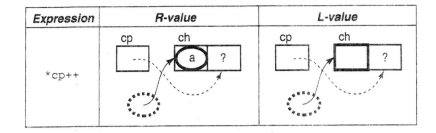	

Using the postfix ++ yields a different result: the R-value and L-value relate to the variable ch, which is where cp originally pointed. Again, the postfix operator uses the original value of its operand in the surrounding expression. The combination of indirection and the postfix ++ is often misunderstood. The precedence table indicates that the postfix ++ has a higher precedence than the *, yet it appears as if the indirection is being performed first. In fact, there are three steps involved: (1) ++ makes a copy of cp, (2) then ++ increments cp, and finally, (3) the indirection is performed on the copy.

This expression is often used in loops to sequentially examine the contents of some array to which the pointer has previously been initialized. Some examples are shown later in this chapter.

Expression	R-value	L-value
++*cp	cp ch [ ]→[b] [?] (b)	Illegal

In this expression, the indirection is evaluated first due to the right-to-left associativity of these operators. Therefore, the location to which cp points is incremented; the result is a copy of the incremented value.

The last three expressions are not used as often as some of the previous ones but deciphering them will increase your skill.

Expression	R-value	L-value
`(*cp)++`		*Illegal*

With the postfix `++`, we need parentheses to make the indirection go first. This expression is evaluated like the previous example except that the result is the value that `ch` had before the increment took place.

Expression	R-value	L-value
`++*++cp`		*Illegal*

This one looks pretty tricky, but it isn't really. There are three operators in this expression, which is what makes it look intimidating. If you analyze them one by one, though, each will be familiar. In fact, we've already evaluated `*++cp` earlier; all we are doing now is to increment its result. But let's start from scratch. Remember that the associativity of these operators is right to left, so the first thing that happens is `++cp`; the dotted oval beneath `cp` illustrates the first intermediate result. Then we apply indirection to this copy, which takes us to the location after `ch`. The second intermediate result is shown with a dotted box because the next operator uses it as an L-value. Finally, we apply `++` to this location, which increments its value. We display the value as `? + 1` because we do not know the original value of the location.

Expression	R-value	L-value
++*cp++	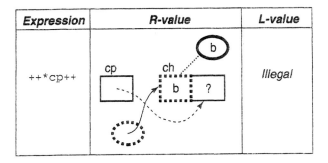	Illegal

The difference between this expression and the previous one is that the first ++ is postfix instead of prefix, so it is evaluated first because of its higher precedence. The indirection then takes us to cp instead of the following location.

6.12 Examples

Here are some sample programs to illustrate a few common pointer expressions. Program 6.1 computes the length of a string. You should never have to write this function because the library contains one, but it is a useful example.

```c
/*
** Compute the length of a string.
*/

#include <stdlib.h>

size_t
strlen( char *string )
{
        int     length = 0;

        /*
        ** Advance through the string, counting characters
        ** until the terminating NUL byte is reached.
        */
        while( *string++ != '\0' )
                length += 1;

        return length;
}
```

Program 6.1   String length   strlen.c

The expression *string++ in the while statement is true until the pointer has reached the terminating NUL byte. It also increments the pointer for the next test. This expression even handles empty strings properly.

If the function is called with a NULL pointer, the indirection in the while statement will fail. Should the function check for this condition before dereferencing the pointer? To be absolutely safe, it should. However, this function does not create the string. If it finds that the argument is NULL, it has really found an error that occurred elsewhere in the program. It seems logical that the pointer should be checked where it was created, because then it need be checked only once. This approach is taken by this function. If the function fails because a careless client didn't bother to check the argument, they deserve what they get.

Programs 6.2 and 6.3 add a level of indirection. They search a collection of strings for a specific character value, but an array of pointers is used to keep track of the strings, as illustrated in Figure 6.1. The arguments to the functions are strings, the pointer to the array of pointers; and value, the character value we're looking for. Notice that the array of pointers ends with a NULL pointer. The functions will check for this value to determine when to stop. The expression in

```
while( ( string = *strings++ ) != NULL ){
```

does three things: (1) it copies the pointer that strings currently points to into the variable string, (2) it increments strings to point to the next value, and (3) it tests whether string is NULL. The inner while loop stops when string points to the terminating NUL byte at the end of the current string.

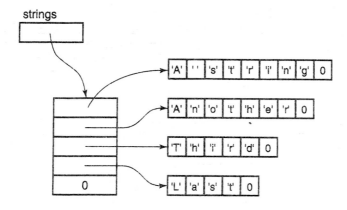

Figure 6.1   Array of pointers to strings

```
/*
** Given a pointer to a NULL-terminated list of pointers, search
** the strings in the list for a particular character.
*/

#include <stdio.h>

#define TRUE     1
#define FALSE    0

int
find_char( char **strings, char value )
{
        char    *string;         /* the string we're looking at */

        /*
        ** For each string in the list ...
        */
        while( ( string = *strings++ ) != NULL ){
                /*
                ** Look at each character in the string to see if
                ** it is the one we want.
                */
                while( *string != '\0' ){
                        if( *string++ == value )
                                return TRUE;

                }
        }
        return FALSE;

}
```

Program 6.2   Search a collection of strings: version one   s_srch1.c

Until then,

```
if( *string++ == value )
```

tests whether the current character matches the desired value and increments
the pointer to the next character.

Program 6.3 performs the same function without making a copy of the
pointer to each string. As a side effect, however, this program destroys the
array of pointers. This side effect makes the function less useful than the previous version, as it can be used only when the strings are searched once.

```
/*
** Given a pointer to a NULL-terminated list of pointers, search
** the strings in the list for a particular character.  This
** version destroys the pointers so it can only be used when
** the collection will be examined only once.
*/

#include <stdio.h>
#include <assert.h>

#define TRUE    1
#define FALSE   0

int
find_char( char **strings, int value )
{
        assert( strings != NULL );

        /*
        ** For each string in the list ...
        */
        while( *strings != NULL ){
                /*
                ** Look at each character in the string to see if
                ** it is the one we want.
                */
                while( **strings != '\0' ){
                        if( *(*strings)++ == value )
                                return TRUE;
                }
                strings++;
        }
        return FALSE;
}
```

Program 6.3 Search a collection of strings: version two   s_srch2.c

There are, however, two interesting expressions in Program 6.3. The first is `**strings`. The first indirection goes to the current pointer in the array of pointers, and the second follows that pointer to the current character in the string. The inner `while` statement tests this character to see whether the end of the string has been reached.

The second interesting expression is `*(*strings)++`. Parentheses are needed in order for the expression to evaluate properly. The first indirection goes to the current pointer in the list. The increment adds one to that location, but the second indirection works on a copy of the original value. The net result is that the current character in the current string is tested to see whether we've reached the end of the string, and the pointer to the current string character is incremented as a side effect.

6.13 Pointer Arithmetic

Programs 6.1–6.3 include expressions involving additions of pointer values and integers. Is it legal to perform any arithmetic with pointers? The answer is a qualified yes; you can do more than just addition but not much more.

The result of a pointer plus an integer is another pointer. The question is, where does it point? If you add one to a character pointer, the result points to the next character in memory. A float occupies more than one byte; what happens if you increment a pointer to a float—does the result point somewhere inside of the float?

Fortunately, no. When arithmetic is performed with a pointer and an integer quantity, the integer is always *scaled* to the proper size before the addition. The "proper size" is the size of whatever type the pointer is pointing at, and the "scaling" is simply multiplication. To illustrate, imagine a machine on which floats occupy four bytes. In evaluating an expression that adds three to a pointer to a float, the value three is scaled (multiplied) by the size of a float, which is four in this example. The value actually added to the pointer is twelve.

Adding three to the pointer increased it by the size of three floats, not by three bytes. This behavior is much more sensible than getting a pointer that points somewhere in the middle of a float. Table 6.2 contains some additional examples. The beauty of scaling is that pointer arithmetic doesn't

Expression	Assuming p Is a Pointer to a ...	... and the Size of *p Is ...	Value Added to the Pointer
p + 1	char	1	1
	short	2	2
	int	4	4
	double	8	8
p + 2	char	1	2
	short	2	4
	int	4	8
	double	8	16

Table 6.2   Pointer arithmetic results

depend on the type of the pointer. In other words, the expression `p + 1` points to the next `char` if `p` was a pointer to a `char`. It points to the next `float` if `p` was a pointer to a `float`, and so forth.

6.13.1 Arithmetic Operations

Pointer arithmetic in C is restricted to exactly two forms. The first form is:

```
pointer ± integer
```

This form is defined by the Standard only for pointers that are pointing at an element of an array, such as this one,

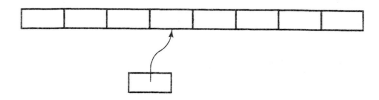

and yields a result of the same type as the pointer. This form also works with dynamically allocated memory obtained from `malloc` (see Chapter 11), though through an oversight the Standard fails to mention this fact.

Elements in an array are stored in consecutive memory locations, and the later elements have larger addresses than the earlier ones. Given this information, it is easy to see that adding one to the pointer moves it to the next element in the array, adding five moves it five elements to the right, and so forth. Subtracting three moves it three elements to the left. Scaling the integer ensures that the addition produces this result no matter what size elements are in the array.

The effect of an addition or a subtraction is undefined if the result points to anything earlier than the first element of the array or if it points to any element more than one beyond the last element of the array. It is legal for the pointer to go one element past the end of the array, but indirection may not be performed on it then.

Time for an example. Here is a loop that initializes all of the elements of an array to zero. (Chapter 8 discusses the efficiency of loops like this one compared to loops that use subscripts.)

```
#define N_VALUES        5
float    values[N_VALUES];
float    *vp;

for( vp = &values[0]; vp < &values[N_VALUES]; )
        *vp++ = 0;
```

The initialization step of the for statement makes vp point to the first element of the array.

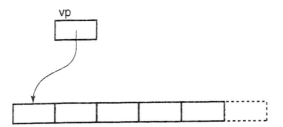

The pointer arithmetic in this example is performed by the ++ operator. The increment value, one, is multiplied by the size of a float, and this value is added to the pointer vp. After the first time through the body of the loop, memory looks like this:

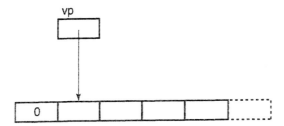

After five times through the loop, vp has gone past the end of the array

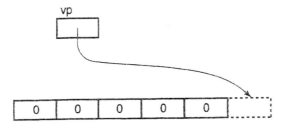

and the loop stops. With subscript values beginning at zero, the last element of an array of five elements will have a subscript of four. Thus

&values[N_VALUES] represents the address of the first location beyond the right end of the array. When vp reaches this value, we know we have reached the end of the array, and the loop terminates.

The pointer in this example goes one element beyond the end of the array. The pointer may legally attain this value but applying indirection to it will access whatever other variable (if any) happens to reside in that location. The programmer generally has no way of determining what variable that might be, which is why indirection is not allowed in this circumstance.

The second type of pointer arithmetic has the form:

```
pointer - pointer
```

Subtracting one pointer from another is allowed only when both point to elements of the same array, like this:

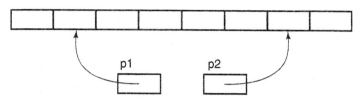

The result of subtracting two pointers is of type **ptrdiff_t**, which will be a signed integral type. The value is the distance (measured in array elements, not bytes) between the two pointers, because the result of the subtraction is divided (scaled) by the size of the array elements. For example, if p1 points to array[i] and p2 points to array[j] then p2 - p1 will have the same value as j - i.

Let's see how this works with a specific type. Suppose the array in the previous diagram consisted of floats occupying four bytes each. If the array began at location 1000, then p1 would contain 1004 and p2 would contain 1024. The result of the expression p2 - p1 would be five, though, because the difference between the pointer values (20) is divided by the size of each element (4).

Once again, scaling makes the result independent of the data's type. The result of this pointer subtraction will be five no matter what type of data the array contains.

Is the expression p1 - p2 legal? Yes, if both pointers are pointing to elements of the same array. In the previous example, its value would be –5.

The result of subtracting two pointers that do not point to the same array is undefined for the same reason that subtracting the addresses of two houses on different streets doesn't tell you the number of houses in between them. The programmer has no way of knowing where the two arrays might have been allocated relative to one another. Without this knowledge, the distance from one pointer to another has no meaning.

In practice, most compilers do not check whether the result of a pointer expression falls within any legal bounds. Therefore, it is up to the programmer to make sure it does. Similarly, the compiler will not prevent you from taking the address of a scalar variable and performing pointer arithmetic on it, even though there is no way to predict what variable the result will point to. Out-of-range pointers and pointers to unknown values are two common causes of errors. When using pointer arithmetic, be very careful that the result points to something meaningful.

6.13.2 Relational Operations

Relational operations on pointers are also constrained. It is possible to compare two pointer values with the relational operators

```
    <       <=       >       >=
```

only if they both point to elements of the same array. Depending on which operator you choose, the comparison will tell you which pointer points earlier or later in the array. The results of comparing arbitrary pointers are not defined by the Standard.

However, you may test for equality or inequality between any pointers, because the results of such comparisons do not depend on where the compiler has chosen to allocate data—the pointers either refer to the same address or to different ones.

Let's look again at the loop to clear the elements of an array.

```
#define N_VALUES        5
float   values[N_VALUES];
float   *vp;

for( vp = &values[0]; vp < &values[N_VALUES]; )
        *vp++ = 0;
```

The for statement uses a relational test to terminate the loop. The test is legal because both vp and the pointer constant point to elements of the same array. (Actually, the pointer constant points one beyond the end of the array, and when the last comparison is made so does vp, but indirection is not performed so we're safe.) Using != instead of < would also work, because both expressions will be false when vp attains its final value.

Now consider this loop:

```
for( vp = &values[N_VALUES]; vp > &values[0]; )
    *--vp = 0;
```

It performs the same job as the previous loop except that the elements are cleared in the opposite order. We initialize vp to point just beyond the right end of the array, but the pointer is decremented just before the indirection occurs. We stop the loop when vp points to the first element of the array, but this occurs after the first element has already been cleared.

Some might object to the expression *--vp on the grounds of readability. But look what happens to this loop when it is "simplified:"

```
for( vp = &values[N_VALUES - 1]; vp >= &values[0]; vp-- )
    *vp = 0;
```

Now vp is initialized to point to the last element of the array and is decremented in the adjustment step of the for statement. There is a problem with this loop—do you see it?

After the first element in the array is cleared, vp is decremented again, and the next comparison is supposed to terminate the loop. But here is where the problem occurs: the comparison vp >= &values[0] is undefined because vp has moved outside of the bounds of the array. The Standard allows for a comparison with a pointer that points just beyond the right side of an array but not for one that points just beyond the left side.

In practice, this loop will work properly on most ANSI C implementations. Nevertheless, it should be avoided because the Standard does not guarantee that it will work, and sooner or later you are bound to run across a machine on which it fails. Such are the problems that give nightmares to programmers responsible for portable code.

6.14 Summary

Each location in the computer's memory is identified by an address. Adjacent locations are often grouped together to allow larger ranges of values to be stored. A pointer is a value that represents a memory address.

Neither you nor the computer can determine the type of a value by examining its bits; the type is implicit in how the value is used. The compiler helps us by ensuring that values are used in a way that is appropriate to how they are declared.

The value of a pointer variable is *not* the value to which it points. Indirection must be applied to a pointer to obtain the value that it points to. The result of applying indirection to a "pointer to integer" is an integer.

Declaring a pointer variable does not automatically allocate any memory in which to store values. Before indirection can be performed on the pointer, it must be initialized to point either to existing memory or to dynamically allocated memory. Indirection on an uninitialized pointer variable is illegal but often goes undetected. The result may be that an unrelated value is modified. These errors are difficult to debug.

The NULL pointer is a value that is defined as pointing to nothing at all. It can be assigned to a pointer variable to indicate that the variable does not point to any value. The result of applying indirection to a NULL pointer is implementation dependent; two common results are to return the value of memory location zero and to abort the program.

A pointer variable, like any other variable, can be used as an L-value. Applying indirection to a pointer also results in an L-value because the expression identifies a specific memory location.

Other than the NULL pointer, there is no built-in notation for expressing pointer constants because the programmer usually has no way of predicting where the compiler will place variables. In the rare cases where they are needed, pointer constants can be created by casting integer values.

Limited arithmetic can be performed on pointer values. You can add an integer value to a pointer, and subtract an integer value from a pointer. In both cases, the integer value is scaled by the size of the pointer's target type. Thus, adding one to a pointer makes it point to the next variable regardless of the size of the variables in memory.

However, this pointer arithmetic is predictable only with arrays. It is illegal (but often not detected) to perform arithmetic on any pointer that does not point to an element of an array. It is also illegal to subtract from a pointer if the result lies before the first element of the array to which it points, and to add to a pointer if the result lies more than one element after the end of the array to which it points. The result of a pointer addition may point one element beyond the end of the array, but it is illegal to apply indirection to this result.

Two pointers may be subtracted from one another only if they both point to elements of the same array. The result of pointer subtraction is scaled by the size of the values in the array, so the result is the number of values separating the original pointers. Subtracting pointers to elements of different arrays is an (often undetected) error.

Any pointers may be compared to each other for equality or inequality. Two pointers that point to elements of the same array may also be compared using the relational operators <, <=, >, and >= to determine their positions in the array relative to each other. The result of a relational comparison between unrelated pointers is undefined.

6.15 Summary of Cautions

1. Dereferencing an uninitialized pointer variable (page 135).

2. Dereferencing a NULL pointer (page 136).

3. NULL pointer arguments to functions (page 149).

4. Unexpected results from errors in pointer expressions that are not detected (page 156).

5. Decrementing a pointer variable past the beginning of an array (page 157).

6.16 Summary of Programming Tips

1. A value should only have one meaning (page 136).

2. Set pointer variables to NULL when they are not pointing to anything useful (page 137).

6.17 Questions

1. If the type of a value cannot be determined simply by looking at its bits, how does the machine know how the value should be manipulated?

2. Why doesn't C have a way of declaring literal pointer constants?

3. Suppose an integer contains the value 244. Why doesn't the machine interpret this value as an address?

4. On some machines, the compiler arranges for memory location zero to contain the value zero. Dereferencing a NULL pointer then accesses this location. What are the consequences of this arrangement?

5. What is the difference (if any) between the work that is required to evaluate
    expressions *(a)* and *(b)*? Assume that the variable `offset` has the value three.

    ```
    int     i[ 10 ];
    int     *p = &i[ 0 ];
    int     offset;

    p += offset;    (a)
    p += 3;         (b)
    ```

6. What (if anything) is wrong with the following code segment?

    ```
    int     array[ARRAY_SIZE];
    int     *pi;

    for( pi = &array[0]; pi < &array[ARRAY_SIZE]; )
            *++pi = 0;
    ```

7. The table below shows the contents of several memory locations. Each loca-
    tion is identified by its address and also by the name of the variable stored
    there. All numbers are shown in decimal.

Variable	Address	Contents	Variable	Address	Contents
a	1040	1028	o	1096	1024
c	1056	1076	q	1084	1072
d	1008	1016	r	1068	1048
e	1032	1088	s	1004	2000
f	1052	1044	t	1060	1012
g	1000	1064	u	1036	1092
h	1080	1020	v	1092	1036
i	1020	1080	w	1012	1060
j	1064	1000	x	1072	1080
k	1044	1052	y	1048	1068
m	1016	1008	z	2000	1000
n	1076	1056			

Using these values, evaluate each of the expressions below four ways. First,
assume that all the variables are integers, and find the expression's R-value.
Then find its L-value, and give the address of the location it specifies. Next,
assume that all the variables are pointers to integers and repeat the exercise.
Note: Do your address arithmetic based on four-byte integers and pointers.

		Integers		Pointers to Integers	
	Expression	*R-value*	*L-value addr*	*R-value*	*L-value addr*
a.	m				
b.	v + 1				
c.	j - 4				
d.	a - d				
e.	v - w				
f.	&c				
g.	&e + 1				
h.	&o - 4				
i.	&(f + 2)				
j.	*g				
k.	*k + 1				
l.	*(n + 1)				
m.	*h - 4				
n.	*(u - 4)				
o.	*f - g				
p.	*f - *g				
q.	*s - *q				
r.	*(r - t)				
s.	y > i				
t.	y > *i				
u.	*y > *i				
v.	**h				
w.	c++				
x.	++c				
y.	*q++				
z.	(*q)++				
aa.	*++q				
bb.	++*q				
cc.	*++*q				
dd.	++*(*q)++				

6.18 Programming Exercises

★★★ 1. Write a function that will search a string for any one of a given set of characters. Your function should match this prototype:

```
char *find_char( char const *source,
    char const *chars );
```

The basic idea is to locate the first character in the source string that
matches any of the characters in the chars string. The function then returns a
pointer to the place in source where the first match was found. If none of the
characters in source match any of the chars, then a NULL pointer is returned.
If either argument is NULL, or either string is empty, then a NULL pointer is
returned.

To illustrate, suppose source points to ABCDEFG. If chars points to
XYZ, JURY, or QQQQ, the function should return NULL. If chars points to
XRCQEF, the function should return a pointer to the C in source. The
strings that the arguments point to are never modified.

As it happens, there is a function in the C library called strpbrk that
behaves almost exactly the same as the one you are to write. But the object of
this program is for you to manipulate the pointers yourself, so:

a.   You may not use any of the library string routines (for example, strcpy,
strcmp, index, etc.), and

b.   you may not use subscripts anywhere in your function.

★★★ 2. Write a function that deletes a portion of a string. Here is its prototype:

```
int del_substr( char *str, char const *substr )
```

The function should first determine whether the string substr occurs in str.
If it does not, the value 0 should be returned. If the substring does appear, the
function should remove it by copying the characters in str that follow the
substring over the substring itself. The value 1 should then be returned. If the
substring appears several times in the first argument, only the first occurrence
should be deleted. The second argument should never be changed.

To illustrate, suppose str points to ABCDEFG. If substr points to
FGH, CDF, or XABC, the function should return 0 and leave str unchanged.
But if substr points to CDE, the function should change str to ABFG by
copying the characters F, G, and the NUL byte. The function should then
return 1. In no event is the second argument string ever modified.

As with the last program:

a.   you may not use any of the library string routines (e.g. strcpy,
strcmp, etc.), and

b.   you may not use any subscripts in your function.

On a philosophical note, the empty string is a substring of every string but removing an empty substring produces no change in the string.

⬦ ★★★ 3.   Write the function `reverse_string`, whose prototype is shown below:

```
void reverse_string( char *string );
```

The function reverses the characters in the argument string. Use pointers rather than subscripts, and do not use any of the C library string functions. *Hint:* There is no need to declare a local array to temporarily hold the argument string.

★★★ 4.   A prime number is one that is divisible only by itself and one. The Sieve of Eratosthenes is an efficient algorithm for the computation of prime numbers. The first step of the algorithm is to write down all the numbers from two to some upper limit. In the rest of the algorithm, you go through the list and cross out numbers that are not prime.

Here are the remaining steps. Starting at the beginning of the list, find the first number that is not crossed out, which will be two. Cross out every second number in the list after two, because they are all multiples of two. Then repeat these steps from the beginning of the list. The first number in the list that is not crossed out is now three, so cross out every third number after three. The next number in the list, four, is already crossed out so it is skipped. When you have finished this process, the numbers that have not been crossed out are prime.

Write a program that implements this algorithm, using an array for your list. The value in each array element keeps track of whether the corresponding number has been crossed out. Set all elements of the array to TRUE initially, then set them FALSE according to the algorithm above to "cross them out." If you are working on a 16-bit machine, think carefully which variables should be declared `long`. Start with an array of 1000 elements. If you use an array of characters, you can find more prime numbers than if you use an array of integers. You can use subscripts to compute pointers to the beginning and end of the array, but you should use pointers to access the array elements.

Note that none of the even numbers are prime except for two. With a little thought, you can make the program more space efficient by keeping track of only the odd numbers with your array. You should then be able to find (roughly) twice as many prime numbers with the same size array.

★★ 5.   Modify the Sieve of Eratosthenes program in the previous problem so that it uses an array of bits rather than characters, using the bit array functions developed in the Chapter 5 programming exercises. This change makes the program even more space efficient, at a cost of time efficiency. What is the largest prime number you can compute in this manner on your system?

★★ 6. Are there as many large prime numbers as there are small ones? In other words, are there as many prime numbers between 50,000 and 51,000 as there are between, say, 1,000,000 and 1,001,000? Use the previous program to determine how many prime numbers there are between 0 and 1000, between 1000 and 2000, and so forth up to 1,000,000 (or as high as you can go on your system). What is the trend in the number of primes per thousand numbers?

7

Functions

There is much about functions in C that is similar to functions in other languages, which is why you've been able to use them thus far with only an informal discussion. However there are some aspects of functions that are less intuitive, so this chapter formally describes functions in C.

7.1 Function Definition

The *definition* of a function specifies the function *body*, the block of statements to be executed when the function is called. In contrast, a function *declaration* is used where the function is being called. A declaration gives the compiler information about the function so that it can be called correctly. Let's look first at definitions.

A function is defined with this syntax:

```
type
name( formal_parameters )
block
```

Recall that a block is a pair of braces enclosing optional declarations followed by optional statements. The minimal function, therefore, looks like this:

```
function_name()
{
}
```

When called, this function simply returns. Nevertheless, it serves a useful purpose as a *stub*, a placeholder for code that has yet to be implemented. Writing stubs, or "stubbing out" code that has not yet been written, lets you compile and test the rest of the program.

The list of formal parameters includes variable names and their type declarations. The block contains declarations for local variables and the statements that are executed when the function is called. Program 7.1 is an example of a simple function.

Writing the function type on a separate line from the function name is a matter of style; it makes it easier to locate the function names when perusing the source code either visually or with some program.

K&R C   In K&R C, the types of formal parameters were declared in a separate list that appeared between the parameter list and the opening brace of the function body, like this:

```
int *
find_int( key, array, array_len )
int key;
int array[];
int array_len;
{
```

```
/*
** Find the place in an array where a particular integer value
** is stored, and return a pointer to that location.
*/
#include <stdio.h>

int *
find_int( int key, int array[], int array_len )
{
        int     i;

        /*
        ** For each location in the array ...
        */
        for( i = 0; i < array_len; i += 1 )
                /*
                ** Check the location for the desired value.
                */
                if( array[ i ] == key )
                        return &array[ i ];

        return NULL;
}
```

Program 7.1   Find an integer in an array   find_int.c

This declaration form is allowed by the Standard mainly so that older programs can be compiled without modification. The newer declaration style is preferred for two reasons. First, it eliminates the redundancy of the old style. More importantly, it allows for the use of function prototypes, discussed later in this chapter, which improve the compiler's error checking of function calls.

7.1.1 Return Statement

When execution reaches the end of the function definition, the function *returns*, that is, execution goes back to where the function was called. The `return` statement allows you to return from anywhere in the function body, not just at its end. Its syntax is shown below.

```
return expression;
```

The `expression` is optional. It is omitted in functions that do not return a value to the calling program, what most other languages call a *procedure*. Functions that return implicitly by reaching the end of their code also do not return a value. Procedure-type functions should be declared with the type `void`.

A true *function* is called from within an expression, and must return a value that is used in evaluating the expression. The `return` statement in these functions must include the `expression`. Usually, the expression will be of the type that the function was declared to return. An expression of a different type is permitted only if the compiler can convert it to the proper type through the usual arithmetic conversions.

Some programmers prefer to write return statements like this:

```
return( x );
```

The syntax does not require parentheses, but you can use them if you prefer because parentheses are always legal around an expression.

In C, both types of subprograms are called functions. It is possible to call a true function (one that returns a value) without using the value in any expression. In this situation, the returned value is just discarded. Calling a procedure-type function from within an expression is a serious error, though, because an unpredictable (garbage) value is used in evaluating the expression. Fortunately, modern compilers usually catch this error because they are stricter about function return types than were earlier compilers.

7.2 Function Declaration

When the compiler encounters a call to a function, it generates code to pass the arguments and call the function, and code to receive the value (if any) sent back by the function. But how does the compiler know what kinds of arguments (and how many) the function expects to get, and what kind of value (if any) that the function returns?

If there isn't any specific information given about the function, the compiler assumes that the call has the correct number and types of arguments. It also assumes that the function will return an integer, which usually leads to errors for functions that return nonintegral types.

7.2.1 Prototypes

It is safer to give the compiler specific information about the function, which we can do two different ways. First, if the definition for the function appears earlier in the same source file, the compiler will remember the number and types of its arguments and the type of its return value. It can then check all subsequent calls to the function (in that source file) to make sure they are correct.

| K&R C |

If a function is defined using the old syntax, with a separate list giving the types of the arguments, then the compiler remembers only the type of the function's return value. No information is saved on the number or types of the arguments. Because of this fact, it is important to use the new function declaration style whenever possible.

The second way to give the compiler information about a function is to use a *function prototype*, which you saw in Chapter 1. A prototype summarizes the declaration at the beginning of the function definition, thus giving the compiler complete information on how the function is to be called. The most convenient (and safest) way to use a prototype is to put it in a separate file and then #include that file wherever it is needed. This technique avoids the possibility of mistyping a prototype. It also simplifies maintenance of the program by only having one physical copy of the prototype. Should the prototype need to be changed, there is only one copy of it to modify.

To illustrate, here is a prototype for the find_int function from the previous example:

```
int *find_int( int key, int array[], int len );
```

Note the semicolon at the end: it distinguishes a prototype from the beginning of a function definition. The prototype tells the compiler the number of arguments, the type of each argument, and the type of the returned value. After the prototype has been seen, the compiler will check calls made to the function to make sure that their arguments are correct and that the returned value is used properly. Where mismatches occur (for example, an argument of the wrong type) the compiler will convert the value to the correct type if such a conversion is possible.

Note that I put argument names in the above prototype. While not required, it is wise to include descriptive parameter names in function prototypes because they give useful information to clients wishing to call the function. For example, which of the following two prototypes do you find more useful?

```
char *strcpy( char *, char * );
char *strcpy( char *destination, char *source );
```

The following code fragment illustrates a dangerous way to use function prototypes.

```
void
a()
{
        int     *func( int *value, int len );
        ...
}

void
b()
{
        int     func( int len, int *value );
        ...
}
```

Look closely at the prototypes and you will see that they are different. The arguments are reversed, and the return values are different types. The problem is that each prototype is written inside the body of a function. They have block scope, so the compiler throws out what it learned from the prototype at the end of each function and never detects the mismatch.

The Standard states that a function prototype must match any earlier prototype for the same function that is in scope, or else an error message is printed. In this example, though, the the scope for the first block does not overlap the second block. Therefore, the mistakes in the prototypes go undetected. One or the other of these prototypes is wrong (maybe both), but the compiler never sees the contradiction so no error messages are produced.

The code fragment below illustrates the preferred way to use prototypes.

```
#include "func.h"

void
a()
{
        . . .
}

void
b()
{
        . . .
}
```

The file `func.h` contains the prototype

```
int     *func( int *value, int len );
```

This technique is better in several ways.

1. The prototype now has file scope so that one copy of it applies to the entire source file, which is easier than writing a separate copy in each place from which the function is called.

2. The prototype is only written once, so there is no chance for disagreements between multiple copies.

3. If the function definition changes, all we have to do is modify the prototype and recompile each source file that includes it.

4. If the prototype is also `#include`'d into the file where the function is defined, the compiler will be able to verify that the prototype matches the function definition.

By writing the prototype once, we eliminate the chance that multiple copies of it differ. However, the prototype must match the function definition. Including the prototype in the file where the function is defined lets the compiler verify that they match.

Consider this declaration, which looks ambiguous:

```
int     *func();
```

It could be either an old-style declaration (giving the return type of `func`) or a new-style prototype for a function with no arguments. Which is it? The declaration must be interpreted as an old-style declaration in order to maintain compatiblity with pre-ANSI programs. A prototype for a function without arguments is written like this:

```
int      *func( void );
```

The keyword void indicates that there aren't any arguments, not that there is one argument of type void.

7.2.2 Default Function Assumptions

When a call is made to a function for which no prototype has been seen, the function is assumed to return an integer value. This can lead to errors for functions which return nonintegral values.

While it is recommended that all functions be prototyped, it is especially important to prototype functions that return nonintegral values. Remember that the type of a value is not inherent in the value itself, but rather in the way that it is used. If the compiler assumes that a function returns an integral value, it will generate integer instructions to manipulate the value. If the value is actually a nonintegral type, floating-point for example, the result will usually be incorrect.

Let's look at an example of this error. Imagine a function xyz that returns the float value 3.14 . The bits used to represent this floating-point number on a Sun Sparc workstation are

```
01000000010010001111010111000011
```

Now assume that the function is called like this:

```
float   f;
...
f = xyz();
```

If there is no prototype for the function, the compiler will assume that it is returning an integer and will generate instructions to convert the value to floating-point before assigning it to f.

The function returns the bits shown above. The conversion instructions interpret them as the integer 1,078,523,331 and convert *this* integer value to floating-point, and the result is stored in f.

Why was this conversion done when the value returned was already in floating-point format? The compiler has no way of knowing it was, because there was no prototype or declaration to tell it so. This example illustrates why it is vital for functions that return values other than integers to have prototypes.

7.3 Function Arguments

All arguments to C functions are passed with a technique known as *call by value*, which means that the function gets a *copy* of the argument value. Thus the function may modify its parameters without fear of affecting the values of the arguments passed from the calling program. This behavior is the same as value (not **var**) parameters in Modula and Pascal.

The rule in C is simple: *all* arguments are passed by value. However, if an array name is passed as an argument and a subscript is used on the argument in the function, then modifying array elements in the function actually changes the elements of the array in the calling program. The function accesses the very same array that exists in the calling program; the array is not copied. This behavior is termed *call by reference* and is how **var** parameters are implemented in many other languages.

```
/*
** Check the value for even parity.
*/

int
even_parity( int value, int n_bits )
{
        int     parity = 0;

        /*
        ** Count the number of 1-bits in the value.
        */
        while( n_bits > 0 ){
                parity += value & 1;
                value >>= 1;
                n_bits -= 1;
        }

        /*
        ** Return TRUE if the low order bit of the count is zero
        ** (which means that there were an even number of 1's).
        */
        return ( parity % 2 ) == 0;
}
```

Program 7.2   Parity check   parity.c

The behavior with array arguments seems to contradict the call by value rule. However there isn't a contradiction—the value of the array name is really a pointer, and a copy of the pointer is passed to the function. A subscript is really a form of indirection and applying indirection to the pointer accesses the locations that it points to. The argument (the pointer) is indeed a copy, but the indirection uses the copy to access the original array values. We return to this point in the next chapter, but for now remember these two rules:

1. Scalar arguments to a function are passed by value.

2. Array arguments to a function *behave* as though they are passed by reference.

Program 7.2 illustrates the call-by-value behavior of scalar function arguments. This function checks whether the first argument has *even parity*, that is, if the number of 1's it contains is an even number. The second argument specifies the number of significant bits in the value. The function works by shifting the value by one bit, over and over, so that every bit appears sooner or later in the right-most position. The bits are added together, one by one, so that after the loop ends we have a count of the number of 1's in the original value. Finally, the count is tested to see if its least significant bit is set. If not, the number of 1's was even.

The interesting feature of this function is that it destroys both of its arguments as the work progresses. This technique works fine, because with call-by-value the arguments are copies of the caller's values. Destroying the copies does not affect the original values.

```c
/*
** Exchange two integers in the calling program (doesn't work!).
*/

void
swap( int x, int y )
{
        int temp;

        temp = x;
        x = y;
        y = temp;
}
```

Program 7.3a   Swap integers: bad version   swap1.c

Program 7.3a is different: it wants to modify the caller's arguments. The intent of this function is to exchange the contents of two arguments in the calling program. It doesn't work, though, because all that is exchanged are the copies of the values that were sent to the function. The original values are untouched.

To access the caller's values you must pass pointers to the locations you wish to modify. The function must then use indirection to follow the pointers and modify the desired locations. Program 7.3b uses this technique. Because the function expects pointers as arguments, we would call it like this:

```
swap( &a, &b );
```

Program 7.4 sets all of the elements of an array to zero. n_elements is a scalar so it is passed by value; modifying its value in the function does not affect the corresponding argument in the calling program. On the other hand, the function does indeed set the elements of the calling program's array to zero. The value of the array argument is a pointer, and the subscript performs indirection with this pointer.

This example also illustrates another feature. It is legal to declare array parameters without specifying a size because memory is not allocated for the array elements in the function; the indirection causes the array elements in the calling program to be accessed instead. Thus, a single function can access

```
/*
** Exchange two integers in the calling program.
*/

void
swap( int *x, int *y )
{
        int temp;

        temp = *x;
        *x = *y;
        *y = temp;
}
```

Program 7.3b   Swap integers: good version   swap2.c

arrays of any size, which should excite Pascal programmers. However, there isn't any way for the function to figure out the actual size of an array argument, so this information must also be passed explicitly if it is needed.

Recall that in K&R C, function parameters were declared like this:

```
int
func( a, b, c )
int a;
char b;
float c;
{
...
```

Another reason to avoid this style is that K&R compilers handled arguments a little differently: char and short arguments were promoted to int before being passed, and float arguments were promoted to double. These conversions are called the *default argument promotions*, and because of them you will frequently see function parameters in pre-ANSI programs declared as int when in fact char values are passed.

To maintain compatibility, ANSI compilers also perform these conversions for functions declared in the old style. They are not done on functions that have been prototyped, though, so mixing the two styles can lead to errors.

```
/*
** Set all of the elements of an array to zero.
*/

void
clear_array( int array[], int n_elements )
{
        /*
        ** Clear the elements of the array starting with the last
        ** and working towards the first.  Note the predecrement
        ** avoids going off the end of the array.
        */
        while( n_elements > 0 )
                array[ --n_elements ] = 0;
}
```

Program 7.4 Set an array to zero   clrarray.c

7.4 ADTs and Black Boxes

C facilitates the design and implementation of *abstract data types*, or *ADTs*, because of its ability to limit the scope of function and data definitions. This technique is also referred to as *black box* design. The basic idea behind an abstract data type is simple—a module has a functional specification, which states the work that the module will perform, and an interface specification, which defines how the module is used. However, users of the module do not need to know any details of its implementation and are prevented from accessing the module in any way other than with the defined interface.

Limiting access to the module is accomplished through the judicious use of the `static` keyword to restrict the accessibility of functions and data that

```
/*
** Declarations for the address list module.
*/


/*
** Data characteristics
**
**      Maximum lengths of the various data (includes space for the
**      terminating NUL byte), and maximum number of addresses.
*/
#define NAME_LENGTH     30          /* longest name allowed */
#define ADDR_LENGTH     100         /* longest address allowed */
#define PHONE_LENGTH    11          /* longest phone # allowed */

#define MAX_ADDRESSES   1000        /* # of addresses allowed */

/*
** Interface functions
**
**      Given a name, find the corresponding address.
*/
char const *
lookup_address( char const *name );

/*
**      Given a name, find the corresponding phone number.
*/
char const *
lookup_phone( char const *name );
```

Program 7.5a Address list module: header file   addrlist.h

are not part of the interface. For example, consider a module that maintains an address/phone number list. The module must provide functions to look up an address and to look up a phone number for a specific name. However, the manner in which the list is stored is implementation dependent, so this information is kept private within the module and is not available to the client.

The next example illustrates one possible implementation of this module. Program 7.5a shows the include file that defines the interface used by the client, and Program 7.5b shows the implementation.[30]

```
/*
** Abstract data type to maintain an address list.
*/

#include "addrlist.h"
#include <stdio.h>

/*
**      The three parts to each address are kept in corresponding
**      elements of these three arrays.
*/
static  char    name[MAX_ADDRESSES][NAME_LENGTH];
static  char    address[MAX_ADDRESSES][ADDR_LENGTH];
static  char    phone[MAX_ADDRESSES][PHONE_LENGTH];

/*
**      This routine locates a name in the array and returns the
**      subscript of the location found.  If the name does not exist,
**      -1 is returned.
*/
static int
find_entry( char const *name_to_find )
{
        int     entry;

        for( entry = 0; entry < MAX_ADDRESSES; entry += 1 )
                if( strcmp( name_to_find, name[ entry ] ) == 0 )
                        return entry;
```

Program 7.5b   Address list module: implementation   *continued . . .*

---

[30] It would be better if each name, address, and phone number were stored in a structure, but structures aren't covered until Chapter 10.

```
                return -1;
}


/*
**      Given a name, look up and return the corresponding address.
**      If the name was not found, return a NULL pointer instead.
*/
char const *
lookup_address( char const *name )
{
        int     entry;

        entry = find_entry( name );
        if( entry == -1 )
                return NULL;
        else
                return address[ entry ];

}


/*
**      Given a name, look up and return the corresponding phone
**      number. If the name was not found, return a NULL pointer
**      instead.
*/
char const *
lookup_phone( char const *name )
{
        int     entry;

        entry = find_entry( name );
        if( entry == -1 )
                return NULL;
        else
                return phone[ entry ];

}
```

Program 7.5b Address list module: implementation   addrlist.c

Program 7.5 is a good example of a black box. The functionality in the box is accessed through the specified interface, which in this case are the functions lookup_address and lookup_phone. However, the user cannot directly access data that relate to the implementation, such as the array or the support function lookup_entry, because these items are declared static.

The power of this type of implementation is that it makes the various parts of the program more independent of one another. For example, as the address list grows larger, the simple sequential search may become too slow, or the table might become full. At that time you can rewrite the finding function to be more efficient, perhaps by using some form of hashed lookup, or you could even scrap the array altogether and dynamically allocate the space for the entries. But if the client program had been able to access the table directly, changing the organization of the table would cause the program to fail in each of these places.

The black box concept removes the temptation to use the implementation details by making those details unavailable. Thus, the only possible way to access the module is through its defined interface.

7.5 Recursion

C supports *recursive* functions through its runtime stack.[31] A recursive function is one that calls itself, either directly or indirectly. Computing factorials and Fibonacci numbers are two applications often used in textbooks to illustrate recursion, which is very unfortunate. Recursion does not offer any advantage for the first, and it is horribly inefficient for the second.

Here is a simple program to illustrate recursion. The objective is to convert an integer from binary to printable characters. For example, from the value 4267 we want to produce the characters '4', '2', '6', and '7', in that order. printf performs this type of processing for the %d format code.

The strategy we use is to repeatedly divide the value by 10 and print the remainders. For example, 4267 mod 10 gives the value 7. We cannot just print this remainder, though; we need to print the value that represents the digit '7' in the machine's character set. In ASCII, the character '7' has the value 55, so we might add 48 to the remainder to get the proper character. However, using character constants rather than integer constants enhances portablility. Consider the relationships below:

```
'0' + 0 = '0'
'0' + 1 = '1'
'0' + 2 = '2'
etc.
```

From these relationships it is easy to see that adding '0' to the remainder

---

[31] Interestingly, the Standard does not require a stack. A stack provides the mandated behavior, though, and is used in many implementations.

produces the code for the corresponding character.[32] Then the remainder is printed. The next step is to get the quotient: 4267 / 10 is 426. The process now begins again with this value.

The only problem with this process is that it generates the digits in the wrong order: they are printed backwards. Program 7.6 uses recursion to correct this problem.

This function is recursive because it contains a call to itself. At first glance, it appears that the function will never stop. When the function is called, it will call itself; this second execution will call itself again, and so forth, forever and ever. This is not the case, though.

The recursion in this program implements a kind of twisted while loop. Just as a while loop must make some progress towards its termination criteria during each execution of the body, so too must a recursive function get closer to a limiting case with each recursive call. The limiting case is the one in which the function does not call itself.

In Program 7.6, the limiting case occurs when the quotient is zero. We divide the value by 10 before each recursive call, so it gets closer and closer to zero each time and eventually the recursion stops.

```
/*
** Take an integer value (unsigned), convert it to characters, and
** print it.  Leading zeros are suppressed.
*/
#include <stdio.h>

void
binary_to_ascii( unsigned int value )
{
        unsigned int    quotient;

        quotient = value / 10;
        if( quotient != 0 )
                binary_to_ascii( quotient );
        putchar( value % 10 + '0' );

}
```

Program 7.6   Convert a binary integer to characters   btoa.c

---

[32] These relationships require that the digits be assigned sequential codes. This characteristic is true of all common character sets.

How does recursion help get the digits to print in the proper order? Here is how to read this function.

1. Divide the value by 10.

2. If the quotient is nonzero, call `binary_to_ascii` *to print those digits now.*

3. Then print the remainder of the division in step 1.

Note that the middle step, printing the digits of a number, is exactly the same problem we were trying to solve in the first place except that the number is smaller. We solve the problem by calling the function that we just wrote, the one that converts integers to digits and prints them. Because the number is smaller, the recursion eventually stops.

Once you understand recursion, the easiest way to read a recursive function is to *not* get hung up on tracing its execution. Just take it on faith that the recursive call will do what it claims to do. If you do the right work for each step, your limiting case is correct, and you get closer to it each time, then the function will work correctly.

7.5.1 Tracing a Recursive Function

But in order to understand how recursion works in the first place, you need to trace the execution of the recursive calls. So let's do that now. The key to following the execution of a recursive function is understanding how the variables declared in a function are stored. When a function is called, space for its variables is created on the runtime stack. The variables belonging to the previous functions remain on the stack, but they are covered up by the new ones and are inaccessible.

When a recursive function calls itself, the same thing happens. A new set of variables is created for the new call, which cover up the variables that belong to the previous call(s) to this function. When tracing the execution of a recursive function, we must keep these different sets of variables separate from one another to avoid confusion.

The function in Program 7.6 has two variables: the argument `value` and the local variable `quotient`. The following diagrams show the state of the stack, with the set of variables currently being accessed on the top of the stack. All other sets of variables are shaded in gray, because they are inaccessible to the function currently executing.

Suppose we call the function with the value 4267. Here is what the stack looks like as the function begins to execute.

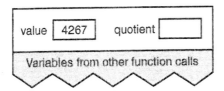

After the division occurs, the stack looks like this.

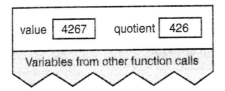

Next, the `if` statement determines that the quotient is not zero and makes a recursive call to the function. Here is what the stack looks like as the second call of the function begins.

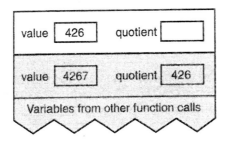

A new set of variables has been created on the stack, hiding the previous set, which will remain inaccessible until this recursive call to the function returns. After the division, the stack looks like this.

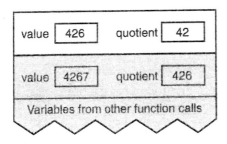

The quotient has the value 42, which is nonzero, so we get another recursive call with another set of variables. After the division, the stack looks like this:

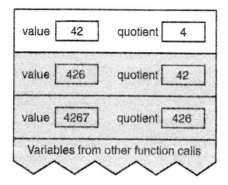

The quotient is still nonzero, so another recursive call is made. After the division, the stack looks like this:

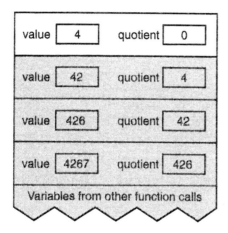

Disregarding the recursive call itself, the only statements that have been executed so far are the division and the test of the quotient. Because the recursive call has caused these statements to be repeated, the effect is similar to that of a loop: while the quotient is nonzero, use it as the initial value and start over again. But the recursion saves information that a loop would not, the stacked values of the variables. This information is about to become important.

The quotient is zero, so the function does not call itself again. Instead, it begins to print output. The function then returns, which begins to remove values from the stack.

Each call to putchar gets the last digit of the value by taking the value modulo ten. The result is an integer in the range zero to nine; the character constant for a zero is added in order to get the ASCII character that corresponds to the digit, which is printed.

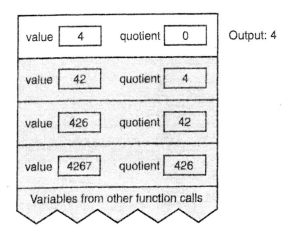

The function then returns, and its variables are discarded from the stack. The previous invocation of the function then continues to execute from the point of the recursive call using its own variables, which are now on the top of the stack. Because its value is 42, the call to putchar prints the digit two.

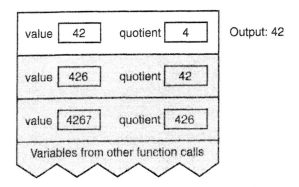

This invocation of the function then returns, which uncovers the variables for the previous invocation. Execution continues there from the point of the recursive call, and a six is printed. Just before the function returns again, the stack looks like this:

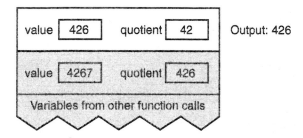

We have now unwound the recursion and are back to the original call to the function. It prints the digit seven, which is the remainder of its `value` divided by ten.

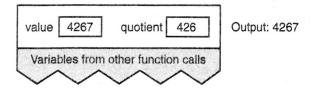

The function then returns to whatever other function called it.

If you put all of the characters that were printed side by side as they would appear on a printer or screen, you will see the correct value: `4267`.

7.5.2 Recursion versus Iteration

Recursion is a powerful technique, but like any technique it can be misused. Here is an example. The definition of a factorial is often stated recursively, like this:

$$\text{factorial}(n) = \begin{cases} n \le 0: & 1 \\ n > 0: & n \times \text{factorial}(n-1) \end{cases}$$

This definition has both of the properties we discussed earlier for recursion: there is a limiting case from which no recursion is performed, and each recursive call gets a little closer to the limiting case.

Definitions like this one often lead people to use recursion to implement a factorial function, such as the one shown in Program 7.7a. This function produces the correct answers, but it is not a good use of recursion. Why? The recursive function calls involve some runtime overhead—arguments must be pushed on the stack, space allocated for local variables (in general, though not

```
/*
** Compute the factorial of n, recursively
*/

long
factorial( int n )
{
        if( n <= 0 )
                return 1;
        else
                return n * factorial( n - 1 );
}
```

Program 7.7a   Recursive factorials   fact_rec.c

for this specific example), registers must be saved, and so forth. When each call to the function returns, all this work must be undone. For all of this overhead, however, recursion does little to simplify the solution to this problem.

Program 7.7b computes the same result with a loop. Although this program with its simple loop does not resemble the mathematical definition of factorial nearly as closely, it computes the same result more efficiently. If you look more closely at the recursive function, you will see that the recursive call

```
/*
** Compute the factorial of n, iteratively
*/

long
factorial( int n )
{
        int     result = 1;

        while( n > 1 ){
                result *= n;
                n -= 1;
        }

        return result;
}
```

Program 7.7b   Iterative factorials   fact_itr.c

is the last thing the function does. This function is an example of *tail recursion*. Because no work is done in the function after the recursive call returns, tail recursion can easily be converted to a simple loop that accomplishes the same task.

Many problems are explained recursively only because it is clearer than a non-recursive explanation. However, an iterative implementation of these problems is often more efficient than a recursive implementation, even though the resulting code is less clear. When a problem is complex enough that an iterative implementation is difficult for someone else to follow, then the clarity of the recursive implementation may justify the runtime overhead that it will incur.

In Program 7.7a, recursion added little to the solution of the problem. Program 7.7b with its loop was just as simple. Here is a more extreme example. Fibonacci numbers are a sequence of numbers in which each value is the sum of the previous two values. This relationship is often described recursively:

$$\text{Fibonacci}(n) = \begin{cases} n \leq 1: & 1 \\ n = 2: & 1 \\ n > 2: & \text{Fibonacci}(n-1) + \text{Fibonacci}(n-2) \end{cases}$$

Again, the recursive definition suggests that the solution should be implemented using recursion, as illustrated in Program 7.8a. Here is the trap: the recursive step computes Fibonacci$(n-1)$ and Fibonacci$(n-2)$. But, the

```
/*
** Compute the value of the n'th Fibonacci number, recursively.
*/

long
fibonacci( int n )
{
        if( n <= 2 )
                return 1;

        return fibonacci( n - 1 ) + fibonacci( n - 2 );
}
```

Program 7.8a   Recursive Fibonacci numbers   fib_rec.c computation of Fibonacci(n − 1) *also computes* Fibonacci(n − 2). How much could one extra computation cost?

The answer is that there is far more than just one redundant computation: each recursive call begins *two more* recursive calls, and each of those calls begins two more, and so forth. Therefore, the number of redundant computations grows very rapidly. For instance, in computing Fibonacci(10), the value of Fibonacci(3) is computed 21 times. But to compute Fibonacci(30) recursively, Fibonacci(3) is computed 317,811 times. Of course, every one of these 317,811 calculations produced exactly the same result, so all but one were wasted. This overhead is horrible!

Consider Program 7.8b, which uses a simple loop instead of recursion. Once again, the loop does not resemble the abstract definition as closely as the recursive version, but it is hundreds of thousands of times more efficient!

Before implementing a function recursively, ask yourself whether the benefit to be gained by using recursion outweights the costs. And be careful: the costs might be more than what they first appear to be.

```
/*
** Compute the value of the n'th Fibonacci number, iteratively.
*/

long
fibonacci( int n )
{
        long    result;
        long    previous_result;
        long    next_older_result;

        result = previous_result = 1;

        while( n > 2 ){
                n -= 1;
                next_older_result = previous_result;
                previous_result = result;
                result = previous_result + next_older_result;
        }
        return result;
}
```

Program 7.8b   Iterative Fibonacci numbers   fib_iter.c

7.6 Variable Argument Lists

A function prototype lists the arguments that the function expects, but a prototype can only show a fixed number of arguments. Is it possible for a function to accept a different number of arguments at different times? Yes, but there are some restrictions. Consider a function that computes the average of a series of values. This task is trivial if the values are stored in an array, so to make the problem more interesting let's assume that they are not. Program 7.9a attempts to do the job.

This function has several problems. First, there isn't a test for too many arguments, but one could easily be added. Second, the function cannot handle more than five values. This problem can only be rectified by adding even more copies of the already redundant code.

But there is a more serious problem which occurs when you try to call the function like this:

```
avg1 = average( 3, x, y, z );
```

There are only four arguments, but the function has six formal parameters. The Standard covers this situation: the behavior is undefined. Thus, the first argument might correspond to the n_values parameter or maybe to the v2

```
/*
** Compute the average of the specified number of values (bad).
*/

float
average( int n_values, int v1, int v2, int v3, int v4, int v5 )
{
        float   sum = v1;

        if( n_values >= 2 )
                sum += v2;
        if( n_values >= 3 )
                sum += v3;
        if( n_values >= 4 )
                sum += v4;
        if( n_values >= 5 )
                sum += v5;
        return sum / n_values;
}
```

Program 7.9a   Compute the average of scalar values: bad version   average1.c

parameter. You can certainly test your implementation to see what it does, but the program is certainly not portable. What is needed is a mechanism to access an unbounded argument list in a well-defined way.

7.6.1 The stdarg Macros

Variable argument lists are implemented using macros defined in the stdarg.h header, which is part of the standard library. The header declares a type va_list and three macros—va_start, va_arg, and va_end.[33] A variable of type va_list is declared and used with the macros to access the argument values.

Program 7.9b uses these macros to correctly accomplish what program 7.9a tried to do. Notice the ellipsis in the argument list: it indicates that an unspecified number of arguments with unspecified types may be passed. The same notation is used when prototyping the function.

The function declares a variable called var_arg with which to access the unspecified portion of the argument list. This variable is initialized by calling va_start. The first parameter is the name of the va_list variable, and the second parameter is the last named argument before the ellipsis. This initialization sets the var_arg variable to point to the first of the variable arguments.

To access an argument, va_arg is used. This macro takes two parameters: the va_list variable and the type of the next value in the list. In this example, the variable arguments are all integers. In some functions, you may have to determine the type of the next argument by examining previously obtained data.[34] va_arg returns the value of this argument and advances var_arg to point to the next variable argument.

Finally, va_end is called after the last access to the variable arguments.

7.6.2 Limitations of Variable Arguments

Note that the variable arguments must be accessed one by one, in order, from start to finish. You can stop early if you wish, but there isn't any way to begin accessing in the middle of the list. In addition, because the variable portion of the argument list is not prototyped, the default argument promotions are performed on all values passed as variable arguments.

---

[33] Macros are implemented by the preprocessor and are discussed in Chapter 14.

[34] For example, printf examines the characters in the format string to determine the types of the arguments it is supposed to print.

```
/*
** Compute the average of the specified number of values.
*/

#include <stdarg.h>

float
average( int n_values, ... )
{
        va_list var_arg;
        int     count;
        float   sum = 0;

        /*
        ** Prepare to access the variable arguments.
        */
        va_start( var_arg, n_values );

        /*
        ** Add the values from the variable argument list.
        */
        for( count = 0; count < n_values; count += 1 ){
                sum += va_arg( var_arg, int );
        }

        /*
        ** Done processing variable arguments.
        */
        va_end( var_arg );

        return sum / n_values;
}
```

Program 7.9b   Compute the average of scalar values: good version   average2.c

You may also have noticed the requirement that there must be at least one named argument in the argument list; you cannot use va_start without it. This argument provides a way to locate the varying portion of the argument list.

There are two fundamental limitations of these macros, both of which are a direct result of the fact that the type of a value cannot be determined simply by examining it.

1.   The macros cannot determine how many arguments actually exist.

2.   The macros cannot determine the type of each argument.

The named argument(s) must answer both of these questions. In Program 7.9b, the named argument specifies how many values were passed, but their types are assumed to be integers. The named argument in `printf` is the format string, which indicates both the number and types of the arguments.

If you specify the wrong type with `va_arg` the results are unpredictable. This error is easy to make because `va_arg` doesn't compensate for the default argument promotions that are performed on variable arguments. `char`, `short`, and `float` values will actually be passed as `int`'s and `double`'s. Be careful to use these latter types with `va_arg`.

7.7 Summary

A function definition specifies both the parameter list and the body of the function, the statements that are executed when the function is called. There are two acceptable forms for writing the parameter list. The K&R style declares the types of the parameters in a separate list that occurs prior to the opening brace of the function's body. The new style, which is preferred, includes the types in the parameter list. A function with no statements in its body, called a stub, is useful in testing incomplete programs.

A function declaration gives limited information about a function, and is used where the function is called. There are two acceptable forms for function declarations. The K&R style, with no parameter list, only declares the type of value returned by the function. The new style, which is preferred, is called a function prototype. It includes declarations of the types of the parameters as well, which allows the compiler to check the types and number of arguments in calls to the function. You can also put parameter names in a function prototype as well. While optional, this practice makes the prototype more useful for other readers because it conveys more information. Prototypes for functions without parameters have just the keyword `void` as a parameter list. The preferred way to use function prototypes is to put the prototype in a separate file which is then `#include`'d wherever the prototype is needed. This technique minimizes the number of separate copies of the prototype that are needed, which simplifies maintenance.

The `return` statement is used to specify the value to be returned from a function. If no value is given in the `return` statement, or if a function does not contain any `return` statements, no value will be returned. Such functions are called procedures in many other languages. In ANSI C, functions that do not return a value should be declared as returning the type `void`.

If a function it is called before any declarations for it have been seen, the compiler assumes that the function returns an integer value. It is important to declare functions that return nonintegral types in order to avoid errors caused by unexpected type conversions. Arguments to functions that are not prototyped undergo the default argument promotions: `char` and `short` arguments are converted to `int`, and `float` arguments are converted to `double`.

Arguments to functions are passed call by value, which makes a copy of each argument. A function can therefore modify its parameters (the copies) without affecting the caller's arguments. Array names are also passed using call by value, but all that is copied is a pointer to the caller's array. When a subscript is used on the array parameter in the function, indirection causes an element in the caller's array to be accessed. Thus, modifying an array element in the function actually modifies the caller's array. This behavior is named call by reference. You can get call by reference semantics with scalar arguments by passing pointers to the arguments and using indirection in the function to access or modify the values.

An abstract data type, or black box, consists of an interface and an implementation. The interface, which is public, specifies how a client uses the functionality provided by the ADT. The implementation, which is private, is where the work is actually done. Keeping the implementation private prevents clients from making their programs dependent on details of the implementation. The implementation can then be changed when necessary without affecting the clients' code.

A recursive function is one that calls itself, either directly or indirectly. For recursion to work, each invocation of the function must make some progress toward a goal. When the goal is reached, no more recursive calls are made. To read a recursive function, do not get hung up on tracing each recursive call. It is easier to understand what is happening if you simply assume that the recursive call performs the work that it claims to do.

Some functions that are described recursively, such as factorial and Fibonacci numbers, can be implemented more efficiently iteratively. When a recursive call is the last thing that is done in a function, it is called tail recursion. Tail recursion can easily be converted to a loop, which is usually more efficient.

Functions with argument lists containing variable numbers and types of arguments can be implemented using the macros defined in the `stdarg.h` header. The varying portion of the parameter list, which follows one or more ordinary (named) parameters, is indicated with an elipsis in the function prototype. The named parameter(s) must somehow indicate the number of arguments passed in the varying part and, if not known in advance, their types. The arguments in the varying portion of the list undergo the default argument promotions when they are passed, and they can only be accessed in order from first to last.

7.8 Summary of Cautions

1. Writing function prototypes within the scope of other functions (page 169).

2. Not prototyping functions that return nonintegral values (page 171).

3. Mixing function prototypes with old-style function definitions (page 175).

4. Using the wrong argument type in `va_arg` gives undefined results (page 192).

7.9 Summary of Programming Tips

1. Putting argument names in function prototypes makes it easier for the client to use the function (page 169).

2. Abstract data types increase reliability by decreasing the program's reliance on implementation details (page 179).

3. Use recursion as a notational tool when the benefit justifies the cost (page 187).

7.10 Questions

1. A function with an empty body is useful as a stub. How might such a function be modified to be more useful?

2. Prototypes for functions are not mandatory in ANSI C. Is this fact an advantage or a disadvantage?

3. What happens if a function that is declared to return a specific type includes a `return` statement with an expression of a different type?

4. What happens if a function that is declared `void` contains a `return` statement with an expression?

5. If a function is called before the compiler has seen a prototype for it, what happens if the function returns some type other than integer?

6. If a function is called before the compiler has seen a prototype for it, what

happens if the types of the arguments do not match those of the formal parameters?

7. What (if anything) is wrong with the following function?

```
int
find_max( int array[10] )
{
        int     i;
        int     max = array[0];

        for( i = 1; i < 10; i += 1 )
                if( array[i] > max )
                        max = array[i];

        return max;
}
```

8. How is recursion similar to a `while` loop?

9. Explain the advantages of putting function prototypes in `#include` files.

10. Enter the recursive Fibonacci function on your system, and add a statement at the beginning of the function that increments a global integer variable. Now write a main function to set the global variable to zero and compute `fibonacci( 1 )`. Repeat for `fibonacci( 2 )` through `fibonacci( 10 )`. How many times was the `fibonacci` function called for each of these computations? Is this progression of values related in any way to the Fibonacci numbers themselves? Based on this information, can you calculate the number of calls that would be needed to compute `fibonacci( 11 )`? `fibonacci( 25 )`? `fibonacci( 50 )`?

7.11 Programming Exercises

★★ 1. The *Hermite Polynomials* are defined as follows:

$$H_n(x) = \begin{cases} n \leq 0: & 1 \\ n = 1: & 2x \\ n \geq 2: & 2xH_n - 1(x) - 2(n-1)H_n - 2(x) \end{cases}$$

For example, the value of $H_3(2)$ is 40. Write a recursive function to compute the value of $H_n(x)$. Your function should match this prototype:

```
int hermite( int n, int x );
```

★★ 2. The *greatest common divisor* of two integers M and N (where $M, N > 0$) can be computed as follows:

$$gcd(M, N) = \begin{cases} M \% N = 0: & N \\ M \% N = R, \; R > 0: & gcd(N, R) \end{cases}$$

Write a function called gcd that takes two integer arguments and returns the greatest common divisor of those numbers. If either of the arguments is not greater than zero, your function should return zero.

🖎 ★★ 3. Write the function for the following prototype:

```
int ascii_to_integer( char *string );
```

The string argument must contain one or more digits, and the function should convert those digits to an integer and return the result. If any nondigit characters are found, return the value zero instead. Do not worry about arithmetic overflow. *Hint:* The technique is simple—for each digit you find, multiply the value you have so far and then add the value represented by the new digit.

★★★ 4. Write a function called max_list that examines an arbitrary number of integer arguments and returns the largest of them. The arguments will be terminated by a value that is less than zero.

★★★★ 5. Implement a bare-bones printf function that is capable of handling the %d, %f, %s, and %c format codes. The behavior for other format codes, in the true spirit of the ANSI Standard, is undefined. You may assume the existence of the functions print_integer and print_float to print values of those types. Use putchar to print everything else.

★★★★ 6. Write a function

```
void written_amount( unsigned int amount, char *buffer );
```

that converts the value in amount to words and stores them in the buffer. This function might be used in a program that prints checks. For example, if value is 16,312, then the string

```
SIXTEEN THOUSAND THREE HUNDRED TWELVE
```

should be stored in the buffer. It is the caller's responsibility to make the buffer large enough.

Some values can be printed in two different ways. For example, 1,200 could be either ONE THOUSAND TWO HUNDRED or TWELVE HUNDRED You may convert these values whichever way you wish.

8

Arrays

You've been using simple, one-dimensional arrays since Chapter 2. This chapter explains more about these arrays and explores more advanced array topics such as multidimensional arrays, arrays and pointers, and array initialization.

8.1 One-Dimensional Arrays

Before we introduce multidimensional arrays, there is a lot more to learn about one-dimensional arrays. Let's begin with a concept that many consider a flaw in the design of the C language, but this concept actually ties some disparate concepts together quite nicely.

8.1.1 Array Names

Consider these declarations:

```
int     a;
int     b[10];
```

We call the variable a a *scalar* because it is a single value. The type of the value is integer. We call the variable b an array because it is a collection of values. A subscript is used with the array name to identify one specific value from that collection; for example, b[0] identifies the first value in the b array, and b[4] identifies the fifth. Each specific value is a scalar and may be used in any context in which a scalar may be used.

The type of b[4] is integer, but what is the type of b? To what does it refer? A logical answer would be that it refers to the whole array, but it doesn't. In C, when the name of an array is used in almost any expression, the value of the name is a *pointer constant* that is the address of the first element of the array. Its type depends on the type of the array elements: if they are int, then the value of the array name is a "constant pointer to int." If they are something else, then the value of the array name is a "constant pointer to *something else*."

Do not conclude from this that arrays and pointers are the same. An array has quite different characteristics than a pointer, for example, an array has a certain number of elements, while a pointer is a scalar. The compiler uses the array name to keep track of these properties. It is only when the array name is used in an expression that the compiler generates the pointer constant.

Note that this value is a pointer constant as opposed to a pointer variable; you cannot change the value of a constant. On reflection this restriction makes sense: the value points to where the array begins in memory, so the only way to change it is to *move* the array somewhere else in memory. But memory for arrays is fixed when the program is linked, so by the time the program is running, it is much too late to move an array. Hence, the values of array names are pointer constants.

There are only two places where this pointer substitution does not occur—when an array name is an operand of either sizeof or the unary operator &. sizeof returns the size of the entire array, not the size of a pointer to the array. Taking the address of an array name gives a pointer to the first element in the array, not a pointer to some substituted pointer constant value.

Now consider this example:

```
int     a[10];
int     b[10];
int     *c;
...
c = &a[0];
```

The expression &a[0] is a pointer to the first element of the array. But that's the value of the array name itself, so the following assignment performs exactly the same job as the one above:

```
c = a;
```

This assignment shows why it is important to understand the true meaning of an array name in an expression. If the name referred to the entire array, this statement would imply that the entire array is being copied to a new array. But this is not at all what happens: what is assigned is a copy of a pointer, making c point to the first element of the array. Thus, assignments such as

```
b = a;
```

are illegal. You cannot use the assignment operator to copy all the elements of one array to another array; you must use a loop and copy one element at a time.

Consider this statement:

```
a = c;
```

With c declared as a pointer variable, this assignment looks like it ought to perform another pointer assignment, copying the value of c into a. But this assignment is illegal: remember that the value of a in this expression is a constant, so it cannot be changed.

8.1.2 Subscripts

In the context of the previous declarations, what is the meaning of this expression?

```
*( b + 3 )
```

First, the value of b is a pointer to an integer, so the value three is scaled to the size of an integer. The addition yields a pointer to the integer that is located three integers beyond the first one in the array. The indirection then takes us to this new location, either to get the value there (R-value) or to store a new one (L-value).

If this process sounds familiar, it is because a subscript does exactly the same thing. We can now explain a statement that was mentioned in Chapter 5: except for its precedence, a subscript is exactly the same as an indirection. For example, the following expressions are equivalent:

```
array[subscript]
*( array + ( subscript ) )
```

Now that you know that the value of an array name is just a pointer constant, you can verify this equivalence. In the subscript expression, the subscript is evaluated first. Then the subscript value selects a specific array element. In the second expression, the inner parentheses guarantee that the subscript is evaluated first, as before. Using pointer arithmetic, the addition produces a pointer to the desired element. The indirection then follows that pointer, and voilá—an array element.

Wherever a subscript is used, the equivalent pointer expression can also be used; and wherever a pointer expression of the form shown above is used, you can also use a subscript.

Here is a little exercise to illustrate this equivalence.

```
int     array[10];
int     *ap = array + 2;
```

Remember the scaling that is performed on the addition; the result is that ap
points at `array[2]`, like this:

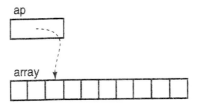

For each of the following expressions involving ap, see if you can think of an
equivalent expression that uses `array`.

ap	This one is easy, you can just read the answer from the initialization: `array + 2`. The expression `&array[2]` is equivalent.
*ap	Another easy one: the indirection follows the pointer to the location it is pointing at, which is `array[2]`. You could also write `*( array + 2 )`.
ap[0]	"You can't do that, ap isn't an array!" If you thought something like this, you're stuck in the "can't do it in *other* languages" rut. Remember, a subscript in C is exactly like an indirection expression, so you can use one anywhere you can use indirection. In this case, the equivalent expression is `*( ap + ( 0 ) )` which, after getting rid of the zero and the parentheses, ends up being identical to the previous expression. Therefore it has the same answer: `array[2]`.
ap + 6	If ap points to `array[2]`, this addition gives a pointer to the location six integers later in the array, which is equivalent to `array + 8` or `&array[8]`.
*ap + 6	Be careful, there are two operators here: which goes first? The indirection. The result of the indirection is then added to six, so this expression is the same as `array[2] + 6`.
*(ap + 6)	The parentheses force the addition to go first, so this time we get the value of `array[8]`. Observe that the indirection used here is in exactly the same form as the indirection of a subscript.

`ap[6]`	Convert this subscript to its indirection form, and you'll see the same expression we just did, so it has the same answer.
`&ap`	This expression is perfectly legal, but there is no equivalent expression involving `array` because you cannot predict where the compiler will locate `ap` relative to `array`.
`ap[-1]`	How's that again, a negative subscript? A subscript is just an indirection expression; convert it to that form and then evaluate it. `ap` points at the third element (the one whose subscript is two), so using an offset of -1 gets us the *previous* element: `array[1]`.
`ap[9]`	This one looks fine but is actually a problem. The equivalent expression is `array[11]`, but the problem is that there are only ten elements in the array. Evaluating the subscript produces a pointer expression that runs off the end of the array, which makes this illegal according to the Standard. However, few compilers detect this error, so the program goes merrily on its way. But what does the expression do? The Standard says that its behavior is undefined, but on most machines it accesses whatever value happens to be stored in the second location beyond the end of the array. You can sometimes figure out what this value is by asking the compiler to produce an assembly language version of the program and examining that code, but there is no universal way to predict what value will be stored there. Thus, this expression will access (or, if used as an L-value, will *change*) the value of some random variable. This result is not likely to be what you wanted.

The last two examples show why subscript checking is a difficult task in C. The Standard does not require that it be done at all; the earliest C compilers didn't check subscripts, and most current ones still don't. The fact that subscripts can be applied to arbitrary pointers, not just array names, makes the job difficult. The validity of a subscript applied to a pointer variable depends on where it happens to be pointing at the time, as well as the value of the subscript.

Consequently, subscript checking in C involves more overhead than you might first think. Instructions must be inserted into the program to verify that the result of the subscript refers to an element in the same array as the pointer. This comparison requires information about the locations and sizes of all arrays in the program, which will take some space. The information must also be updated as the program runs to reflect automatic and dynamically allocated arrays, which will take some time. Thus, compilers that offer subscript check-ing usually also offer a way to turn it off.

Here's an interesting, though admittedly arcane, tangent. In the context of the previous declarations, what is the meaning of this expression?

```
2[array]
```

The answer may surprise you: it is legal. Convert it to the equivalent indirec-tion expression and you will see its validity:

```
*( 2 + ( array ) )
```

The inner parentheses are redundant, so we can delete them. Also, addition is commutative, so this expression has exactly the same meaning as

```
*( array + 2 )
```

meaning that the original, funny-looking expression is identical to `array[2]`.

This quirk exists because of the way that subscripts are implemented in C. Either form is fine as far as the compiler is concerned. However, you should *never* write `2[array]`: it only makes the program harder for others to read.

8.1.3 Pointers versus Subscripts

If you can use indirection expressions and subscripts interchangeably, which should you use? As usual, there is no simple answer. Subscripts are easier for most people to understand, especially with multidimensional arrays, so there is some benefit gained in readability by using them. On the other hand, this choice may affect runtime efficiency.

Assuming that they are both used correctly, subscripts are never more efficient than pointers, but pointers are sometimes more efficient than subscripts.

To understand this efficiency issue let's examine two loops that perform the same work. First, we clear the elements of an array using subscripts.

```
int     array[10], a;

for( a = 0; a < 10; a += 1 )
        array[a] = 0;
```

To evaluate this subscript, the compiler inserts instructions in the program to take the value of a and multiply it by the size of an integer (say, four). This multiplication takes both space and time.

Now consider this loop, which does exactly the same work.

```
int     array[10], *ap;

for( ap = array; ap < array + 10; ap++ )
        *ap = 0;
```

The multiplication is still in here somewhere, even though there is no longer any subscript. Look closely now and see if you can find it.

The multiplication is now performed in the adjustment step of the `for` statement; the value one must be scaled to the size of an integer before it is added to the pointer. But there is a big difference here: the same two values (1 × 4) are multiplied each time through the loop. As a result, this multiplication is performed once at compile time—the program now contains an instruction to add four to the pointer. No multiplications are performed at run time.

This example illustrates the type of situation in which pointers are more efficient than subscripts—when moving through an array by one (or any other fixed amount). The multiplication is performed on the fixed amount at compile time, so there are fewer instructions to execute at run time. On most machines the program is smaller and faster.

Now consider these two fragments of code:

```
a = get_value();          a = get_value();
array[a] = 0;             *( array + a ) = 0;
```

There is no difference in the code generated for these statements. a could be any value, so the multiplication instruction is needed in both places to scale it. This example illustrates the type of situation in which pointers and subscripts are equally efficient.

8.1.4 Pointer Efficiency

I stated earlier that pointers are sometimes more efficient than subscripts, *assuming that they are used correctly.* As they say on TV, your results may vary; it depends on your compiler and machine. However, the efficiency of your program depends primarily on the code you write, and it is just as easy to write bad code with pointers as it is with subscripts. In fact, it is probably easier.

To illustrate some bad techniques as well as good ones, let's look at a simple function that copies the contents of one array into a second array using subscripts. We will analyze the assembly code produced for this function by one particular compiler for a computer using a processor from the Motorola

M68000 family. We will then modify the function in various ways to use pointers and see what effect each modification has on the resulting object code.

Before beginning the example, two cautions are in order. First, the way you write your program affects not only its runtime efficiency but also its readability. It is important not to sacrifice readability for negligible gains in efficiency. More will be said about this issue later.

Second, the assembly language shown is obviously specific to the 68000 family of processors. Other machines (and other compilers) may translate the programs differently. If you need the utmost efficiency for your environment, you can experiment as I've done here to see how various source code idioms are implemented.

First, the following declarations apply to all versions of the function.

```
#define SIZE    50
int     x[SIZE];
int     y[SIZE];
int     i;
int     *p1, *p2;
```

Here is the subscript version of the function.

```
void
try1()
{
        for( i = 0; i < SIZE; i++ )
                x[i] = y[i];

}
```

This version is pretty straightforward. The compiler produced the following assembly language code.

```
00000004    42b90000 0000    _try1:     clrl      _i
0000000a    6028                         jra       L20
0000000c    20390000 0000    L20001:    movl      _i,d0
00000012    e580                         asll      #2,d0
00000014    207c0000 0000               movl      #_y,a0
0000001a    22390000 0000               movl      _i,d1
00000020    e581                         asll      #2,d1
00000022    227c0000 0000               movl      #_x,a1
00000028    23b00800 1800               movl      a0@(0,d0:L),a1@(0,d1:L)
0000002e    52b90000 0000               addql     #1,_i
00000034    7032             L20:       moveq     #50,d0
00000036    b0b90000 0000               cmpl      _i,d0
0000003c    6ece                         jgt       L20001
```

Let's walk through these instructions, one by one. First, the location containing the variable i is cleared, which implements the assignment to zero. Then execution jumps to the instruction labeled L20, which, with the following instruction, tests whether i is less than 50. If it is, execution jumps back up to the instruction labeled L20001.

The instruction labeled L20001 begins the body of the loop. i is copied to register d0 where it is shifted left by two bits. The shift is used because it produces the same result as a multiplication by four but is faster. The address of the array y is then copied to address register a0.

Now the same calculation that was previously performed on i is done again, but this time the result is put in register d1. Then the address of the array x is put into address register a1.

The movl instruction with the complicated operands is what really does the work: the value that a0 + d0 points at is copied to the location that a1 + d1 points at. Then i is incremented, and compared to 50 to see if the loop should repeat.

Does it seem silly that the compiler evaluates the expression i * 4 twice, when i has not changed between the expressions? Well, this compiler is fairly old, and its optimizer isn't very smart. Modern compilers may do a better job, but maybe not. It is better to write good source code in the first place than to depend on the compiler to produce efficient object code from bad source code. Remember, though, that efficiency is not the only factor; usually the clarity of the code is more important.

Switching to Pointers

Now let's rewrite the function with pointers.

```
void
try2()
{
        for( p1 = x, p2 = y; p1 - x < SIZE; )
               *p1++ = *p2++;
}
```

I've replaced the subscripts with pointer variables. One of the pointers is tested to determine when to exit the loop, so the counter is no longer needed.

```
00000046   23fc0000 00000000  _try2:    movl    #_x,_p1
           0000
00000050   23fc0000 00000000            movl    #_y,_p2
           0000
0000005a   601a                         jra     L25
```

```
0000005c   20790000 0000    L20003:   movl      _p2,a0
00000062   22790000 0000              movl      _p1,a1
00000068   2290                       movl      a0@,a1@
0000006a   58b90000 0000              addql     #4,_p2
00000070   58b90000 0000              addql     #4,_p1
00000076   7004             L25:      moveq     #4,d0
00000078   2f00                       movl      d0,sp@-
0000007a   20390000 0000              movl      _p1,d0
00000080   04800000 0000              subl      #_x,d0
00000086   2f00                       movl      d0,sp@-
00000088   4eb90000 0000              jbsr      ldiv
0000008e   508f                       addql     #8,sp
00000090   7232                       moveq     #50,d1
00000092   b280                       cmpl      d0,d1
00000094   6ec6                       jgt       L20003
```

These changes do not give much of an improvement over the first version.
The code needed to copy an integer and increment the pointers has decreased,
but the initialization code has increased. The shifts to scale the subscript are
gone, and the movl instruction that does the real work no longer uses indexing.
But the code to check for the end of the loop has increased a lot, because the
subtraction of two pointers must be scaled (in this case, divided by 4). The
division is performed by pushing the values on the stack and calling a subroutine named ldiv. If this machine had a 32-bit divide instruction, the division
might have been done more efficiently.

Bringing Back the Counter

Let's try another approach.

```
void
try3()
{
        for( i = 0, p1 = x, p2 = y; i < SIZE; i++ )
            *p1++ = *p2++;

}
```

I've used the counter again to control when the loop should exit to get rid of
the pointer subtraction and the resulting long sequence of code.

```
0000009e   42b90000 0000    _try3:    clrl      _i
000000a4   23fc0000 00000000          movl      #_x,_p1
           0000
000000ae   23fc0000 00000000          movl      #_y,_p2
```

```
                  0000
000000b8          6020                          jra     L30
000000ba          20790000 0000    L20005:      movl    _p2,a0
000000c0          22790000 0000                 movl    _p1,a1
000000c6          2290                          movl    a0@,a1@
000000c8          58b90000 0000                 addql   #4,_p2
000000ce          58b90000 0000                 addql   #4,_p1
000000d4          52b90000 0000                 addql   #1,_i
000000da          7032             L30:         moveq   #50,d0
000000dc          b0b90000 0000                 cmpl    _i,d0
000000e2          6ed6                          jgt     L20005
```

This version has the shorter code to copy the integer and increment the pointers, and to control when the loop breaks. But we're still copying the pointer variables into address registers before the indirection.

Register Pointer Variables

We can eliminate copying the pointer values by using register variables for the pointers. However, they must be declared as local variables.

```
void
try4()
{
        register int *p1, *p2;
        register int i;

        for( i = 0, p1 = x, p2 = y; i < SIZE; i++ )
                *p1++ = *p2++;
}
```

This change improves more than just eliminating the copying of the pointers.

```
000000f0          7e00             _try4:       moveq   #0,d7
000000f2          2a7c0000 0000                 movl    #_x,a5
000000f8          287c0000 0000                 movl    #_y,a4
000000fe          6004                          jra     L35
00000100          2adc             L20007:      movl    a4@+,a5@+
00000102          5287                          addql   #1,d7
00000104          7032             L35:         moveq   #50,d0
00000106          b087                          cmpl    d7,d0
00000108          6ef6                          jgt     L20007
```

Note that the pointer variables exist in registers a4 and a5 from the start. We can increment them directly with the hardware's autoincrement addressing mode (which behaves very much like the C postfix ++ operator). The initialization and loop termination code is, for the most part, unchanged. This code is looking better.

Eliminating the Counter

If we can find a way to terminate the loop without using the pointer subtraction that caused trouble earlier, we can eliminate the counter.

```
void
try5()
{
        register int *p1, *p2;

        for( p1 = x, p2 = y; p1 < &x[SIZE]; )
                *p1++ = *p2++;
}
```

Instead of the subtraction to see now many elements we've copied, this loop checks to see whether the pointer p1 has reached the end of the source array. Functionally this test is just as good, but it should be more efficient because it does not do a subtraction. Furthermore, the expression &x[SIZE] can be evaluated at compile time, because SIZE is a literal constant. Here is the result.

```
0000011c   2a7c0000 0000    _try5:    movl    #_x,a5
00000122   287c0000 0000              movl    #_y,a4
00000128   6002                       jra     L40
0000012a   2adc             L20009:   movl    a4@+,a5@+
0000012c   bbfc0000 00c8    L40:      cmpl    #_x+200,a5
00000132   65f6                       jcs     L20009
```

This code is compact and fast and rivals what an assembly language programmer would have produced. The counter and its associated instructions are gone. The comparison instruction contains the expression _x+200, which is the expression &x[SIZE]. This computation was done at compile time because SIZE is a constant. This code is about as tight as we can get on this machine.

Conclusions

What can we learn from these experiments?

1. Pointer variables can result in more efficient code than subscripts when you are moving through an array by some fixed increment. This point is

especially true when the increment is one and the machine has an autoin-crement addressing mode.

2. Pointers declared as register variables are often more efficient than pointers in static memory or on the stack (the amount of improvement depends on the particular machine you're working with).

3. If you can check for loop termination by testing something that is already being initialized and adjusted for the loop, then you don't need a separate counter.

4. Expressions that must be evaluated at run time are more expensive than constant expressions such as `&array[SIZE]` or `array + SIZE`.

The previous examples must now be put into perspective. Is it worth replacing the first loop, which is easily understood, with the last one, which one reader called "utter gibberish," just to save a few dozen microseconds of execution time? Occasionally yes, but in most cases the answer is *definitely not!* The cost of gaining runtime efficiency in this way is to make the program more difficult to write in the first place and more difficult to maintain later. If the program doesn't work or cannot be maintained, its execution speed is irrelevant.

It is easy to argue that experienced C programmers will have little trouble with the pointer loop, but there are two fallacies to this argument. First, "little trouble" actually means "some trouble." Using complex idioms naturally involves more risk than using simple ones. Second, the maintenance programmers who work on the code later may not be as experienced as you are. Program maintenance is the major cost of a software product, so programming techniques that make maintenance more difficult must be used with care.

Also, some machines are designed with specific instructions to perform array subscripting, with the intent of making this common operation very fast. A compiler for such a machine will implement subscript expressions with these specialized instructions but may not use them to implement pointer expressions, even though it should. On such a machine, then, a subscript may indeed be more efficient than a pointer.

Then what is the point of these experiments with efficiency? You may have to read some "gibberish" that someone else wrote, so it is important that you understand it. But there are also a few places where peak efficiency is vital, such as real-time programs that must respond quickly to events as they occur. But any program that is too slow can benefit from these techniques. The key is to identify the sections of code that are taking the most time and concentrate your energies on improving them, for that is how you achieve the biggest gains for your effort. Techniques for identifying these sections of code are discussed in Chapter 18.

8.1.5 Arrays and Pointers

Pointers and arrays are not equivalent. To illustrate this idea, consider these declarations:

```
int     a[5];
int     *b;
```

Can a and b be used interchangeably? Both have pointer values, and you can use indirection and subscripts on either one. They are, nevertheless, quite different.

Declaring an array sets aside space in memory for the indicated number of elements, and then creates the array name whose value is a constant that points to the beginning of this space. Declaring a pointer variable reserves space for the pointer itself, but that is all. Space is not allocated for any integers. Furthermore, the pointer variable is not initialized to point to any existing space. If it is an automatic variable it is not initialized at all. These two declarations look very different when diagrammed.

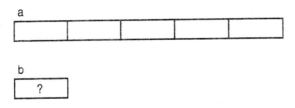

Thus, after the declarations the expression *a is perfectly legal, but the expression *b is not. *b will access some indeterminate location in memory or cause the program to terminate. On the other hand, the expression b++ will compile, but a++ will not because the value of a is a constant.

It is important that you understand this distinction clearly, because the next topic may muddy the waters.

8.1.6 Array Names as Function Arguments

What happens when an array name is passed as an argument to a function? You now know that the value of an array name is a pointer to the first element of the array, so it makes sense that a copy of this pointer value is passed to the function. A subscript used in the function will perform indirection on this pointer, and it is through this indirection that the function can access or modify the elements of the calling program's array.

Now I can explain the apparent contradiction about argument passing in C. I stated earlier that all arguments to functions are passed by value but that arrays behave as though they were passed by reference. Call by reference is implemented by passing a pointer to the desired argument and then using indirection in the function to access the data through the pointer. The array name is a pointer, and subscripts perform indirection.

So where is the call-by-value behavior with arrays? The function is passed a *copy* of the argument (a copy of the pointer to the beginning of the array) so the function is free to manipulate its pointer parameter without fear of modifying the corresponding argument's value.

So there is no contradiction after all: *all* arguments are passed by value. Of course, when you pass a pointer to a variable and the function uses indirection on the pointer, the function can modify the variable. Though it was not obvious at first glance, this process occurs with array name arguments. The argument, a pointer, is actually passed by value, and the function gets a copy of the pointer, which can be modified without fear of changing the caller's argument.

Program 8.1 is a simple function that illustrates these points. It copies the string contained in the second argument to the buffer to which the first argument points. The caller's buffer is modified because of the indirection, yet the arguments (the pointers) are modified without changing the caller's pointer arguments.

Note the expression `*string++` in the `while` statement. It fetches the character to which `string` points and, as a side effect, modifies `string` to point to the next character. Changing the parameter in this way does not affect the argument in the calling program, because only the function's copy is changed.

```
/*
** Copy the string contained in the second argument to the
** buffer specified by the first argument.
*/
void
strcpy( char *buffer, char const *string )
{
        /*
        ** Copy characters until a NUL byte is copied.
        */
        while( (*buffer++ = *string++) != '\0' )
                ;
}
```

Program 8.1   String copy   strcpy.c

There are two other points about this function that are worth mentioning (or reiterating). First, the parameter is declared as a pointer to const characters. Why is this declaration important for a function that is not going to modify the characters in the first place? There are at least three reasons. First, it is good documentation. Someone wishing to use this function can see from the prototype that the data will not be changed, without reading the code (which might not be available). Second, the compiler will be able to catch any programming error that causes accidental modification. Lastly, the declaration allows const arguments to be passed to the function.

The second point to be made about this function is the declaration of the argument and the local variable as register variables. On many machines register variables will result in code that executes faster than if they were in static memory or on the stack, as illustrated earlier with the array copy functions. Runtime efficiency is especially important with a function such as this one, which is likely to be called quite often because it performs such a useful task.

However, it depends on your environment whether using register variables will result in an improvement. Many current compilers can do a better job of register allocation than the programmer. With such a compiler, using register declarations can actually cause a decrease in efficiency. Check the documentation that comes with your compiler to see if it performs its own register allocation.

8.1.7 Declaring Array Parameters

Here is an interesting question. What is the correct way to declare a function parameter if you intend to pass it an array name argument? Is it declared as a pointer, or as an array?

As you have seen, a pointer is actually passed, so the function parameter is really a pointer. But to make things a little easier for the novice programmer, the compiler will also accept an array declaration for a function parameter. Thus, the following function prototypes are equivalent:

```
int     strlen( char *string );
int     strlen( char string[] );
```

This equivalence implies that a pointer and an array name are really identical after all but don't be fooled—these two declarations are equivalent *in this context only!* Everywhere else they are quite different, as discussed earlier. But for array parameters, you may use either declaration.

You can use either declaration, but which is "more correct?" The pointer. The argument is really a pointer, not the array. Also, the expression `sizeof string` will produce the size of a pointer to a character, not the size of the array.

It should now be clear why a parameter for a one-dimensional array in a function prototype does not need a dimension—space is not being allocated for the array in the function; the parameter is simply a pointer to space that was previously allocated elsewhere. This fact explains why an array parameter is compatible with arrays of any size—all that is passed is a pointer to the first element. On the other hand, this implementation makes it impossible for the function to determine the size of the array. If the array size is needed in the function, it must be passed as an explicit argument.

8.1.8 Initialization

Just as scalar variables can be initialized in their declarations, so too can arrays. The only difference is that a series of values is needed to initialize an array. A series is easily specified: the values are written as a comma-separated list enclosed in braces, as in this example:

```
int     vector[5] = { 10, 20, 30, 40, 50 };
```

The values given in the initializer list are assigned to the elements of the array one by one, so `vector[0]` gets the value 10, `vector[1]` gets the value 20, and so forth.

Static and Automatic Initialization

The way array initialization takes place is analogous to the way scalars are initialized—it depends upon their storage class. Arrays stored in static memory are initialized once, before the program begins to execute. No instructions are executed to put the values in the proper places, they just start out there. This magic is accomplished by having the linker initialize the array elements to their proper values in the file containing the executable program. If the array was not initialized, the initial values will be zero. When this file is loaded into memory for execution, the initialized array values are loaded in exactly the same way as the program instructions. Thus when execution begins, static arrays are already initialized.

The situation is not as rosy with automatic variables, however. Because they reside on the runtime stack, automatic variables may use different memory locations each time the block in which they are declared is entered. There isn't any way that the compiler can initialize these locations before the program begins, so automatic variables are uninitialized by default. If initial values are given, the variables are initialized with implicit assignment statements each time execution enters the scope in which they were declared. The implicit assignment statements take up space and take time to execute just as ordinary assignments would. The problem for arrays is that there may be many values in the initializer list, resulting in just as many assignments. For very large arrays, the initialization could take considerable time.

Here is the tradeoff, then. When initializing an array that is local to a function (or a block), think carefully about whether it should be reinitialized each time the function (or block) is entered. If the answer is no, then declare the array static so that the initialization can be performed once before the program begins.

8.1.9 Incomplete Initialization

What happens with these two declarations?

```
int     vector[5] = { 1, 2, 3, 4, 5, 6 };
int     vector[5] = { 1, 2, 3, 4 };
```

In both cases, the number of initializers does not match the size of the array. The first declaration is an error; there is no way to pack six integer values into five integer variables. The second, however, is legal. It provides values for the first four elements of the array; the last element is initialized to zero.

Can the middle values be omitted from the list as well?

```
int     vector[5] = { 1, 5 };
```

The compiler can only tell that there are not enough initializers, but it has no way to figure out which ones are missing. Therefore, only trailing initializers can be omitted.

8.1.10 Automatic Array Sizing

Here is an example of another useful technique.

```
int     vector[] = { 1, 2, 3, 4, 5 };
```

If the array size is missing, the compiler makes the array just big enough to hold the initializers that were given. This technique is particularly helpful if the initializer list is frequently modified.

8.1.11 Character Array Initialization

From what we have said so far, you might think that character arrays are initialized like this:

```
char    message[] = { 'H', 'e', 'l', 'l', 'o', 0 };
```

This code works, but it is cumbersome for all but the shortest strings. Therefore, the language Standard provides a shorthand notation for initializing character arrays:

```
char    message[] = "Hello";
```

Although this looks like a string literal, *it is not.* It is simply an alternate way of writing the initializer list in the previous example.

How can you tell the difference between string literals and these shorthand initializer lists if they look exactly the same? They are distinguished from one another by the context in which they're used. When initializing a character array, it is an initializer list. Everywhere else it is a string literal.

Here is an example:

```
char    message1[] = "Hello";
char    *message2 = "Hello";
```

The initializers look alike, but they have different meanings. The first initializes the elements of a character array, but the second is a true string literal. The pointer variable is initialized to point to wherever the literal is stored, as illustrated below:

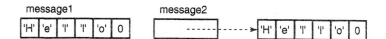

8.2 Multidimensional Arrays

An array is called *multidimensional* if it has more than one dimension. For example, the declaration

```
int     matrix[6][10];
```

creates a matrix containing 60 elements. However, is this six rows of ten elements each, or ten rows of six elements each?

To answer this question, you need to look at multidimensional arrays from a different viewpoint. Consider this progression of declarations:

```
int      a;
int      b[10];
int      c[6][10];
int      d[3][6][10];
```

a is a single integer. By adding the dimension to the next declaration, b is a vector containing ten integer elements.

But all that has been done for c is to add another dimension, so we can view c as a vector containing six elements, except that each of those elements happens to be a vector of ten integers. In other words, c is a one-dimensional array of one-dimensional arrays. The same can be said of d: it is an array of three elements, each of which is a matrix. Wait, "matrix" is the wrong viewpoint. d is an array of three elements, each of which is an array of six elements, and each of those is an array of ten integers. More concisely, d is an array of three arrays of six arrays of ten integers each.

It is important that you understand this viewpoint, because it is the basis for C's implementation of multidimensional arrays. To reinforce this idea, let's talk about the order in which array elements are stored in memory.

8.2.1 Storage Order

Consider this array:

```
int      array[3];
```

It contains three elements, as shown in this diagram.

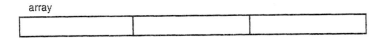

But now suppose you are told that each of these elements is in fact an array of six elements? Here is the new declaration:

```
int      array[3][6];
```

and here is how it looks:

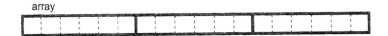

The solid boxes show the three elements of the first dimension, and the dotted divisions show the six elements of the second dimension. The subscripts of the elements above, from left to right, are:

```
0,0  0,1  0,2  0,3  0,4  0,5  1,0  1,1  1,2
1,3  1,4  1,5  2,0  2,1  2,2  2,3  2,4  2,5
```

This example illustrates what is called the *storage order* of array elements. In C, elements of a multidimensional array are stored in the order given by varying their rightmost subscript most rapidly, called *row major* order. Knowing the storage order helps you answer some useful questions, for example, the order in which to write the values in an initializer list.

What values does the following code print?

```
int     matrix[6][10];
int     *mp;
...
mp = &matrix[3][8];
printf( "First value is %d\n", *mp );
printf( "Second value is %d\n", *++mp );
printf( "Third value is %d\n", *++mp );
```

It is obvious that the first value printed will be the contents of `matrix[3][8]`, but what is printed next? The storage order determines the answer—the next element is the one whose rightmost subscript has changed, namely `matrix[3][9]`. What about the next one? Column nine is the last column in the row. Because the rows of the matrix are stored one after another, the next element printed will be `matrix[4][0]`.[35]

Here is a related question. Does `matrix` have three rows of ten columns each, or ten rows of three columns each? The answer may surprise you—in some contexts, it could be either way.

Either way? How could it be two different things? Easy. If you use subscripts to put data into the array and you later use subscripts to look up values in the array, then it makes no difference whether you interpret the first subscript as the row number or the column number. *As long as you do it the same way each time,* it will work with either interpretation.

However, interpreting the first subscript as a row or as a column cannot change the storage order of the array. If you use the first subscript as the row number and the second as the column number, then accessing the elements one after another in their storage order will give you the data row by row. On the other hand, if you use the first subscript as the column number, then the same kind of access will give you your data in order column by column. You can

---

[35] This example used a pointer to an integer to traverse the memory locations used to hold a two-dimensional array of integers. Called *flattening the array*, this technique is actually illegal, because moving from one row to the next involves leaving the subarray that contains the first row. Though it usually works, it should be avoided if possible.

choose whichever interpretation makes the most sense for your application. You cannot, however, change the way the elements are actually stored in memory. That order is defined by the Standard.

8.2.2 Array Names

The value of the name of a one-dimensional array is a pointer constant, its type is "pointer to *element-type*," and it points to the first element of the array. Multidimensional arrays are almost as easy. The only difference is that an element in the first dimension of a multidimensional array is another array. For example, the declaration:

```
int     matrix[3][10];
```

creates `matrix`, a one-dimensional array containing three elements. Each of these elements happens to be an array of ten integers.

The value of the name `matrix` is a pointer to the first element, so `matrix` points to an array of ten integers.

| K&R C | The idea of a pointer to an array was a fairly late addition to K&R C, and some older compilers do not fully implement it. However, the notion of a pointer to an array is crucial to the understanding of subscripts with multidimensional arrays.

8.2.3 Subscripts

To identify a single element from a multidimensional array, one subscript must be given for each dimension, in the same order that the dimensions were given in the declaration, and each subscript is enclosed in its own set of brackets. With this declaration:

```
int     matrix[3][10];
```

the expression

```
matrix[1][5]
```

accesses this element:

matrix

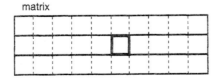

But subscripts are really indirection expressions in disguise, even with multidimensional arrays. Consider the expression

```
matrix
```

Its type is "pointer to an array of ten integers," and its value is:

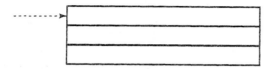

It points to the first array of ten integers.
  The expression

```
matrix + 1
```

is also a "pointer to an array of ten integers," but it points to a different row of the matrix:

Why? Because the value one is scaled by the size of an array of ten integers. Applying indirection follows the arrow and selects this array:

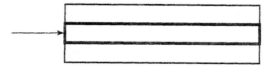

So the expression

```
*( matrix + 1 )
```

really identifies a particular array of ten integers. The value of an array name is a constant pointer to the first element in the array, and the same is true of this expression. Its type is "pointer to integer," and we can now show its value in the context of the next dimension:

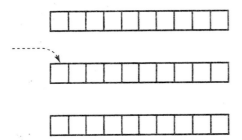

Now hold on to your hat. What is the result of this expression?

```
*( matrix + 1 ) + 5
```

The previous expression pointed to an integer, so value five is scaled by the size of an integer. The result points five integers after the original expression:

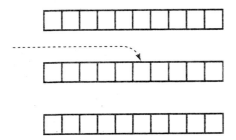

Applying indirection,

```
*( *( matrix + 1 ) + 5 )
```

takes us to the integer in question. If used as an R-value, you would get the value stored there. As an L-value, the location would receive a new value.

This intimidating expression is actually our old friend, the subscript. We can rewrite the subexpression *(matrix + 1) as matrix[1]. Substituting this subexpression into the original expression gives us:

```
*( matrix[1] + 5 )
```

This expression is perfectly valid. matrix[1] selects an array of ten integers, so its type is a pointer to an integer. To this pointer we add five, and then apply indirection.

But once again, we have the subscript form of indirection, so we can substitute and get

```
matrix[1][5]
```

Thus, subscripts are simply another form of indirection expression even for multidimensional arrays.

The point of this exercise is to illustrate how subscripts work for multidimensional arrays and how they depend on the notion of a pointer to an array. Subscripts are evaluated from left to right. The array name is a pointer to the first element of the first dimension, so the first subscript value is scaled by the size of that element. The result points to the desired element in that dimension. The indirection then selects that specific element. Because the element is an array, the type of this expression is a pointer to the first element of the next dimension. The next subscript is scaled by that size, and the process is repeated until all of the subscripts have been evaluated.

In many other languages, multiple subscripts are written as a comma-separated list of values. Some languages allow both forms. Not so in C: writing

```
matrix[4,3]
```

looks perfectly fine, but almost certainly does not accomplish what you want. Remember that the comma operator evaluates the first expression but *throws away its value*. The result is the value of the second expression. Thus, the previous expression is equivalent to

```
matrix[3]
```

The problem is that the expression may compile without any error or warning. The expression is perfectly legitimate, it just doesn't mean what you had intended.

8.2.4 Pointers to Arrays

Are these declarations legal?

```
int     vector[10], *vp = vector;
int     matrix[3][10], *mp = matrix;
```

The first is legal. It allocates a vector of integers, and then declares vp to be a pointer to an integer and initializes the pointer to point to the first element in vector. Both vector and vp have the same type: pointer to integer. The second declaration is illegal, however. It creates the matrix correctly and declares mp to be a pointer to an integer, but the initialization of mp is incorrect because matrix is not a pointer to an integer, it is a pointer to an array of integers. How would we declare a pointer to an array of integers?

```
int      (*p) [10];
```

This declaration is more complex than those you have seen before, but it really isn't too difficult. Just pretend that it is an expression and evaluate it. Subscripts have a higher precedence than indirection, but the parentheses surrounding the indirection force it to go first. So p is a pointer to something, but to what?

The subscript is applied next, so p points to some kind of array. There aren't any more operators in the declaration expression, so each element of the array is an integer.

The declaration doesn't tell you directly what p is, but it is not difficult to figure out—when we applied indirection to p we got an array, and putting a subscript on that expression produced an integer. So p is a pointer to an array of integers.

Adding initialization to the declaration gives us:

```
int      (*p) [10] = matrix;
```

which makes p point to the first row of matrix.

p is a pointer to an array of ten integers. Adding an integer to p will cause the integer value to be scaled by the size of ten integers before the addition takes place. So we can use this pointer to step through the matrix row by row.

What should you do if you want a pointer that will go through the matrix integer by integer rather than row by row? Both of the following declarations create a simple integer pointer, initialized in two different ways to point to the first integer in the matrix.

```
int      *pi = &matrix[0] [0];
int      *pi = matrix[0];
```

Incrementing this pointer advances it to the next integer.

If you intend to perform any arithmetic with the pointer, avoid this kind of declaration:

```
int      (*p) [] = matrix;
```

p is still a pointer to an array of integers, but the array size is missing. Integers involved in pointer arithmetic with this variable will be scaled by the size of an empty array (that is, multiplied by zero), which is probably not what you had in mind. Some compilers catch this error and some don't.

8.2.5 Multidimensional Arrays as Function Arguments

A multidimensional array name used as an argument to a function is passed the same as a one-dimensional array name—a pointer to the first element of the array is passed. However, the difference between them is that each element of the multidimensional array is another array, and the compiler needs to know its dimensions in order to evaluate subscripts for the array parameter in the function. Here are two examples to illustrate the difference:

```
int      vector[10];
...
func1( vector );
```

The type of the argument `vector` is a pointer to an integer, so `func1` can be prototyped in either of the following ways:

```
void func1( int *vec );
void func1( int vec[] );
```

Pointer arithmetic on `vec` in the function uses the size of an integer for its scale factor.

Now let's look at a matrix.

```
int      matrix[3][10];
...
func2( matrix );
```

Here the type of the argument `matrix` is a pointer to an array of ten integers. What should the prototype for `func2` look like? Either of the following forms could be used:

```
void func2( int (*mat)[10] );
void func2( int mat[][10] );
```

In the function, the first subscript used with `mat` is scaled by the size of an array of ten integers; the second subscript is then scaled by the size of an integer, just as it would be for the original matrix.

The key here is that the compiler must know the sizes of the second and subsequent dimensions in order to evaluate subscripts, thus the prototype must declare these dimensions. The size of the first dimension isn't needed because it is not used in the calculation of subscripts.

You can write the prototype for a one-dimensional array parameter either as an array or as a pointer. For multidimensional arrays, you only have this choice for the first dimension, though. Specifically, it is incorrect to prototype `func2` like this:

```
void func2( int **mat );
```

This example declares mat to be a pointer to a pointer to an integer, which is not at all the same thing as a pointer to an array of ten integers.

8.2.6 Initialization

The storage order of array elements becomes important when initializing multidimensional arrays. There are two ways to write the initializer list. The first is to just give a long list of initializers, as in the following example.

```
int matrix[2][3] = { 100, 101, 102, 110, 111, 112 };
```

The storage order has the rightmost subscript varying most rapidly, so this initialization produces the the same result as these assignments:

```
matrix[0][0] = 100;
matrix[0][1] = 101;
matrix[0][2] = 102;
matrix[1][0] = 110;
matrix[1][1] = 111;
matrix[1][2] = 112;
```

The second way is based on the idea that a multidimensional array is really a one-dimensional array of complicated elements. For example, here's a declaration for a two-dimensional array:

```
int     two_dim[3][5];
```

View two_dim as an array of three (complicated) elements. To initialize an array of three elements, we use a list containing three initializers:

```
int     two_dim[3][5] = { *, *, * };
```

But each of these elements is actually an array of five integers, so each of the *'s should be a list of five values enclosed in braces. Replacing each * with such a list results in code that looks like this:

```
int     two_dim[3][5] = {
        { 00, 01, 02, 03, 04 },
        { 10, 11, 12, 13, 14 },
        { 20, 21, 22, 23, 24 }
};
```

Of course, the indenting and spacing we have used are not required, although they do make the list easier to read.

If you erase all but the outermost braces from this example, you will see that what is left is a simple initializer list like the first one. The braces merely delimit the initializer list by row.

Figures 8.1 and 8.2 illustrate initializing three- and four-dimensional arrays. In these examples, the digits of each initializer show the subscript values of the location in which it is stored.[36]

Why go to all the trouble of putting in these braces when the initialization works exactly the same way without them? There are two reasons. The first is organization. A single, long list of numbers makes it difficult to see which value belongs to each location of the array, thus the braces act as signposts and make it easier to verify that the right values appear in the right places.

Second, the braces are valuable for incomplete initialization. Without them, only trailing initializers may be omitted. Even if only a few elements of a large multidimensional array were to be initialized, the list might still be quite long because only the trailing initializers can be omitted. With the braces, though, trailing initializers may be omitted from *each* list. Also, the initializers for *each* dimension also form a list.

To illustrate this point, let's revisit the four-dimensional array initialization in Figure 8.2 and change our requirements a little. Suppose we only need to initialize two elements in the array. Element `[0][0][0][0]` should be 100 and element `[1][0][0][0]` should be 200. All other elements should be left

```
int     three_dim[2][3][5] = {
        {
                { 000, 001, 002, 003, 004 },
                { 010, 011, 012, 013, 014 },
                { 020, 021, 022, 023, 024 }
        },
        {
                { 100, 101, 102, 103, 104 },
                { 110, 111, 112, 113, 114 },
                { 120, 121, 122, 123, 124 }
        }
};
```

Figure 8.1   Initializing a three-dimensional array

---

[36] If these examples were compiled, the initializers that begin with zero would actually be interpreted as octal numbers. Ignore this point, and look only at the individual digits of each initializer.

```
int     four_dim[2][2][3][5] = {
        {
                {
                        { 0000, 0001, 0002, 0003, 0004 },
                        { 0010, 0011, 0012, 0013, 0014 },
                        { 0020, 0021, 0022, 0023, 0024 }
                },
                {
                        { 0100, 0101, 0102, 0103, 0104 },
                        { 0110, 0111, 0112, 0113, 0114 },
                        { 0120, 0121, 0122, 0123, 0124 }
                }
        },
        {
                {
                        { 1000, 1001, 1002, 1003, 1004 },
                        { 1010, 1011, 1012, 1013, 1014 },
                        { 1020, 1021, 1022, 1023, 1024 }
                },
                {
                        { 1100, 1101, 1102, 1103, 1104 },
                        { 1110, 1111, 1112, 1113, 1114 },
                        { 1120, 1121, 1122, 1123, 1124 }
                }
        }
};
```

Figure 8.2   Initializing a four-dimensional array

to their default values. Here is how we can accomplish this task:

```
int     four_dim[2][2][3][5] = {
        {
                {
                        { 100 }
                }
        },
        {
                {
                        { 200 }
                }
        }
};
```

Without the braces, you would need this longer initializer list:

```
int     four_dim[2][2][3][5] = { 100, 0, 0,
0, 0, 0, 0, 0, 0, 0, 0, 0, 0, 0, 0, 0, 0,
0, 0, 0, 0, 0, 0, 0, 0, 0, 0, 0, 0, 0, 200 };
```

This list is not only harder to read but also more difficult to get right in the first place.

8.2.7 Automatic Array Sizing

With multidimensional arrays, only the *first* dimension of the array can be implied by the initializer list. The remaining ones are needed so that the compiler can determine the size of each subordinate dimension. For example:

```
int     two_dim[][5] = {
        { 00, 01, 02 },
        { 10, 11 },
        { 20, 21, 22, 23 }
};
```

The leftmost dimension is determined to be three by counting the number of initializers it contains.

Why can't the other dimension be determined automatically by counting the values in its longest initializer list? In principle, the compiler could figure it out, but then at least one of the initializers in each list would have to be full size in order for the dimension to be determined accurately. By requiring that all dimensions after the first one be given, all of the initializer lists can be incomplete.

8.3 Arrays of Pointers

Aside from its type, a pointer variable is like any other variable. Just as you can create arrays of integers, you can also declare arrays of pointers. Here is an example:

```
int     *api[10];
```

To figure out this complex declaration, pretend that it is an expression and evaluate it.

Subscripts have a higher precedence than indirection, so in this expression, the subscript would be applied first. Therefore, api is an array of something (and oh, by the way, there are ten of them). After getting one element of the array, the indirection is applied next. There aren't any more operators, so the result of this expression is an integer.

So what is api? We got an integer by applying indirection to an element of an array, so api must be an array of pointers to integers.

Where would you ever use an array of pointers? Here is one example:

```
char     const    *keyword[] = {
        "do",
        "for",
        "if",
        "register",
        "return",
        "switch",
```

```
/*
** Determine whether the argument matches any of the words in
** a list of keywords, and return the index to the one it matches.
** If no match is found, return the value -1.
*/

#include <string.h>

int
lookup_keyword( char const * const desired_word,
    char const *keyword_table[], int const size )
{
        char     const **kwp;

        /*
        ** For each word in the table ...
        */
        for( kwp = keyword_table; kwp < keyword_table + size; kwp++ )
                /*
                ** If this word matches the one we're looking for,
                ** return its position in the table.
                */
                if( strcmp( desired_word, *kwp ) == 0 )
                        return kwp - keyword_table;

        /*
        ** Not found.
        */
        return -1;
}
```

Program 8.2   Keyword lookup   keyword.c

```
            "while"
    };
    #define N_KEYWORD         \
            ( sizeof( keyword ) / sizeof( keyword[0] ) )
```

Notice the use of sizeof to automatically count the number of elements in the array. sizeof(keyword) gives the number of bytes in the entire array, and sizeof(keyword[0]) is the number of bytes in one element. The resulting division gives the number of elements.

This array would be useful in a program that counts keywords in C source files. Each word from the input would be compared to the strings in the list, and all matches would be counted. Program 8.2 goes through the list of keywords looking for a match with the argument string. When a match is found, the offset into the list is returned. The calling program must know that zero means do, one means for, and so forth, and it also has to know that -1 is returned for a nonkeyword. This information would probably be obtained via symbols defined in an included file.

We could also store the keywords in a matrix, like this:

```
char    const    keyword[][9] = {
        "do",
        "for",
        "if",
        "register",
        "return",
        "switch",
        "while"
};
```

What is the difference between this declaration and the preceding one? The second declaration creates a matrix whose rows are each long enough to hold the longest keyword (plus its terminating NUL byte). The matrix looks like this:

keyword

'd'	'o'	0	0	0	0	0	0	0
'f'	'o'	'r'	0	0	0	0	0	0
'i'	'f'	0	0	0	0	0	0	0
'r'	'e'	'g'	'i'	's'	't'	'e'	'r'	0
'r'	'e'	't'	'u'	'r'	'n'	0	0	0
's'	'w'	'i'	't'	'c'	'h'	0	0	0
'w'	'h'	'i'	'l'	'e'	0	0	0	0

The first declaration creates an array of pointers, which are initialized to point
to various string literals, as illustrated below.

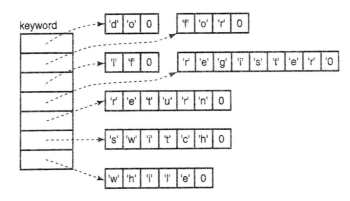

Notice the difference in the amount of memory used. The matrix looks
inefficient because every row must be long enough to store the longest keyword. But it does not need any pointers. On the other hand, the array of
pointers takes space, but each of the string literals is only as long as it needs to
be.

What would we need to change in Program 8.2 to use the matrix instead
of the array of pointers? It may surprise you to learn that only the declarations
for the table parameter and the local variable would be different. The code
wouldn't change at all. Because the value of an array name is a pointer, the
body of the function will work with either a pointer variable or an array name.

Which is better? It depends on the specific words you wish to store. If
they are all nearly the same length, the matrix is more compact because there
is no space needed for pointers. However, if the words are different lengths,
or worse yet, most of them are short but a few are quite long, then the array of
pointers may be more compact. It depends on whether the space consumed by
the pointers is less than the space wasted by using fixed-length rows for each
word.

In practice, these differences are so slight as to be unimportant for all but
the largest of tables. More often than not, the array of pointers is used, but
with a twist:

```
char    const    *keyword[] = {
        "do",
        "for",
        "if",
        "register",
        "return",
        "switch",
```

```
        "while",
        NULL
    };
```

Here we add a NULL pointer to the end of the table. The NULL lets functions that search the table detect the end of the table without knowing its size in advance, like this:

```
for( kwp = keyword_table; *kwp != NULL; kwp++ )
```

8.4 Summary

The value of an array name in most expressions is a pointer to the first element of the array. There are only two exceptions to this rule. `sizeof` returns the number of bytes in the entire array rather than the size of a pointer. The unary `&` operator returns a pointer to the first element of the array, not a pointer to a pointer to the first element.

Except for their precedence, the subscript expression `array[value]` is the same as the indirection expression `*( array + ( value ) )`. Thus, subscripts may be used with pointer expressions as well as with array names, which makes it difficult for the compiler to check the validity of subscripts. Pointer expressions may be more efficient than subscripts, but subscripts are never more efficient than pointer expressions. However, reducing program maintainability to gain runtime efficiency is rarely a good idea.

Pointers and arrays are not equivalent. The properties of an array and a pointer variable are quite different. Declaring an array creates space to store the array elements, while declaring a pointer variable only creates space to store the pointer.

When an array name is passed as a function argument, a pointer to the first element is passed to the function. This parameter is a copy, so the function can manipulate it without affecting the actual argument. However, applying indirection to the pointer parameter allows the function to modify the original array elements. Array parameters may be declared either as array names or pointers; both declaration forms are equivalent *for function parameters only.*

An array may be initialized with a list of values enclosed in braces. Static variables (including arrays) receive their initial values when the program is loaded into memory. Automatic variables (including arrays) must be reinitialized with implicit assignment statements each time execution enters the block in which they are declared. If an initializer list has fewer values than the size of the array, the last elements of the array are initialized with the default value. If the dimension of an initialized array is omitted, the compiler will make the array just large enough to hold the values given in the initializer list. Character arrays may be initialized with a shorthand notation that resembles a string literal.

Multidimensional arrays are actually one-dimensional arrays whose elements are each an array. The values in multidimensional arrays are stored in row major order, with the rightmost subscript varying most rapidly. The value of a multidimensional array name is a pointer to its first element, which will be a pointer to an array. Arithmetic with this pointer will be scaled by the size of the array. Subscripts for multidimensional arrays are also pointer expressions. When the name of a multidimensional array is passed as an argument to a function, the corresponding function parameter must be declared with the sizes of the second and subsequent dimensions. Because a multidimensional array is really a one-dimensional array of complex elements, the initializer list for a multidimensional array contains a list of initializers for the complex elements. Each of these lists may also contain nested lists, as needed by the number of dimensions in the array. The interior braces may be omitted if the initializer lists are all complete. Only the first dimension of a multidimensional array may be automatically sized from the initializer list.

It is possible to create arrays of pointers. Lists of strings may be stored in a matrix, or as a list of pointers to vectors or string literals. In a matrix, each row must be as long as the longest string, however no pointers are stored. The list of pointers takes space, but each of the strings need only be as long as necessary.

8.5 Summary of Cautions

1. Using commas to separate subscripts when accessing a multidimensional array (page 221).

2. Doing arithmetic with a pointer to an unsized array (page 222).

8.6 Summary of Programming Tips

1. Writing good code in the first place is better than depending on the compiler to fix up bad code (page 205).

2. Source code readability is nearly always more important than runtime efficiency (page 209).

3. Pointer parameters to functions should be declared `const` whenever possible (page 212).

4. Using `register` variables increases runtime efficiency in some environments (page 212).

5. Using braces to fully enclose the initializers of a multidimensional array increases readability (page 225).

8.7 Questions

1. Given the declarations and data shown below, evaluate each of the expressions and state its value. Evaluate each expression with the original data shown (that is, the results of one expression do not affect the following ones). Assume that the `ints` array begins at location 100 and that integers and pointers both occupy four bytes.

```
int      ints[20] = {
         10, 20, 30, 40, 50, 60, 70, 80, 90, 100,
         110, 120, 130, 140, 150, 160, 170, 180, 190, 200
};
(Other declarations)
int      *ip = ints + 3;
```

Expression	Value	Expression	Value
ints		ip	
ints[4]		ip[4]	
ints + 4		ip + 4	
*ints + 4		*ip + 4;	
*(ints + 4)		*(ip + 4)	
ints[-2]		ip[-2]	
&ints		&ip	
&ints[4]		&ip[4]	
&ints + 4		&ip + 4	
&ints[-2]		&ip[-2]	

2. Are the expressions array[i + j] and i + j[array] equivalent?

3. The following declarations are an attempt to access the array data using sub-scripts that start at one. Will it work?

```
int     actual_data[ 20 ];
int     *data = actual_data - 1;
```

4. Rewrite the following loop, which tests whether a string is a palindrome, to use pointer variables instead of subscripts.

```
char    buffer[SIZE];
int     front, rear;
...
front = 0;
rear = strlen( buffer ) - 1;
while( front < rear ){
        if( buffer[front] != buffer[rear] )
                break;

        front += 1;
        rear -= 1;
}
if( front >= rear ){
        printf( "It is a palindrome!\n" );
}
```

5. The potential efficiency of pointers over subscripts is a motivation to use them. When is it reasonable to use subscripts despite the possible loss of runtime speed?

6. Compile the functions try1 through try5 on your machine, and analyze the resulting assembly code. What is your conclusion?

7. Test your conclusion for the previous question by running each of the functions and timing their execution. Making the arrays several thousand elements long increases the accuracy of the experiment because the copying takes far more time than the irrelevant parts of the program. Also, call the functions from within a loop that iterates enough times so that you can accurately time the entire execution. Compile the programs twice for this experiment—once without any optimization at all, and once with optimization. If your compiler offers a choice, select optimization for best speed.

✎ 8. The following declarations were found in one source file:

```
int     a[10];
int     *b = a;
```

But in a different source file, this code was found:

```
extern  int     *a;
extern  int     b[];
int     x, y;
...
x = a[3];
y = b[3];
```

Explain what happens when the two assignment statements are executed. (Assume that integers and pointers both occupy four bytes).

9. Write a declaration that will initialize an array of integers called coin_values to the values of current U.S. coins.

10. Given the declaration

```
int     array[4][2];
```

give the value of each of the following expressions. Assume that the array begins at location 1000 and that integers occupy two bytes of memory.

Expression	Value
array	_____
array + 2	_____
array[3]	_____
array[2] - 1	_____
&array[1][2]	_____
&array[2][0]	_____

11. Given the declaration

```
int     array[4][2][3][6];
```

compute the value of each of the following expressions. Also, show the declaration that would be needed for the variable x in order for the expression to be assigned to x without using a cast. Assume that the array begins at location 1000 and that integers occupy four bytes of memory.

Expression	Value	Type of x
array	_____	_____
array + 2	_____	_____
array[3]	_____	_____
array[2] - 1	_____	_____
array[2][1]	_____	_____
array[1][0] + 1	_____	_____
array[1][0][2]	_____	_____
array[0][1][0] + 2	_____	_____
array[3][1][2][5]	_____	_____
&array[3][1][2][5]	_____	_____

12. Arrays in C are stored in row-major order. When is this information relevant?

13. Given the declaration:

```
int     array[4][5][3];
```

convert the following pointer expressions to use subscripts.

Expression	Subscript Expression
*array	_____
*(array + 2)	_____
*(array + 1) + 4	_____
*(*(array + 1) + 4)	_____
*(*(*(array + 3) + 1) + 2)	_____
*(*(*array + 1) + 2)	_____
*(**array + 2)	_____
**(*array + 1)	_____
***array	_____

14. The subscripts for a multidimensional array must each be given in its own set of brackets. Under what conditions would the following code fragment compile without producing any warnings or errors?

```
int     array[10][20];
...
i = array[3,4];
```

15. Given the declarations:

    ```
    unsigned int    which;
    int             array[ SIZE ];
    ```

    which of the following statements makes more sense, and why?

    ```
    if( array[ which ] == 5 && which < SIZE ) ...
    if( which < SIZE && array[ which ] == 5 ) ...
    ```

16. What is the difference (if any) between the variables `array1` and `array2` in this program?

    ```
    void function( int array1[10] ){
            int     array2[10];
            ...
    }
    ```

♻ 17. Explain the significant differences between the following two uses of the `const` keyword.

    ```
    void function( int const a, int const b[] ){
    ```

18. How else could the following function prototype be written to achieve the same results?

    ```
    void function( int array[3][2][5] );
    ```

19. In Program 8.2, the keyword lookup example, the array of pointers to characters was modified by adding a NULL pointer to the end of it, thus eliminating the need to know the size of the table. How could the matrix of keywords be modified to achieve the same result? Show the `for` statement that would be used to access the modified matrix.

8.8 Programming Exercises

★ 1. Write a declaration for an array that initializes certain locations of the array to specific values. The array should be called `char_values` and contain 3 × 6 × 4 × 5 unsigned characters. The following locations should be statically initialized to these values:

Loc	Value	Loc	Value	Loc	Value
1,2,2,3	`'A'`	1,1,1,1	`' '`	1,3,2,2	`0xf3`
2,4,3,2	`'3'`	1,4,2,3	`'\n'`	2,2,3,1	`'\121'`
2,4,3,3	`3`	2,5,3,4	`125`	1,2,3,4	`'X'`
2,1,1,2	`0320`	2,2,2,2	`'\''`	2,2,1,1	`'0'`

Locations other than those mentioned above should be initialized to binary (not the character) zero. *Note:* Static initialization is to be used; there can be no executable code in your solution!

Although it will not be part of the solution, you will probably want to write a program to check your initialization by printing out the array. Because some of the values are not printable characters, print the values as integers (octal or hexadecimal output would be convenient).

Note: Solving this problem twice, once using nested braces in the initializer list and once without, will give you a greater appreciation of the usefulness of the nested braces.

★★ 2. The U.S. federal income tax for single people in 1995 was computed according to the following rules:

If Your Taxable Income Is Over	But Not Over	Your Tax Is	of the Amount Over
$0	$23,350	15%	$0
23,350	56,550	$3,502.50 + 28%	23,350
56,550	117,950	12,798.50 + 31%	56,550
117,950	256,500	31,832.50 + 36%	117,950
256,500	—	81,710.50 + 39.6%	256,500

Write the function prototyped below:

```
float single_tax( float income );
```

The argument is taxable income, and the function returns the appropriate amount of tax.

★★ 3. An *identity matrix* is a square matrix whose values are all zero except for those on the main diagonal, which are one. For example:

```
1  0  0
0  1  0
0  0  1
```

is a 3 × 3 identity matrix. Write a function called `identity_matrix` that takes a 10 × 10 matrix of integers as its only argument and returns a boolean value indicating whether the matrix is an identity matrix.

★★★ 4. Modify the `identity_matrix` function from the previous problem so that it can take matrices of any size by flattening the array. The first argument should be a pointer to an integer, and you will need a second argument that specifies the size of the matrix.

★★★★ 5. If A is a matrix of x rows and y columns and B is a matrix of y rows and z columns, then A and B can be multiplied together and the result will be a matrix C with x rows and z columns. Each element of this matrix is determined with the following formula:

$$C_{i,j} = \sum_{k=1}^{y} A_{i,k} \times B_{k,j}$$

For example:

$$\begin{bmatrix} 2 & -6 \\ 3 & 5 \\ 1 & -1 \end{bmatrix} \times \begin{bmatrix} 4 & -2 & -4 & -5 \\ -7 & -3 & 6 & 7 \end{bmatrix} = \begin{bmatrix} 50 & 14 & -44 & -52 \\ -23 & -21 & 18 & 20 \\ 11 & 1 & -10 & -12 \end{bmatrix}$$

The value 14 in the answer was the result of adding 2×-2 and -6×-3.

Write a function to multiply two matrices. The function should have this prototype:

```
void matrix_multiply( int *m1, int *m2, int *r,
    int x, int y, int z );
```

`m1` will be a matrix with x rows and y columns; `m2` will be a matrix with y rows and z columns. These matrices should be multiplied together, and the results should be stored in `r`, which will be a matrix with x rows and z columns. Remember to modify the formula as necessary to account for the fact that subscripts in C begin with zero, not one!

★★★★★ 6. As you know, the C compiler allocates arrays with subscripts that always begin at zero and does not check subscripts when array elements are accessed. In this project, you will write a function that allows the user to access "pseudo-arrays" whose subscripts can be in any ranges, with complete error checking. Here is a prototype for the function you will write:

```
int array_offset( int arrayinfo[], ... );
```

The function takes a set of information describing the dimensions of a pseudo-array and a set of subscript values. It then uses the information to translate the subscript values into an integer that can be used as a subscript on a vector. With this function, the user can allocate space either as a vector or with `mal-loc`, but then access that space as a multidimensional array. The array is called a "pseudo-array" because the compiler thinks that it is a vector, even though this function allows it to be accessed as a multidimensional array.

The function's arguments are:

Argument	Meaning
arrayinfo	A variable-length array of integers that contains information about the pseudo-array. arrayinfo[0] specifies how many dimensions the pseudo-array has, which must be a value in the range 1–10, inclusive. arrayinfo[1] and arrayinfo[2] give the low and high limits for the first dimension, arrayinfo[3] and arrayinfo[4] give the low and high limits for the second dimension, and so forth.
. . .	The variable portion of the argument list may contain up to ten integers, which are subscript values that identify a particular location in the pseudo-array. You must use va_ argument macros to access them. When the function is called, arrayinfo[0] arguments will be passed.

The formula to use for computing an array location from its subscripts is given below. The variables s_1, s_2, etc. represent the subscript arguments s1, s2, etc. The variables lo_1 and hi_1 represent the low and high limits for subscript s1, from the arrayinfo argument, and so forth for the remaining dimensions. The variable *loc* represents the desired location in the pseudo-array, as an integer offset from the beginning of a vector. For a one-dimensional pseudo-array:

$$loc = s_1 - lo_1$$

For a two-dimensional pseudo-array:

$$loc = (s_1 - lo_1) \times (hi_2 - lo_2 + 1) + s_2 - lo_2$$

For a three-dimensional pseudo-array:

$$loc = \left[(s_1 - lo_1) \times (hi_2 - lo_2 + 1) + s_2 - lo_2 \right] \times (hi_3 - lo_3 + 1) + s_3 - lo_3$$

For a four-dimensional pseudo-array:

$$loc = \left\{ \left[(s_1 - lo_1) \times (hi_2 - lo_2 + 1) + (s_2 - lo_2) \right] \times (hi_3 - lo_3 + 1) + s_3 - lo_3 \right\} \times (hi_4 - lo_4 + 1) + s_4 - lo_4$$

and so forth up to ten dimensions.

You may assume that `arrayinfo` is a valid pointer and that the correct number of subscript arguments are passed to `array_offset`. Everything else must be checked for errors. A few of the possible errors are: number of dimensions not in the range 1–10, a subscript is less than its *low* value, a *low* value is greater than the corresponding *high* value, etc. If these or any other errors are detected, the value -1 should be returned.

Hint: Copy the subscript arguments into a local array. You can then code the calculation as a loop with an iteration for each dimension.

Example: Assume that the `arrayinfo` array contains the values 3, 4, 6, 1, 5, -3, and 3. These values indicate that we are working with a three-dimensional pseudo-array. The first subscript is a value from 4 through 6, the second subscript is a value from 1 through 5, and the third subscript is a value from -3 through 3. In this example, `array_offset` will be called with three subscript arguments. Several sets of subscripts are shown below along with the offsets that they represent.

Subscripts	Offset	Subscripts	Offset	Subscripts	Offset
4, 1, -3	0	4, 1, 3	6	5, 1, -3	35
4, 1, -2	1	4, 2, -3	7	6, 3, 1	88

★★★ 7. Modify the `array_offset` function from Problem 6 so that it accesses pseudo-arrays whose elements are allocated in column major order, that is, with the leftmost subscript varying most rapidly. This new function, `array_offset2`, should otherwise work the same as the original function.

The formulas for calculating subscripts for these arrays are given below. For a one-dimensional pseudo-array:

$$loc = s_1 - lo_1$$

For a two-dimensional pseudo-array:

$$loc = (s_2 - lo_2) \times (hi_1 - lo_1 + 1) + s_1 - lo_1$$

For a three-dimensional pseudo-array:

$$loc = \left[(s_3 - lo_3) \times (hi_2 - lo_2 + 1) + s_2 - lo_2 \right] \times (hi_1 - lo_1 + 1) + s_1 - lo_1$$

For a four-dimensional pseudo-array:

$$loc = \left\{ \left[(s_4 - lo_4) \times (hi_3 - lo_3 + 1) + (s_3 - lo_3) \right] \right.$$
$$\left. \times (hi_2 - lo_2 + 1) + s_2 - lo_2 \right\} \times (hi_1 - lo_1 + 1) + s_1 - lo_1$$

and so forth up to ten dimensions.

Example: Assume that the `arrayinfo` array contains the values 3, 4, 6, 1, 5, -3, and 3. These values indicate that we are working with a three-dimensional pseudo-array. The first subscript is a value from 4 through 6, the second subscript is a value from 1 through 5, and the third subscript is a value from -3 through 3. In this example, `array_offset2` will be called with three subscript arguments. Several sets of subscripts are shown below along with the offsets that they represent.

Subscripts	Offset	Subscripts	Offset	Subscripts	Offset
4, 1, -3	0	4, 2, -3	3	4, 1, -1	30
5, 1, -3	1	4, 3, -3	6	5, 3, -1	37
6, 1, -3	2	4, 1, -2	15	6, 5, 3	104

★★★★★ 8. The queen is the most powerful piece in the game of chess. On the board shown below, the queen can capture any piece on any square covered by the eight arrows.

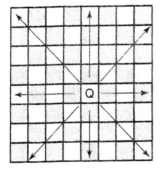

Is it possible to place eight queens on a chessboard in such a way that none of them can attack any of the others? This question is called The Eight Queens Problem. Your task is to write a program to find all solutions to the Eight Queens Problem. How many solutions are there?

Hint: The program is easy if you use a technique called *backtracking.* Write a function that places a queen in the first column of one row and then checks to make sure that there are no conflicts with any other queens on the board. If there is a conflict, the function should move the queen to the next column of that row and try again. If there is a conflict in every column, the function should return.

If the queen can be placed, though, the function should then call itself recursively to place a queen in the next row. When the recursive call returns, the function then moves its queen to the next column. Whenever a queen is placed successfully in the last row, the function should print the chessboard, showing the locations of the eight queens.

9

Strings, Characters, and Bytes

Strings are an important type of data, yet C does not have an explicit string data type because strings are stored in character arrays or as string literals. Literals are appropriate for strings that the program does not need to modify. All other strings must be stored in character arrays or dynamically allocated memory (see Chapter 11). This chapter describes the library functions that deal with strings and characters and a related group of functions with similar capabilities that deal with both string and nonstring data.

9.1 String Basics

First, let's review the basics of strings. A *string* is a sequence of zero or more characters followed by a NUL byte, which is a byte whose bits are all zero. Therefore, it is not possible for a string to *contain* a NUL as one of its characters. This restriction rarely causes problems because there isn't a printable character associated with NUL, which is why it was chosen as a terminator. The NUL terminates the string but is not considered a part of it, so the length of a string does not include the NUL.

The header file string.h contains the prototypes and declarations needed to use the string functions. Although its use is not required, it is a good idea to include this header file because with the prototypes it contains the compiler can do a better job error checking your program.[37]

---

[37] Old C programs often did not include this file. Without function prototypes, all that could be declared was the type returned by each function, and the values returned by most of these functions are ignored anyway.

9.2 String Length

The length of a string is the number of characters it contains. The length is easily computed by counting the characters, as is done in Program 9.1. This implementation illustrates the type of processing used when dealing with strings, but in fact you rarely need to write string functions because the ones provided in the standard library usually will do the job. Should you wish to write a string function, though, be aware that the Standard reserves all function names that begin with `str` for future expansion of the library.

The prototype for the library `strlen` is:

```
size_t  strlen( char const *string );
```

Note that `strlen` returns a value of type `size_t`. This type is defined in the include file `stddef.h` and is an unsigned integer type. Using unsigned values in expressions can lead to unexpected results. For example, the following two statements appear to be equivalent,

```
if( strlen( x ) >= strlen( y ) ) ...
if( strlen( x ) - strlen( y ) >= 0 ) ...
```

but they are not. The first works as you would expect, but the second one is *always* true. The result of `strlen` is unsigned, so the expression on the left of the `>=` is unsigned, and unsigned values can never be negative.

```c
/*
** Compute the length of the string argument.
*/
#include <stddef.h>

size_t
strlen( char const *string )
{
        int length;

        for( length = 0; *string++ != '\0'; )
                length += 1;

        return length;
}
```

Program 9.1   String length   strlen.c

Expressions containing both signed and unsigned values can also produce strange results. The following statements are not equivalent for the same reason as the previous pair.

```
if( strlen( x ) >= 10 ) ...
if( strlen( x ) - 10 >= 0 ) ...
```

Casting the value returned by strlen to an int eliminates this problem.

It is tempting to write your own strlen function, making judicious use of register declarations and clever tricks to make it faster than the library function. It rarely works. The standard library functions are sometimes implemented in assembly language in order to exploit the speed of special string manipulation instructions provided by certain machines. Even on machines without such instructions, your time is better spent concentrating on the algorithms for other parts of your program. Finding a better algorithm is more effective than tuning a bad one, and it is more efficient to reuse existing software than to reinvent it.

9.3 Unrestricted String Functions

The most commonly used string functions are "unrestricted," meaning that they determine the length of their string arguments solely by looking for the terminating NUL byte. When using these functions, it is the programmer's responsibility to make sure that the resulting string does not overflow the memory in which it is supposed to fit. This problem is described in more detail for each of the functions discussed in this section.

9.3.1 Copying Strings

Strings are copied using **strcpy** whose prototype is shown below.

```
char    *strcpy( char *dst, char const *src );
```

This function copies the string from the src argument into the dst argument. If the src and dst arguments overlap, the result is undefined. Because it is modified, dst must be a character array or a pointer to an array or to dynamically allocated memory. A string literal may not be used. The function returns a value, which is described in Section 9.3.3.

The previous contents of the destination argument are overwritten and are lost. Even if the new string is shorter than the old contents of dst, the last characters of the previous string are effectively erased because they appear after the terminating NUL byte of the new string.

Consider this example:

```
char    message[] = "Original message";
...
if( ... )
        strcpy( message, "Different" );
```

If the condition is true and the copy is performed, the array will contain the following:

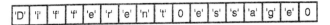

The characters after the first NUL byte are never accessed by the string functions and are, for all practical purposes, lost.

It is up to the programmer to make sure that the destination array is large enough to hold the string. If the string is longer than the array, the excess characters will be copied anyway and will overwrite whatever values happen to be after the array in memory. strcpy is unable to avoid this problem because it cannot determine the size of the destination array.

For example:

```
char    message[] = "Original message";
...
strcpy( message, "A different message" );
```

The second string is too long to fit in the array, so the strcpy will run off the end of the array and overwrite whatever variables happen to follow it in memory. You can avoid a lot of debugging by making sure that the destination argument is large enough before calling strcpy.

9.3.2 Concatenating Strings

To append (concatenate) one string to the end of another, **strcat** is used. Its prototype is:

```
char    *strcat( char *dst, char const *src );
```

strcat requires that dst already contain a (possibly empty) string. It finds the end of this string, and appends to it a copy of the string from src. If the src and dst strings overlap, the result is undefined.

The following example shows a common use of this function.

```
strcpy( message, "Hello " );
strcat( message, customer_name );
strcat( message, ", how are you?" );
```

Each of the arguments to strcat are appended to the string already in message. The result is a string such as this one:

```
Hello Jim, how are you?
```

Once again, the programmer must ensure that there is enough space remaining in the destination array to hold the entire source string. But this time it is incorrect to simply compare the length of the source string with the size of the array. You must also account for the length of the existing string.

9.3.3 Function Return Value

Both strcpy and strcat return a copy of their first argument, which is a pointer to the destination array. Because of this value, you can nest calls to these functions, as illustrated in the following example.

```
strcat( strcpy( dst, a ), b );
```

The strcpy is performed first. It copies the string from a into dst and returns the value dst. The returned value becomes the first argument to strcat, which appends the string in b to dst.

This nested style does not have a functional advantage over the more readable

```
strcpy( dst, a );
strcat( dst, b );
```

Indeed, the values returned by the vast majority of calls to these functions are simply ignored.

9.3.4 String Comparisons

Comparing two strings involves comparing the corresponding characters in them, one by one, until a mismatch is found. The string from which the "lower" character (that is, the character nearer the beginning of the character set) came is said to be "less than" the other string. If one string is a prefix of the other, it will be "less than" the other string because its terminating NUL is reached first. Called a *lexicographic* comparison, this process gives the same result as an everyday alphabetic ordering for strings containing only uppercase or only lowercase characters.

The library function **strcmp** compares two string arguments. Its prototype is:

```
int     strcmp( char const *s1, char const *s2 );
```

strcmp returns a value less than zero if s1 is less than s2; a value greater than zero if s1 is greater than s2; and zero if the two strings are equal.

Beginners often write

```
if( strcmp( a, b ) )
```

and assume that the result returned will be true if the strings are equal. The result is just the opposite though, because zero (false) is returned in this case. However, it is bad style to test this value as if it were boolean because it has three distinct outcomes: less, equal, and greater. Comparing the value to zero is therefore preferred.

Note that the Standard does not specify the specific values used to indicate inequalities. It only states that the value returned be greater than zero if the first string is greater than the second and be less than zero if the first string is less than the second. A common mistake is to assume that the values 1 and -1 will be returned, but this assumption is not always correct.

Because strcmp does not change either of its arguments, there isn't any danger of overflowing an array. However, as with the other unrestricted string functions, the string arguments must be NUL terminated. If they are not, strcmp will continue comparing bytes beyond the end of the data, and the result will have no meaning.

9.4 Length-Restricted String Functions

The library includes several functions that deal with strings in a different way. This group of functions takes an explicit length argument that limits how many characters can be copied or compared. These functions provide an easy mechanism to prevent unexpectedly long strings from overflowing their destinations.

The prototypes for these functions are shown on the next page. Like their unrestricted cousins, the results from strncpy and strncat are undefined if the source and destination arguments overlap.

```
char    *strncpy( char *dst, char const *src, size_t len );
char    *strncat( char *dst, char const *src, size_t len );
int     strncmp( char const *s1, char const *s2, size_t len );
```

Like `strcpy`, **strncpy** copies characters from the source string to the destination array. However, it always writes exactly *len* characters to `dst`. If `strlen( src )` is less than *len*, then `dst` is padded to a length of *len* with additional NUL characters. If `strlen( src )` is greater than or equal to *len*, then only *len* characters will be written to `dst`, *and the result will not be NUL-terminated!*

The result of a call to `strncpy` might not be a string, because strings must be terminated with a NUL byte. What happens if an unterminated sequence of characters is used where a string is required, for example, as an argument to `strlen`? The function will be unable to tell that the NUL is missing, so it will continue looking, character by character, until it finds one. It might not find one until hundreds of characters later, and the value returned by `strlen` will essentially be a random number. Or, the program might crash trying to access memory beyond what was allocated to it.

This problem only occurs when you create strings with the `strncpy` function, and then either use them with the `str---` functions or print them with the `%s` format code of `printf`. Before using the unrestricted functions, you must first ensure that the string is actually NUL-terminated. For example, consider this code fragment:

```
char    buffer[BSIZE];
...
strncpy( buffer, name, BSIZE );
buffer[BSIZE - 1] = '\0';
```

If the contents of `name` fit into `buffer`, the assignment has no effect. If `name` is too long, though, the assignment ensures that the string in `buffer` is properly terminated. Subsequent calls to `strlen` or other unrestricted string functions on this array will work properly.

Although **strncat** is also a length-restricted function, it works differently than `strncpy`. It appends up to *len* characters from *src* to the destination string. But `strncat` always appends a NUL character to the end of the result, and it does not pad the result with NULs like `strncpy`. Note that the length of the existing string in the destination array is *not* accounted for by `strncat`. It can write up to *len* characters plus a terminating NUL byte regardless of whether the initial contents of the destination argument leave enough room for them.

Finally, **strncmp** compares up to *len* characters of two strings. If the strings are unequal before or at the *len*'th character, the comparison stops as it would with strcmp. If the first len characters of the strings are equal, value zero is returned.

9.5 Basic String Searching

There are many functions in the library that search strings in various ways. This wide variety of tools gives the C programmer great flexibility.

9.5.1 Finding a Character

The easiest way to locate a specific character in a string is with the **strchr** and **strrchr** functions, whose prototypes are:

```
char    *strchr( char const *str, int ch );
char    *strrchr( char const *str, int ch );
```

Note that the second argument is an integer. It contains a character value, however. strchr searches the string str to find the first occurrence of the character ch. Then a pointer to this position is returned. If the character does not appear at all in the string, a NULL pointer is returned. strrchr works exactly the same except that it returns a pointer to the *last* (rightmost) occurrence of the character.

Here is an example:

```
char    string[20] = "Hello there, honey.";
char    *ans;

ans = strchr( string, 'h' );
```

ans will get the value string + 7 because the first 'h' appears in this position. Note that case is significant.

9.5.2 Finding Any of Several Characters

The **strpbrk** function is more general. Instead of searching for one specific character, it looks for the first occurrence of any of a group of characters. Its prototype is:

```
char      *strpbrk( char const *str, char const *group );
```

This function returns a pointer to the first character in `str` that matches *any* of the characters in `group`, or NULL if none matched.

In the following code fragment,

```
char      string[20] = "Hello there, honey.";
char      *ans;

ans = strpbrk( string, "aeiou" );
```

`ans` will get the value `string + 1` because this position is the first that contains any of the characters in the second argument. Once again, case is significant.

9.5.3 Finding a Substring

To locate a substring, **strstr** is used. Its prototype is:

```
char      *strstr( char const *s1, char const *s2 );
```

This function finds the first place in `s1` where the entire string `s2` begins and returns a pointer to this location. If `s2` does not appear in its entirety anywhere in `s1`, then NULL is returned. If the second argument is an empty string, then `s1` is returned.

The standard library includes neither a **strrstr** nor a **strrpbrk** function, but they are easy to implement if you need them. Program 9.2 shows one way of implementing `strrstr`. The same technique could be used for `strrpbrk`.

9.6 Advanced String Searching

The next group of functions simplify the location and extraction of individual substrings from a string.

9.6.1 Finding String Prefixes

The **strspn** and **strcspn** functions count characters at the beginning of a string. Their prototypes are shown at the top of page 253.

```
/*
** Look in the string s1 for the rightmost occurrence of the string
** s2, and return a pointer to where it begins.
*/
#include <string.h>

char    *
my_strrstr( char const *s1, char const *s2 )
{
        register char    *last;
        register char    *current;

        /*
        ** Initialize pointer for the last match we've found.
        */
        last = NULL;

        /*
        ** Search only if the second string is not empty.  If s2 is
        ** empty, return NULL.
        */
        if( *s2 != '\0' ){
                /*
                ** Find the first place where s2 appears in s1.
                */
                current = strstr( s1, s2 );

                /*
                ** Each time we find the string, save the pointer to
                ** where it begins.  Then look after the string for
                ** another occurrence.
                */
                while( current != NULL ){
                        last = current;
                        current = strstr( last + 1, s2 );
                }
        }

        /*
        ** Return pointer to the last occurrence we found.
        */
        return last;
}
```

Program 9.2   Find rightmost occurrence of a substring   mstrrstr.c

```
size_t strspn( char const *str, char const *group );
size_t strcspn( char const *str, char const *group );
```

The `group` string specifies one or more characters. `strspn` returns the number of characters at the beginning of `str` that match any of these characters. For example, if `group` contained the whitespace characters space, tab, and so forth, this function would return the number of whitespace characters found at the beginning of `str`. The next character of `str` would be the first non-whitespace character.

Consider this example:

```
int     len1, len2;
char    buffer[] = "25,142,330,Smith,J,239-4123";

len1 = strspn( buffer, "0123456789" );
len2 = strspn( buffer, ",0123456789" );
```

Of course, the buffer would not normally be initialized in this manner; it would contain data read in at run time. But with this value in the buffer, the variable `len1` would be set to two, and the variable `len2` would be set to 11. The following code will compute a pointer to the first non-whitespace character in a string.

```
ptr = buffer + strspn( buffer, " \n\r\f\t\v" );
```

`strcspn` works similarly except that only characters that are *not* in `group` are counted. The `c` in the name `strcspn` comes from the notion that the character group is *complemented*, that is, exchanged for all of the characters it did not originally contain. If you used the string " \n\r\f\t\v" for the `group` argument, this function would return the number of non-whitespace characters found at the beginning of the first argument.

9.6.2 Finding Tokens

A string often contains several individual parts that are somehow separated from each other. To process these parts one at a time, you must first extract them from the string.

This task is exactly what the **strtok** function accomplishes. It isolates individual parts, called *tokens*, from a string and discards the separators. Its prototype is:

```
char    *strtok( char *str, char const *sep );
```

The sep argument is a string that defines the set of characters that are used as separators. The first argument specifies a string that is assumed to contain zero or more tokens separated from one another by one or more characters from the sep string. strtok finds and NUL-terminates the next token in str, and returns a pointer to the token.

While it is doing its work, strtok modifies the string that it is processing. If the string must not be changed, copy it and use strtok on the copy.

If the first argument to strtok is not NULL, the function finds the first token in the string. strtok also saves its position in the string. If the first argument to strtok is NULL, the function uses the saved position to find the *next* token from the same string as before. strtok returns a NULL pointer when there aren't any more tokens in the string. Typically, a pointer to a string is passed on the first call to strtok. The function is then called repeatedly with a NULL first argument until it returns NULL.

Program 9.3 is a short example. This function extracts tokens from its argument and prints them one per line. The tokens are separated by white space. Do not be confused by the appearance of the for statement. It was broken onto three lines because of its length.

```
/*
** Extract whitespace-delimited tokens from a character array and
** print them one per line.
*/
#include <stdio.h>
#include <string.h>

void
print_tokens( char *line )
{
        static  char    whitespace[] = " \t\f\r\v\n";
        char    *token;

        for( token = strtok( line, whitespace );
            token != NULL;
            token = strtok( NULL, whitespace ) )
                printf( "Next token is %s\n", token );
}
```

Program 9.3   Extract tokens   token.c

If you wish, you may use different separator sets in each call to strtok. This technique is handy when different parts of a string are separated by different groups of characters.

 Because strtok saves local state information about the string it is parsing, you cannot use it to parse two strings concurrently. Thus, Program 9.3 would fail if the body of the for loop called a function that also called strtok.

9.7 Error Messages

When calls are made to the operating system to perform functions, such as opening files, errors that occur are reported by setting an external integer variable called errno to an error code. The **strerror** function takes one of these error codes as an argument and returns a pointer to a message describing the error. The prototype of this function is:

```
char *strerror( int error_number );
```

In fact, the returned value ought to be declared const, because you are not supposed to modify it.

9.8 Character Operations

The library includes two groups of functions that operate on individual characters, prototyped in the include file ctype.h. The first group is used in classifying characters, and the second group transforms them.

9.8.1 Character Classification

Each classification function takes an integer argument that contains a character value. The function tests the character and returns an integer true or false value.[38] Table 9.1 lists the classification functions and the test that each performs.

---

[38] Note that the Standard does not specify any particular value, so any nonzero value might be returned.

Function	Returns True if Its Argument Is
iscntrl	any control character.
isspace	a whitespace character: space ' ', form feed '\f', newline '\n', carriage return tab '\t', or vertical tab '\v'.
isdigit	a decimal digit 0 through 9.
isxdigit	a hexadecimal digit, which includes the decimal digits and the letters a through f and A through F.
islower	a lowercase letter a through z.
isupper	an uppercase letter A through Z.
isalpha	an alphabetic character a through z or A through Z.
isalnum	an alphabetic or a numeric character a through z, A through Z, or 0 through 9.
ispunct	punctuation: any character with a graphic (printable symbol) associated with it that is not alphanumeric.
isgraph	any character with a graphic associated with it.
isprint	any printing character, which includes the graphic characters and the space character.

Table 9.1   Character classification functions

9.8.2 Character Transformation

The transformation functions translate uppercase characters to lowercase and vice versa.

```
int tolower( int ch );
int toupper( int ch );
```

toupper returns the uppercase equivalent of its argument, and **tolower** returns the lowercase equivalent of its argument. If the argument to either function is not a character of the appropriate case, then it is returned unchanged.

Testing or manipulating characters directly reduces a program's portability. For example, consider the following statement, which attempts to test whether ch contains an uppercase character.

```
if( ch >= 'A' && ch <= 'Z' )
```

This statement works on machines using the ASCII character set, but fails on machines using the EBCDIC character set. On the other hand, the statement

```
if( isupper( ch ) )
```

will work correctly with any character set.

9.9 Memory Operations

By definition, a string is terminated with a NUL byte, so strings may not contain any NULs. However, it is not uncommon for nonstring data to contain zeros. You cannot use the string functions to process this kind of data because they would stop working when they reached the first NUL.

There is a related set of functions whose operations are similar to some of the string functions, but these functions deal with arbitrary sequences of bytes. Here are their prototypes.

```
void    *memcpy( void *dst, void const *src, size_t length );
void    *memmove( void *dst, void const *src, size_t length );
void    *memcmp( void const *a, void const *b, size_t length );
void    *memchr( void const *a, int ch, size_t length );
void    *memset( void *a, int ch, size_t length );
```

Each prototype includes an explicit argument to indicate how many bytes to process, but unlike the *strn---* functions, their operations do not stop if they encounter a NUL byte.

memcpy copies *length* bytes, beginning at src, into the memory beginning at dst. You can copy any type of value in this manner, so long as the third argument specifies the length of the value in bytes. The result is undefined if src and dst overlap in any way.

For example:

```
char    temp[SIZE], values[SIZE];
...
memcpy( temp, values, SIZE );
```

copies the SIZE bytes from the array values into the array temp.

But what if both were arrays of integers? Then the following statement would do the job:

```
memcpy( temp, values, sizeof( values ) );
```

No casts are needed on the first two arguments because the prototype calls for void pointers, and any type of pointer can be converted to a void *.

If only part of the array is to be copied, the desired count may be given for the third argument. For data that is larger than one byte, be sure to multiply the count by the size of each datum, for example:

```
memcpy( saved_answers, answers,
    count * sizeof( answers[ 0 ] ) );
```

You can also copy structures or arrays of structures with this technique.

memmove behaves exactly the same as memcpy except that its source and destination operands may overlap. Though it need not be implemented this way, the result of memmove is the same as the result obtained by copying the source operand to a temporary location that overlaps neither the source nor the destination, then copying from this temporary location to the destination operand. memmove usually cannot be implemented using the special byte-string handling instructions provided on some machines, so it may be slower than memcpy. However, memmove should be used when there is a real possibility of overlapping arguments, as in the following example.

```
/*
** Shift the values in the x array left one position.
*/
memmove( x, x + 1, ( count - 1 ) * sizeof( x[ 0 ] ) );
```

memcmp compares the *length* bytes of memory beginning at a to the bytes beginning at b. The values are compared byte by byte as unsigned characters, and the function returns the same type of value as strcmp—a negative value if a is less than b, a positive value if a is greater than b, and zero if they are equal. Because the values are compared as sequences of unsigned bytes, memcmp may give unexpected results if it is used to compare nonbyte data such as integers or floats.

memchr searches the *length* bytes beginning at a for the first occurrence of the character ch and returns a pointer to that location. If the character does not occur, NULL is returned.

Finally, **memset** sets each of the *length* bytes beginning at a to the character value ch. For example,

```
memset( buffer, 0, SIZE );
```

initializes the first SIZE bytes of the buffer to zero.

9.10 Summary

A string is a sequence of zero or more characters. The sequence is terminated by a NUL byte. The length of a string is the number of characters it contains. The standard library provides a host of functions that process strings; their prototypes are in the file string.h.

The strlen function computes the length of a string. The value that is returned is unsigned, so be careful when using it in expressions. strcpy copies a string from one location to another, and `strcat` appends a copy of a string to the end of another string. Both of these functions assume that their arguments are valid strings, and the results of both are undefined if the source and destination strings overlap. `strcmp` performs a lexicographic comparison of two strings. Its return value indicates whether the first string is less than, equal to, or greater than the second string.

The length-restricted functions `strncpy`, `strncat`, and `strncmp` are similar to their unrestricted counterparts. The difference is that these functions take a length argument. With `strncpy`, the length specifies how many characters will be written to the destination array. If the source string is longer than the length, the result will not be NUL terminated. The length argument to `strncat` indicates the maximum number of characters that will be copied from the source string, but the result is always NUL terminated. The length argument to `strncmp` limits the number of characters that are compared. If the strings do not differ within this length, they are considered equal.

There are several functions that search strings. `strchr` searches a string for the first occurrence of a character, and `strrchr` searches a string for the last occurrence of a character. `strpbrk` searches a string for the first occurrence of any character in a specified set. The `strstr` function searches a string for the first occurrence of another string.

More advanced string searches are also provided. The `strspn` function counts the number of characters at the beginning of a string that match any character in a specified set. `strcspn` counts the number of characters at the beginning of a string that do not match any of the characters in a specified set. The `strtok` function breaks a string into tokens. Each time it is called, it returns a pointer to the next token in the string. The tokens are separated by one or more characters from a specified set.

The `strerror` takes an error code as an argument. It returns a pointer to a string that describes the error.

A variety of functions are supplied for testing and transforming characters. Programs that use these functions are more portable than those that perform their own tests or transformations of characters. The `toupper` function converts a lowercase character to uppercase, and the `tolower` function converts a character the other way. The `iscntrl` function checks whether its argument is a control character, and `isspace` tests for white space. `isdigit` checks for a decimal digit, and `isxdigit` checks for hexadecimal digits. `islower` and `isupper` check for lowercase and uppercase characters, respectively. `isalpha` looks for alphabetic characters, `isalnum` looks for alphanumeric characters, and `ispunct` looks for punctuation characters. Finally, `isgraph` checks whether its argument has a printable graphic associated with it, and `isprint` checks for either a graphic character or a space.

The memxxx functions provide capabilities similar to some of the string functions, but process arbitrary byte values, including NUL. Each of the functions takes a length argument. memcpy copies bytes from a source to a destination. memmove performs the same function, but its behavior is well-defined when the source and destination arguments overlap. memcmp compares two sequences of bytes, and memchr searches a sequence of bytes for a specific value. Finally, memset stores a specified value in a sequence.

9.11 Summary of Cautions

1. Using strlen in expressions that should be signed (page 244).

2. Mixing signed and unsigned quantities in expressions (page 245).

3. Overflowing a short array by using strcpy to copy a long string into it (page 246).

4. Overflowing an array by appending a string that is too long using strcat (page 247).

5. Testing the result returned by strcmp as a boolean (page 248).

6. Comparing the value returned by strcmp to 1 or -1 (page 248).

7. Using character sequences that are not NUL terminated (page 248).

8. Producing unterminated strings with strncpy (page 249).

9. Mixing strncpy with strxxx (page 249).

10. Forgetting that strtok modifies the string that it processes (page 254).

11. The strtok function is not reentrant (page 255).

9.12 Summary of Programming Tips

1. Don't try to beat the library string functions by writing your own (page 245).

2. Using the library character classification and transformation functions enhances portability (page 256).

9.13 Questions

✎ 1. Is the absence of an explicit string data type in C an advantage or a disadvantage?

2. `strlen` returns an unsigned (`size_t`) quantity. Why is an unsigned value more appropriate than a signed value? Why is an unsigned value less appropriate?

3. Would there be any advantage in having `strcat` and `strcpy` return a pointer to the *end* of the destination string rather than returning a pointer to its beginning?

✎ 4. What is the simplest way to copy 50 bytes from the array `x` into the array `y`?

5. Suppose you have an array called `buffer` that is `BSIZE` bytes long, and you have copied a string into this array with the following statement:

```
strncpy( buffer, some_other_string, BSIZE - 1 );
```

Is it guaranteed that the result in `buffer` is a valid string?

6. What are the advantages of using

```
if( isalpha( ch ) ){
```

instead of the explicit test

```
if( ch >= 'A' && ch <= 'Z' ||
    ch >= 'a' && ch <= 'z' ){
```

7. How can the following code be simplified?

```
for( p_str = message; *p_str != '\0'; p_str++ ){
    if( islower( *p_str ) )
            *p_str = toupper( *p_str );
}
```

✎ 8. How do the expressions below differ?

```
memchr( buffer, 0, SIZE ) - buffer
strlen( buffer )
```

9.14 Programming Exercises

★ 1. Write a program that reads from the standard input and computes the percentage of characters it finds in each of the following categories:

> control characters
> whitespace characters
> digits
> lower case letters
> upper case letters
> punctuation characters
> non-printable characters

Use the character categories that are defined for the ctype.h functions.

✍ ★ 2. Write a function called my_strnlen that is similar to strlen but is able to handle unterminated strings created with the *strn---* functions. You will have to pass an argument containing the size of the array that holds the string to be tested.

★ 3. Write a function called my_strcpy that is similar to strcpy but will not overflow the destination array. The result of the copy must be a true string.

★ 4. Write a function called my_strcat that is similar to strcat but will not overflow the destination array. The result must be a true string.

★ 5. Write the function

```
void my_strncat( char *dest, char *src, int dest_len );
```

which concatenates the string in src to the end of the string in dest, making sure not to overflow the dest array, which is dest_len bytes long. Unlike strncat, this function takes into account the length of the string already in dest thereby insuring that the array bounds are not exceeded.

✍ ★ 6. Write a strcpy replacement called my_strcpy_end that returns a pointer to the end of the destination string (that is, a pointer to the NUL byte) rather than a pointer to the beginning of the destination string.

★ 7. Write a function called my_strrchr with this prototype:

```
char *my_strrchr( char const *str, int ch );
```

The function is similar to strchr except that it returns a pointer to the last (rightmost) occurrence of the character.

★ 8. Write a function called `my_strnchr` with this prototype:

```
char *my_strnchr( char const *str, int ch, int which );
```

The function is similar to `strchr` except that the third argument specifies which occurrence of the character is desired. For example, if the third argument is one, the function behaves exactly like `strchr`. If the third argument is two, the function returns a pointer to the second occurrence of `ch` in the string `str`.

★★ 9. Write a function with this prototype:

```
int count_chars( char const *str,
    char const *chars );
```

The function should look through the first argument and return the number of characters that match characters in the second argument.

★★★ 10. Write this function:

```
int palindrome( char *string );
```

which returns a true value if the argument string is a palindrome and false otherwise. A palindrome is a string that reads the same forwards and backwards.[39] The function should ignore all nonalphabetic characters, and character comparisons should be case independent.

⌂ ★★★ 11. Write a program that scans the standard input and counts the number of times the word "the" appears. The comparison should be case independent, so "The" and "THE" don't count. You may assume that words will be separated from each other by one or more white-space characters and that the input lines will be less than 100 characters in length. The count should be written to the standard output.

★★★ 12. There is a technique for encrypting data that uses a word as its key. Here is how it works. First, a word is chosen as the key, for example, TRAIL-BLAZERS. If the word contains any duplicate letters, only the first of each is kept; the rest are discarded. Now the modified word is written beneath the alphabet, as shown here:

```
A B C D E F G H I J K L M N O P Q R S T U V W X Y Z
T R A I L B Z E S
```

---

[39] When the spacing, punctuation, and capitalization are ignored. An example is what Adam might have said when he first met Eve: "Madam, I'm Adam."

Finally, the bottom line is completed by filling in the remaining letters of the alphabet:

```
A B C D E F G H I J K L M N O P Q R S T U V W X Y Z
T R A I L B Z E S C D F G H J K M N O P Q U V W X Y
```

To encrypt a message, each letter in the message is located in the top row, and the corresponding character from the bottom row is used instead. Thus, ATTACK AT DAWN would be encrypted using this key as TPPTAD TP ITVH.

In this first of three programs, you will write the function

```
int prepare_key( char *key );
```

which accepts a string containing the desired key word and converts it as described above to the array of encoded characters. Assume that the key argument is an array at least 27 characters long. The function must convert all the characters in the key to either upper- or lowercase (your choice), eliminate any duplicate letters from the word, and then fill in the rest of the alphabet in the same case you chose earlier. If the processing succeeds, the function returns a true result. If the key argument is empty or contains any nonalphabetic characters, the function should return a false result.

★★ 13. Write the function

```
void encrypt( char *data, char const *key );
```

which uses a key produced by prepare_key to encrypt the characters in data. Nonalphabetic characters in data are not changed, but alphabetic characters are encrypted using the key provided by replacing the original character with the coded character. The case of alphabetic characters should be preserved.

★★ 14. The final part of this problem is to write the function

```
void decrypt( char *data, char const *key );
```

which takes an encrypted string and reconstructs the original message. Except for decrypting, this function should work the same as encrypt.

★★★ 15. The standard I/O library does not provide a mechanism for putting commas in large integers when they are printed. For this exercise you will write a program that provides this capability for dollar amounts. The function will convert a string of digits (representing an amount in pennies) to dollars as illustrated by the following examples.

Input	Output	Input	Output
(empty)	$0.00	12345	$123.45
1	$0.01	123456	$1,234.56
12	$0.12	1234567	$12,345.67
123	$1.23	12345678	$123,456.78
1234	$12.34	123456789	$1,234,567.89

Here is a prototype for the function:

```
void dollars( char *dest, char const *src );
```

src will point to the characters to be formatted. (You may assume that these are all digits.) Your function should format the characters as shown in the examples, leaving the resulting string in dest. Be sure that the string you create is terminated with a NUL byte. src should not be modified. Use pointers rather than subscripts.

Hint: First find the length of the string in the second argument. This value will help determine where the commas should be inserted. Also, the decimal point and last two digits should be the only special case you need to handle.

★★★ 16. This program is similar to the previous one but is more general. It formats a string of digits as specified by a format string, similar to the "print using" statement found in many implementations of BASIC. The function should have this prototype:

```
int format( char *format_string,
    char const *digit_string );
```

Working from right to left, the digits in digit_string are copied into the format_string according to the characters initially found in format_string. Note that format_string is modified as a result of this process. Make sure that the format_string is still NUL-terminated when you are finished with it. The returned value is either true or false depending on whether any errors occurred in formatting.

The format string may contain the following characters:

\#   Working from right to left in both strings, each pound sign in the format string is replaced by the next digit from the digit string. If the digit string runs out, all remaining pound signs in the format string are replaced with blanks (but see the discussion for periods below).

,   A comma is not changed if there will be at least one digit to its left in the result, otherwise it is replaced with a blank.

. A period is always left as a period. If there isn't a digit to the left of the period, zeros are filled in from where the digits ended to the position just to the left of the period.

The following examples illustrate several calls to this function. The ¤ symbol is used to indicate a blank space.

Format	Digits	Resulting Format
#####	12345	12345
#####	123	¤¤123
##,###	1234	¤1,234
##,###	123	¤¤¤123
##,###	1234567	34,567
#,###,###.##	123456789	1,234,567.89
#,###,###.##	1234567	¤¤¤12,345.67
#,###,###.##	123	¤¤¤¤¤¤¤¤1.23
#,###,###.##	1	¤¤¤¤¤¤¤¤0.01
#####.#####	1	¤¤¤¤0.00001

To simplify the project, you may assume that the format string is correctly formed. There will always be at least one pound sign to the left and to the right of a period and every comma, and commas will never appear to the right of a period. The only errors you need to check for are:

a. more digits in the digit string than there are pound signs in the format string (as in the bottom left example above), and

b. an empty digit string.

Either of these errors result in the function returning FALSE, otherwise it should return TRUE. If the digit string is empty, the format string should be returned unchanged. You will learn more if you use pointers rather than subscripts.

Hint: Start by getting pointers to the end of both the format string and the digit string, then work from right to left. You must retain the pointer values that were passed as arguments so that you can determine when you have reached the left end of these strings.

★★★★ 17. This program is similar to the previous two but more general still. It allows the caller to put commas in large numbers, suppress leading zeros, provide a floating dollar sign, and so forth.

The function is similar in operation to the Edit and Mark instruction on the IBM 370 computer. It has this prototype:

```
char *edit( char *pattern, char const *digits );
```

The basic idea is simple. The pattern is a picture of what the result should look like. Characters from the digit string are copied into the pattern string *from left to right* in a manner determined by this picture.

The first significant digit in the digit string is important. All characters in the result that are to the left of the first significant digit are replaced by a "fill" character, and the function will return a pointer to the place in the result where the first significant digit was stored. (The calling program can use the returned pointer to put a floating dollar sign immediately to the left of the value.) The resulting output looks like what you may have seen printed on checks—all of the space to the left of the value is filled in with stars or some other character.

Before the detailed workings of the function are described, it will be helpful to see some examples of its operation. For clarity, the ¤ character is used to represent a space. The underline in the result indicates the character to which the returned value points. If there isn't an underlined character, the returned value was NULL.

Pattern	Digits	Result
*#,###	1234	*1,234
*#,###	123456	*1,234
*#,###	12	*1,2
*#,###	0012	****12
*#,###	¤¤12	****12
*#,###	¤1¤¤	***100
*X#Y#Z	(empty)	**
¤#,##!.##	¤23456	¤¤¤234.56
¤#,##!.##	023456	¤¤¤234.56
$#,##!.##	¤¤¤456	$$$$4.56
$#,##!.##	0¤¤¤¤6	$$$$0.06
$#,##!.##	0	$$$
$#,##!.##	1	$1,
$#,##!.##	Hi¤there	$H,i0t.he

Now, the details. The first argument is the pattern, and the first character in the pattern is the "fill character." The function uses the digit string to modify the remaining characters of the pattern to produce the output string. The pattern is overwritten in this process. The output string cannot be longer than the original pattern, so there is no danger of (and no need to check for) overflowing the first argument.

The pattern is processed character by character from left to right. For each character after the fill character, one of three things happens: (a) the character is left unchanged, (b) it is replaced by a character from the digit string, or (c) it is replaced by the fill character.

The digit string is also processed from left to right, but it is never modified in any way. Although it is called a "digit string," it can contain any characters, as one of the above examples illustrates. However, every space in the digit string should be treated (and produce the same results) as if it were the digit 0.

The function must keep a "significance" flag, which remembers whether any significant digits have been copied from the digit string. Leading spaces and 0's in the digit string are not significant; all other characters are.

It is an error for either the pattern or digit arguments to be NULL. In this case, the function should immediately return NULL.

The following table lists all processing that is required. The columns headed `signif` refer to the significance flag. "Pattern" and "Digit" refer to the next character in the pattern string and digit string, respectively. The left side of the table lists all of the different cases that might occur. The right side describes the processing needed for each case. For example, if the next pattern character is '#', the significance indicator is false, and the next character in the digit string is '0', replace the '#' in the pattern with a copy of the fill character and don't change the significance indicator.

If you find this . . .			_Then you do this . . ._		
Pattern	signif	**Digit**	**Pattern**	signif	**Notes**
'\0'	(doesn't matter)	(not used)	(unchanged)	(unchanged)	Return saved pointer
	(doesn't matter)	'\0'	'\0'	(unchanged)	Return saved pointer
'#'	false	'0' or ' '	fill char	(unchanged)	
		any other	the digit	true	Save pointer to this char
	true	any	the digit	(unchanged)	
'!'	(doesn't matter)	'\0'	'\0'	(unchanged)	Return saved pointer
	false	any	the digit	true	Save pointer to this char
	true	any	the digit	(unchanged)	
anything else	false	(not used)	fill char	(unchanged)	
	true	(not used)	(unchanged)	(unchanged)	

10

Structures and Unions

Data frequently exists in groups. For example, an employer must keep track of the name, age, and salary of each employee. Accessing these values is simplified if they can be stored together. However, if the values are different types, as they are in this example, they cannot be stored together in an array. In C, values with dissimilar types can be stored together using a structure.

10.1 Structure Basics

An *aggregate* data type is one that can hold more than one individual piece of data at a time. C provides two types of aggregate data, arrays and structures. Arrays are collections of elements of the same type, and individual elements are selected through a subscript or indirection on a pointer.

A *structure* is also a collection of values, called *members*, but the members of a structure may be of different types. A structure is quite similar to a *record* in Pascal or Modula.

Array elements can be accessed via a subscript only because all of the elements are the same size. The situation is different with structures. Because a structure's members can be of different sizes, subscripts cannot be used to access them. Instead, structure members are given names and are accessed by those names.

This distinction is important. A structure is not an array of its members. Unlike an array name, the name of a structure variable is not replaced with a pointer when it is used in an expression. Subscripts cannot be used on a structure variable to select specific members.

A structure variable is a scalar, so you can perform the same kinds of operations with it that you can with other scalars. Structures may be passed as arguments to functions, they may be returned by functions, and structures of

269

the same type may be assigned to one another. You can declare pointers to structures, take the address of structure variables, and declare arrays of structures. However, we must first cover a few more basics before discussing these issues.

10.1.1 Structure Declarations

Structures are declared by listing the members that they will contain. This list includes the type and the name of each member.

```
struct tag { member-list } variable-list ;
```

This structure declaration syntax requires some explanation. The optional fields cannot all be omitted—at least two of them must appear.[40]

Here are several examples.

```
struct {
        int     a;
        char    b;
        float   c;
} x;
```

This declaration creates a single variable named x, which contains three members: an integer, a character and a float.

```
struct {
        int     a;
        char    b;
        float   c;
} y[20], *z;
```

This declaration creates an array y of twenty structures and z, which is a pointer to a structure of this type.

These two declarations are treated by the compiler as entirely different types, even though their member lists are identical. Thus, the variables y and z are a different type than x, so the statement

```
z = &x;
```

---

[40] An exception to this rule is the incomplete declaration of structure tag, described later in this chapter.

is illegal. But does this fact mean that all structures of a given type must be created in a single declaration?

Fortunately, no. The *tag* field allows a name to be given to the member list so that it can be referenced in subsequent declarations. The tag allows many declarations to use the same member list and thus create structures of the same type. Here is an example.

```
struct   SIMPLE   {
         int     a;
         char    b;
         float   c;
};
```

The declaration associates the tag SIMPLE with this member list. The declaration doesn't have a variable list, so it doesn't create any variables.

This declaration is similar to making a cookie cutter. A cookie cutter determines the shape of cookies yet to be made, but the cookie cutter is not a cookie. The tag identifies a pattern for declaring future variables, but neither the tag nor the pattern are variables.

```
struct   SIMPLE  x;
struct   SIMPLE  y[20], *z;
```

These declarations use the tag to create variables. They create the same variables as the first two examples but with one important difference—now x, y, and z are all the same kind of structure.

Another good technique for declaring structures is to create a new type with a typedef, as in the following example.

```
typedef struct   {
         int     a;
         char    b;
         float   c;
} Simple;
```

This technique has almost the same effect as declaring a structure tag. The difference is that Simple is now a type name rather than a structure tag, so subsequent declarations would look like this one:

```
Simple  x;
Simple  y[20], *z;
```

If you want to use a particular structure in more than one source file, you should put the tag declaration or typedef in a header file. You can then #include the declaration wherever it is needed.

10.1.2 Structure Members

In the examples so far, I have used only simple types for members. But any kind of variable that can be declared outside of a structure may also be used as a structure member. Specifically, structure members can be scalars, arrays, pointers, and even other structures.

Here is a more complex example:

```
struct  COMPLEX {
        float    f;
        int      a[20];
        long     *lp;
        struct  SIMPLE  s;
        struct  SIMPLE  sa[10];
        struct  SIMPLE  *sp;
};
```

The members of a structure may have names that are identical to members of other structures, so the member a of this structure doesn't conflict with the member a which is a part of the struct SIMPLE s. As you will see next, the way in which members are accessed allows either member to be specified without ambiguity.

10.1.3 Direct Member Access

The members of a structure variable are accessed with the dot operator, which takes two operands. The left operand is the name of a structure variable and the right operand is the name of the desired member. The result of this expression is the designated member. For instance, consider the declaration

```
struct  COMPLEX comp;
```

The member named a is an array, so the expression comp.a selects that member. This expression *is* an array name, so you can use it in any context in which an array name could be used. Similarly, the member s is a structure, so the expression comp.s *is* the name of a structure variable and may be used in any way that we might use an ordinary structure variable. Specifically, we can use this expression as the left operand of another dot operator, as in (comp.s).a, to select the member named a of the structure s, which is a member of the structure comp. The dot operator associates from left to right so we do not need the parentheses; the expression comp.s.a is equivalent.

Here is a more complex example. The member sa is an array of structures, so comp.sa is an array name whose value is a pointer constant.

Applying a subscript to this expression, as in `(comp.sa) [4]`, yields one element of the array. But this element is a structure, so we can use another dot operator to get one of its members. Here is the expression:

```
( (comp.sa) [4] ) .c
```

The subscript and dot operators have the same precedence and all associate left to right, so we don't need these parentheses either. The expression

```
comp.sa[4].c
```

is equivalent.

10.1.4 Indirect Member Access

How do you access the members of a structure if all you have is a pointer to it? The first step is to apply indirection to the pointer, which takes you to the structure. Then you use the dot operator to select a member. However, the dot operator has higher precedence than the indirection, so you must use parentheses to ensure that the indirection is evaluated first. As an example, suppose an argument to a function is a pointer to a structure, as in this prototype:

```
void    func( struct COMPLEX *cp );
```

The function can access the member f of the structure to which this variable points with this expression:

```
(*cp).f
```

The indirection follows the pointer to the structure; once there the dot operator selects a member.

Because this notation is a nuisance, C provides a more convenient operator to do this job—the `->` or arrow operator. Like the dot, the arrow takes two operands, but the left operand must be a *pointer* to a structure. The arrow operator applies indirection to the left operand to follow the pointer, and then selects the member specified by the right operand exactly like the dot operator. The indirection is built into the arrow operator, though, so we don't need an explicit indirection or the accompanying parentheses. Here are a few examples using the same pointer as before.

```
cp->f
cp->a
cp->s
```

The first expression accesses the floating-point member. The second is an array name, and the third is a structure. Shortly you will see numerous additional examples to clarify accessing structure members.

10.1.5 Self-Referential Structures

Is it legal for a structure to contain a member that is the same type as the structure? Here is an example to illustrate this idea.

```
struct  SELF_REF1 {
        int     a;
        struct  SELF_REF1 b;
        int     c;
};
```

This type of self reference is not legal, because the member b is another complete structure that will contain its own member b. This second member is yet another complete structure and contains its own member b, and so forth, forever. The problem is somewhat like a recursive program that never stops recursing. But the following declaration is legal. Can you see the difference?

```
struct  SELF_REF2 {
        int     a;
        struct  SELF_REF2 *b;
        int     c;
};
```

The difference between this declaration and the previous one is that b is now a pointer rather than a structure. The compiler knows the size of a pointer to a structure even before the size of the structure has been determined, so this self reference is legal.

If the idea of a structure containing a pointer to itself seems strange, keep in mind that it will actually be pointing to a *different* structure of the same type. More advanced data structures, such as linked lists and trees, are implemented with this technique. Each structure points to the next element on the list or down this branch of a tree.

Watch out for this trap:

```
typedef struct   {
        int     a;
        SELF_REF3 *b;
        int     c;
} SELF_REF3;
```

The intent of this declaration is to create SELF_REF3 as the type name for this structure. It fails, however. The type name SELF_REF3 only becomes defined at the end of the declaration, so it is undefined inside of the declaration.

The solution is to define a structure tag to use in declaring b, as shown next.

```
typedef struct   SELF_REF3_TAG {
          int      a;
          struct   SELF_REF3_TAG *b;
          int      c;
} SELF_REF3;
```

10.1.6 Incomplete Declarations

Occasionally you will have to declare structures that are mutually dependent, that is, each contains one or more members of the other type. As with self referential structures, at least one of the structures must refer to the other only through pointers. The problem is in the declaration: if each structure refers to the other's structure tag, which one is declared first?

The solution to this problem is the *incomplete declaration*, which declares an identifier to be a structure tag. We can then use the tag in declarations where the size of the structure is not needed, such as declaring pointers to it. A subsequent declaration associates a member list with the tag.

Consider this example, in which two different structure types each contain a pointer to the other.

```
struct  B;

struct  A        {
        struct  B        *partner;
        /* other declarations */
};

struct  B        {
        struct  A        *partner;
        /* other declarations */
};
```

The incomplete declaration of the tag B is needed in the member list of A. Once A has been declared, the member list for B can be declared.

10.1.7 Initializing Structures

Structures can be initialized in much the same way as arrays. A comma-separated initializer list enclosed in braces is used to specify the values for the structure members. The values are written in the order given in the member list. Missing values cause the remaining members to get default initialization.

Structures containing array or structure members are initialized similar to multidimensional arrays. A complete initializer list for the aggregate member is nested within the initializer list for the structure. Here is an example:

```
struct   INIT_EX {
         int      a;
         short    b[10];
         Simple   c;
} x = {
         10,
         { 1, 2, 3, 4, 5 },
         { 25, 'x', 1.9 }
};
```

10.2 Structures, Pointers, and Members

The operators for accessing structures and their members directly and through pointers are quite simple, but they can become confusing when applied in complicated situations. Here are some examples to help you better understand how the operators work. The examples use the following declarations.

```
typedef struct   {
         int      a;
         short    b[2];
} Ex2;
typedef struct EX {
         int      a;
         char     b[3];
         Ex2      c;
         struct   EX       *d;
} Ex;
```

Structures of type Ex will be pictured like this:

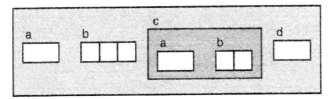

The structures are pictured this way to make the examples clearer. In fact, the diagram is not completely accurate, because the compiler avoids wasting space between the members whenever it can.

The first examples will use these declarations:

```
Ex      x = { 10, "Hi", { 5, { -1, 25 } }, 0 };
Ex      *px = &x;
```

which produce the following variables:

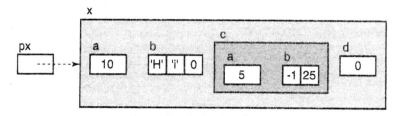

We will now examine and diagram different expressions using the notation from Chapter 6.

10.2.1 Accessing the Pointer

Let's begin with the pointer variable. The R-value of the expression `px` is:

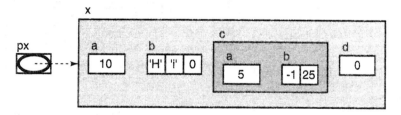

`px` is a pointer variable but there isn't any indirection operator, so the value of the expression is the contents of `px`. The L-value of this expression is:

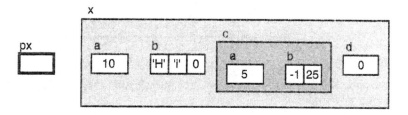

which shows that the old value of `px` is about to be replaced by a new value.

Now consider the expression px + 1. This expression is not a legal L-value because its value is not stored in any identifiable memory location. The expression's R-value is more interesting. If px had been pointing to an element of an array of structures, this expression would point to the next structure in the array. As it is, the expression is illegal because there is no way of telling whether what comes next in memory is one of these structures or something else. The compiler is not able to detect such errors, so it is up to you to determine when pointer arithmetic is meaningful.

10.2.2 Accessing the Structure

We can apply indirection to the pointer with the * operator. The R-value of the expression *px is the entire structure to which px points.

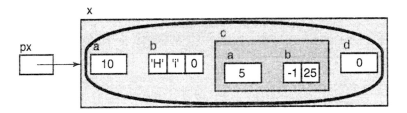

The indirection follows the arrow, which is shown as a solid line, and the result is the whole structure. You can assign this expression to another structure of the same type, or you can use it as the left operand of the dot operator to select a specific member. You can also pass it as an argument to a function or return it as the value of a function (though there are some efficiency concerns about these last two operations that will be discussed later). The L-value of the expression *px is:

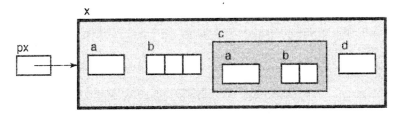

Here, the structure is about to receive a new value, or more precisely, new values for all of its members. As an L-value, it is the *place* that is important, not the values contained in the place.

The expression *px + 1 is illegal, because the result of *px is a structure. Addition is not defined between structures and integers. But what about the expression * (px + 1)? If x had been an element of an array, this expression would refer to the structure that followed it. But x is a scalar, so this expression is actually illegal.

10.2.3 Accessing Structure Members

Now let's look at the arrow operator. The R-value of the expression px->a is

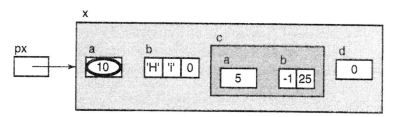

The -> operator applies indirection to px (indicated by the solid arrow) in order to get the structure, and then selects the a member. The expression px->a is used when you have a pointer to a structure but do not know its name. If you knew the name of this structure, you could use the equivalent expression x.a instead.

Let's pause here and compare the expressions *px and px->a to each other. In both cases, the address in px is used to find the structure. But the first member in the structure is a, so the address of a is the same as the address of the structure. It would seem, then, that px points to the structure *and* to the first member of the structure: after all, they both have the same address. This analysis is only half correct, though. Although both addresses have the same value, they have different types. The variable px was declared as a pointer to a structure, so the result of the expression *px is the whole structure, not its first member.

Let's create a pointer to an integer.

```
int     *pi;
```

Can we make pi point to the integer member a? If pi had the same value as px, then the result of the expression *pi would be the member a. But the assignment

```
pi = px;
```

is illegal because their types do not match. Using a cast works,

```
pi = (int *)px;
```

but is dangerous because it circumvents the compiler's type checking. The correct expression is simpler—to get a pointer to px->a, use the & operator:

```
pi = &px->a;
```

The precedence of the -> operator is higher than that of &, so parentheses are not needed in this expression. Let's examine a diagram of &px->a:

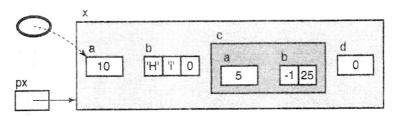

Note how the value in the oval points directly to the a member of the structure, as opposed to px, which points to the entire structure. After the assignment above, pi and px will have the same value. But their types are different, so the result of applying indirection to them will also be different: *px is the whole structure, and *pi is a single integer.

Here is another example using the arrow operator. The value of px->b is a pointer constant because b is an array. This expression is not a legal L-value. Here is its R-value.

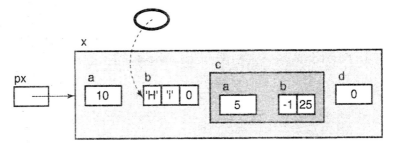

If we add indirection to this expression, it selects the first element of the array. With a subscript or pointer arithmetic, other elements of the array can be obtained as well. The expression px->b[1] selects the second array element, like this:

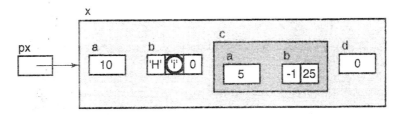

10.2.4 Accessing a Nested Structure

To access the member c, which is a structure, use the expression px->c. Its
R-value is the entire structure.

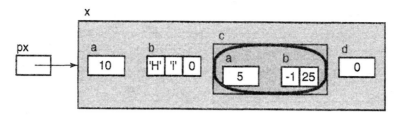

The dot operator can be added to this expression to access specific members of
c. For example, the expression px->c.a has the following R-value:

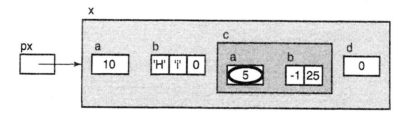

This expression contains both the dot and arrow operators. The arrow is used
because px is not a structure, it *points to* a structure. Then the dot operator is
used because px->c does not point to a structure, it *is* a structure.

Here is a more complex expression:

```
*px->c.b
```

Examining this expression is easy if you take one step at a time. There are
three operators, and the arrow goes first. px->c gives the structure c. Adding
.b to the expression selects the member b from structure c. b is an array, so
px->c.b is a (constant) pointer to the first element of the array. Finally, the
indirection is applied to this pointer, so the result is the first element of the
array. The expression is diagrammed below.

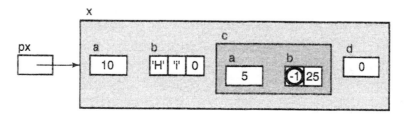

10.2.5 Accessing a Pointer Member

The expression px->d gives the result you would expect—its R-value is 0, and its L-value is the location itself. The expression *px->d is more interesting. Here indirection is applied to the pointer value found in the member d. But d contains the null pointer, so it doesn't point to anything. Dereferencing a null pointer is an error, but as discussed earlier, some environments will not catch it at run time. On these machines, the program will access whatever is at location zero as if it were one of these structures, and then continue merrily on as if nothing were wrong. This example illustrates the importance of checking to see that pointers really point to something before dereferencing them.

Let's create another structure and set x.d to point to it.

```
Ex      y;
x.d = &y;
```

Now we can evaluate *px->d.

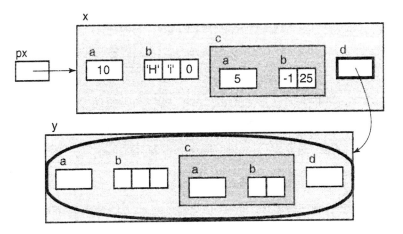

The member d points to a structure, so applying indirection to it yields the entire structure. The new structure was not initialized explicitly, so no values are shown for its members in the diagram.

As you may expect, members of this new structure can be selected by adding more operators to the expression. We use the arrow because d points to a structure. What do these expressions accomplish?

```
px->d->a
px->d->b
px->d->c
px->d->c.a
px->d->c.b[1]
```

Here is a diagram of the R-value of the last expression.

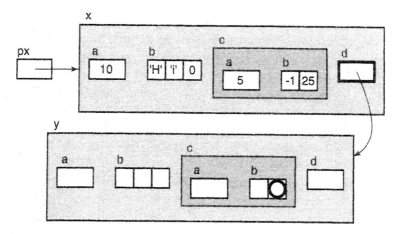

10.3 Structure Storage Allocation

How are structures actually stored in memory? The diagrams in the previous examples imply that structures contain a lot of empty space. This picture is not entirely accurate. Memory is allocated for each of the members, one after another, in the order given by the member list. Extra memory is used only when needed to get the correct boundary alignment of a member.

To illustrate, consider this structure:

```
struct   ALIGN    {
         char     a;
         int      b;
         char     c;
};
```

On a machine whose integers occupy four bytes and must begin at a byte whose address is evenly divisible by four, this structure would appear like this in memory:

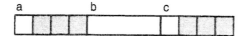

The compiler is forbidden to skip bytes for boundary alignment at the beginning of a structure, so all structures must begin on whatever boundary is required for the most stringent data type. Thus, the member a, shown by the leftmost box, begins at an address divisible by four. The next member is an integer, so three bytes (shown in gray) must be skipped to reach an appropriate boundary. After the integer comes the last character.

If a second variable of the same type were declared, it would have to begin on a boundary of four as well, so three more bytes would be skipped at the end of the structure. Thus, each structure would require twelve bytes of memory but would only use six of them, which is not very good utilization.

You can minimize the space lost to boundary alignment in structures by rearranging the member list in the structure declaration so that the members with the strictest boundary requirements appear first and those with the weakest requirements appear last. For example, this structure

```
struct  ALIGN2  {
        int     b;
        char    a;
        char    c;
};
```

contains the same members as the previous structure, but requires only eight bytes, a savings of 33%. The two characters can be stored adjacent to one another, so the only wasted space is the two bytes skipped after the structure.

There may be good reasons why we might not want to rearrange the members of a structure to reduce the memory lost to alignment. For example, we may want to keep related structure members together for easier maintenance and readability. Lacking any such reasons, however, the members of a structure should be arranged according to their boundary needs in order to minimize the memory that will be lost to alignment.

When the program will be creating hundreds or thousands of the structures, the need to reduce wasted memory can become more important than readability concerns. In this type of situation, adding comments to the declaration may help regain much of the lost readability.

`sizeof` gives the total size of a structure, which includes any bytes that are skipped for boundary alignment. If you must determine the actual position of a member in a structure, taking into account boundary alignment, use the **offsetof** macro (which is defined in `stddef.h`).

```
offsetof( type, member )
```

type is the type of the structure, and *member* is the name of the member you want. The result is a `size_t` value specifying the number of bytes from the beginning of the structure where the specified member begins. For example, with the declaration above,

```
offsetof( struct ALIGN, b )
```

returns four.

10.4 Structures as Function Arguments

A structure variable is a scalar and can be used wherever any other scalar can be used. Thus it is legal to pass a structure as an argument to a function, but this technique is often inappropriate.

The following code fragments are from a program written to operate an electronic cash register. Here is the declaration for a structure that contains information about an individual transaction.

```
typedef struct  {
        char      product[PRODUCT_SIZE];
        int       quantity;
        float     unit_price;
        float     total_amount;
} Transaction;
```

When a transaction occurs, there are many steps involved, one of which is printing the receipt. Let's look at some different ways to perform this task.

```
void
print_receipt( Transaction trans )
{
        printf( "%s\n", trans.product );
        printf( "%d @ %.2f total %.2f\n", trans.quantity,
            trans.unit_price, trans.total_amount );
}
```

If current_trans is a Transaction structure, we could call the function like this:

```
print_receipt( current_trans );
```

This approach produces the correct result, but it is inefficient because the call-by-value argument passing of C requires that a copy of the argument be given to the function. If PRODUCT_SIZE is 20 and we are using a machine with four-byte integers and floats, this particular structure occupies 32 bytes. To pass it as an argument, 32 bytes must be copied onto the stack and then discarded later.

Compare the previous function with this one:

```
void
print_receipt( Transaction *trans )
{
        printf( "%s\n", trans->product );
        printf( "%d @ %.2f total %.2f\n", trans->quantity,
            trans->unit_price, trans->total_amount );
}
```

which would be called in this manner:

```
print_receipt( &current_trans );
```

Here, a pointer to the structure is passed. The pointer is smaller than the entire structure and therefore more efficient to push on the stack. The price paid for passing a pointer is that we must use indirection in the function to access the members of the structure. The bigger the structure, the more efficient it is to pass a pointer to it.

On many machines, you can improve the efficiency of the pointer version by declaring the parameter to be a register variable. On some machines, this declaration requires an extra instruction at the beginning of the function to copy the argument from the stack (where it was passed) to the register in which it will be used. But if the function performs indirection on the pointer more than two or three times, then the savings realized in the indirections will be greater than the cost of the additional instruction.

A drawback of passing a pointer is that the function is now able to modify the values in the calling program's structure variable. If it is not supposed to do this, you can use the const keyword in the function to prevent such modifications. Here is what the function prototype looks like with these two changes:

```
void print_receipt( register Transaction const *trans );
```

Let's move on to another step in processing a transaction: computing the total amount due. You would expect that the function compute_total_-amount would modify the total_amount member of the structure. There are three ways to accomplish this task. Let's look at the least efficient way first. The following function

```
Transaction
compute_total_amount( Transaction trans )
{
        trans.total_amount =
            trans.quantity * trans.unit_price;
        return trans;
}
```

would be called in this manner:

```
current_trans = compute_total_amount( current_trans );
```

A copy of the structure is passed as an argument and modified. Then a copy of the modified structure is returned, so the structure is copied twice.

A slightly better method is to return only the modified value rather than the entire structure. This approach is used by the second function.

```
float
compute_total_amount( Transaction trans )
{
        return trans.quantity * trans.unit_price;
}
```

However, this function must be invoked in this manner:

```
current_trans.total_amount =
    compute_total_amount( current_trans );
```

This version is better than returning the entire structure, but the technique only works when a single value is to be computed. If we wanted the function to modify two or more members of the structure, this approach fails. Besides, there is still the overhead of passing the structure as an argument. Worse, it requires that the calling program have knowledge of the contents of the structure, specifically, the name of the total field.

The third approach, passing a pointer, is better:

```
void
compute_total_amount( register Transaction *trans )
{
        trans->total_amount =
            trans->quantity * trans->unit_price;
}
```

This function is called like this:

```
compute_total_amount( &current_trans );
```

Now, the `total_amount` field in the caller's structure is modified directly; there is no need to pass the entire structure into the function or to copy the modified structure as the return value. This version is more efficient than either of the other two functions. In addition, the caller no longer needs to know about the internals of the structure, so modularity is also improved.

When *should* you pass a structure, rather than a pointer, as an argument to a function? Rarely. Only when a structure is extremely small (the size of a pointer, or smaller) is it as efficient to pass the structure as it is to pass a pointer to it. For most structures, it is more efficient to pass a pointer. If you want the function to be able to modify any of the structure's members, a pointer is also preferred.

With very early K&R C compilers, you couldn't pass structures as arguments—the compiler simply did not allow it. Later K&R compilers did allow structure arguments. However, these compilers did not support const, so the only way to prevent a function from modifying a structure argument was to pass a copy of the structure.

10.5 Bit Fields

One last thing to mention about structures is their capability for implementing *bit fields*. A bit field is declared exactly like a structure except that its members are fields of one or more *bits*. These variable length fields are actually stored in one or more integer variables.

The declaration of a bit field is the same as the declaration of any ordinary structure member with two exceptions. First, bit field members must be declared as int, signed int, or unsigned int. Second, a colon and an integer appear after the member name, and the integer value specifies the number of bits in that field.

It is a good idea to explicitly declare bit fields as either signed or unsigned integers. It is implementation dependent whether bit fields declared as int are interpreted as signed or unsigned values.

Programs that are intended to be portable should avoid bit fields. Because of the following implementation dependencies, bit fields may work differently on various systems.

1.   Whether an int bit field is treated as signed or unsigned.

2.   The maximum number of bits in a bit field. Many compilers limit bit field members to the size of an integer, so a bit field declaration that works on a machine with 32-bit integers may not work on one that uses 16-bit integers.

3.   Whether the members in a bit field are allocated from left to right or from right to left in memory.

4.   When a declaration specifies two bit fields and the second is too large to fit in the bits left over from the first, the compiler may either put the second bit field in the next word of memory or immediately after the first field, overlapping the boundary between memory locations.

Here is an example of a bit field declaration:

```
struct  CHAR    {
        unsigned ch     : 7;
        unsigned font   : 6;
        unsigned size   : 19;
};
struct  CHAR    ch1;
```

This declaration is from a text formatting program that is capable of manipulating up to 128 different character values (for which seven bits are required), up to 64 different fonts (which takes six bits), in sizes from 0 to 524,287 units. The size field is too large to be held in a short integer, but the other fields are both smaller than a character. The bit field lets the programmer use the bits left over from `ch` and `font` to increase the number of bits for `size`, thus avoiding the need to declare a whole integer to store `size`.

Many compilers for machines with 16-bit integers will flag this declaration as illegal because the last field is too large. But on a 32-bit machine, this declaration would create `ch1` as one of these two possibilities.

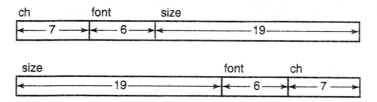

This example illustrates a good reason to use bit fields: the ability to pack odd-sized data together to save storage. This savings becomes particularly important when thousands of these structures are being used.

The other reason to use bit fields is because they make it convenient to access parts of an integer. Let's examine an example that might be found in an operating system. The code to operate the floppy disk must communicate with the controller for the disk. Often these device controllers contain several registers, each of which contains many different values all packed together into one integer. A bit field is a convenient way to access the individual values.

Suppose one of the registers for the controller was defined as:

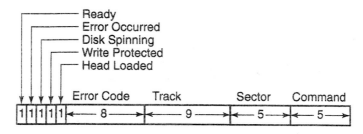

The first five fields are one bit each, and the remaining fields are larger. On a machine that allocated bit fields from right to left, the following declaration would allow easy access to the various fields in this register.

```
struct  DISK_REGISTER_FORMAT    {
        unsigned        command         : 5;
        unsigned        sector          : 5;
        unsigned        track           : 9;
        unsigned        error_code      : 8;
        unsigned        head_loaded     : 1;
        unsigned        write_protect   : 1;
        unsigned        disk_spinning   : 1;
        unsigned        error_occurred  : 1;
        unsigned        ready           : 1;
};
```

If the disk register is accessed at memory address 0xc0200142, we would declare the following pointer constant:

```
#define DISK_REGISTER    \
    ((struct DISK_REGISTER_FORMAT *)0xc0200142)
```

With this preparation, the code needed to actually access the disk register is simple, as shown in this code fragment.

```
/*
** Tell the controller which sector and track,
** and start the read operation.
*/
DISK_REGISTER->sector = new_sector;
DISK_REGISTER->track = new_track;
DISK_REGISTER->command = READ;

/*
** Wait until the operation is done,
** indicated by ready becoming true.
*/
while( ! DISK_REGISTER->ready )
        ;

/*
** Check for errors.
*/
if( DISK_REGISTER->error_occurred ){
        switch( DISK_REGISTER->error_code ){
        ...
```

Bit fields are a convenience. Any task that can be completed with bit fields can also be accomplished through shifting and masking. For example, the following code accomplishes exactly the same thing as the first assignment in the previous example.

```
#define DISK_REGISTER    (unsigned int *)0xc0200142

*DISK_REGISTER &= 0xfffffc1f;
*DISK_REGISTER |= ( new_sector & 0x1f ) << 5;
```

The first assignment uses a bitwise AND to clear all of the bits in the sector field to zero without affecting the other bits. The second takes the value of new_sector, AND's it to make sure that the value does not exceed the width of the field, shifts it left to the proper position, and then uses a bitwise OR to set the field to the desired value.

The bit field expresses this process more simply in the source code, but there isn't any difference in the object code. The same shifting and masking operations are required whether or not the bit field is used. The only advantage provided by the bit field is simplifying the source code. This advantage must be weighed against the bit field's lack of portability.

10.6 Unions

A *union* is a different animal altogether. A union is declared like a structure but doesn't work like a structure. All of the members of a union refer to *the same location(s) in memory*. Unions are used when you need to store different things in one place at different times.

First, let's look at a simple example.

```
union    {
         float   f;
         int     i;
} fi;
```

On a machine in which floats and integers both occupy 32 bits, the variable fi occupies only one 32-bit word of memory. If the member f is used, the word is accessed as a floating-point value; if the member i is used, the word is accessed as an integer. So this code

```
fi.f =   3.14159;
printf( "%d\n", fi.i );
```

first stores the floating-point representation of π into fi, and then interprets *those same bits* as if they were an integer and prints out that value. Note that

both members are referring to the same bits; the only difference is that the type
of each member determines how the bits are interpreted.

Why would anyone ever want to do anything like this example? It would
be helpful if you wanted to see how floating-point numbers are stored on a
particular machine but probably not for anything else. Here is a more realistic
example. One task of a BASIC interpreter is to keep track of the values of variables used in the program. BASIC provides several different types of variables,
so the type of each variable must be stored along with its value. Here is a
structure that saves this information, but it is not too efficient.

```
struct  VARIABLE         {
        enum    { INT, FLOAT, STRING } type;
        int     int_value;
        float   float_value;
        char    *string_value;
};
```

When a variable in the BASIC program is created, the interpreter creates one of
these structures and records the type of the variable. Then, based on the type,
one of the three value fields is used to store the variable's value.

What is inefficient about this structure is the amount of memory used—
every VARIABLE contains two value fields that are not used. A union can
reduce this waste by storing each of the three value fields in the same memory.
The three fields will not conflict because each variable can only have one type,
thus only one of the fields in the union will ever be needed at a time.

```
struct  VARIABLE         {
        enum    { INT, FLOAT, STRING } type;
        union   {
                int     i;
                float   f;
                char    *s;
        } value;
};
```

Now, for an integer variable, you would store INT in the type field and the
integer value in the value.i field. For a floating-point value, you would use
the value.f field. When obtaining the value of this variable later, the type
field would be checked to determine which value field to use. This choice
determines how the memory location will be accessed, so one location can be
used to store any of these three different kinds of values. Note that the compiler doesn't check the type field to verify that the proper union member is
used. It is up to the programmer to maintain the type field and to check it.

If the members of a union are different sizes, the union will be as large
as the largest member. The next section discusses this situation.

10.6.1 Variant Records

Let's examine an example that implements what Pascal and Modula call a *variant record*. Conceptually, this is the same situation we just discussed—a particular area in memory will store different types of values at different times. In this case, however, the values are more complex than simple integers or floats. Each is an entire structure.

I took the following example from an inventory system that keeps track of two different kinds of entities: parts and subassemblies. A part is a gadget that is purchased from another manufacturer. It has various characteristics such as who we buy it from, how much it costs, and so forth. A subassembly is something that we make, and is a combination of a bunch of parts and other subassemblies.

The first two structures specify what must be stored for a part and for a subassembly.

```
struct   PARTINFO       {
         int     cost;
         int     supplier;
         ...
};

struct   SUBASSYINFO    {
         int     n_parts;
         struct  {
                 char    partno[10];
                 short   quan;
         } parts[MAXPARTS];
};
```

The inventory record contains common information for each entry and a union to store either part information or subassembly information.

```
struct   INVREC  {
         char    partno[10];
         int     quan;
         enum    { PART, SUBASSY }       type;
         union   {
                 struct  PARTINFO        part;
                 struct  SUBASSYINFO     subassy;
         } info;
};
```

Here are some statements that manipulate an INVREC structure variable called rec.

```
if( rec.type == PART ){
        y = rec.info.part.cost;
        z = rec.info.part.supplier;
}
else {
        y = rec.info.subassy.nparts;
        z = rec.info.subassy.parts[0].quan;
}
```

Although not very realistic, this code illustrates how to access each of the members of the union. The first part of the statement gets the cost and the supplier for a part, and the second part of the statement gets the number of different parts in a subassembly and the quantity of the first part.

In a union whose members are different sizes, the amount of memory allocated for the union is determined by the size of its largest member. Thus, a union will always be big enough to store its largest member. If the members are wildly different sizes, there will be a lot of wasted memory when storing the shorter members. In this type of situation, it might be preferable for the union to store pointers to the different members rather than the members themselves. The pointers would all be the same size thus avoiding the problem of wasted memory. When it is decided which member is needed, the right amount of memory can be obtained to store it. Chapter 11, which deals with dynamic memory allocation, contains an example illustrating this technique.

10.6.2 Initializing Unions

A union variable can be initialized, but the value must be appropriate for the type of the first member of the union, and it must be enclosed in braces. For example,

```
union {
        int     a;
        float   b;
        char    c[4];
} x = { 5 };
```

initializes x.a to have the value five.

It is not possible to initialize this variable to a floating-point or a character value. If an initializer of any other type is given, it is converted (if possible) to an integer and assigned to x.a.

10.7 Summary

Values of different types can be stored together in a structure. The values in a structure, called members, are accessed by name. A structure variable is a scalar, and can appear wherever an ordinary scalar variable can appear.

The declaration of a structure lists the members that the structure will contain. Different declarations are considered to be different types even if their member lists are identical. A structure tag is a name associated with a member list. You can use different declarations to declare structures of the same type by using a structure tag rather than repeating the member list in the declarations. A typedef may also be used to accomplish this goal.

Structure members may be scalars, arrays, or pointers. A structure may also contain members which are structures. There is no conflict between identically named members of different structures. You use the dot operator to access the members of a structure variable. If you have a pointer to a structure, you use the arrow operator to access the structure's members.

A structure may not contain a member that is the same type of structure, but may contain a member that is a pointer to the same type of structure. This technique is often used in linked data structures. To declare two structures that each contain a pointer to the other type, an incomplete declaration is needed to define a structure tag name. Structure variables may be initialized by giving a list of values enclosed in braces. The type of each value must be appropriate for the member that it initializes.

The compiler allocates memory for the members of a structure variable in accordance with their boundary alignment requirements. Memory may be wasted in the structure to achieve the proper alignment. Listing the structure members in decreasing order of their alignment requirements minimizes the amount of wasted memory in the structure. The value returned by sizeof includes any wasted memory in a structure.

Structures may be passed as arguments to functions and returned from functions. However, it is usually more efficient to pass a pointer to the structure instead. The const keyword can be used in the declaration of a pointer argument to prevent the function from modifying the structure.

Bit fields are structure members whose size is specified in bits. Bit field declarations are inherently nonportable due to the many factors that are implementation dependent. However, bit fields allow you to pack odd sized values together to conserve space. They also simplify the source code needed to access arbitrary runs of bits from within a value.

The members of a union are all stored in the same memory. By accessing union members of different types, the same bits in memory can be interpreted differently. Unions are useful in implementing variant records, though the programmer is responsible for keeping track of which variant has been stored and for selecting the proper union member to access the data. A union variable can be initialized, but the value must match the type of its first member.

10.8 Summary of Cautions

1. Structure declarations with identical member lists produce variables of different types (page 270).

2. Be careful using `typedef` to define a name for a self-referential structure (page 274).

3. Passing structures as arguments is inefficient (page 285).

10.9 Summary of Programming Tips

1. Put structure tag declarations and `typedef`'s into header files, which can be `#include`'d wherever needed (page 271).

2. The best arrangement of structure members may not be the one that wastes the least amount of space due to boundary alignment (page 284).

3. Explicitly declare bit field members as either `signed int` or `unsigned int` (page 288).

4. Bit fields are not portable (page 288).

5. Bit fields allow bit operations to be expressed more clearly in the source code (page 291).

10.10 Questions

1. How are structure members different from array elements?

2. How is a structure name different from an array name?

3. The syntax for structure declarations shows some optional components. List all the legal forms of a structure declaration, and explain what is accomplished by each.

4. What (if anything) is wrong with the following program fragment?

```
struct abc {
        int     a;
        int     b;
        int     c;
```

```
        };
        ...
        abc.a = 25;
        abc.b = 15;
        abc.c = -1
```

5. What (if anything) is wrong with the following program fragment?

```
        typedef struct {
                int     a;
                int     b;
                int     c;
        } abc;
        ...
        abc.a = 25;
        abc.b = 15;
        abc.c = -1
```

6. Complete the following declaration to initialize x so that the member a is three, b is the string hello, and c is zero. You may assume that x is stored in static memory.

```
        struct   {
                int     a;
                char    b[10];
                float   c;
        } x =
```

7. Consider the following declarations and data.

```
        struct NODE {
                int a;
                struct NODE *b;
                struct NODE *c;
        };

        struct NODE      nodes[5] = {
                 { 5,     nodes + 3,      NULL },
                 { 15,    nodes + 4,      nodes + 3 },
                 { 22,    NULL,           nodes + 4 },
                 { 12,    nodes + 1,      nodes },
                 { 18,    nodes + 2,      nodes + 1 }
        };
        (Other declarations...)
        struct NODE      *np      = nodes + 2;
        struct NODE      **npp     = &nodes[1].b;
```

Evaluate each of the expressions below and state its value. Also, state any side effects that occur when the expression is evaluated. You should evaluate each expression with the original values shown (that is, don't use the results of one expression to evaluate the next one). Assume that the nodes array begins at location 200 and that integers and pointers are four bytes on this machine.

Expression	Value	Expression	Value
nodes		&nodes[3].c->a	
nodes.a		&nodes->a	
nodes[3].a		np	
nodes[3].c		np->a	
nodes[3].c->a		np->c->c->a	
*nodes		npp	
*nodes.a		npp->a	
(*nodes).a		*npp	
nodes->a		**npp	
nodes[3].b->b		*npp->a	
*nodes[3].b->b		(*npp)->a	
&nodes		&np	
&nodes[3].a		&np->a	
&nodes[3].c		&np->c->c->a	

8. How much space is wasted in the following structure due to boundary alignment on a machine with 16-bit integers? On a machine with 32-bit integers?

```
struct  {
        char    a;
        int     b;
        char    c;
};
```

9. Name at least two reasons why bit field declarations are not portable.

10. Write a declaration that allows easy access to the individual parts of a floating-point in the following format.

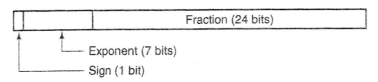

Fraction (24 bits)

Exponent (7 bits)

Sign (1 bit)

11. How would you accomplish the same result as the following code without using bit fields? Assume that you have a 16-bit machine that allocates bit fields from left to right.

```
struct   {
            int      a:4;
            int      b:8;
            int      c:3;
            int      d:1;
} x;
...
x.a = aaa;
x.b = bbb;
x.c = ccc;
x.d = ddd;
```

12. What does the following code fragment print?

```
struct   {
            int      a:2;
} x;
...
x.a = 1;
x.a += 1;
printf( "%d\n", x.a );
```

13. What (if anything) is wrong with the following code fragment?

```
union    {
            int      a;
            float    b;
            char     c;
} x;
...
x.a = 25;
x.b = 3.14;
x.c = 'x';
printf( "%d %g %c\n", x.a, x.b, x.c );
```

14. Suppose some information has been assigned to a union variable. How can this information be retrieved correctly?

15. The following structure could be used by a BASIC interpreter to keep track of the type and value of variables.

```
struct   VARIABLE           {
```

```
        enum    { INT, FLOAT, STRING } type;
        union   {
                int     i;
                float   f;
                char    *s;
        } value;
};
```

What would be different if the structure were written like this instead:

```
struct  VARIABLE        {
        enum    { INT, FLOAT, STRING } type;
        union   {
                int     i;
                float   f;
                char    s[MAX_STRING_LENGTH];
        } value;
};
```

10.11 Programming Exercises

✍ ★★ 1. The information saved by the telephone company when you make a long distance phone call includes the date and time you placed the call. It also includes three phone numbers: the one you called, the one you are calling from, and the one that will be billed. Each of these phone numbers has three parts: the area code, the exchange, and the station number. Write a structure declaration for this billing information.

★★ 2. Write a declaration for an information system that records sales at an auto dealer. The following data must be saved for every sale. The maximum length of string values given does not include space for the terminating NUL byte.

customer's name	string (20)
customer's address	string (40)
model	string (20)

Three different types of transactions are possible: all-cash sales, sales involving a loan, and leases. For all-cash sales, the following additional information must be saved:

manufacturer's suggested retail price	float
actual selling price	float
sales tax	float
licensing fee	float

For leases, the following additional information must be saved:

manufacturer's suggested retail price	float
actual selling price	float
down payment	float
security deposit	float
monthly payment	float
lease term	int

For sales involving a loan, the following additional information must be saved:

manufacturer's suggested retail price	float
actual selling price	float
sales tax	float
licensing fee	float
down payment	float
loan duration	int
interest rate	float
monthly payment	float
name of bank	string (20)

★★★ 3. One of the computer's tasks is to decode each instruction in the program that is running to determine what operation to perform. On many machines, the decoding process is complicated by the fact that different instructions have different formats. On one particular machine, each instruction is 16 bits long, and the following different formats are implemented. Bits are numbered from right to left.

Single Operand (sgl_op)		Double Operand (dbl_op)		Branch (branch)	
Bits	**Field Name**	**Bits**	**Field Name**	**Bits**	**Field Name**
0–2	dst_reg	0–2	dst_reg	0–7	offset
3–5	dst_mode	3–5	dst_mode	8–15	opcode
6–15	opcode	6–8	src_reg		
		9–11	src_mode		
		12–15	opcode		

Register Source (reg_src)		Miscellaneous (misc)	
Bits	**Field Name**	**Bits**	**Field Name**
0–2	dst_reg	0–15	opcode
3–5	dst_mode		
6–8	src_reg		
9–15	opcode		

Your task is to write a declaration that will allow a program to interpret an instruction in any of these formats. Your declaration must also have an unsigned short field called `addr` that accesses all 16 bits. Use a `typedef` in your declaration to create a new type called `machine_inst`.

Given the declaration:

```
machine_inst    x;
```

the expressions below should access the indicated bits.

Expression	Bits
x.addr	0–15
x.misc.opcode	0–15
x.branch.opcode	8–15
x.sgl_op.dst_mode	3–5
x.reg_src.src_reg	6–8
x.dbl_op.opcode	12–15

11

Dynamic Memory Allocation

The elements of an array are stored in contiguous locations in memory. When an array is declared, its memory is allocated at compile time. However, you can also allocate the memory at runtime with dynamic memory allocation. In this chapter, we will examine the differences between these techniques and see when and how to use dynamic memory allocation.

11.1 Why Use Dynamic Allocation

When declaring arrays, the array size must be given as a compile-time constant. Often, the actual size needed for the array is not known until run time because the amount of space depends upon the input data. For example, a program that computes student grades and averages might need to store data for all of the students in a class, but different classes will have different numbers of students. In these situations, the usual approach is to declare an array that is as big as it ever will need to be.

This approach has the advantage of being simple, but it has several disadvantages. First, such declarations build an artificial limitation into the program, making it incapable of handling problems larger than the size used in the declaration. The obvious solution is to make the array even bigger, but the second problem then becomes even worse. Nearly all of the memory used for a huge array is wasted when the number of elements actually required is small. A third disadvantage is that the program must respond in a reasonable way when there is more input than the array can hold. It should not fail with an exception, and it *must not* print answers that look valid but in fact are wrong. The required logic is simple enough, but the assumption that "the array will never overflow" makes it very tempting to not bother implementing it.

11.2 Malloc and Free

The C library provides two functions, **malloc** and **free**, that perform dynamic memory allocation and deallocation. These functions maintain a pool of available memory. When a program needs additional memory, it calls malloc, which takes an appropriate piece of memory from the pool and returns a pointer to this block of memory to the program. The memory is not initialized in any way. If it is important that the memory be initialized, you must either do it yourself or use the calloc function (described in the next section). When a previously allocated piece of memory is no longer needed, free is called to return it to the pool for later reuse.

The prototypes for these two functions are shown below, and are in stdlib.h.

```
void    *malloc( size_t size );
void    free( void *pointer );
```

The argument to malloc is the number of bytes (characters) of memory that are needed.[41] If the desired amount of memory is available, malloc returns a pointer to the beginning of the allocated block.

malloc allocates contiguous blocks of memory. For example, a request for 100 bytes will be satisfied with 100 adjacent bytes, never with two or more separate chunks of memory. Also, malloc may actually allocate a chunk of memory slightly larger than requested. However, this behavior is implementation dependent, so you should not count on getting more memory than you requested.

What if the pool of memory is empty, or it does not contain a big enough block? In this case, malloc calls the operating system to obtain more memory and begins allocating pieces from this new chunk. If the operating system is unable to give more memory to malloc, then a NULL pointer is returned. Thus it is vital that the pointer returned by every call to malloc be checked to ensure that it is not NULL.

The argument to free must either be NULL or a value that was previously returned from malloc, calloc, or realloc (described below). Passing a NULL argument to free has no effect.

---

[41] Note that the type of this argument is size_t, which is an unsigned type. It is defined in stdlib.h.

How does `malloc` know whether you want to store integers, floating-point values, structures, or arrays in the memory you've requested? It doesn't—`malloc` returns a pointer of type `void *` for precisely this reason. The Standard states that a `void *` pointer can be converted to any other pointer type. Some compilers though, especially older ones, may require you to use a cast for the conversion.

On machines with boundary alignment requirements, the memory returned by `malloc` will always begin on a boundary that is suitable for the data type with the most stringent alignment requirements.

11.3 Calloc and Realloc

There are two additional memory allocation functions, **calloc** and **realloc**. Their prototypes are shown below.

```
void    *calloc( size_t num_elements,
            size_t element_size );
void    *realloc( void *ptr, size_t new_size );
```

`calloc` also allocates memory. The major difference between `malloc` and `calloc` is that the latter initializes the memory to zero before returning a pointer to it. This initialization is often convenient, but is a waste of time if the first thing your program does is to store values into the array. A minor difference between `calloc` and `malloc` is the way the amount of memory is requested. `calloc` takes the number of elements desired and the number of bytes in each element. From these values it computes the total number of bytes needed.

The `realloc` function is used to change the size of a previously allocated block of memory. You can make a block larger or smaller with this function. If a block is made larger, its old contents remain unchanged and additional memory is added to the end of the block. The new memory is not initialized in any way. If the block is made smaller, then memory is taken off of the end. What remains of the original contents are unchanged.

If the original block cannot be resized, `realloc` will allocate a different block of the right size and copy the contents of the old block to the new one. Thus, you must not use the old pointer to the block after a call to `realloc`. Use the new pointer that is returned instead.

Finally, if the first argument to `realloc` is NULL, then it behaves exactly like `malloc`.

11.4 Using Dynamically Allocated Memory

Here is an example that obtains a chunk of memory from `malloc`.

```
int      *pi;
...
pi = malloc( 100 );
if( pi == NULL ){
        printf( "Out of memory!\n" );
        exit( 1 );
}
```

The symbol `NULL` is defined in `stdio.h` as the literal constant zero. It acts as a visual reminder that the value being tested is a pointer type rather than an integer.

If there was memory available, we will now have a pointer to 100 bytes. On a machine with 4-byte integers, the memory will be treated as an array of 25 integers because `pi` is a pointer to an integer.

If your goal is to get enough memory for 25 integers, though, here is a much better technique for obtaining it.

```
pi = malloc( 25 * sizeof( int ) );
```

This approach is better because it is portable. It works properly even on machines with different size integers.

Now that you have a pointer, how do you use the memory? Of course you can use indirection and pointer arithmetic to access different integer locations in this array, as in this loop, which sets each element of the newly allocated array to zero:

```
int      *pi2, i;
...
pi2 = pi;
for( i = 0; i < 25; i += 1 )
        *pi2++ = 0;
```

As you have seen, you can use a subscript on the pointer as well. This second loop performs the same work as the previous one.

```
int      i;
...
for( i = 0; i < 25; i += 1 )
        pi[i] = 0;
```

11.5 Common Dynamic Memory Errors

There are many errors that can occur in programs that use dynamic memory allocation. These include dereferencing NULL pointers, going outside the bounds of the memory that was allocated, freeing memory blocks that were not dynamically allocated, attempting to free a portion of a dynamic block, and continuing to use dynamic memory after it has been freed.

The most common error with dynamic memory allocation is forgetting to check whether the requested memory was allocated. Program 11.1 presents a technique that makes this error checking almost foolproof. The MALLOC macro takes the number of elements and type of each element, computes the total number of bytes needed, and calls alloc to obtain the memory.[42] alloc calls malloc and then checks to make sure that the pointer returned was not NULL.

The final piece of this puzzle is the very first #define. It prevents accidental calls directly to malloc by substituting junk into the program. If an accidental call is made, the program will not compile due to syntax errors. The #undef is needed in alloc so that it can call malloc without error.

The second biggest source of error with dynamically allocated memory is going outside of the bounds of the memory that was allocated. For example, if you have obtained an array of 25 integers, accessing elements with subscripts less than zero or greater than 24 can cause two types of problems.

The first problem is obvious: the memory being accessed might be holding some other variable. Changing it here will destroy the variable, and changing the variable will destroy any value you store here. These kinds of bugs are very difficult to track down.

The second problem is not so obvious. Some implementations of malloc and free keep the pool of available storage as a linked list. Modifying

```
/*
** Definitions for a less error-prone memory allocator.
*/
#include <stdlib.h>

#define malloc                  DON'T CALL malloc DIRECTLY!
#define MALLOC(num,type)        (type *)alloc( (num) * sizeof(type) )
extern  void    *alloc( size_t size );
```

Program 11.1a   Error checking allocator: interface   alloc.h

---

[42] #define macros are described in detail in Chapter 14.

```
/*
** Implementation for a less error-prone memory allocator.
*/
#include <stdio.h>
#include "alloc.h"
#undef  malloc

void    *
alloc( size_t size )
{
        void    *new_mem;

        /*
        ** Ask for the requested memory, and check that we really
        ** got it.
        */
        new_mem = malloc( size );
        if( new_mem == NULL ){
                printf( "Out of memory!\en" );
                exit( 1 );
        }
        return new_mem;
}
```

Program 11.1b   Error checking allocator: implementation   alloc.c

```
/*
** A program that uses the less error-prone memory allocator.
*/
#include "alloc.h"

void
function()
{
        int     *new_memory;

        /*
        ** Get space for a bunch of integers
        */
        new_memory = MALLOC( 25, int );
        /* ... */
}
```

Program 11.1c   Using the error checking allocator   a_client.c

locations outside the bounds of allocated memory can corrupt this list, which can cause exceptions that terminate the program.

When a program that uses dynamically allocated memory fails, it is tempting to blame the problems on `malloc` and `free`. They are rarely the culprit, though. In practice, the problem is nearly always in your program and is frequently caused by accessing data outside of the allocated memory.

Different errors can occur when using `free`. The pointer passed to `free` must be a pointer that was obtained from `malloc`, `calloc`, or `realloc`. Calling `free` with a pointer to memory that was not dynamically allocated can cause the program to terminate either right away or at some later time. Similar problems can be caused by attempting to free only a portion of a dynamically allocated block, like this:

```
/*
** Get 10 integers
*/
pi = malloc( 10 * sizeof( int ) );
...
/*
** Free only the last 5 integers; keep the first 5
*/
free( pi + 5 );
```

Freeing a portion of a block is not allowed; the whole block must be freed. However, the `realloc` function can make a dynamically allocated chunk of memory smaller, effectively freeing the end of it.

Finally, you must be careful not to access memory that has been `free`'d. This warning may seem obvious, but there is a subtle problem here after all. Suppose copies are made of the pointer to a dynamically allocated block, and these copies are sent off to many different parts of the program. It is difficult to make sure that none of these other areas in the program use their copies of the pointer after the memory has been freed. Conversely, you must be sure that all parts of the program are finished using a chunk of memory before freeing it.

11.5.1 Memory Leaks

Dynamically allocated memory should be freed when it is no longer needed so that it can be reused later for other purposes. Allocating memory but not freeing it later causes a *memory leak*. With operating systems that share a common pool of memory among all executing programs, memory leaks dribble away the available memory so that eventually there isn't any left. Rebooting the computer is the only recovery for this situation.

Other operating systems keep track of which pieces of memory each program currently has, so that when a program terminates all of the memory that it had allocated but had not freed is returned to the pool. Memory leaks are a serious problem even on these systems, because a program that continually allocates memory without ever freeing any will eventually exhaust the available memory. At this point, the defective program will not be able to continue executing, and its failure may result in the loss of the work completed so far.

11.6 Memory Allocation Examples

A common use for dynamic memory allocation is obtaining space for arrays whose sizes are not known until run time. Program 11.2 reads a list of integers, sorts them into ascending sequence, and prints the list.

```
/*
** Read, sort, and print a list of integer values.
*/
#include <stdlib.h>
#include <stdio.h>

/*
**      Function called by 'qsort' to compare integer values
*/
int
compare_integers( void const *a, void const *b )
{
        register int    const *pa = a;
        register int    const *pb = b;

        return *pa > *pb ? 1 : *pa < *pb ? -1 : 0;
}

int
main()
{
        int     *array;
        int     n_values;
        int     i;

        /*
        ** See how many numbers there will be.
```

Program 11.2 Sort a list of integers   *continued . . .*

```
        */
        printf( "How many values are there? " );
        if( scanf( "%d", &n_values ) != 1 || n_values <= 0 ){
                printf( "Illegal number of values.\n" );
                exit( EXIT_FAILURE );
        }

        /*
        ** Get memory to store them.
        */
        array = malloc( n_values * sizeof( int ) );
        if( array == NULL ){
                printf( "Can't get memory for that many values.\n" );
                exit( EXIT_FAILURE );
        }

        /*
        ** Read the numbers.
        */
        for( i = 0; i < n_values; i += 1 ){
                printf( "? " );
                if( scanf( "%d", array + i ) != 1 ){
                        printf( "Error reading value #%d\n", i );
                        exit( EXIT_FAILURE );
                }
        }

        /*
        ** Sort the values.
        */
        qsort( array, n_values, sizeof( int ), compare_integers );

        /*
        ** Print them out.
        */
        for( i = 0; i < n_values; i += 1 )
                printf( "%d\n", array[i] );

        /*
        ** Free the memory and exit.
        */
        free( array );
        return EXIT_SUCCESS;
}
```

Program 11.2   Sort a list of integers   sort.c

Memory to hold the list is dynamically allocated so that when you are writing the program you don't have to guess how many values the user might wish to sort. The only limit on the number of values that can be sorted is the amount of dynamic memory available to the program. When small lists are sorted, though, only as much memory as is actually needed is allocated, so memory is not wasted.

Now consider a program that reads strings. If you don't know the length of the longest string in advance you cannot use an ordinary array as a buffer. Instead, use dynamically allocated memory. When you find an input line that doesn't fit, reallocate a larger buffer and read the remainder of the line into it. The implementation of this technique is left as a programming exercise.

```c
/*
** Make a copy of a string in dynamically allocated memory.  Note:
** caller is responsible for checking whether the memory was
** allocated!  This allows the caller to respond to an error in
** any way they wish.
*/
#include <stdlib.h>
#include <string.h>

char *
strdup( char const *string )
{
        char    *new_string;

        /*
        ** Ask for enough memory to hold the string and its
        ** terminating NUL byte.
        */
        new_string = malloc( strlen( string ) + 1 );

        /*
        ** If we got the memory, copy the string.
        */
        if( new_string != NULL )
                strcpy( new_string, string );

        return new_string;
}
```

Program 11.3   Duplicate a string   strdup.c

The input is read into this buffer, one line at a time. The length of the string is determined, and then memory is allocated to hold it. Finally, the string is copied into the new memory so the buffer can be used to read the next line.

The function in Program 11.3, called strdup, returns a copy of its input string in dynamically allocated memory. The function first tries to obtain enough memory to hold the copy. The additional byte beyond the string length is needed to hold the NUL byte that terminates the string. If the memory was successfully allocated, the string is copied into the new memory. Finally, a pointer to the new memory is returned. Notice that new_string will be NULL if the allocation failed for some reason, so a NULL pointer would be returned in this case.

This function is very handy. It is so useful, in fact, that many environments include it as part of the library even though the Standard does not mention it.

Our final example illustrates how you can use dynamic memory allocation to eliminate wasted memory with variant records. Program 11.4 is a modification of the inventory system example from Chapter 10. Program 11.4a contains the declarations for the inventory records.

As before, the inventory system must handle two types of records, those for parts and those for subassemblies. The first structure holds the information specific to a part (only a portion of this structure is shown), and the second holds information about subassemblies. The last declaration is for the inventory record. It contains some common data needed for both subassemblies and parts and a variant portion.

Because the different fields in the variant part are different sizes (in fact, the subassembly record is variable size), the union contains pointers to structures rather than the structures. Dynamic allocation lets the program create an inventory record that is the correct size for the item being stored, so there is no wasted memory.

Program 11.4b is a function that creates an inventory record for a subassembly. This task depends on the number of different parts the subassembly contains, so this value is passed as an argument.

This function allocates three things: the inventory record, the subassembly structure, and the array of parts in the subassembly structure. If any of these allocations fails, any memory that was already obtained is freed and a NULL pointer is returned. Otherwise, the type and info.subassy->n_parts fields are initialized and a pointer to the record is returned.

Obtaining memory for an inventory record to store a part is a little easier than for a subassembly because only two allocations are needed. This function is therefore not illustrated here.

```
/*
** Declarations for the inventory record.
**
**       Structure that contains information about a part.
*/
typedef struct {
        int     cost;
        int     supplier;
        /* etc. */
} Partinfo;

/*
**       Structure to hold information about a subassembly.
*/
typedef struct {
        int     n_parts;
        struct  SUBASSYPART {
                char    partno[10];
                short   quan;
        } *part;
} Subassyinfo;

/*
**       Structure for an inventory record, which is a variant record.
*/
typedef struct {
        char    partno[10];
        int     quan;
        enum    { PART, SUBASSY }        type;
        union   {
                Partinfo        *part;
                Subassyinfo     *subassy;
        } info;
} Invrec;
```

Program 11.4a   Inventory system declarations   inventor.h

```
/*
** Function to create a SUBASSEMBLY inventory record.
*/

#include <stdlib.h>
```

Program 11.4b   Dynamic creation of a variant record   *continued . . .*

```
#include <stdio.h>
#include "inventor.h"

Invrec *
create_subassy_record( int n_parts )
{
        Invrec  *new_rec;

        /*
        ** Try to get memory for the Invrec portion.
        */
        new_rec = malloc( sizeof( Invrec ) );
        if( new_rec != NULL ){
                /*
                ** That worked; now get the SUBASSYINFO portion.
                */
                new_rec->info.subassy =
                    malloc( sizeof( Subassyinfo ) );
                if( new_rec->info.subassy != NULL ){
                        /*
                        ** Get an array big enough for the parts.
                        */
                        new_rec->info.subassy->part = malloc(
                            n_parts * sizeof( struct SUBASSYPART ) );
                        if( new_rec->info.subassy->part != NULL ){
                                /*
                                ** Got the memory; fill in the fields
                                ** whose values we know and return.
                                */
                                new_rec->type = SUBASSY;
                                new_rec->info.subassy->n_parts =
                                    n_parts;
                                return new_rec;
                        }

                        /*
                        ** Out of memory: free what we've got so far.
                        */
                        free( new_rec->info.subassy );
                }
                free( new_rec );
        }
        return NULL;
}
```

Program 11.4b   Dynamic creation of a variant record   invcreat.c

Program 11.4c contains the last part of this example: a function that destroys inventory records. This function works for either type of inventory record. It uses a `switch` statement to determine the type of record it was given and then frees all dynamically allocated fields in the record. Finally, the record is deleted.

A common mistake made in situations like this one is to free the record before freeing the memory pointed to by fields in the record. After the record has been freed, you may no longer safely access any of the fields that it contains.

```c
/*
** Function to discard an inventory record.
*/

#include <stdlib.h>
#include "inventor.h"

void
discard_inventory_record( Invrec *record )
{
        /*
        ** Delete the variant parts of the record
        */
        switch( record->type ){
        case SUBASSY:
                free( record->info.subassy->part );
                free( record->info.subassy );
                break;

        case PART:
                free( record->info.part );
                break;
        }

        /*
        ** Delete the main part of the record
        */
        free( record );
}
```

Program 11.4c   Destruction of a variant record   invdelet.c

Although it is a little less obvious, the following code fragment is a slightly more efficient implementation of Program 11.4c.

```
if( record->type == SUBASSY )
        free( record->info.subassy->part );

free( record->info.part );
free( record );
```

This code does not distinguish between subassemblies and parts when freeing the variant part of the record. Either member of the union can be used, as free does not care which type of pointer it gets.

11.7 Summary

When an array is declared, its size must be known at compile time. Dynamic allocation allows a program to create space for an array whose size isn't known until runtime.

The malloc and calloc functions both allocate memory and return a pointer to it. The argument to malloc is the number of bytes of memory needed. In contrast, calloc requires the number of elements you want and the size of each element. calloc initializes the memory to zero before returning, whereas malloc leaves the memory uninitialized. The realloc function is called to change the size of an existing block of dynamically allocated memory. Increases in size may be accomplished by copying the data from the existing block to a new, larger block. When a dynamically allocated block is no longer needed, free is called to return it to the pool of available memory. Memory must not be accessed after it has been freed.

The pointer returned by malloc, calloc, and realloc will be NULL if the requested allocation could not be performed. Erroneously accessing memory outside of an allocated block may cause the same errors as accessing memory outside of an array, but can also corrupt the pool of available memory and lead to a program failure. You may not pass a pointer to free that was not obtained from an earlier call to malloc, calloc, or realloc. Nor may you free a portion of a block.

A memory leak is memory that has been dynamically allocated but has not been freed and is no longer in use. Memory leaks increase the size of the program, and may lead to a crash of the program or the system.

11.8 Summary of Cautions

1. Not checking the pointer returned from `malloc` for NULL (page 307).

2. Accessing outside the bounds of dynamically allocated memory (page 307).

3. Passing a pointer to `free` that did not originally come from `malloc` (page 309).

4. Accessing dynamic memory after it has been `freed` (page 309).

11.9 Summary of Programming Tips

1. Dynamic allocation helps eliminate built-in limitations in the program (page 303).

2. Using `sizeof` to compute the size of data types enhances portability (page 306).

11.10 Questions

1. What is the largest static array that you can declare on your system? The largest dynamically allocated piece of memory?

2. What is the total amount of memory that you can dynamically allocate on your system when you ask for it 500 bytes at a time? When you ask for it 5000 bytes at a time? Is there a difference? If so, how do you explain it?

3. In a program that reads strings from a file, is there any value that can logically be used for the size of the input buffer?

4. Some C implementations provide a function called **alloca**, which differs from `malloc` in that it allocates memory on the stack. What are the advantages and disadvantages of this type of allocation?

5. The following program, which is supposed to read integers in the range one through `size` from the standard input and return counts of how many times each value occurs, contains several errors. What are they?

```
#include <stdlib.h>

int *
frequency( int size )
{
        int     *array;
        int     i;
```

```
/*
** Get enough memory to hold the counts.
*/
array = (int *)malloc( size * 2 );

/*
** Adjust the pointer back one integer so we
** can use subscripts in the range 1 - size.
*/
array -= 1;

/*
** Clear the values to zero.
*/
for( i = 0; i <= size; i += 1 )
        array[i] = 0;

/*
** Count how many times each value appears,
** then return the answers.
*/
while( scanf( "%d", &i ) == 1 )
        array[ i ] += 1;

free( array );
return array;
}
```

6. Suppose you are writing a program and wish to minimize the amount of stack space it uses. Will allocating arrays dynamically help? How about scalars?

7. What would be the effect of deleting the two calls to `free` in Program 11.4b?

11.11 Programming Exercises

★ 1. Write your own version of the `calloc` function, using `malloc` to obtain memory.

⌂ ★★ 2. Write a function that reads a list of integers from the standard input and returns the values in a dynamically allocated array. The end of the input list is determined by watching for EOF. The first number in the array should be a count of how many values the array contains. This number is followed by the values.

★★★ 3. Write a function that reads a string from the standard input and returns a copy of the string in dynamically allocated memory. The function may not impose any limit on the size of the string being read!

★★★ 4. Write a program to create the data structure in the following diagram. The last three objects are structures which are dynamically allocated. The first object, which may be static, is a pointer to a structure. You do not need to make this program general—we will discuss this data structure in the next chapter.

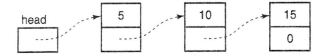

Using Structures and Pointers

You can create powerful data structures by combining structures and pointers. In this chapter we take a closer look at some techniques for using structures and pointers. We spend a lot of time with a data structure called a linked list, not only because it is very useful but also because many of the techniques used to manipulate linked lists are applicable to other data structures.

12.1 Linked Lists

For those of you who are not familiar with linked lists, here is a brief introduction. A *linked list* is a collection of independent structures (often called *nodes*) that contain data. The individual nodes in the list are connected by links, or pointers. A program accesses the nodes in the list by following the pointers. Usually the nodes are dynamically allocated, though occasionally you will find linked lists constructed among elements of an array of nodes. Even in this case, though, a program traverses the list by following the pointers.

12.2 Singly Linked Lists

In a *singly linked list*, each node contains a pointer to the next node in the list. The pointer field of the last node in the list contains NULL to indicate that there are no more nodes in the list. After you have found the first node on a list, the pointers will lead you to the remaining nodes. To keep track of where the list begins, a *root* pointer is used. The root pointer points to the first node on the list. Notice that the root is a pointer and it does not contain any data.

Here is a diagram of a singly linked list.

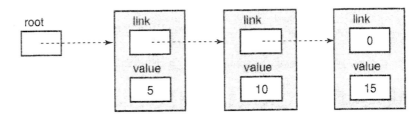

The nodes in this example are structures created with the following declaration.

```
typedef struct   NODE    {
          struct   NODE    *link;
          int               value;
} Node;
```

The data stored in each node is an integer. This list contains three nodes. If you begin at the root and follow the pointer to the first node, you can access the data stored in that node. Following the pointer in the first node takes you to the second node, where you can get its data. Finally, the next pointer brings you to the last node. The value zero is used to indicate a NULL pointer; here it means that there are no more nodes in the list.

In the diagram the nodes are shown as adjacent to display the *logical* ordering that the links provide. In fact, the nodes might actually be scattered all through memory. It doesn't make any difference to a program processing such a list whether the nodes are physically adjacent or not, because the program always uses the links to get from one node to the next.

A singly linked list can be traversed from start to end by following the links, but the list cannot be traversed backwards. In other words, once your program has reached the last node in the list, the only way to get back to any earlier node is to start again from the root pointer. Of course, the program could save a pointer to the current node before advancing to the next one, or it could even save pointers to the preceding few nodes. However, these linked lists are dynamic and can grow to hold hundreds or thousands of nodes, so it is not feasible to save pointers to all of the preceding nodes in a list.

The nodes in this particular list are linked so that the data values are in ascending order. This ordering is important for some applications, such as organizing appointments by time of day. It is also possible to create an unordered list for applications that do not require any ordering.

12.2.1 Inserting into a Singly Linked List

How would we insert a new node into an ordered singly linked list? Suppose we had a new value, say 12, to insert into the previous list. Conceptually this task is easy: start at the beginning of the list, follow the pointers until you find the first node whose value is larger than 12, and then insert the new value into the list just before that node.

In practice the algorithm is more interesting. We traverse the list and stop when we reach the node containing 15, the first value greater than 12. We know that the new value should be added to the list just before this node, but the pointer field of the *previous* node must be modified to accomplish the insertion. However, we've passed this node, and we cannot go back. The solution is to always save a pointer to the previous node in the list.

We will now develop a function to insert a node into an ordered, singly linked list. Program 12.1 is our first attempt.

```c
/*
** Insert into an ordered, singly linked list.  The arguments are
** a pointer to the first node in the list, and the value to
** insert.
*/
#include <stdlib.h>
#include <stdio.h>
#include "singly_linked_list_node.h"

#define FALSE   0
#define TRUE    1

int
sll_insert( Node *current, int new_value )
{
        Node    *previous;
        Node    *new;

        /*
        ** Look for the right place by walking down the list
        ** until we reach a node whose value is greater than
        ** or equal to the new value.
        */
        while( current->value < new_value ){
                previous = current;
                current = current->link;
        }
}
```

Program 12.1   Insert into an ordered, singly linked list: first try

continued . . .

```
/*
** Allocate a new node and store the new value into it.
** In this event, we return FALSE.
*/
new = (Node *)malloc( sizeof( Node ) );
if( new == NULL )
        return FALSE;
new->value = new_value;

/*
** Insert the new node into the list, and return TRUE.
*/
new->link = current;
previous->link = new;
return TRUE;
}
```

Program 12.1   Insert into an ordered, singly linked list: first try   insert1.c

We call the function in this manner:

```
result = sll_insert( root, 12 );
```

Let's trace this code and see whether it correctly inserts the new value 12 into the list. First, the function is called with the value of the root variable, a pointer to the first node in the list. Here is the state of the list when the function begins:

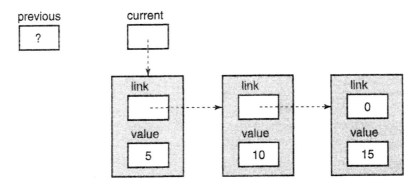

This diagram does not show the root variable because the function cannot access it. A copy of its value came into the function as the parameter current, but the function cannot access root. Now current->value is 5, which is less than 12, so the body of the loop is executed once. When we get back to the top of the loop, our pointers will have advanced.

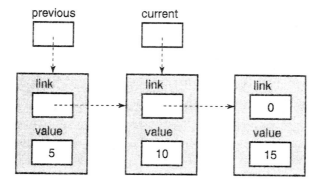

current->value is now 10, so the body of the loop executes again, with this result:

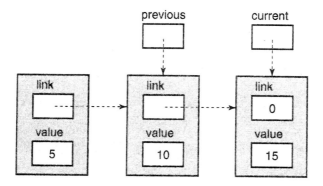

Now current->value is greater than 12 so the loop breaks.

At this point the previous pointer is the important one, because it points to the node that must be changed to insert the new value. But first, a new node must be obtained to hold the value. The next diagram shows the state of the list after the value is copied into the new node.

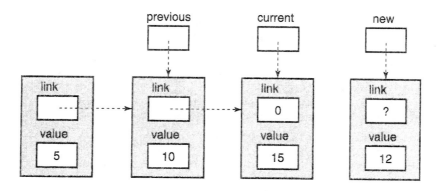

Linking the new node into the list requires two steps. First,

```
new->link = current;
```

makes the new node point to what will be the next node in the list, the first one we found with a value larger than 12. After this step, the list looks like this:

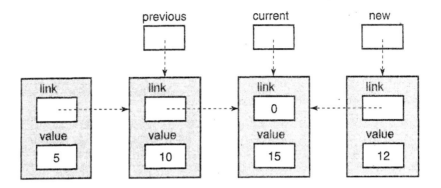

The second step is to make the `previous` node, the last one whose value was smaller than 12, point to the new node. The following statement performs this task.

```
previous->link = new;
```

The result of this step is:

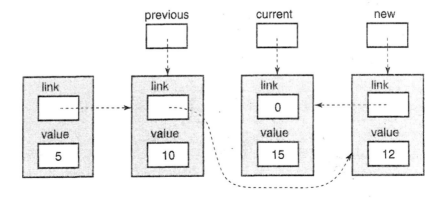

The function then returns, leaving the list looking like this:

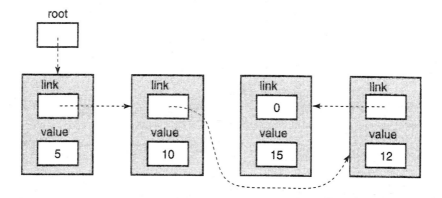

Starting at the `root` pointer and following the links verifies that the new node has been correctly inserted.

Debugging the Insert Function

Unfortunately, the insert function is incorrect. Try inserting the value 20 into the list and you will see one problem: the `while` loop runs off the end of the list and then applies indirection to a NULL pointer. To solve this problem, we must test `current` to make sure that it is not NULL before evaluating `current->value`:

```
while( current != NULL && current->value < value ){
```

The next problem is tougher. Trace the function to insert the value 3 into the list. What happens?

In order to add a node to the beginning of the list, the function must change the root pointer. The function, however, cannot access the variable `root`. The easiest way to fix this problem is to just make `root` a global variable so that the insertion function can modify it. Unfortunately, this approach is also the *worst* way to fix the problem, because then the function works only for that one list.

The better solution is to pass a pointer to `root` as an argument. Then the function can use indirection both to obtain the value of `root` (the pointer to the first node of the list), and to store a new pointer into it. What is the type of this parameter? `root` is a pointer to a `Node`, so the parameter is of type `Node **`: a pointer to a pointer to a `Node`. The function in Program 12.2 contains these modifications. We must now call the function like this:

```
result = sll_insert( &root, 12 );
```

```
/*
** Insert into an ordered, singly linked list.  The arguments are
** a pointer to the root pointer for the list, and the value to
** insert.
*/
#include <stdlib.h>
#include <stdio.h>
#include "singly_linked_list_node.h"

#define FALSE   0
#define TRUE    1

int
sll_insert( Node **rootp, int new_value )
{
        Node    *current;
        Node    *previous;
        Node    *new;

        /*
        ** Get the pointer to the first node.
        */
        current = *rootp;
        previous = NULL;

        /*
        ** Look for the right place by walking down the list
        ** until we reach a node whose value is greater than
        ** or equal to the new value.
        */
        while( current != NULL && current->value < new_value ){
                previous = current;
                current = current->link;
        }

        /*
        ** Allocate a new node and store the new value into it.
        ** In this event, we return FALSE.
        */
        new = (Node *)malloc( sizeof( Node ) );
        if( new == NULL )
                return FALSE;
        new->value = new_value;

        /*
```

Program 12.2   Insert into an ordered, singly linked list: second try   *continued . . .*

```
** Insert the new node into the list, and return TRUE.
*/
new->link = current;
if( previous == NULL )
        *rootp = new;
else
        previous->link = new;
return TRUE;
}
```

Program 12.2   Insert into an ordered, singly linked list: second try   insert2.c

This second version contains some additional statements.

```
previous = NULL;
```

is needed so that we can check later whether the new value will be the first node in the list.

```
current = *rootp;
```

uses indirection on the root pointer argument to get the value of `root`, a pointer to the first node in the list. Finally

```
if( previous == NULL )
        *rootp = new;
else
        previous->link = new;
```

was added to the end of the function. It checks whether the new value should be added to the beginning of the list. If so, we use indirection on the root pointer to make `root` point to the new node.

This function works, and in many languages it is as good as you can get. However, we can do better because C allows you to get the address of (a pointer to) existing objects.

Optimizing the Insert Function

It appears that inserting a node at the beginning of the list *must* be a special case. After all, the pointer that must be adjusted to insert the first node is the root pointer. For every other node, the pointer to be adjusted is the link field of the previous node. These seemingly different operations are really the same.

The key to eliminating the special case is to realize that every node in the list has a pointer somewhere pointing to it. For the first node, it is the `root` pointer, and for every other node it is the link field of the preceding node. The important point is that there is a pointer somewhere pointing to each node. Whether the pointer is or is not contained in a node is irrelevant.

Let's look at the list once more to clarify this point. Here is the first node and its corresponding pointer.

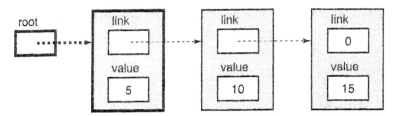

If the new value is inserted before the first node, then this pointer must be changed.

Here is the second node and its pointer.

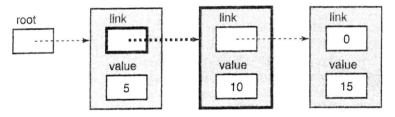

If the new value is inserted before the second node, then *this* pointer must be changed. Note that we're concerned only with the pointer; the node that contains it is irrelevant. The same pattern holds for every node in the list.

Now let's take a look at the modified function as it begins to execute. Here are its variables as they appear just after the first assignment statement.

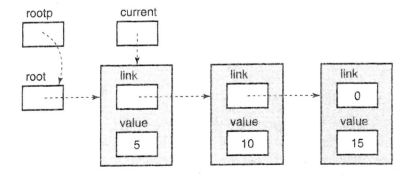

We have a pointer to the current node and a pointer to the link that points to the current node. We don't need anything else! If the value in the current node is larger than the new value, the `rootp` pointer tells us which link field must be changed to link the new node into the list. If insertions elsewhere in the list can be expressed the same way, the special case disappears. The key is the pointer/node relationship we saw earlier.

When moving to the next node, save a pointer to the *link* that points to the next node instead of keeping a pointer to the previous *node*. It is easy to diagram what is desired.

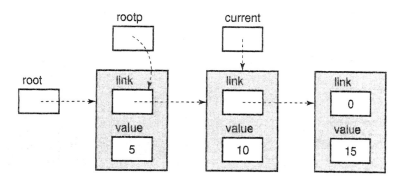

Notice here that `rootp` is not pointing to the node; it points to the link field within the node. This fact is the key to simplifying the insert function, but it depends upon our being able to obtain the address of the link field of the current node. This operation is easy in C. The expression `&current->link` does the trick. Program 12.3 is the final version of our insertion function. The `rootp` parameter is now called `linkp`, because it points to many different links now, not just the root. We don't need `previous` any more, because our link pointer takes care of locating the link that needs to be modified. The special case at the end of the function is gone because we always have a pointer to the link field that needs to be changed—we modify the root variable in exactly the same way as the link field of a node. Finally, `register` declarations have been added to the pointer variables to improve the efficiency of the resulting code.

The `while` loop in this final version is trickier because of the embedded assignment to `current`. Here is an equivalent, though slightly longer loop.

```
/*
** Look for the right place.
*/
current = *linkp;
while( current != NULL && current->value < value ){
        linkp = &current->link;
```

```
/*
** Insert into an ordered, singly linked list.  The arguments are
** a pointer to the first node in the list, and the value to
** insert.
*/
#include <stdlib.h>
#include <stdio.h>
#include "singly_linked_list_node.h"

#define FALSE   0
#define TRUE    1

int
sll_insert( register Node **linkp, int new_value )
{
        register Node   *current;
        register Node   *new;

        /*
        ** Look for the right place by walking down the list
        ** until we reach a node whose value is greater than
        ** or equal to the new value.
        */
        while( ( current = *linkp ) != NULL &&
            current->value < new_value )
                linkp = &current->link;

        /*
        ** Allocate a new node and store the new value into it.
        ** In this event, we return FALSE.
        */
        new = (Node *)malloc( sizeof( Node ) );
        if( new == NULL )
                return FALSE;
        new->value = new_value;

        /*
        ** Insert the new node into the list, and return TRUE.
        */
        new->link = current;
        *linkp = new;
        return TRUE;
}
```

Program 12.3   Insert into an ordered, singly linked list: final version   insert3.c

```
            current = *linkp;
    }
```

To begin, `current` is set to point to the first node in the list. The `while` test checks whether we've reached the end of the list. If not, it then checks whether we are at the proper place for the insertion. If not, the body of the loop executes, which sets `linkp` to point to the link field in the current node, and advances `current` to the next node.

   The fact that the last statement in the loop body is identical to the statement just prior to the loop leads to the "simplification" of embedding the assignment to `current` within the `while` expression. The result is a more complex but more compact loop, because we have eliminated the redundant assignment to `current`.

Eliminating the special case made this function simpler. There are two factors that make this improvement possible. The first factor is our ability to interpret the problem correctly. Unless you can identify the commonality in seemingly different operations, you will be stuck writing extra code to handle special cases. Often this knowledge is acquired only after you have worked with the data structure for a while and understand it more clearly. The second factor is that the C language provides the right tools for you to exploit the commonality.

   The improved function depends on C's ability to obtain the address of existing objects. Like many C features, this ability is both powerful and dangerous. In Modula and Pascal, for example, there isn't an "address of" operator, so the only pointers that exist are those produced by dynamic memory allocation. It is not possible to obtain a pointer to an ordinary variable or even to a field of a dynamically allocated structure. Pointer arithmetic is not allowed, and there isn't any means for casting a pointer from one type to another. These restrictions are advantageous in that they prevent the programmer from making mistakes such as subscripting off the end of an array and generating pointers of one type that in fact point to objects of some other type.

There are far fewer restrictions on pointers in C, which is why we were able to improve the insertion function. On the other hand, C programmers must be more careful when using pointers to avoid mistakes. The Pascal philosophy to pointers is sort of like saying, "You might hurt yourself with a hammer, so we won't give you one." The C philosophy is, "Here is a hammer. In fact, here are several kinds of hammers. Good luck." With this power, C programmers can get into more trouble than Pascal programmers, but good C programmers can produce smaller, more efficient, and more maintainable code than their Pascal or Modula counterparts. This is one of the reasons why C is so popular in industry, and why experienced C programmers are in such demand.

12.2.2 Other List Operations

To make singly linked lists really useful, we need more operations such as searching and deletion. However, the algorithms for these operations are straightforward and easily implemented using the techniques illustrated in the insertion function. These functions are left as exercises.

12.3 Doubly Linked Lists

An alternative to singly linked lists is the *doubly linked list*. In a doubly linked list, each node has two pointers—one to the next node in the list and one to the previous node. The back pointer lets us traverse doubly linked lists in either direction. We can even go back and forth. The following diagram illustrates a doubly linked list.

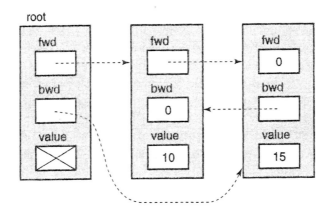

Here is the declaration for the node type.

```
typedef struct   NODE    {
         struct  NODE    *fwd;
         struct  NODE    *bwd;
         int             value;
} Node;
```

The root is now two pointers: one points to the first node in the list, and the other points to the last node. These two pointers let us begin a traversal at either end of the list.

We might declare the two root pointers as separate variables, but then we would have to pass pointers to both of them to the insertion function. It is more convenient to declare an entire node for the root pointers, one whose value field is never used. In our example, this technique only wastes the memory for one integer. Separate pointers might be better for lists whose value field is large. Alternatively, we might use the value field of the root node to store other information about the list, for example, the number of nodes it currently contains.

The fwd field of the root node points to the first node in the list, and the bwd field of the root node points to the last node in the list. Both of these fields will be NULL if the list is empty. The bwd field of the first node in the list and the fwd field of the last node will be NULL. In an ordered list, nodes are stored in increasing order of the value field.

12.3.1 Inserting into a Doubly Linked List

This time, we develop a function that inserts a value into an ordered, doubly linked list. dll_insert takes two arguments: a pointer to the root node and an integer value.

The singly linked insertion function we wrote earlier adds duplicate values to the list. It may be more appropriate for some applications to not add duplicates. dll_insert will add a new value only if is not already in the list.

Let's take a more disciplined approach to developing this function. There are four cases that can occur when inserting a node into a linked list:

1.   The value might have to be inserted in the middle of the list.

2.   The value might have to be inserted at the beginning of the list.

3.   The value might have to be inserted at the end of the list.

4.   The value might have to be inserted at both the beginning and the end (that is, inserted into an empty list).

In each of these cases, four pointers must be modified.

*   In cases (1) and (2), the fwd field of the new node must be set to point to the next node in the list, and the bwd field of the next node in the list must be set to point to the new node. In cases (3) and (4), the fwd field of the new node must be set to NULL, and the bwd field of the root node must be set to point to the new node.

*   In cases (1) and (3), the bwd field of the new node must be set to point to the previous node in the list, and the fwd field of the previous node must be set to point to the new node. In cases (2) and (4), the bwd field of the new node must be set to NULL, and the fwd field of the root node must be set to point to the new node.

If this description seems unclear, the straightforward implementation in Program 12.4 should help.

```
/*
** Insert a value into a doubly linked list.  rootp is a pointer to
** the root node, and value is the new value to be inserted.
** Returns: 0 if the value is already in the list, -1 if there was
** no memory to create a new node, 1 if the value was added
** successfully.
*/
#include <stdlib.h>
#include <stdio.h>
#include "doubly_linked_list_node.h"

int
dll_insert( Node *rootp, int value )
{
        Node    *this;
        Node    *next;
        Node    *newnode;

        /*
        ** See if value is already in the list; return if it is.
        ** Otherwise, allocate a new node for the value ("newnode"
        ** will point to it). "this" will point to the node that the
        ** new value should follow, and "next" will point to the one
        ** after it.
        */
        for( this = rootp; (next = this->fwd) != NULL; this = next ){
                if( next->value == value )
                        return 0;
                if( next->value > value )
                        break;
        }
        newnode = (Node *)malloc( sizeof( Node ) );
        if( newnode == NULL )
                return -1;
        newnode->value = value;

        /*
        ** Add the new node to the list.
        */
        if( next != NULL ){
                /*
                ** Case 1 or 2: not at end of the list
                */
                if( this != rootp ){            /* Case 1: not at front */
                        newnode->fwd = next;
```

Program 12.4   Straightforward doubly linked list insert function   *continued . . .*

```
                                this->fwd = newnode;
                                newnode->bwd = this;
                                next->bwd = newnode;
                        }
                        else {                          /* Case 2: at front */
                                newnode->fwd = next;
                                rootp->fwd = newnode;
                                newnode->bwd = NULL;
                                next->bwd = newnode;
                        }
                }
                else {
                        /*
                        ** Case 3 or 4: at end of the list
                        */
                        if( this != rootp ){            /* Case 3: not at front */
                                newnode->fwd = NULL;
                                this->fwd = newnode;
                                newnode->bwd = this;
                                rootp->bwd = newnode;
                        }
                        else {                          /* Case 4: at front */
                                newnode->fwd = NULL;
                                rootp->fwd = newnode;
                                newnode->bwd = NULL;
                                rootp->bwd = newnode;
                        }
                }
        }
        return 1;
}
```

Program 12.4   Straightforward doubly linked list insert function   dll_ins1.c

The function begins by making `this` point to the root node. The `next` pointer always points to the node after `this`; the idea is to advance these pointers together until the new node should be inserted between them. The `for` loop checks the value in the `next` node to determine when this position has been reached.

If the new value is found in the list, the function simply returns. Otherwise, the loop ends when the end of the list is reached or when the proper position for insertion is reached. In either case, the new node should be inserted after the `this` node. Note that space for the new node is not allocated until after we determine whether the value should actually be added to the list.

Allocating the new node first would cause a potential memory leak for duplicate values.

The four cases have been implemented separately. Let's trace case 1 by inserting the value 12 into the list. The following diagram shows the state of our variables just after the `for` loop breaks.

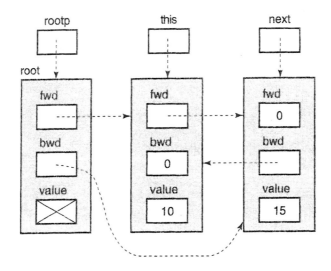

A new node is then allocated. After executing the statements

```
newnode->fwd = next;
this->fwd = newnode;
```

the list looks like this:

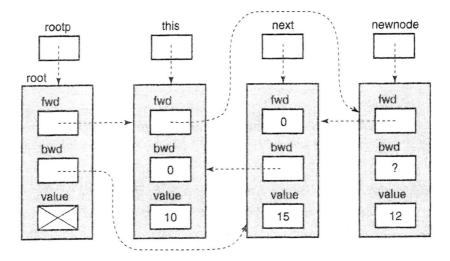

Then, the statements

```
newnode->bwd = this;
next->bwd = newnode;
```

finish linking the new value into the list:

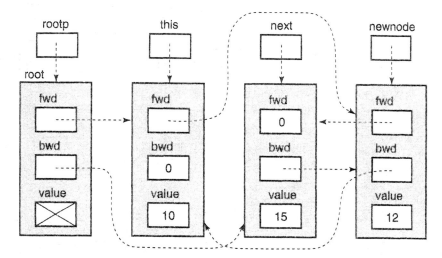

Study the code to determine how the remaining cases work, and convince
yourself that each case is completed properly.

Simplifying the Insert Function

The observant programmer will notice that there is a lot of similarity among
the groups of statements in the nested `if` statements in the function, and the
good programmer will be bothered by all of the duplication. So we will now
eliminate the duplication using two techniques. The first is *statement factoring*,
and is illustrated in the following example.

```
if( x == 3 ){
        i = 1;
        something;
        j = 2;
}
else {
        i = 1;
        something different;
        j = 2;
}
```

Notice that the statements i = 1; and j = 2; will be executed whether the expression x == 3 is true or false. Doing i = 1; before the if will not affect the result of the test x == 3, so both pairs of assignments can be factored out, leaving the simpler, but completely equivalent, statements:

```
i = 1;
if( x == 3 )
        something;
else
        something different;
j = 2;
```

Be careful not to factor a statement above the if that changes the result of the test. For example, in

```
if( x == 3 ){
        x = 0;
        something;
}
else {
        x = 0;
        something different;
}
```

the statement x = 0; cannot be factored out because it would affect the result of the comparison.

Factoring the innermost of the nested if's in Program 12.4 yields the code fragment in Program 12.5. Compare this code to the previous function and convince yourself that it is equivalent.

The second simplification technique is easily illustrated with an example:

```
if( pointer != NULL )
        field = pointer;
else
        field = NULL;
```

The intent here is to set a variable equal to pointer, or to NULL if pointer doesn't point to anything. But look at this statement:

```
field = pointer;
```

If pointer is not NULL, field gets a copy of its value, as before. But if

```
/*
** Add the new node to the list.
*/
if( next != NULL ){
        /*
        ** Case 1 or 2: not at end of the list
        */
        newnode->fwd = next;
        if( this != rootp ){          /* Case 1: not at front */
                this->fwd = newnode;
                newnode->bwd = this;
        }
        else {                        /* Case 2: at front */
                rootp->fwd = newnode;
                newnode->bwd = NULL;
        }
        next->bwd = newnode;
}
else {
        /*
        ** Case 3 or 4: at end of the list
        */
        newnode->fwd = NULL;
        if( this != rootp ){          /* Case 3: not at front */
                this->fwd = newnode;
                newnode->bwd = this;
        }
        else {                        /* Case 4: at front */
                rootp->fwd = newnode;
                newnode->bwd = NULL;
        }
        rootp->bwd = newnode;
}
```

Program 12.5   Factored doubly linked list insertion logic   dll_ins2.c

pointer is NULL, field gets a copy of the NULL from pointer, which has
the same effect as assigning the constant NULL. This statement performs the
same work as the previous one and is obviously simpler.

The key to applying this technique to the code in Program 12.5 is to
identify the statements that perform the same work even though they look different and rewrite them so that they are identical. We can rewrite the first
statement in cases 3 and 4 as

```
newnode->fwd = next;
```

because the `if` statement has just determined that `next == NULL`. This change makes the first statement on both sides of the `if` statement identical, so we can factor it out. Write down this change, and study what remains.

Did you see it? Both nested `if`'s are now identical, so they can also be factored. The result of these changes is shown in Program 12.6.

We can improve this code still further. The first statement in the `else` clause of the first `if` can be rewritten as

```
this->fwd = newnode;
```

because the `if` statement has already decided that `this == rootp`. The rewritten statement and its mate can now be factored out, too.

Program 12.7 is the entire function after all of the changes have been implemented. It does the same work as the original but is much smaller. The local pointers have been declared register variables to improve the size and speed of the code even further.

```
/*
** Add the new node to the list.
*/
newnode->fwd = next;

if( this != rootp ){
        this->fwd = newnode;
        newnode->bwd = this;
}
else {
        rootp->fwd = newnode;
        newnode->bwd = NULL;
}
if( next != NULL )
        next->bwd = newnode;
else
        rootp->bwd = newnode;
```

Program 12.6   Further factored doubly linked list insertion logic   dll_ins3.c

```
/*
** Insert a value into a doubly linked list.  rootp is a pointer to
** the root node, and value is the new value to be inserted.
** Returns: 0 if the value is already in the list, -1 if there was
** no memory to create a new node, 1 if the value was added
** successfully.
*/
#include <stdlib.h>
#include <stdio.h>
#include "doubly_linked_list_node.h"

int
dll_insert( register Node *rootp, int value )
{
        register Node    *this;
        register Node    *next;
        register Node    *newnode;

        /*
        ** See if value is already in the list; return if it is.
        ** Otherwise, allocate a new node for the value ("newnode"
        ** will point to it). "this" will point to the node that the
        ** new value should follow, and "next" will point to the one
        ** after it.
        */
        for( this = rootp; (next = this->fwd) != NULL; this = next ){
                if( next->value == value )
                        return 0;
                if( next->value > value )
                        break;
        }
        newnode = (Node *)malloc( sizeof( Node ) );
        if( newnode == NULL )
                return -1;
        newnode->value = value;

        /*
        ** Add the new node to the list.
        */
        newnode->fwd = next;
        this->fwd = newnode;

        if( this != rootp )
                newnode->bwd = this;
        else
```

Program 12.7 Fully simplified doubly linked list insertion function   *continued . . .*

```
              newnode->bwd = NULL;

if( next != NULL )
              next->bwd = newnode;
else
              rootp->bwd = newnode;


return 1;
}
```

Program 12.7   Fully simplified doubly linked list insertion function   dll_ins4.c

This function cannot be made significantly better, though we can make the source code smaller. The purpose of the first if statement is to determine the right side of an assignment. We can replace the if with a conditional expression. We can also replace the second if with a conditional, though this change is less obvious.

The code in Program 12.8 is certainly smaller, but is it really better? Although there are fewer statements, the number of comparisons and assignments that must be made is the same as before, so this code isn't any faster than what we had before. There are two minor differences: newnode->bwd and ->bwd = newnode are both written once rather than twice. Will these differences result in smaller code? Possibly, depending on how well your compiler can optimize. But the difference will be small at best, and this code is less readable than before, particularly for an inexperienced C programmer. Thus, Program 12.8 may be more trouble to maintain.

If the program size or execution speed were really important, the only thing left to try would be to hand code the function in assembly language. Even this drastic option does not guarantee any significant improvement, and the difficulty of writing, reading, and maintaining assembly code suggests that this approach should be used only as a last resort.

```
/*
** Add the new node to the list.
*/
newnode->fwd = next;
this->fwd = newnode;
newnode->bwd = this != rootp ? this : NULL;
( next != NULL ? next : rootp )->bwd = newnode;
```

Program 12.8   Insert function using conditional expressions   dll_ins5.c

12.3.2 Other List Operations

As with singly linked lists, more operations are needed for doubly linked lists. The exercises will give you practice in writing them.

12.4 Summary

A singly linked list is a data structure that stores values using pointers. Each node in the list contains a field which points to the next node. A separate pointer, called the root, points to the first node. When the nodes are dynamically allocated, they may be scattered throughout memory. However, the list is traversed by following the pointers, so the physical arrangement of the nodes is irrelevant. A singly linked list can only be traversed in one direction.

To insert a new value into an ordered, singly linked list, you must first find the proper position in the list. New values may be inserted into unordered lists anywhere. There are two steps to link a new node into the list. First, the new node's link field must be set to point to what will be the next node. Second, the previous link field must be changed to point to the new node. In many other languages, an insertion function would save a pointer to the previous node to accomplish the second step. However, this technique makes inserting at the beginning of the list a special case. In C, you can eliminate the special case by saving a pointer to the link field that must be changed instead of a pointer to the previous node.

Each node in a doubly linked list contains two link fields: one points to the next node in the list, and the other points to the previous node. Two root pointers are used to point to the first and the last nodes in the list. Thus, traversals of doubly linked lists may begin from either end of the list and may proceed in either direction. To insert a new node into a doubly linked list, four links must be changed. The new node's forward and backward links must be set, and the previous node's forward pointer and the next node's backward pointer must both be changed to point to the new node.

Statement factoring is a technique that simplifies a program by removing redundant statements from it. If the "then" and the "else" clauses of an if end with identical sequences of statements, they can be replaced by a single copy of the sequence after the if. Identical sequences of statements can also be factored from the beginning of an if statement unless their execution changes the test performed by the if. If different statements actually perform the same work, you may be able to rewrite them identically. You may then be able to apply statement factoring to simplify the program.

12.5 Summary of Cautions

1. Falling off the end of a linked list (page 327).

2. Be especially careful with pointers, because C does not provide a safety net for their use (page 333).

3. Factoring a statement out of an `if` that changes the result of the test (page 340).

12.6 Summary of Programming Tips

1. Eliminating special cases makes code easier to maintain (page 333).

2. Eliminate duplicate statements from `if` statements by factoring them (page 339).

3. Do not judge the quality of code solely by its size (page 344).

12.7 Questions

1. Can Program 12.3 be written without using a `current` variable? If so, compare the resulting function to the original.

2. Some data structures textbooks suggest using a "header node" in a singly linked list. This dummy node is always the first element in the list and eliminates the special case code for inserting at the beginning of the list. Discuss the pros and cons of this technique.

3. Where would the insertion function in Program 12.3 put a node with a duplicate value? What would be the effect of changing the comparison from < to <=?

4. Discuss techniques for omitting the value field from the root node of a doubly linked list.

5. What would be the result if the call to `malloc` in Program 12.7 were performed at the beginning of the function?

6. Is it possible to sort the nodes in an unordered, singly linked list?

7. A *concordance list* is an alphabetic list of the words that appear in a book or article. You can implement a concordance list using an ordered, singly linked list of strings with an insertion function that does not add duplicate words to the list. The problem with this implementation is that the time it takes to search the list increases as the list grows in size.

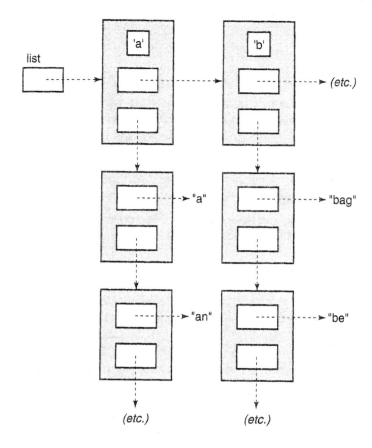

Figure 12.1   A concordance list

Figure 12.1 illustrates an alternative data structure for storing the concordance list. The idea is to break the large list into 26 smaller lists—one list of words for each letter of the alphabet. Each of the nodes in the primary list contains a letter and points to an ordered, singly linked list of words (stored as strings) that begin with this letter.

How does the time to search this structure for a specific word compare to the time to search an ordered, singly linked list containing all of the words?

12.8 Programming Exercises

  ✦ ★ 1. Write a function that counts the number of nodes in a singly linked list. It should take a pointer to the first node in the list as its only argument. What must you know in order to write this function? What other jobs can this function perform?

★ 2. Write a function to locate a particular value in an unordered, singly linked list, and return a pointer to that node. You may assume that the node structure is defined in the file `singly_linked_list_node.h`.

Are any changes needed in order to make the function work on an ordered, singly linked list?

★★★ 3. Rewrite Program 12.7, `dll_insert`, so that the head and tail pointers are passed in as separate pointers rather than as part of a root node. What effect does this change have on the logic of the function?

★★★★ 4. Write a function that reverses the order of the nodes in a singly linked list. The function should have the following prototype:

```
struct NODE * sll_reverse( struct NODE *first );
```

Declare the node structure in the file `singly_linked_list_node.h`.

The argument points to the first node in the list. After the list is rearranged, the function returns a pointer to the new head of the list. The link field of the last node in the list will contain NULL, and in the event of an empty list (`first == NULL`) the function should return NULL.

△ ★★★ 5. Write a program to remove a node from a singly linked list. The function should have the following prototype:

```
int sll_remove( struct NODE **rootp, struct NODE *node );
```

You may assume that the node structure is defined in the file `singly_linked_list_node.h`. The first argument points to the root pointer of the list, and the second points to the node that is to be removed. The function returns false if the list does not contain the indicated node, otherwise it removes the node and returns true.

Is there any advantage in taking a pointer to the node to remove as opposed to taking the value?

★★★ 6. Write a program to remove a node from a doubly linked list. The function should have the following prototype:

```
int
dll_remove( struct NODE *rootp, struct NODE *node );
```

You may assume that the node structure is defined in the file `doubly_linked_list_node.h`. The first argument points to a node containing the root pointers for the list (the same as with Program 12.7), and the second points to the node that is to be removed. The function returns false if the list does not contain the indicated node, otherwise it removes the node and returns true.

★★★★★ 7. Write a function to insert a new word into the concordance list described in Question 7. The function should take a pointer to the `list` pointer and a string as its arguments. The string is assumed to contain a single word. If the word does not already exist in the list, it should be copied into dynamically allocated memory and then inserted. The function should return true if the string was inserted; and false if the string already existed in the list, did not begin with a letter, or if anything else went wrong.

The function should maintain the primary list in order by the letter of the node and the secondary lists in order by the words.

13

Advanced Pointer Topics

This chapter is a collection of various techniques involving pointers. Some of them are very useful, others are of more academic interest, and a few are just fun, but all are good illustrations of various principles in the language.

13.1 More Pointers to Pointers

We used pointers to pointers in the last chapter to simplify the function that inserts a new value into a singly linked list. There are many other areas where having a pointer to a pointer is also valuable.

Here is a general example.

```
int     i;
int     *pi;
int     **ppi;
```

These declarations create the following variables in memory. If these are automatic variables, we cannot make any assumptions about their initial values.

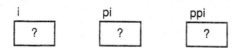

Given this information, what is the effect of each of these statements?

```
①  printf( "%d\n", ppi );
②  printf( "%d\n", &ppi );
③  *ppi = 5;
```

351

① If `ppi` is an automatic variable, it is uninitialized and a random value is printed. If it is a static variable, zero is printed.

② This statement prints, as a decimal integer, the address where `ppi` is stored. This value is not very useful.

③ The result of this statement is unpredictable. Indirection should not be performed on `ppi` because it is not yet initialized.

The next two statements are more useful.

```
ppi = &pi;
```

This statement initializes `ppi` to point to the variable `pi`. We can now safely apply indirection to `ppi`.

```
*ppi = &i;
```

This statement initializes `pi` (which is accessed indirectly through `ppi`) to point to `i`. After these last two statements, the variables look like this:

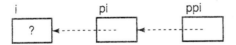

Now, each of the following statements has the same effect:

```
i = 'a';
*pi = 'a';
**ppi = 'a';
```

Why would anyone ever use the more complicated versions with indirection if a simple assignment to `i` does the job? Because the simple assignment is not always possible, such as in the linked list insertion. We could not use a simple assignment in that function because the variable name was not known within the scope of the function. All the function had was a pointer to the location that needed to be changed, so indirection was used on the pointer to access the desired variable.

In the previous example, the variable `i` is an integer, and `pi` is a pointer to an integer. But `ppi` is pointing at `pi`, so it is a pointer to a pointer to an integer. Suppose we wanted another variable, one that would point to `ppi`. Its type, of course, would be "pointer to a pointer to a pointer to an integer," and it would be declared in this way:

```
int     ***pppi;
```

The more levels of indirection, the less often you will need to use it. But once you truly understand indirection, it is easy to apply as many levels of indirection as you need for any situation.

Use only as many levels of indirection as you really need. Otherwise, your programs will end up being larger, slower, and harder to maintain.

13.2 Advanced Declarations

Before using more advanced pointer types, we must see how they are declared. Earlier chapters introduced the idea of a declaration expression and how variables in C are declared by inference. We saw some examples of declaration by inference when we declared pointers to arrays in Chapter 8. Let's explore this topic by looking at a sequence of increasingly complex declarations.

We'll start with some easy ones.

```
int     f;      /* an integer */
int     *f;     /* a pointer to an integer */
```

Remember how the second declaration works, though: it declares the *expression* *f to be an integer. From this fact you must deduce that f is a pointer to an integer. This interpretation of C declarations is validated by the declaration

```
int*    f, g;
```

which does not declare two pointers. Despite the spacing, the star is associated with f, and only f is a pointer. g is an ordinary integer.

Here is another one you have seen before:

```
int     f();
```

It declares f to be a function that returns an integer. The old-style declaration says nothing about the function's parameters. It only declares the type of value that f will return. I will use this style for now to keep the examples simpler and return to full prototypes later.

Here's a new one:

```
int     *f();
```

To figure this one out, you must determine how the expression *f() is evaluated. The function call operator () goes first because its precedence is higher than that of indirection, so f is a function that returns a pointer to an integer.

If "declaration by inference" seems like a nuisance, consider that the expressions used for declaring variables are evaluated with the same rules used for ordinary expressions. You don't need to learn a separate syntax for declarations. If you can evaluate complex expressions, you can also figure out complex declarations because they work the same way.

The next declaration is more interesting.

```
int     (*f)();
```

Figuring out what the parentheses mean is an important step in deciphering this declaration. There are two sets of parentheses, and each has a different meaning. The second set of parentheses is the function call operator, but the first set is used only for grouping. It forces the indirection to be applied before the function call, making f a pointer to a function that returns an integer.

A pointer to a function? Yes, each function in a program begins at some address in memory, so it is possible for a variable to point to that location. The initialization and use of pointers to functions is covered later in this chapter.

The next declaration should now be easy:

```
int     *(*f)();
```

It is the same as the previous example except that in order to get an integer, indirection is applied to the value returned by the function. Here f is a pointer to a function that returns a pointer to an integer.

Now let's consider arrays, too.

```
int     f[];
```

indicates that f is an array of integers. The size has been omitted for now because we're not concerned with the array's size, only its type.[43]

How about this one?

```
int     *f[];
```

Again, there are two operators. The subscript has the higher precedence, so f is now an array of pointers to integers.

The next example is a trick question, but try to figure it out anyway.

```
int     f()[];
```

f appears to be a function that returns an array of integers. The trick is that it is illegal—functions can only return scalars, not arrays.

---

[43] Even without a size, these declarations are still legal if they are external or are function parameters.

Here is another one that will require some thought:

```
int      f[]();
```

Now f appears to be an array of functions that return integers. This declaration is also illegal because array elements must all be the same size, but it is quite reasonable for different functions to be different sizes.

The next declaration is legal, though:

```
int      (*f[])();
```

You must first find all of the operators and then apply them in the correct order. Once again, there are two sets of parentheses with different meanings. The parenthesized expression *f[] is evaluated first, so f is an array of pointers to something. The trailing () is the function call operator, so f must be an array of pointers to functions that return integers.

If you got that last one right, then this one should be easy:

```
int      *(*f[])();
```

The only change is one final indirection, so this declaration creates an array of pointers to functions that return *pointers to* integers.

Up to now, I've used old-style declarations to keep the examples simple. But ANSI C lets us use full function prototypes to make the declaration more specific. For example:

```
int      (*f)( int, float );
int      *(*g[])( int, float );
```

declares f to be a pointer to a function that takes two arguments, an integer and a float, and returns an integer. g is an array of pointers to functions that take two arguments, an integer and a float, and return a pointer to an integer. Despite the increased complexity in the declaration, the prototype form is greatly preferred because of the additional information it gives the compiler.

If you have a UNIX system and have access to the Internet, you can get cdecl, a program that converts between C declarations and English. It can explain an existing C declaration:

```
cdecl> explain int (*(*f)())[10];
declare f as pointer to function returning pointer to
    array 10 of int
```

or give you the syntax for a declaration:

```
cdecl> declare x as pointer to array 10 of pointer to
    function returning int
int (*(*x)[10])()
```

The source code for cdecl can be found in Volume 14 of the archives for the comp.sources.unix newsgroup.

13.3 Pointers to Functions

You will not use pointers to functions every day. However, they have their uses, and the two most common are jump tables and passing a function pointer as an argument in a function call. We'll explore both of these techniques this section. First, though, it is important to point out a common error.

Simply declaring a pointer to a function does not make it usable. Like any other pointer, a pointer to a function must be initialized to point to something before indirection can be performed on it. The following code fragment illustrates one way to initialize a pointer to a function.

```
int     f( int );
int     (*pf)( int ) = &f;
```

The second declaration creates pf, a pointer to a function, and initializes it to point to the function f. The initialization can also be accomplished with an assignment statement. It is important to have a prototype for f prior to the initialization, for without it the compiler would be unable to check whether the type of f agreed with that of pf.

The ampersand in the initialization is optional, because the compiler always converts function *names* to function *pointers* wherever they are used. The ampersand does explicitly what the compiler would have done implicitly anyway.

After the pointer has been declared and initialized, there are three ways to call the function:

```
int     ans;

ans = f( 25 );
ans = (*pf)( 25 );
ans = pf( 25 );
```

The first statement simply calls the function f by name, though its evaluation is probably not what you expected. The function name f is first converted to a pointer to the function; the pointer specifies where the function is located. The function call operator then invokes the function by executing the code beginning at this address.

The second statement applies indirection to pf, which converts the function pointer to a function name. This conversion is not really necessary, because the compiler converts it back to a pointer before applying the function call operator. Nevertheless, this statement has exactly the same effect as the first one.

The third statement has the same effect as the first two. Indirection is not needed, because the compiler wants a pointer to the function anyway. This example shows how function pointers are usually used.

When would anyone ever want to use a pointer to a function? As mentioned earlier, the two most common uses of pointers to functions are passing a function pointer as an argument in a function call and jump tables. Let's look at an application of each.

13.3.1 Callback Functions

Here is a simple function that locates a value in a singly linked list. Its arguments are a pointer to the first node in the list and the value to locate.

```
Node *
search_list( Node *node, int const value )
{
        while( node != NULL ){
                if( node->value == value )
                        break;
                node = node->link;
        }
        return node;
}
```

This function looks simple enough, but it works only with linked lists whose values are integers. If you also had a linked list of strings, you would need to write a different function, identical in every respect to this one except for the type of the parameter value and the manner in which the node values are compared.

A more general approach is to make the searching function typeless so that it will work on lists with values of any type. We must revise two aspects of the function to make it typeless. First, we must change how the comparison is performed so that the function can compare values of any type. This goal sounds impossible. If you write statements to compare integer values, how can they possibly work with other types such as strings? The solution uses a pointer to a function. The caller writes a function to compare two values and passes a pointer to it as an argument to the search function. The search function then calls the comparison function to make comparisons. In this way, values of any type may be compared.

The second aspect we must change is to pass a *pointer* to the value rather than the value. The function will receive this argument in a void * parameter. The pointer to the value is then passed to the comparison function. This change also enables string and array objects to be used. Strings and arrays cannot be passed as arguments, but pointers to them can.

Functions used in this manner are *callback functions* because the user passes a pointer to a function to some other routine, which then "calls back" to the user's function. You can use the technique any time you are writing a function that must be able to perform different types of work at a given point or perform work that can be defined only by the function's caller. Many windowing systems use callback functions to connect actions, such as dragging the mouse and clicking buttons, to specific functions in the user's program.

We cannot write an accurate prototype for the callback function in this context because we don't know what type of values are being compared. Indeed, we want the search function to work with any type of value. The solution to this dilemma is to declare the arguments as void *, which means "a pointer to something whose type we do not know."

Before using the pointers in the comparison function, they must be cast to the correct type. Because a cast circumvents the usual type checking, be extremely careful that the function is called with the proper type of arguments.

In this case, the callback function compares two values. The search function passes pointers to the two values to be compared and checks the returned value; for example, zero for equal values and nonzero for unequal values. The search function is now typeless because it doesn't perform the actual comparison. It is true that the caller must now write the necessary comparison function, but doing so is easy because the caller knows what type of values are contained in the list. And if several lists with different types of values are used, writing one comparison function for each type allows a single search function to operate on all of the lists.

Program 13.1 is an implementation of a typeless search function. Note that the third parameter to the function is a pointer to a function. The full prototype is used to declare this parameter. Note also that the parameter node is not declared const even though the function never modifies any of the nodes to which it points. If node were declared const the function would have to return a const result, which would restrict the caller from modifying the node that was located.

```
/*
** Function to search a linked list for a specific value.  Arguments
** are a pointer to the first node in the list, a pointer to the
** value we're looking for, and a pointer to a function that compares
** values of the type stored on the list.
*/
#include <stdio.h>
#include "node.h"

Node *
search_list( Node *node, void const *value,
    int (*compare)( void const *, void const * ) )
{
        while( node != NULL ){
                if( compare( &node->value, value ) == 0 )
                        break;
                node = node->link;
        }
        return node;
}
```

Program 13.1   Typeless linked list search   search.c

Pointers to the value argument and &node->value are passed to the comparison function. The latter is the value in the node we are currently examining. I chose the counter-intuitive convention of having the comparison function return zero for equal operands in order to be compatible with the specification for comparison functions used by several functions in the standard library. In this specification, unequal operands are reported more explicitly—a negative value indicates that the first argument was less than the second, and a positive value indicates that it was greater.

To search a particular linked list, the user would write the appropriate comparison function and pass pointers to it and to the desired value. For example, here is a comparison function for searching a list of integers.

```
int
compare_ints( void const *a, void const *b )
{
        if( *(int *)a == *(int *)b )
                return 0;
        else
                return 1;
}
```

The function would be used like this:

```
desired_node = search_list( root, &desired_value,
    compare_ints );
```

Note the casts: The arguments to the comparison function must be declared void * to match the prototype of the search function; they are then cast to int * in order to compare the values as integers.

If you wish to search a list of strings, this code will do the job:

```
#include <string.h>
...
desired_node = search_list( root, "desired_value",
    strcmp );
```

It happens that the library function strcmp does exactly the comparison we need, though some compilers will issue warnings because its arguments are declared char * rather than void *.

13.3.2 Jump Tables

Jump tables are best explained with an example. The following code fragment is from a program that implements a pocket calculator. Other parts of the program have already read in two numbers (op1 and op2) and an operator (oper). This code tests the operator to determine which function to invoke.

```
switch( oper ){
case ADD:
        result = add( op1, op2 );
        break;

case SUB:
        result = sub( op1, op2 );
        break;

case MUL:
        result = mul( op1, op2 );
        break;

case DIV:
        result = div( op1, op2 );
        break;
...
```

For a fancy calculator with a hundred or so operators, this `switch` statement will become extremely large.

Why are functions being called to perform these operations? It is good design to separate the operations from the code that chooses among them. The more complex operations will certainly be implemented as separate functions because of their size, but even the simple operations may have side effects, such as saving a constant value for later operations.

In order to use a `switch`, the codes that represent the operators must be integers. If they are consecutive integers starting with zero, we can use a *jump table* to accomplish the same thing. A jump table is just an array of pointers to functions.

There are two steps in creating a jump table. First, an array of pointers to functions is declared and initialized. The only trick is to make sure that the prototypes for the functions appear before the array declaration.

```
double  add( double, double );
double  sub( double, double );
double  mul( double, double );
double  div( double, double );
...
double  (*oper_func[])( double, double ) = {
        add, sub, mul, div, ...
};
```

The proper order for the functions' names in the initializer list is determined by the integer codes used to represent each operator in the program. This example assumes that ADD is zero, SUB is one, MUL is two, and so forth.

The second step is to replace the entire `switch` statement with this one!

```
result = oper_func[ oper ]( op1, op2 );
```

`oper` selects the correct pointer from the array, and the function call operator executes it.

An out-of-bounds subscript is just as illegal on a jump table as it is on any other array, but it is much more difficult to diagnose. There are three places where the program might terminate when this error occurs. First, if the subscript value is far enough out of bounds, the location that it identifies might be outside of the memory allocated to the program. Some operating systems detect this error and abort the program, but others do not. If the program is terminated, the fault will be reported near the jump table statement, making the problem fairly easy to diagnosis.

If the program does not abort, the value identified by the illegal subscript is fetched, and the processor jumps to that location. This unpredictable value may or may not represent a valid address for the program. If it does not, the program may also abort, but the address reported for the fault is essentially a random number, making debugging more difficult.

If the program hasn't failed yet, the machine will begin to execute instructions at the bogus address obtained with the illegal subscript, and debugging the error becomes much harder. If the random address is in an area in memory that contains data, the program usually aborts very quickly due to an illegal instruction or an illegal operand address (although data values sometimes represent valid instructions, they do not often make any sense). The only clue to how the computer got where it did is the return address stored on the stack by the function call made in the jump table. If any of the random instructions modified the stack or changed the stack pointer when they were executed, this clue is lost.

Worse still is if the random address happens to be in the middle of a function. Then the function executes merrily along, changing who knows what data, until it is finished. But the return address isn't where the function expects it to be on the stack, so another random value is used instead. This value becomes the address of the next instruction to execute, and the computer goes to a different random location and continues to execute whatever it finds there.

The problem is that the instructions destroy the last clue as to how the computer got to where the fault finally occurs. Without this information, it is difficult to pinpoint the source of the problem. If you are suspicious of a jump table, then print a message before and after its function call. It will then be obvious if the called function never returns. The trick is to realize that a fault in one part of the program might be caused by an error in a jump table in some distant, unrelated part of the program.

It is much easier to make sure that the subscript used in a jump table is within range in the first place. In the calculator example, the function that reads in the operator and converts it to its corresponding integer should verify that the operator is valid.

13.4 Command Line Arguments

Processing command line arguments is another application of pointers to pointers. Some operating systems, including UNIX and MS-DOS, let the user write arguments on the command that initiates the execution of a program. These arguments are passed to the program, which can process them in any way it sees fit.

13.4.1 Passing Command Line Arguments

How are these arguments passed to the program? The `main` function of a C program has two parameters.[44] The first, often called `argc`, is a count of the number of arguments in the command line. The second, often called `argv`, points to the values of the arguments. Because there isn't an inherent limit on the number of arguments, `argv` points to the first element of what is essentially an array. Each of these elements is a pointer to the text of one argument. If the program needs to access the command line arguments, the main function is declared with these parameters:

```
int
main( int argc, char **argv )
```

Note that the names `argc` and `argv` are frequently used but are not magical in any way. They could be called "fred" and "ginger" if you so desired, though the program would be harder to read.

Figure 13.1 shows how the arguments in this command line would be passed:

```
$ cc -c -O main.c insert.c -o test
```

Note the array of pointers: Each element of this array is a pointer to a character, and the array is terminated by a NULL pointer. The value in `argc` and this

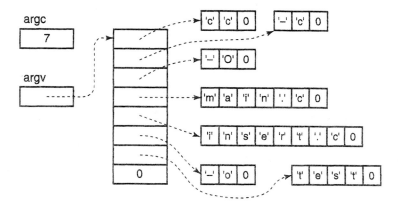

Figure 13.1   Command line arguments

---

[44] Actually, some operating systems also pass a third parameter to the `main` function, a pointer to a list of environment variables and their values. Consult your compiler's or operating system's documentation for details.

NULL may both be used to determine how many arguments were passed. `argv` points to the first element of this array, which is why it is declared as a pointer to a pointer to a character.

One last thing to observe is that the very first argument is the name of the program. What is the purpose of passing the program name as an argument? Surely the program knows what it is. Usually this argument is ignored, but it can be useful for programs that are commonly invoked with different sets of options. The UNIX `ls` command, which lists the files in a directory, is such a program. On many UNIX systems, the command has several different names. When invoked with the name `ls`, it produces a brief listing of files. When invoked with the name `l`, it produces a multicolumn brief listing, and the name `ll` produces a detailed listing. The program examines the first argument to determine which name was used to invoke it and selects options based on the name.

On some systems, the argument strings are stored one right after the other, so advancing a pointer to the first argument past the end of the string will take you to the beginning of the next one. This arrangement is implementation dependent, though, so you must not depend upon it. To find the beginning of an argument, use the appropriate pointer from the array.

```
/*
** A program to print its command line arguments.
*/
#include <stdio.h>
#include <stdlib.h>

int
main( int argc, char **argv )
{
        /*
        ** Print arguments until a NULL pointer is reached (argc is
        ** not used). The program name is skipped.
        */
        while( *++argv != NULL )
                printf( "%s\n", *argv );
        return EXIT_SUCCESS;
}
```

Program 13.2   Print command line arguments   echo.c

How does a program access these arguments? Program 13.2 is a very simple example—it simply prints out all of its arguments (except for the program name) much like the UNIX *echo* command.

The `while` loop increments `argv` and then checks `*argv` to see if the end of the argument list has been reached. It is looking for the NULL that terminates the list. If there is another argument, the body of the loop is executed and prints it. By incrementing `argv` first in the loop, the program name is automatically skipped.

The `%s` code used in the format string of `printf` requires an argument that is a pointer to a character. `printf` assumes that this character is the first of a NUL-terminated string. Applying indirection on `argv` yields the value to which it points, a pointer to a character—just what the format requires.

13.4.2 Processing Command Line Arguments

Let's write a program that processes command line arguments more realistically. This program will handle a very common paradigm—option arguments followed by file name arguments. After the program name, there may be zero or more options, followed by zero or more file names, like this:

```
prog -a -b -c name1 name2 name3
```

Each option argument is a dash followed by a single letter that identifies which of several possible options is desired. Each file name argument is processed in some way. If there are no file names, the standard input is processed instead.

To make these examples generic, our program sets variables to remember which options were found. Other parts of a real program might then test these variables to determine what processing was requested. In a real program, the processing required for an option might also be done when the option is discovered in the arguments.

```c
/*
** Process command-line arguments
*/
#include <stdio.h>
#define TRUE    1

/*
**          Prototypes for functions that do the real work.
```

Program 13.3   Processing command line arguments   *continued . . .*

```
*/
void    process_standard_input( void );
void    process_file( char *file_name );

/*
**      Option flags, default initialization is FALSE.
*/
int     option_a, option_b /* etc. */ ;

void
main( int argc, char **argv )
{
        /*
        ** Process option arguments: skip to next argument, and
        ** check that it begins with a dash.
        */
        while( *++argv != NULL && **argv == '-' ){
                /*
                ** Check the letter after the dash.
                */
                switch( *++*argv ){
                case 'a':
                        option_a = TRUE;
                        break;

                case 'b':
                        option_b = TRUE;
                        break;

                /* etc. */
                }
        }

        /*
        ** Process file name arguments
        */
        if( *argv == NULL )
                process_standard_input();
        else {
                do {
                        process_file( *argv );
                } while( *++argv != NULL );
        }
}
```

Program 13.3   Processing command line arguments   cmd_line.c

Program 13.3 resembles Program 13.2 because it contains a loop that goes through all of the arguments. The main difference is that we must now distinguish between option arguments and file name arguments. The loop stops when it reaches an argument that does not begin with a dash. A second loop processes the file names.

Notice the test that was added to the `while` loop in Program 13.3:

```
**argv == '-'
```

The double indirection accesses the first character of the argument, as illustrated in Figure 13.2. If this character is not a dash then there aren't any more options and the loop breaks. Note that it is important to test `*argv` before testing `**argv`. If `*argv` were NULL, the second indirection in `**argv` would be illegal.

The `*++*argv` expression in the `switch` statement is one you have seen before. The first indirection goes to where `argv` points, and this location is incremented. The last indirection follows the incremented pointer, as diagrammed in Figure 13.3. The `switch` statement sets a variable depending on which option letter was found, and the `++` in the `while` loop advances `argv` to the next argument for the next iteration of the loop.

When there aren't any more options, the file names are handled. If `argv` is pointing to the NULL, there aren't any and the standard input is processed. Otherwise, each name is processed one by one. The function calls in this program are generic so they don't show any of the work that a real program might perform. Nevertheless, this design is good. The main program deals with the arguments so that the functions doing the processing don't have to worry about parsing options or looping through file names.

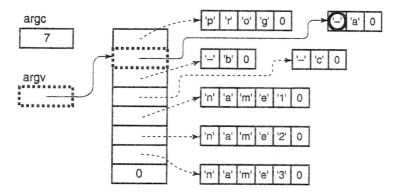

Figure 13.2   Accessing the argument

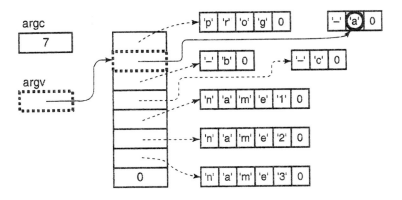

Figure 13.3   Accessing the next character in the argument

Some programs allow the user to put multiple option letters in one argument, like this:

```
prog -abc name1 name2 name3
```

At first you might think that this change will complicate our program, but it turns out to be fairly easy to process. Each argument may now contain multiple options, so we use another loop to process them. The loop should terminate when it encounters the trailing NUL byte at the end of the argument.

The switch statement in Program 13.3 is replaced by the following code fragment:

```
while( ( opt = *++*argv ) != '\0' ){
        switch( opt ){
        case 'a':
                option_a = TRUE;
                break;
        /* etc. */
        }
}
```

The test in the loop advances the argument pointer beyond the dash and makes a copy of the character found there. If this character is not the NUL byte, then the switch statement is used as before to set the appropriate variable. Note that the option character is saved in a local variable opt to avoid having to evaluate **argv in the switch statement.

Be aware that the command line arguments may only be processed once in this manner because the pointers to the arguments are destroyed by the inner loop. If the arguments must be processed more than once, make a copy of each pointer that you must increment as you go through the list.

There are other possibilities for processing options. For example, the options might be words rather than single letters, or there might be values associated with some options, as in this example:

```
cc -o prog prog.c
```

One of the chapter problems expands on this idea.

13.5 String Literals

It is time to take a closer look at a topic mentioned earlier: string literals. When a string literal appears in an expression, its value is a pointer constant. The compiler stores a copy of the specified characters somewhere in memory, and the pointer points to the first of these characters. But when array names are used in expressions, their values are also pointer constants. We can perform subscripting, indirection, and pointer arithmetic on them. Are these operations meaningful on string literals, too? Let's look at some.

What is the meaning of this expression?

```
"xyz" + 1
```

To most programmers, it looks like gibberish. It appears to be trying to perform some kind of addition on a string. But when you remember that the string literal is a pointer, the meaning becomes clear. This expression computes the sum of the pointer value plus one. The result is a pointer to the second character in the literal: y.

How about this expression?

```
*"xyz"
```

When indirection is applied to a pointer, the result is the thing to which it points. The type of a string literal is "pointer to character," so the result of the indirection is the character to which it points: x. Note that the result is *not* the entire string, just the first character.

This next example also looks strange, but by now you should be able to figure out that the value of this expression is the character z.

```
"xyz"[2]
```

The last example contains an error. The offset of four goes off the end of the string, so the result is an unpredictable character.

```
*( "xyz" + 4 )
```

When would anyone ever want to use expressions like these? The function in Program 13.4 is one useful example. Can you figure out what this mystery function does? Here is a hint: Trace the function with several different input values and see what is printed. The answer is given at the end of the chapter.

In the meantime, let's look at another example. Program 13.5 contains a function that converts binary values to characters and prints them. You first saw this function as Program 7.6. For this example, we'll modify it to print values in hexadecimal. The first change is easy: just divide by 16 instead of 10. But now the remainder might be any value from 0 to 15, and the values from 10 to 15 should be printed as the letters A to F. The following code is a typical approach to this new problem.

```
remainder = value % 16;
if( remainder < 10 )
        putchar( remainder + '0' );
else
        putchar( remainder - 10 + 'A' );
```

I've used a local variable to save the remainder rather than computing it three separate times. For remainders in the range 0 through 9, a digit is printed the

```
/*
** Mystery function
**
**      The argument is a value in the range 0 through 100.
*/
#include <stdio.h>

void
mystery( int n )
{
        n += 5;
        n /= 10;
        printf( "%s\n", "**********" + 10 - n );
}
```

Program 13.4   Mystery function   mystery.c

```
/*
** Take an integer value (unsigned), convert it to characters, and
** print it.  Leading zeros are suppressed.
*/
#include <stdio.h>

void
binary_to_ascii( unsigned int value )
{
        unsigned int    quotient;

        quotient = value / 10;
        if( quotient != 0 )
                binary_to_ascii( quotient );
        putchar( value % 10 + '0' );
}
```

Program 13.5   Convert a binary integer to characters   btoa.c

same as before. But the other remainders are printed as letters. The test is
needed because the letters A through F do not immediately follow the digits in
any common character set.

   The following code solves the problem in a different way.

```
putchar( "0123456789ABCDEF"[ value % 16 ] );
```

Once again the remainder will be a value in the range of 0 through 15, but this
time it is used as a subscript to select one of the characters from the string
literal to print. The previous code is complicated because the letters and digits
are not adjacent in the character set. This solution avoids the complication by
defining a string in which they are adjacent. The remainder selects the right
digit from this string.

   This second approach is faster than the traditional one, because fewer
operations are needed. The code may or may not be smaller than the original,
however. The decrease in instructions is offset by the addition of the 17-byte
string literal.

However, a large reduction in readability is a big price to pay for a small
improvement in execution speed. When you use an unusual technique or statement, be sure that you include a comment describing how it works. Once this
example has been explained, it is actually easier to follow than the traditional
code because it is shorter.

Now back to the mystery function. Did you figure it out? It prints a number of stars proportional to the value of the argument. It prints 0 stars if the argument was 0, 10 stars if the argument was 100, and an intermediate number of stars for intermediate values. In other words, this function prints one bar of a histogram, and it does it much more easily and efficiently than the more traditional loop.

13.6 Summary

If declared properly, a pointer variable may point to another pointer variable. Like any other pointer variable, a pointer to a pointer must be initialized before it can be used. Two indirection operations are needed on a pointer to a pointer to obtain the target object. More levels of indirection are allowed (for example, a pointer to a pointer to a pointer to an int), but are needed less often than simpler pointers. You may also create pointer variables that point to functions and arrays, and create arrays of such pointers.

Declarations in C are by inference. The declaration

```
int     *a;
```

declares the expression *a to be an integer. You must then infer that a is a pointer to an integer. With declaration by inference, the rules for reading declarations are the same as those for reading expressions.

You can use pointers to functions to implement callback functions. A pointer to your callback function is passed as an argument to another function, which calls your function using the pointer. With this technique, you can create generic functions that perform common operations such as searching a linked list. Any work that is specific to one instance of the problem, such as comparing values in the list, is performed in a callback function supplied by the client.

Jump tables also use pointers to functions. A jump table performs a selection much like a switch statement. The table consists of an array of pointers to functions (which must have identical prototypes). One pointer is selected with a subscript, and the corresponding function is called. Always verify that the subscript value is in the proper range, because debugging errors in jump tables is difficult.

If an execution environment implements command line arguments, the arguments are passed to the main function via two parameters, often called argc and argv. argc is an integer and contains a count of the number of arguments. argv is a pointer to a sequence of pointers to characters. Each pointer in the sequence points to a command line argument. The sequence is terminated with a NULL pointer. The first argument is the name of the program. A program can access its command line arguments by using indirection on argv.

The value of a string literal that appears in an expression is a constant pointer to the first character in the literal. Like array names, you can use string literals in pointer expressions and with subscripts.

13.7 Summary of Cautions

1. Applying indirection to an uninitialized pointer (page 356).

2. Using an out-of-bounds subscript in a jump table (page 361).

13.8 Summary of Programming Tips

1. Avoid using more levels of indirection than necessary (page 353).

2. The cdecl program is helpful for deciphering complicated declarations (page 355).

3. Be careful when casting from void * to other pointer types (page 358).

4. Always validate the subscript used in a jump table (page 362).

5. Destructively processing command line arguments prevents them from being processed again later (page 369).

6. Unusual code should always be accompanied by a comment describing what it does and how it works (page 371).

13.9 Questions

1. A list of declarations is shown below.

```
a.   int      abc();

b.   int      abc[3];

c.   int      **abc();

d.   int      (*abc)();

e.   int      (*abc)[6];
```

```
f.    int      *abc();
g.    int      **(*abc[6])();
h.    int      **abc[6];
i.    int      *(*abc)[6];
j.    int      *(*abc())();
k.    int      (**(*abc)())();
l.    int      (*(*abc)())[6];
m.    int      *(*(*(*abc)())[6])();
```

Match each of the declarations with the best description from this list.

I.   Pointer to an `int`.

II.   Pointer to a pointer to an `int`.

III.   Array of `int`.

IV.   Pointer to array of `int`.

V.   Array of pointer to `int`.

VI.   Pointer to array of pointer to `int`.

VII.   Array of pointer to pointer to `int`.

VIII.   Function returning `int`.

IX.   Function returning pointer to `int`.

X.   Function returning pointer to pointer to `int`.

XI.   Pointer to function returning `int`.

XII.   Pointer to function returning pointer to `int`.

XIII.   Pointer to function returning pointer to pointer to `int`.

XIV.   Array of pointer to function returning `int`.

XV.   Array of pointer to function returning pointer to `int`.

XVI.   Array of pointer to function returning pointer to pointer to `int`.

XVII.   Function returning pointer to function returning `int`.

XVIII. Function returning pointer to pointer to function returning `int`.

XIX.   Function returning pointer to function returning pointer to `int`.

XX.   Pointer to function returning pointer to function returning `int`.

XXI.   Pointer to function returning pointer to pointer to function returning `int`.

XXII. Pointer to function returning pointer to function returning pointer to `int`.

XXIII. Pointer to function returning pointer to array of `int`.

XXIV. Pointer to function returning pointer to array of pointer to `int`.

XXV. Pointer to function returning pointer to array of pointer to function returning pointer to `int`.

XXVI. Illegal

2. Given the following declarations:

```
char    *array[10];
char    **ptr = array;
```

what is the effect of adding one to the variable `ptr`?

3. Suppose you are writing a function that begins like this:

```
void func( int ***arg ){
```

What is the type of the argument? Draw a diagram that shows how this variable would be correctly used. What expression would you use to get the integer that the argument is referring to?

4. How can the following code fragment be improved?

```
Transaction *trans;
trans->product->orders += 1;
trans->product->quantity_on_hand -= trans->quantity;
trans->product->supplier->reorder_quantity
    += trans->quantity;
if( trans->product->export_restricted ){
        . . .
}
```

5. Given the following declarations:

```
typedef         struct  {
        int     x;
        int     y;
} Point;

Point   p;
Point   *a = &p;
Point   **b = &a;
```

determine the value of each of the following expressions.

    a.   a

    b.   *a

    c.   a->x

    d.   b

    e.   b->a

    f.   b->x

    g.   *b

    h.   *b->a

    i.   *b->x

    j.   b->a->x

    k.   (*b)->a

    l.   (*b)->x

    m.   **b

6. Given the following declarations:

```
typedef          struct  {
        int     x;
        int     y;
} Point;

Point   x, y;
Point   *a = &x, *b = &y;
```

explain the meaning of each of these statements.

    a.   x = y;

    b.   a = y;

    c.   a = b;

    d.   a = *b;

    e.   *a = *b;

7. Many implementations of ANSI C include a function called getopt. This function helps process command line arguments. However, getopt is not mentioned in the Standard. What are the advantages and disadvantages of having such a function?

8. What (if anything) is wrong with this code fragment, and how would you fix it?

```
char     *pathname = "/usr/temp/XXXXXXXXXXXXXXX";
...
/*
** Insert the filename into the pathname.
*/
strcpy( pathname + 10, "abcde" );
```

9. What (if anything) is wrong with the following code fragment, and how would you fix it?

```
char     pathname[] = "/usr/temp/";
...
/*
** Append the filename to the pathname.
*/
strcat( pathname, "abcde" );
```

10. What (if anything) is wrong with the following code fragment, and how would you fix it?

```
char     pathname[20] = "/usr/temp/";
...
/*
** Append the filename to the pathname.
*/
strcat( pathname, filename );
```

△ 11. The Standard states that the effects of modifying a string literal are undefined. What problems might be caused if you did modify string literals?

13.10 Programming Exercises

△ ★★ 1. Write a program that reads from the standard input and computes the percentage of characters it finds in each of the following categories:

> control characters
> whitespace characters
> digits
> lower case letters
> upper case letters
> punctuation characters
> non-printable characters

The character categories are to be as they are defined for the ctype.h functions. Do not use a series of if statements.

★ 2. Write a general-purpose function to traverse a singly linked list. It should take two parameters: a pointer to the first node in the list and a pointer to a callback function. The callback function should take a single argument, a pointer to a list node, and should be invoked once for each node in the list. What does the function need to know about the nodes in the list?

★★ 3. Convert the following code fragment so that it uses a jump table instead of a switch statement.

```
Node    *list;
Node    *current;
Transaction *transaction;
typedef enum    { NEW, DELETE, FORWARD, BACKWARD,
    SEARCH, EDIT } Trans_type;
...
switch( transaction->type ){
case NEW:
        add_new_trans( list, transaction );
        break;

case DELETE:
        current = delete_trans( list, current );
        break;

case FORWARD:
        current = current->next;
        break;

case BACKWARD:
        current = current->prev;
        break;

case SEARCH:
        current = search( list, transaction );
        break;

case EDIT:
        edit( current, transaction );
        break;

default:
        printf( "Illegal transaction type!\n" );
        break;
}
```

★★★★ 4. Write a function called `sort` that will sort an array of any kind of value. To make the function generic, one of its arguments must be a pointer to a callback comparison function that the caller will supply. The comparison function will take two arguments, which are pointers to the values being compared. It will return an integer that is zero if the two values are equal, less than zero if the first value is less than the second, and greater than zero if the first value is greater than the second.

The arguments to `sort` will be:

1. a pointer to the first value in the array to be sorted,

2. the number of values in the array,

3. the size of each array element, and

4. a pointer to the comparison callback function.

The `sort` function does not return a value.

You will not be able to declare the array argument with its real type because the function can be called to sort different types of array. If you treat the data as if it were an array of characters, you can use the third argument both to locate the beginning of each element of the actual array and to interchange two array elements one byte at a time.

You may use the following algorithm for a simple exchange sort, or you may feel free to use any better algorithm you know.

```
for i = 1 to number-of-records - 1 do
    for j = i + 1 to number-of-records do
        if record i > record j then
            interchange records i and j
```

★★★★★ 5. Writing the code to process command line arguments is tedious, which suggests that there ought to be a standard function to do it. Different programs handle their arguments in different ways, however, so the function must be flexible in order for it to be useful in more than just a couple of programs. For this project, you will write such a function. Your routine will provide flexibility by locating and extracting the arguments. Callback functions provided by the user will perform the actual processing.

Here is a prototype for your function. Note that the fourth and fifth arguments prototype callback functions.

```
char **
do_args( int argc, char **argv, char *control,
    void (*do_arg)( int ch, char *value ),
    void (*illegal_arg)( int ch ) );
```

The first two parameters are those received by the main function, which are passed unchanged to do_args. The third is a string that identifies what command line arguments are expected. The last two parameters are pointers to functions provided by the user.

do_args processes command line arguments like this:

```
Skip past the program name argument
While the next argument begins with a dash
        For each character in the argument after the dash
                Process the character
Return a pointer to the next argument pointer.
```

To "process the character," you must first see whether the character is in the control string. If it is not there, call the function to which illegal_arg points, passing the character as an argument. If it is there but *is not* followed by a plus, call the function to which do_arg points, passing the character and a NULL pointer as arguments.

If the character is in control and *is* followed by a plus, then there should be a value associated with the character. If there are any more characters in the current argument, they are the desired value. Otherwise, the next argument is the value. In either case, you should call the function to which do_arg points, passing as arguments the character and a pointer to the value. If there wasn't a value (no additional characters *and* no next argument), then you should call the illegal_arg function instead. *Note: Be sure that the characters in the value are not processed as arguments later!*

When all the arguments that begin with a dash have been processed, you should return a pointer to the pointer to the next command line argument (that is, a value such as &argv[4] or argv + 4). If all of the command line arguments began with dashes, you will return a pointer to the NULL that terminates the command line argument list.

The function must not modify either the command line argument pointers or the arguments. To illustrate, suppose that the program *prog* calls this function: the following examples show the results with several different sets of arguments.

Command line:	$ prog -x -y z
control:	"x"
do_args calls:	(*do_arg)(´x´, 0)
	(*illegal_arg)(´y´)
and returns:	&argv[3]

Command line:	$ prog -x -y -z
control:	"x+y+z+"
do_args calls:	(*do_arg)(´x´, "-y")

	`(*illegal_arg)( ´z´ )`
and returns:	`&argv[4]`

Command line:	`$ prog -abcd -ef ghi jkl`
control:	`"ab+cdef+g"`
do_args calls:	`(*do_arg)( ´a´, 0 )`
	`(*do_arg)( ´b´, "cd" )`
	`(*do_arg)( ´e´, 0 )`
	`(*do_arg)( ´f´, "ghi" )`
and returns:	`&argv[4]`

Command line:	`$ prog -a b -c -d -e -f`
control:	`"abcdef"`
do_args calls:	`(*do_arg)( ´a´, 0 )`
and returns:	`&argv[2]`

The Preprocessor

There are many steps involved in compiling a C program. The first step is called *preprocessing*. The C *preprocessor* performs textual manipulations on the source code before it is compiled. The major tasks include deleting comments, inserting the contents of #include'd files into the code, defining and substituting #define'd symbols, and deciding whether or not certain parts of the code should be compiled based on conditional compilation directives.

14.1 Predefined Symbols

Table 14.1 summarizes the symbols defined by the preprocessor. The values are all either string literals or decimal constants. __FILE__ and __LINE__ are useful in identifying the source of debugging output. __DATE__ and __TIME__ are often used to encode version information into the compiled program. __STDC__ is used in conjunction with conditional compilation (described later in this chapter) for programs that must be compiled in both ANSI and non-ANSI environments.

Symbol	Sample Value	Meaning
__FILE__	"name.c"	Name of the source file being compiled.
__LINE__	25	Line number of the current line in the file.
__DATE__	"Jan 31 1997"	Date that the file was compiled.
__TIME__	"18:04:30"	Time that the file was compiled.
__STDC__	1	1 if the compiler conforms to ANSI C, else undefined.

Table 14.1   Preprocessor symbols

14.2 #define

You have already seen simple uses of the #define directive that give symbolic names to numeric values. In this section, I'll introduce more uses of #define. Let's start by looking at a more formal description of it.

```
#define name    stuff
```

Whenever the symbol *name* appears after this directive, the preprocessor replaces it with *stuff*.

K&R C   Early C compilers required that the # appear at the beginning of a line, although it could be followed by white space. In ANSI C, this restriction is removed.

The replacement text need not be limited to numeric literal constants. *Any* text can be substituted into the program with a #define. Here are a few examples:

```
#define reg          register
#define do_forever   for(;;)
#define CASE          break;case
```

The first definition merely creates a short alias for the register keyword. This shorter name makes it easier to line up declarations with tabs. The second is a more descriptive synonym for the variant of the for statement that implements an infinite loop. Finally, the last one is a shorthand notation for use with switch statements. It automatically puts a break before each case thus making the switch statement appear to be more like case statements in other languages.

If the *stuff* in the definition is long, it can be split over multiple lines by ending each line of the definition, except the last one, with a backslash, as in this example:

```
#define DEBUG_PRINT    printf( "File %s line %d:" \
                        " x=%d, y=%d, z=%d", \
                        __FILE__, __LINE__, \
                        x, y, z )
```

I'm taking advantage of the fact that adjacent string literals are concatenated into one string. This type of declaration is useful when debugging a program with many different computations involving a set of variables. It makes inserting a debugging statement to print their current values easier.

```
x *= 2;
y += x;
z = x * y;
DEBUG_PRINT;
```

The statement invoking DEBUG_PRINT ends with a semicolon, so you shouldn't have a semicolon at the end of the macro definition. If you do, the result will be two statements—a printf followed by an empty statement. Having two statements will cause problems in contexts where only one statement is allowed, for example:

```
if( ... )
        DEBUG_PRINT;
else
        . . .
```

You can also use a #define to insert a sequence of statements into the program. Here is a declaration for an entire loop:

```
#define PROCESS_LOOP                      \
        for( i = 0; i < 10; i += 1 ){     \
                sum += i;                 \
                if( i > 0 )               \
                        prod *= i;        \
        }
```

Don't misuse this technique. If the same code is needed in several areas of the program, it is usually better to implement it as a function. I'll discuss the tradeoffs between #define's and functions in detail later in the chapter.

14.2.1 Macros

The #define mechanism includes a provision to substitute arguments into the text, implementing what are often called *macros* or *defined macros*. Here is how macros are declared:

```
#define  name(parameter-list)   stuff
```

The parameter-list is a comma-separated list of symbols that may appear in the stuff. The opening parenthesis of the parameter list must be adjacent to the name. If there is any white space between them, the parameter list will be interpreted as part of stuff.

When the macro is invoked, the name is followed by a comma-separated list of values, one for each parameter, enclosed in parentheses. The actual value given for each parameter is substituted into the *stuff* whenever the parameter appears.

Here is a macro that takes one parameter:

```
#define SQUARE(x)        x * x
```

If you put

```
SQUARE( 5 )
```

in the program after this declaration, the preprocessor substitutes

```
5 * 5
```

in its place.

There is a problem with this macro, however. Look at this fragment of code:

```
a = 5;
printf( "%d\n", SQUARE( a + 1 ) );
```

At first glance, you would expect that this code would print 36. In fact, it prints 11. To see why, look at the macro text that is substituted. The parameter x is replaced with the text a + 1, so the statement is actually

```
printf( "%d\n", a + 1 * a + 1 );
```

The problem is now clear: the expression resulting from the substitution is not being evaluated in the intended order.

This error is easy to correct by adding parentheses to the macro definition:

```
#define SQUARE(x)        (x) * (x)
```

The preprocessor now substitutes this statement, which has the expected result, in the previous example.

```
printf( "%d\n", ( a + 1 ) * ( a + 1 ) );
```

Here is another macro definition.

```
#define DOUBLE(x)        (x) + (x)
```

The parentheses are in place to avoid the earlier problem, but a different error can occur with this macro. What value is printed by the following code?

```
a = 5;
printf( "%d\n", 10 * DOUBLE( a ) );
```

It looks like it should print 100, but in fact it prints 55. Again, the text resulting from the macro substitution reveals the problem:

```
printf( "%d\n", 10 * ( a ) + ( a ) );
```

The multiplication is performed before the addition defined in the macro is completed. This error is also easy to fix: surround the entire expression with parentheses when the macro is defined.

```
#define DOUBLE(x)          ( (x) + (x) )
```

All macro definitions that evaluate numeric expressions should be parenthesized in this manner to avoid unexpected interactions with operators in the arguments or with operators adjacent to where the macro is used.

Here is an interesting pair of macros:

```
#define repeat          do
#define until( x )      while( ! (x) )
```

These create a "new" loop, which works the same as the repeat/until loop in other languages. It is used like this:

```
repeat {
        statements
} until( i >= 10 );
```

The preprocessor substitutes the following code.

```
do {
        statements
} while( ! ( i >= 10 ) );
```

The parentheses around the expression make sure that it is completely evaluated before the ! operator complements its value.

It is possible to create suites of #define macros in order to write C programs that look like other languages. In most cases, you should avoid this temptation because the resulting programs are difficult for other C programmers to understand. They must constantly look up the definitions to see what is really happening. Even if everyone working on the project now *and for the rest of the project's life* is familiar with the other language, this technique may cause confusion because of aspects of the other language cannot be mimicked exactly.

14.2.2 #define Substitution

There are several steps involved in expanding #define'd symbols and macros in the program.

1. For macro invocations, the arguments are first examined to see if they contain any #define'd symbols. If so, they are replaced first.

2. The substitution text is then inserted into the program in place of the original text. For macros, the argument names are replaced by their values.

3. Finally, the resulting text is scanned again to see if it contains any #define'd symbols; if so, the process is repeated.

Thus, macro arguments and #define definitions may contain other #define'd symbols. Macros may not be recursive, however.

String literals are not examined when the preprocessor is searching for #define'd symbols. There are two techniques that are useful in injecting macro argument values into string literals. First, the concatenation of adjacent strings makes it easy to break a string into pieces, one of which is actually a macro argument. Here is an example of this technique:

```
#define PRINT(FORMAT,VALUE)                    \
        printf( "The value is " FORMAT "\n", VALUE )
...
PRINT( "%d", x + 3 );
```

This technique only works if a string literal is given as the macro argument.

The second technique uses the preprocessor to convert a macro argument to a string. The construct #argument is translated by the preprocessor into "argument". This translation lets you write code like this:

```
#define PRINT(FORMAT,VALUE)                    \
        printf( "The value of " #VALUE   \
        " is " FORMAT "\n", VALUE )
...
PRINT( "%d", x + 3 );
```

which produces this output:

```
The value of x + 3 is 25
```

The ## construct performs a different task. It causes the two tokens on either side of it to be concatenated. Among other uses, this capability allows macro definitions to construct identifiers from separate pieces of text. The following example uses concatenation to add a value to one of several variables:

```
#define ADD_TO_SUM( sum_number, value ) \
        sum ## sum_number += value
...
ADD_TO_SUM( 5, 25 );
```

The last statement adds the value 25 to the variable sum5. Note that the concatenation must result in a legal construct, otherwise the result is undefined.

14.2.3 Macros versus Functions

Macros are frequently used to perform simple computations, such as finding the larger (or smaller) of two expressions:

```
#define MAX( a, b )      ( (a) > (b) ? (a) : (b) )
```

Why not use a function to accomplish this task? There are two reasons. First, the code needed to call and return from a function is likely to be larger than the code that actually performs this small amount of work, so the macro makes the program both smaller and faster than using a function.

More important, though, is the fact that a function's parameters must be declared to be a specific type, so it can only be called with expressions of the proper type. On the other hand, this particular macro can be used for integers, longs, floats, doubles, and any other type whose values may be compared with the > operator. In other words, macros are typeless.

The disadvantage to using macros as opposed to functions is that a copy of the code is inserted into the program each time the macro is used. Unless the macro is very short, using macros can greatly increase the size of the program.

There are some tasks that functions simply cannot accomplish. Let's take a closer look at the macro defined in Program 11.1a. The second argument to the macro is a type, which cannot be passed as a function argument.

```
#define MALLOC(n,type)  \
        ( (type *)malloc( (n) * sizeof( type ) ) )
```

You can now see exactly how this macro works. The first statement in the following example is converted by the preprocessor to the second statement.

```
pi = MALLOC( 25, int );
pi = ( ( int * )malloc( ( 25 ) * sizeof( int ) ) );
```

Again, notice that the definition of the macro does not end with a semicolon. The semicolon appears on the statement that invokes the macro.

14.2.4 Macro Arguments with Side Effects

When macro parameters appear more than once in the definition, there is the danger of unexpected results when the macro is used with arguments that have side effects. A *side effect* is a permanent effect caused by evaluating the expression. For example, the expression

```
x + 1
```

can be evaluated hundreds of times and the same result will be obtained each time. This expression doesn't have any side effects. But

```
x++
```

has a side effect: it increments x. The next time this expression is evaluated, it will produce a different result. The MAX macro demonstrates the problems caused by arguments with side effects. Trace the following code. What do you think it will print out?

```
#define MAX( a, b )      ( (a) > (b) ? (a) : (b) )
...
x = 5;
y = 8;
z = MAX( x++, y++ );
printf( "x=%d, y=%d, z=%d\n", x, y, z );
```

This problem is not easy. Keep in mind that the first expression in the conditional determines which one of the other two expressions will be evaluated. The other expression is not evaluated at all. The result is x=6, y=10, z=9.

As usual, the strange result becomes clearer by examining the code that is substituted for the macro:

```
z = ( ( x++ ) > ( y++ ) ? ( x++ ) : ( y++ ) );
```

Although the smaller value is incremented once, the larger value is incremented twice—once during the comparison and again when the expression after the ? is evaluated.

Side effects are not limited only to changing the values of variables. The expression

```
getchar()
```

has a side effect. Calling the function consumes a character of input, so subsequent calls retrieve different characters. The expression must not be evaluated repeatedly unless the intent is to consume input characters.

Consider the following macro.

```
#define EVENPARITY( ch )                            \
           ( ( count_one_bits( ch ) & 1 ) ?         \
           ( ch ) | PARITYBIT : ( ch ) )
```

It uses the `count_one_bits` function from Program 5.1 that returns the number of one-bits in its argument. The purpose of the macro is to generate a character with even parity.[45] It first counts the number of ones in the character, and if the result is an odd number the PARITYBIT value (a one-bit) is OR'ed in with the character; otherwise the character is used unchanged. But imagine what happens when the macro is used in this manner:

```
ch = EVENPARITY( getchar() );
```

The statement looks reasonable: read a character and compute its parity. However, it fails because it actually reads *two* characters!

14.2.5 Naming Conventions

#define'd macros behave differently than true functions in a number of ways, as summarized in Table 14.2. Because of these differences, it is very important that the programmer knows whether an identifier is a macro or a function. Unfortunately, the syntax for using macros is identical to the syntax for functions, so the language doesn't help highlight the difference.

This confusion is one reason it is important to adopt a naming convention for macros (and for most other #define'd symbols as well). A common convention is to make macro names all uppercase letters. In the statement

```
value = max( a, b );
```

it is not apparent whether `max` is a function or a macro. You have to probe the source file and any header files it included to find out for sure. On the other hand, in

---

[45] *Parity* is an error detection mechanism. Before data is stored or transmitted over a communications line, a parity bit is computed with a value that makes the total number of one-bits an even number. Later, the data can be verified by counting the number of one-bits; if the result is odd, an error has occurred. This technique is called *even parity. Odd parity* works the same way, except that the parity bit is computed so that the total number of one-bits is an odd number.

Property	#define *Macro*	*Function*
Code size	Macro code is inserted into the program each time the macro is used. Program ends up being larger for all but the smallest macros.	Function code appears only once; calls to the function appear each time the function is used.
Execution speed	Faster.	Extra overhead of function call/return.
Operator precedence	Macro arguments are evaluated in the context of any surrounding expression; unless parenthesized, the precedence of adjacent operators can yield unexpected results.	Function arguments are evaluated once when the function is called; the resulting value is passed to the function. Expression evaluation is more predictable.
Argument evaluation	Arguments evaluated every time they are used in the macro definition; arguments with side effects can produce unexpected results due to multiple evaluations.	Arguments evaluated only once before function is called; multiple uses of arguments in the function do not cause multiple evaluations. Side effects in arguments do not pose any special problems.
Argument types	Macros are typeless; work with any argument type for which the operations performed are legal.	Function arguments are typed; separate functions are needed for different argument types even if the work performed is identical.

Table 14.2 Differences between macros and functions

```
value = MAX( a, b );
```

the naming convention makes it obvious. This convention is especially important in macros that might be used with arguments that have side effects, because it alerts the programmer to the need to evaluate the argument into a temporary variable before using it in the macro.

14.2.6 #undef

This directive un-#define's a name by removing its definition.

```
#undef    name
```

If an existing name is to be redefined, the old definition must first be removed with #undef.

14.2.7 Command Line Definitions

Many C compilers provide the ability to define symbols on the command line that initiates the compilation. This feature is useful when compiling different versions of a program from the same source file. For example, suppose a particular program declares an array of a certain size. On machines with limited memory the array must be small, but on machines with lots of memory you'd prefer to make the array larger. If the array is declared using a symbol like this,

```
int      array[ARRAY_SIZE];
```

then the value for ARRAY_SIZE can be given on the command line when the program is compiled.

On UNIX compilers, the -D option does this job. There are two ways to use this option.

```
-Dname
-Dname=stuff
```

The first form defines the symbol *name* to have the value one. The second form defines the symbol's value to be the *stuff* after the equal sign. The Borland C compilers for MS-DOS provide the same capability with the same syntax. Consult your compiler's documentation for information about your system.

To return to our example, the command line to compile this program on a UNIX system might look like this:

```
cc -DARRAY_SIZE=100 prog.c
```

This example illustrates another benefit that you get by parameterizing quantities such as array sizes in the program. If the array size were given as a literal constant in the declaration, or if the array were ever accessed within a loop that used a literal constant as a limit, the technique would not work. The symbolic constant must be used wherever you need to reference the size of the array.

Compilers that offer command-line definition of symbols usually offer command-line un-definition of symbols. On UNIX compilers, the -U option performs this. Specifying -Uname causes the initial definition of *name* in the program to be ignored. This feature is useful in conjunction with conditional compilation.

14.3 Conditional Compilation

It is often handy to be able to select whether certain statements or groups of statements should be translated or ignored when compiling a program. Statements used solely in the debugging of a program are an obvious example. They should not appear in production versions of the program, yet you would rather not physically remove them from the source code as they might be needed for debugging again after the program has undergone some maintenance modifications.

Conditional compilation is perfect for this purpose. With conditional compilation, selected parts of the code can be either compiled normally or completely ignored. The basic construct to support conditional compilation is the **#if** directive with its matching **#endif**. The syntax for its simplest form is shown below.

```
#if constant-expression
        statements
#endif
```

The `constant-expression` is evaluated by the preprocessor. If its value is nonzero (true), then the `statements` are compiled normally; otherwise the preprocessor silently deletes them.

A *constant expression* is one whose terms are either literal constants or #define'd symbols. Variables that do not attain their values until execution time are not legal in constant expressions because their values cannot be predicted at compile time.

For example, bracketing all your debugging code like this:

```
#if DEBUG
        printf( "x=%d, y=%d\n", x, y );
#endif
```

makes it easy to either compile or ignore the code. To compile it,

```
#define DEBUG    1
```

would be used. To ignore it, this symbol would be defined as 0 instead. The code remains in the source file in either case.

Another use of conditional compilation is to select between different alternatives when compiling. To support this capability, the #if directive has optional **#elif** and **#else** clauses. The complete syntax looks like this:

```
#if constant-expression
        statements
#elif constant-expression
        other statements ...
#else
        other statements
#endif
```

There may be any number of #elif clauses. The *constant-expression* in each is evaluated only if none of the previous ones are true. The statements in the #else clause are compiled only when all of the expressions are false, otherwise they are ignored.

K&R C

The original K&R C did not have an #elif directive. However, directives can be nested to achieve the same result with such compilers.

The following example is from a program that is sold in several different versions. Each version has a different set of optional features. The challenge in writing this code was figuring out how to produce the various versions. You must avoid at all costs writing a different set of source files for each version! Most of the code in each set would be identical and maintaining the program would be a nightmare. Fortunately, conditional compilation does the job.

```
    if( feature_selected == FEATURE1 )
#if     FEATURE1_ENABLED_FULLY
        feature1_function( arguments );
#elif   FEATURE1_ENABLED_PARTIALLY
        feature1_partial_function( arguments );
#else
        printf( "To use this feature, send $39.95;"
            " allow ten weeks for delivery.\n" );
#endif
```

There is only one single set of source files. When they are compiled, symbols for each of the desired features (or feature levels) are defined as one, and the remaining symbols are defined as zero.

14.3.1 If Defined

It is also possible to test whether or not a symbol is defined. This task is often more convenient for conditional compilation because the symbol controlling the compilation need not be defined at all unless the feature it controls is wanted. This test can be made in any of the following ways:

```
#if      defined(symbol)
#ifdef   symbol

#if      !defined(symbol)
#ifndef  symbol
```

The members of each of these pairs are equivalent to each other, but the `#if` form is more versatile because the constant expression may contain additional terms, as in:

```
#if X > 0 || defined( ABC ) && defined( BCD )
```

K&R C   Depending upon how old they are, some K&R C compilers may not include all of this capability.

14.3.2 Nested Directives

These directives may be nested within one another, as in the following code fragment:

```
#if      defined( OS_UNIX )
         #ifdef   OPTION1
                 unix_version_of_option1();
         #endif
         #ifdef   OPTION2
                 unix_version_of_option2();
         #endif
#elif    defined( OS_MSDOS )
         #ifdef   OPTION2
                 msdos_version_of_option2();
         #endif
#endif
```

In this example, the choice of operating systems determines which alternatives are available for the different options. The example also illustrates that preprocessor directives may be indented for readability by preceding them with white space.

To help the reader keep track of complicated nested directives, it is helpful to label each `#endif` with the expression from the `#if` to which it applies. This practice is particularly useful when the enclosed statements are lengthy. For example:

```
#ifdef  OPTION1
        lengthy code for option1;
#else
        lengthy code for alternative;
#endif  /* OPTION1 */
```

Some compilers allow a symbol to appear on an `#endif` directive, even though it has no effect. The Standard doesn't mention the legality of this practice, so it is safer to use a comment.

14.4 File Inclusion

As you have already seen, the `#include` directive causes the contents of another file to be compiled as if they actually appeared in place of the `#include` directive. The way this substitution is performed is simple: the preprocessor removes the directive and substitutes the contents of the named file. Thus, a header file that is included into ten other source files is actually compiled ten times.

This fact suggests that using `#include` files involves some overhead, but there are two very good reasons why you should not worry about it. First, there is actually not much extra overhead. If a set of declarations is needed in two source files, it will take nearly the same amount of time to compile those source files if the declarations are duplicated as it would if the declarations were `#include`'d in the files. Also, the overhead occurs only when the program is being compiled, so runtime efficiency is not affected. More importantly, though, the advantages of having the declarations in a header file are significant. They do not have to be replicated in every file in which they are needed, so maintaining them is easier.

The fact that everything in the header file is compiled each time it is `#include`'d suggests that each header file should only contain declarations for one set of functions or data. It is better to use several header files, each containing the declarations appropriate for a particular function or module, than to put all of the declarations for a program in one giant header file.

The principles of program design and modularity support this approach as well. It is better to include into a file only the necessary declarations so that the statements in the file cannot accidentally access functions or variables that should be private. Also, it is easier to maintain a set of declarations if you don't have to wade through hundreds of lines of unrelated code to find them.

14.4.1 Library Includes

The compiler supports two different types of #include's: library files and local files. In fact, there is little difference between them.

Library header files are included using the following syntax.

```
#include <filename>
```

There aren't any restrictions on the *filename*, although by convention the names of the standard library header files end with a .h suffix.[46]

The compiler searches for library header files by looking in a "series of standard locations" defined by the implementation. The documentation for your particular compiler should indicate what the standard locations are and how you can change them or add other locations to the list. For example, C compilers on UNIX systems typically look for library header files in a directory called /usr/include. A command line option to the compiler lets you add additional directories to this list so that you can create your own libraries of header files. Again, consult your compiler's documentation to see how your system behaves.

14.4.2 Local Includes

Here is the other form of the #include directive.

```
#include "filename"
```

The Standard lets each implementation decide whether to treat the local form of #include differently than the library form. If any special processing that is provided for the local form fails for a given file, then the compiler searches for the file as if a library #include had been used. A common strategy for processing local includes is to look in the current directory for the file. If the file is not found, then the standard locations are searched as usual.

You can write all of your #include statements with quotation marks instead of angle brackets. However, some compilers would waste a small amount of time when trying to locate library include files. A better reason to use the angle bracket form for library files is the information that it gives the reader. The angle brackets make it obvious that

---

[46] Technically, library header files need not be stored as files at all, though this won't be apparent to the programmer.

```
#include <errno.h>
```

references a library file. With the alternate form

```
#include "errno.h"
```

it is not clear whether the library header or a local file of the same name is being used. The only way to find out for sure is to examine the directory in which the compilation is performed.

A variant supported on UNIX systems and the Borland C compilers is the *absolute pathname*, which identifies not only the name of a file but its location. An absolute pathname on a UNIX system begins with a slash, like this:

```
/home/fred/C/my_proj/declaration2.h
```

On MS-DOS systems, backslashes are used instead of slashes. If an absolute pathname is used in either form of #include, then the usual directory searching is skipped because the pathname specifies the location of the file.

14.4.3 Nested File Inclusion

It is possible to put #include directives in files that are included. For example, consider a collection of functions that read input and then perform various input validation tasks. The validated data is then returned. When end of file is reached, the constant EOF is returned instead.

Prototypes for these functions would be put in a header file and #include'ed into each source file that uses the functions. However, every file that uses these functions must also include stdio.h to get the declaration for EOF. Therefore, the header file containing the prototypes may also contain:

```
#include <stdio.h>
```

so that including the header file automatically brings in the standard I/O declarations as well.

The Standard requires that nested #include files be supported to a depth of at least eight, but it doesn't impose a maximum limit on nesting depth. In practice, there is little reason to nest #include's to depths greater than one or two.

A disadvantage of nested #include files is that they make it difficult to determine the true dependencies of source files on one another. Some programs, such as the UNIX make utility, must know these dependencies in order to determine which files need to be compiled after some files are modified.

Another disadvantage of nested #include's is the possibility of one header file being included multiple times. To illustrate this error, consider this code:

```
#include "x.h"
#include "x.h"
```

It is obvious here that the file x.h is being included twice. No one would ever write this code intentionally. But this code

```
#include "a.h"
#include "b.h"
```

seems fine. If both a.h and b.h contain a nested #include of x.h, then x.h is once again being included twice, only this time it is not as obvious.

Multiple inclusion occurs most often in larger programs with a multitude of header files, thus it is not easy to find. A simple solution to the problem is provided by the conditional compilation feature. If all header files are written as:

```
#ifndef _HEADERNAME_H
#define _HEADERNAME_H 1
/*
** All the stuff that you want in the header file
*/
#endif
```

then the risks of multiple inclusion are eliminated. The first time the header file is included, it is processed normally and the symbol _HEADERNAME_H is defined to be one. If the header is included again, its entire contents are ignored by the conditional compilation directives. The symbol _HEADERNAME_H is named after the filename of the include file in order to avoid conflicts with similar symbols in other header files.

Note that the definition in the previous example can also be written

```
#define _HEADERNAME_H
```

with exactly the same effect. Even though its value is now the empty string rather than "1", the symbol is still defined.

Keep in mind, though, that the preprocessor must still read the entire header file, even if the whole file is ignored. Because this processing slows down compilation, multiple inclusion, whether by nested #include's or not, should be avoided when possible.

14.5 Other Directives

There are a few additional directives supported by the preprocessor. First, the **#error** directive lets you generate error messages when the program is compiled. Here is its syntax:

```
#error   text of error message
```

The following code fragment shows how you might use this directive.

```
#if      defined( OPTION_A )
         stuff needed for option A
#elif    defined( OPTION_B )
         stuff needed for option B
#elif    defined( OPTION_C )
         stuff needed for option C
#else
         #error No option selected!
#endif
```

Somewhat less useful is the **#line** directive, which has this form:

```
#line         number   "string"
```

It informs the preprocessor that *number* is the line number of the next line of input. If the optional *"string"* is given, the preprocessor takes it as the name of the current file. Specifically, this directive modifies the value of the _ _LINE_ _ symbol and, optionally, the _ _FILE_ _ symbol as well.

This directive is most often used in programs that translate other languages to C code. Error messages produced by the C compiler can reference the file name and line numbers of the original source file instead of the intermediate C source file produced by the translating program.

The **#pragma** directive is a mechanism that supports implementation-dependent directives. Its syntax is implementation dependent. An environment may provide #pragma's to allow options or other processing not available any other way. For example, some compilers use #pragma's to turn listings on or off during compilation or to insert assembly code into C programs. Pragmas are inherently not portable. Unrecognized #pragma directives are ignored by the preprocessor, and two different compilers might interpret the same #pragma in different ways.

Finally, the *null directive* is a line that begins with a pound sign but contains nothing else. These directives are simply deleted by the preprocessor. The null directives in the following example emphasize the #include directive by separating it from the surrounding code.

```
#
#include <stdio.h>
#
```

The same effect can be achieved with blank lines.

14.6 Summary

The first step in compiling a C program is to preprocess it. The preprocessor maintains five symbols, which are described in Table 14.1.

The #define directive attaches a symbolic name to an arbitrary sequence of characters. For example, these characters may be literal constants, expressions, or program statements. The sequence is terminated by the end of the line. Long sequences of characters may be split over multiple lines by ending each line except the last one with a backslash. Macros are defined sequences into which argument values are substituted. When a macro is invoked, values are given for each of its arguments. To prevent errors with macros that may appear in expressions, surround the entire definition of the macro with parentheses. Also, surround each occurrence of the macro parameters in the definition with parentheses. #define may be used to "rewrite" the C language so that it resembles another language.

The #argument construct is converted by the preprocessor into the string literal "argument". The ## operator concatenates the text appearing on each side of it.

Some tasks can be implemented with both macros and functions. However, macros are typeless, which can be an advantage. Macros execute faster than functions because there is no overhead used calling or returning from the function, however using macros rather than functions usually increases the size of the program. Also, arguments with side effects can cause unexpected results with macros. The behavior of these arguments with functions is more predictable. Because of these differences, it is important to use a naming convention that lets the programmer determine whether an identifier is a function or a macro.

With many compilers, symbols can be defined from the command line. The #undef directive causes the initial definition for a name to be ignored.

You can create different versions of a program from a single set of source files by using conditional compilation. The #if directive either includes or ignores a sequence of code according to the result of a compile-time test. When the #elif and #else directives are also used, you can select one of several sequences of code to compile. In addition to testing constant expressions, these directives can test whether or not symbols are defined. The `#ifdef` and `#ifndef` directives also perform this task.

The `#include` directive performs file inclusion. It has two forms. If the filename is enclosed in angle brackets, the compiler searches for the file in an implementation-defined standard place. This form is usually used when including library headers. In the other form, the filename is enclosed in quotation marks. Each implementation may process this form differently. However, if any special processing for this form fails to locate the file, then the standard place is searched instead. This form is usually used for including files that you have written. File inclusion may be nested, though there is usually little need for nesting that is more than one or two levels deep. Nested includes increase the risk of including a file more than once, and make it harder to determine which include files a given source file depends on.

The `#error` directive generates an error message at compile time containing text of your choice. The `#line` directive allows you to tell the compiler the line number of the next line of input and, optionally, the name of the file it came from. The implementation-dependent `#pragma` directive allows compilers to provide nonstandard processing such as inserting inline assembly code into a function.

14.7 Summary of Cautions

1. Do not put a semicolon at the end of a macro definition that forms an entire statement (page 385).

2. Using macro arguments in the definition without surrounding them with parentheses (page 386).

3. Not surrounding the entire macro definition with parentheses (page 387).

14.8 Summary of Programming Tips

1. Avoid using a `#define` for long sequences of code that can be implemented as a function (page 385).

2. In macros that evaluate expressions, parenthesize all occurrences of the macro arguments, and surround the entire definition with parentheses (page 387).

3. Avoid using `#define` macros to create a new language (page 387).

4. Adopt a naming convention that makes it obvious when a `#define` macro is being used (page 391).

5. Use file inclusion wherever it is appropriate; do not worry about overhead (page 397).

6. A header file should only contain declarations for one set of functions and/or data (page 397).

7. Separate header files for different sets of declarations improves information hiding (page 397).

8. Nesting `#include` files makes it more difficult to determine the dependencies among source files (page 399).

14.9 Questions

1. The preprocessor defines five symbols that give the name of the file being compiled, the current line number in that file, the current date and time, and whether the compiler is an ANSI compiler. Name one way in which each of these symbols might be useful.

2. Name two advantages of using `#define`'d names in place of literal constants.

3. Write a macro for debugging that will print arbitrary expressions. It should be called with two arguments. The first is a `printf` format code, and the second is the expression to be printed.

4. What will the following program print? Be sure to expand the `#define`'s carefully!

```
#define MAX(a,b)      (a)>(b)?(a):(b)
#define SQUARE(x)     x*x
#define DOUBLE(x)     x+x

main()
{
        int     x, y, z;

        y = 2; z = 3;
        x = MAX(y,z);
/* a */ printf( "%d %d %d\n", x, y, z );

        y = 2; z = 3;
        x = MAX(++y,++z);
```

```
/* b */ printf( "%d %d %d\n", x, y, z );

        x = 2;
        y = SQUARE(x);
        z = SQUARE(x+6);
/* c */ printf( "%d %d %d\n", x, y, z );

        x = 2;
        y = 3;
        z = MAX(5*DOUBLE(x),++y);
/* d */ printf( "%d %d %d\n", x, y, z );
        }
```

5. The putchar function is defined in the file stdio.h as a macro, despite the fact that it is fairly long. Why do you think it was defined this way?

6. What, if anything, is wrong with the following program fragment?

```
/*
** Process all the values in the array.
*/
result = 0;
i = 0;
while( i < SIZE ){
        result += process( value[ i++ ] );
}
```

7. What, if anything, is wrong with the following program fragment?

```
#define SUM( value )    ( ( value ) + ( value ) )
int     array[SIZE];
...
/*
** Sum all the values in the array.
*/
sum = 0;
i = 0;
while( i < SIZE )
        sum += SUM( array[ i++ ] );
```

8. What, if anything, is wrong with the following code fragments?

In file header1.h:
```
#ifndef _HEADER1_H
#define _HEADER1_H
#include "header2.h"
```

> *other declarations*
> ```
> #endif
> ```
>
> *In file header2.h:*
> ```
> #ifndef _HEADER2_H
> #define _HEADER2_H
> #include "header1.h"
> ```
> *other declarations*
> ```
> #endif
> ```

9. In an attempt to improve portability, one programmer wrote the following declarations.

```
#if sizeof( int ) == 2
        typedef long int32;
#else
        typedef int int32;
#endif
```

What, if anything, is wrong with them?

14.10 Programming Exercises

⌂ ★★ 1. The company you are working for markets a program that handles financial transactions and prints reports about them. To broaden the potential market, the program is sold in several editions, each with various combinations of options—the more options, the higher the price. Your task is to implement the code for a certain printing function so that it can be easily compiled to produce the different versions of the program.

Your function will be named print_ledger. It takes a single int argument, and does not return any value. It should call one or more of the following functions depending on which (if any) symbols are defined when the function is compiled.

If this symbol is defined . . .	Then you call this function.
OPTION_LONG	print_ledger_long
OPTION_DETAILED	print_ledger_detailed
(neither)	print_ledger_default

Each of these functions also takes a single int argument. Pass the value you received to whichever function(s) you call.

★★ 2. Write a function that returns a value indicating the type of computer on which it is running. The function will be used in a program that runs on a wide variety of computers.

We will use conditional compilation to accomplish this magic. Your function should be called cpu_type, and should not take any arguments. When your function is compiled, one of the symbols in the "Defined" column of the table below may be defined. Your function should return the corresponding symbol from the "Returned" column. If none of the symbols in the left column were defined, then the value CPU_UNKNOWN should be returned. If more than one of the symbols was defined, the result is undefined.

Defined	Returned
VAX	CPU_VAX
M68000	CPU_68000
M68020	CPU_68020
I80386	CPU_80386
X6809	CPU_6809
X6502	CPU_6502
U3B2	CPU_3B2
(none)	CPU_UNKNOWN

The symbols in the "Returned" column will be #define'd as various integer values in an include file called cpu_types.h .

15

Input/Output Functions

One of the biggest advantages of ANSI C over earlier implementations is that the library is included in the specification. Every ANSI implementation will have the mandated set of functions, and they will have the required interface and work in the prescribed manner. This situation is a great improvement over the early days of C when different implementations "improved" the common library functions by modifying or extending their functionality. These changes may have been useful on the particular system for which they were made, but they inhibited portability because code that depended on the changes would fail on other implementations that lacked them (or had different changes).

ANSI implementations aren't prohibited from having additional functions in their libraries. However, the standard functions must operate as defined by the Standard. If you are concerned with portability, simply avoid any nonstandard functions.

This chapter covers ANSI C input and output (I/O). However, we begin with two very useful functions to report and react to errors.

15.1 Error Reporting

The **perror** function reports errors in a simple, uniform way. Many of the functions in the ANSI C library call the operating system to perform some work, especially the I/O functions. Any time the operating system is asked to do something, there is the chance that it might fail. For instance, if a program attempts to read from a disk file that does not exist, there is not much the operating system can do except indicate that something went wrong. The library functions pass this indication to the user's program after saving a code in the external integer variable **errno** (defined in errno.h) to indicate exactly why the operation failed.

The `perror` function simplifies reporting these specific errors to the user. Its prototype from `stdio.h` is shown below.

```
void perror( char const *message );
```

If `message` is not NULL and points to a nonempty string, the string is printed and is followed by a colon and a space. A message explaining the error code currently in `errno` is then printed.

`perrno`'s best feature is its ease of use. Good programming practice dictates that any operation that might result in an error should be checked afterwards to determine whether or not it succeeded. Even operations that are supposedly "guaranteed" to work should be checked, because sooner or later they will fail. The small amount of extra work needed to do this checking will be repaid to you many times over in saved debugging time. `perror` is illustrated in examples throughout this chapter.

Note that `errno` is set only when a library function fails. When the functions are successful, `errno` is not modified at all. This behavior means that `errno` cannot be tested to determine whether an error occurred. Instead, check `errno` only when the function that was called indicates that it failed.

15.2 Terminating Execution

Another useful function is **exit**, which is used to terminate the execution of a program. Its prototype, found in `stdlib.h`, is shown below.

```
void exit( int status );
```

The `status` argument is returned to the operating system and is an indication of whether or not the program completed normally. This value is the same as the integer status returned by the `main` function. The predefined symbols **EXIT_SUCCESS** and **EXIT_FAILURE** indicate successful and unsuccessful termination, respectively. Other values may be used, but their meanings are implementation dependent.

This function is particularly useful when error conditions that prevent the program from continuing to execute are discovered. You will often follow calls to `perror` with a call to `exit`. Although terminating the program is not the right way to handle all errors, it is better than letting a doomed program continue to execute and abort later.

Note that this function never returns. When `exit` is finished, the program has disappeared, so there is nothing to return to.

15.3 The Standard I/O Library

The earliest implementations of K&R C had little in the way of library functions to support input and output. As a result, every programmer who wanted more sophisticated I/O functionality than that provided had to implement their own.

This situation was greatly improved by the *Standard I/O Library*, a collection of I/O functions that implemented much of the added functionality that programmers had been implementing on their own. This library expanded on existing functions, such as `printf`, creating different versions that could be used in a variety of situations. The library also introduced the notion of buffered I/O, which increases the efficiency of most programs.

There were two major drawbacks to this library. First, it was implemented on one specific type of machine without much consideration of other machines with different characteristics. This fact led to situations where code that worked fine on one machine could not be made to work on another solely because of architectural differences between the machines. The second drawback is directly related to the first. When implementors discovered these deficiencies, they attempted to fix them by modifying the library functions. As soon as they did so, though, the library was no longer "standard," and program portability was reduced.

The I/O functions in the ANSI C library are direct descendents of those from the old Standard I/O Library except that the ANSI functions have been improved. Portability and completeness were key considerations in the design of the ANSI library. However, backward compatibility with existing programs was another consideration. Most of the differences between ANSI functions and their older counterparts are the additions that enhance portability or functionality.

One last comment on portability: These functions are the result of considerable evolution, but there are probably additional revisions that could make them even better. A major advantage to ANSI C is that any such changes will have to be implemented as *different* functions rather than modifications to the existing functions. Therefore, program portability will not suffer as it has in the past.

15.4 ANSI I/O Concepts

The include file **stdio.h** contains declarations relevant to the I/O portion of the ANSI library. Its name comes from the old Standard I/O Library. Although a few I/O functions may be used without including this file, most functions will require it.

15.4.1 *Streams*

Computers today have a large variety of devices on which I/O may be performed. CD-ROM drives, hard and floppy disk drives, network connections, communications ports, and video adapters are a few of the more common devices. Each device has different characteristics and operating protocols. The operating system takes care of the details of communicating with these different devices and provides a simpler, more uniform I/O interface to the programmer.

ANSI C abstracts the notion of I/O even further. As far as C programs are concerned, all I/O is simply a matter of moving bytes into or out of the program. This stream of bytes, not surprisingly, is called a *stream*. The program is only concerned with creating the correct bytes of data for output and interpreting the bytes of data that come in as input. Details of the specific I/O device are hidden from the programmer.

Most streams are *fully buffered*, which means that "reading" and "writing" actually copy data out of and into an area in memory called the *buffer*. Copying to and from memory is very fast. The buffer for an output stream is *flushed* (physically written) to the device or file only when it becomes full. Writing a full buffer is more efficient than writing the data in little bits and pieces as the program produces it. Similarly, input buffers are refilled when they become empty by reading the next large chunk of input from the device or file into the buffer.

This buffering could cause confusion with the standard input and standard output, so they are fully buffered only if the operating system can determine that they are not associated with interactive devices. Otherwise, their buffering state is implementation dependent. A common (but not universal) strategy is to tie the standard output to the standard input in such a way that the output buffer is flushed when input is requested. Then, any prompts or other output previously written to the output buffer will appear on the screen before the user must enter the input.

Although this buffering is usually desirable, it can cause confusion when you are debugging your program. A common debugging strategy is to sprinkle calls to `printf` throughout the program to determine the specific area in which an error is occurring. However, the output from these calls is buffered and does not immediately show up on the screen. In fact if the program aborts, the buffered output may not be written at all, which leads the programmer to incorrect conclusions about where the error occurred. The solution to this problem is to always follow debugging `printf`'s with a call to `fflush`, like this:

```
printf( "something or other" );
fflush( stdout );
```

`fflush` (described in more detail later in the chapter) forces the buffer to be
written immediately whether or not it is full.

Text Streams

There are two types of streams, *text* and *binary*. Text streams have certain
characteristics that may vary from system to system. One of these is the maximum length of a text line. The Standard requires that this limit be at least 254
characters. Another is the manner in which text lines are terminated. For
example, the convention for text files on MS-DOS systems is that each line is
terminated with a carriage return character and a newline (also called a
linefeed) character. However, UNIX systems use only a newline.

The Standard defines a text line to be zero or more characters followed by a
terminating newline character. On systems where the external representation of
a text line differs from this definition, the library functions take care of
translating between the external and internal forms. On MS-DOS systems, for
example, a newline is written as the carriage return/newline pair. On input, the
carriage return character is discarded. The ability to manipulate text without
regard to its external appearance simplifies the creation of portable programs.

Binary Streams

The bytes in a binary stream, on the other hand, are written to the file or
device exactly as the program wrote them and are delivered to the program
exactly as they were read from the file or device. They are not changed in any
manner. This type of stream is appropriate for nontextual data, but binary
streams may also be used for text files if you do not want the I/O functions to
modify the end-of-line characters.

15.4.2 FILEs

One of the declarations contained in `stdio.h` is for the **FILE** structure. Not
to be confused with a data file stored on a disk, a FILE is a data structure used
to access a stream. If you have several different streams active at a time, each
will have its own FILE associated with it. To perform some operation on a
stream, you call the appropriate function and pass it the FILE associated with
that stream.

The runtime environment must provide at least three streams to every ANSI C program—the *standard input*, the *standard output*, and the *standard error*. The names of these streams are **stdin**, **stdout**, and **stderr**, respectively, and they are simply pointers to FILE structures. The standard input is where input comes from by default, and the standard output is the default output device. The defaults depend on the implementation; often the standard input is a keyboard device and the standard output is a terminal or screen.

Many operating systems let the user change the standard input and output from their default devices when a program is executed. For example, MS-DOS and UNIX systems both support input/output redirection using this notation:

```
$ program < data > answer
```

When this program executes, it will read its standard input from the file data instead of the keyboard, and it will write its standard output to the file answer instead of the screen. Refer to your system's documentation for details on how (or whether) I/O redirection is performed.

The standard error is the place where error messages are written. perror writes its output here. On many systems the standard error and the standard output default to the same location, but having a separate stream for error messages means that they will still appear on the screen or other default output device even if the standard output has been redirected somewhere else.

15.4.3 Standard I/O Constants

There are numerous constants defined in stdio.h that are related in some way to input and output. EOF, which you have already seen, is the value returned by many functions to indicate that end of file has been reached. The actual value chosen for EOF uses more bits than a character in order to prevent binary character values from mistakenly being interpreted as EOF.

How many files can a program have open at once? It depends on the implementation, but you are guaranteed of being able to simultaneously open at least **FOPEN_MAX** files. This constant, which includes the three standard streams, must be at least eight.

The constant **FILENAME_MAX** is an integer that indicates how large a character array should be to hold the longest legal file name that the implementation supports. If there isn't a practical limit to the length of a file name, then this value is the recommended size for such strings. The remaining constants are described later in this chapter along with the functions with which they are used.

15.5 Overview of Stream I/O

The standard library functions make it very convenient to perform I/O to and from files in C programs. Here is a general overview of file I/O.

1. The program declares a pointer variable of type FILE * for each file that must be simultaneously active. This variable will point to the FILE structure used by the stream while it is active.

2. The stream is *opened* by calling the **fopen** function. To open a stream, you must specify which file or device is to be accessed and how it is to be accessed (for example, reading, writing, or both). fopen and the operating system verify that the file or device exists (and, on some operating systems, that you have permission to access it in the manner you specify) and initializes the FILE structure.

3. The file is then read and/or written as desired.

4. Finally, the stream is *closed* with the **fclose** function. Closing a stream prevents the associated file from being accessed again, guarantees that any data stored in the stream buffer is correctly written to the file, and releases the FILE structure so that it can be used again with another file.

I/O on the standard streams is simpler because they do not have to be opened or closed.

The I/O functions deal with data in three basic forms: individual characters, text lines, and binary data. A different set of functions is used to process each form. Table 15.1 lists the function or function family used for each form of I/O. Function families, listed in the table in italic, are groups of functions whose members each perform the same basic work in a slightly different way. The functions differ in where the input is obtained or where the output goes. The variants are to perform the work:

| Type of Data | Function or Family Name | | Description |
	Input	Output	
Character	*getchar*	*putchar*	Read (write) a single character
Line	*gets* *scanf*	*puts* *printf*	Unformatted input (output) of a line Formatted input (output)
Binary	fread	fwrite	Read (write) binary data

Table 15.1 Functions to perform character, line, and binary I/O

Family Name	*Purpose*	*To Any Stream*	*Only* stdin *and* stdout	*String in Memory*
getchar	Character input	fgetc, getc	getchar	①
putchar	Character output	fputc, putc	putchar	①
gets	Line input	fgets	gets	②
puts	Line output	fputs	puts	②
scanf	Formatted input	fscanf	scanf	sscanf
printf	Formatted output	fprintf	printf	sprintf

①   Use a subscript or indirection on a pointer to get/put single characters to/from memory.

②   Use strcpy to get/put lines to/from memory.

Table 15.2   Input/output function families

1.   only with stdin or stdout,

2.   with a stream given as an argument,

3.   using character strings in memory rather than streams.

The functions that require a stream argument will accept stdin or stdout as arguments. Some families do not have functions for the string variants, because it is so easy to accomplish the same result with other statements or functions. Table 15.2 lists the functions in each family. The individual functions are described later in this chapter.

15.6 Opening Streams

The fopen function opens a specific file and associates a stream with the file. Its prototype is shown below.

```
FILE *fopen( char const *name, char const *mode );
```

The arguments are both strings. name is the name of the file or device that you wish to open. The rules for constructing filenames vary from system to system, which is why fopen takes the filename in one string rather than in separate arguments for path name, drive letter, file extension, and so forth. This argument specifies the file to open—the name of the FILE * variable that the program uses to save the value returned by fopen does not influence which file is opened.

The `mode` argument indicates whether the stream will be used for input, output, or both and whether the stream will be text or binary. The modes used most frequently are shown in the following table.

	Read	Write	Append
Text	"r"	"w"	"a"
Binary	"rb"	"wb"	"ab"

The modes begin with r, w, or a to indicate that the stream is to be opened for reading, writing, or appending, respectively. A file opened for reading must already exist, whereas a file opened for writing is truncated if it already exists and created if it does not. If a file opened for appending does not exist, it will be created; if it already exists, it is *not* truncated. In either case, data can only be written to the end of the file.

Adding a + to the mode opens the file for update, and both reading and writing are allowed on the stream. However, if you have been reading from the file, you must call one of the file positioning functions (`fseek`, `fsetpos`, and `rewind`, which are described later in this chapter) before you may begin writing to it. After writing to the file, you must call either `fflush` or one of the file positioning functions before you may begin reading from it.

If it is successful, `fopen` returns a pointer to the `FILE` structure for the newly created stream. Otherwise a `NULL` pointer is returned and `errno` will indicate the nature of the problem.

Always check the value returned by `fopen`! If the function fails, a `NULL` value is returned. If the program does not check for errors, the `NULL` pointer will be given to subsequent I/O functions. They will perform indirection on it and fail.

The following example illustrates the use of `fopen`.

```
FILE     *input;

input = fopen( "data3", "r" );
if( input == NULL ){
        perror( "data3" );
        exit( EXIT_FAILURE );
}
```

First, the `fopen` function is called; the file to be opened is named `data3` and it is to be opened for reading. This step is followed by the all-important check to see whether the open succeeded. If it did not, the error is reported to the user and the program terminates. The exact output produced by this call to `perror` will vary depending on the operating system in use, but it might look something like this:

```
data3: No such file or directory
```

This type of message clearly indicates to the user that something has gone wrong and gives the user a good indication of what the problem is. It is especially important to report these errors in programs which read filenames or take them from the command line. Whenever the user enters a filename, there is the possibility that they may make a mistake. Clear, descriptive error messages help the user determine what went wrong and how to fix it.

The **freopen** function is used to open (or reopen) a specific stream on a file. Its prototype is:

```
FILE *freopen( char const *filename, char const *mode, FILE *stream );
```

The last argument is the stream to be opened. It may be a stream that was previously returned by fopen, or it may be one of the standard streams stdin, stdout, or stderr.

The function first attempts to close the stream. It then opens the stream with the given file and mode. If the open fails, the value NULL is returned, otherwise the third argument value is returned.

15.7 Closing Streams

Streams are closed with the **fclose** function, which has this prototype:

```
int fclose( FILE *f );
```

For output streams, fclose flushes the buffer before the file is closed. fclose returns zero if it was successful and EOF otherwise.

Program 15.1 interprets its command line arguments as a list of filenames. It opens each file and processes them, one by one. If any file cannot be opened, an error message that includes the name of the file is printed, and the program continues to the next name in the list. The exit status is based on whether any errors occurred.

I said earlier that any operation that might fail should be checked to see whether or not it succeeded. In this program, the value returned by fclose is checked to see if anything went wrong. Many programmers do not bother with this test, arguing that there is no reason why the close will fail to work. Furthermore, they're finished with the file, so it doesn't matter even if it did fail. However, this analysis is not entirely correct.

```
/*
** Process each of the files whose names appear on the command line.
*/
#include <stdlib.h>
#include <stdio.h>

int
main( int ac, char **av )
{
        int     exit_status = EXIT_SUCCESS;
        FILE    *input;

        /*
        ** While there are more names ...
        */
        while( *++av != NULL ){
                /*
                ** Try opening the file.
                */
                input = fopen( *av, "r" );
                if( input == NULL ){
                        perror( *av );
                        exit_status = EXIT_FAILURE;
                        continue;
                }

                /*
                ** Process the file here ...
                */

                /*
                ** Close the file (don't expect any errors here).
                */
                if( fclose( input ) != 0 ){
                        perror( "fclose" );
                        exit( EXIT_FAILURE );
                }
        }

        return exit_status;
}
```

Program 15.1   Opening and closing files   open_cls.c

The `input` variable might have changed because of a program bug between the `fopen` and the `fclose`. This bug would certainly cause a failure. In programs that do not check the result of an `fopen`, `input` might even be NULL. Either of these conditions will cause the `fclose` to fail. But if either of these conditions existed, the I/O would have failed as well, and the program probably would have terminated long before `fclose` was called.

So should you check `fclose` (or any other operation, for that matter) for errors or not? When making this decision, ask yourself two questions.

1.   What should be done if the operation succeeded?

2.   What should be done if the operation failed?

If the answers to these questions are different, then you should check for the error. It is reasonable to skip the error checking only in cases where both questions have the same answer.

15.8 Character I/O

After a stream is open, it can be used for input and output. The simplest form is character I/O. Character input is performed by the *getchar* family of functions, whose prototypes are shown below.

```
int fgetc( FILE *stream );
int getc( FILE *stream );
int getchar( void );
```

The desired stream is given as the argument to `getc` and `fgetc`, but `getchar` always reads from the standard input. Each function reads the next character from the stream and returns it as the value of the function. If there aren't any more characters on the stream, the constant EOF is returned instead.

These functions are supposed to read characters, yet they all return an `int` rather than a `char`. Although codes that represent characters are just small integers, the real reason for returning an `int` is to allow the functions to report end of file. If a `char` were returned, then one of the 256 character values would have to be chosen to designate end of file. If this character appeared in a file, it would be impossible to read beyond its position because the character would seem to signal the end of the file.

Having the functions return an `int` solves the problem. EOF is defined as an integer whose value is outside of the range of possible character values. This solution lets us use these functions to read binary files, where all characters may occur, as well as text files.

To write individual characters to a stream, functions in the *putchar* family are used. Their prototypes are:

```
int fputc( int character, FILE *stream );
int putc( int character, FILE *stream );
int putchar( int character );
```

The first argument is the character to be printed. The functions truncate the integer argument to an unsigned character before printing, so

```
putchar( 'abc' );
```

only prints one character (which one is implementation dependent).

These functions return the value EOF if they fail for any reason, such as writing to a stream that has been closed.

15.8.1 Character I/O Macros

fgetc and fputc are true functions, but getc, putc, getchar, and putchar are #define'd macros. The macros are slightly more efficient in terms of execution time, and the functions will be more efficient in terms of program size. Having both types available allows you to choose the right one depending on whether size or speed is more important. This distinction is rarely a matter of great concern, because the differences observed in actual programs using one or the other are usually not significant.

15.8.2 Undoing Character I/O

You cannot tell what the next character on a stream will be until you've read it. Thus, you will occasionally read one character beyond what you wanted. For example, suppose you must read a sequence of digits from a stream one by one. Because you cannot see what the next character will be without reading it, you must keep reading until you get a nondigit. But what do you do with the extra character to avoid losing it?

The **ungetc** function solves this type of problem. Here is its prototype.

```
int ungetc( int character, FILE *stream );
```

ungetc returns a character previously read back to the stream so that it can be read again later. Program 15.2 illustrates ungetc. It reads characters from the standard input and converts them to an integer. Without an ungetc capability,

```
/*
** Convert a series of digits from the standard input to an integer.
*/

#include <stdio.h>
#include <ctype.h>

int
read_int()
{
        int     value;
        int     ch;

        value = 0;

        /*
        ** Convert digits from the standard input; stop when we get a
        ** character that is not a digit.
        */
        while( ( ch = getchar() ) != EOF && isdigit( ch ) ){
                value *= 10;
                value += ch - '0';
        }

        /*
        ** Push back the nondigit so we don't lose it.
        */
        ungetc( ch, stdin );
        return value;
}
```

Program 15.2   Converting characters to an integer   char_int.c

this function would have to return the excess character to the caller, who
would then be responsible for sending it to whatever part of the program reads
the next character. The special cases and extra logic involved in handling the
extra character make the program significantly more complex.

Each stream allows at least one character to be pushed back (ungotten).
If more characters are pushed back on a stream that allows it, they will be read
in the opposite order that they were pushed. Note that pushing characters back
to a stream is not the same as writing to the stream. The external storage associated with a stream is not affected by an ungetc.

"Ungotten" characters are associated with the current position in the stream, so changing the stream's position with `fseek`, `fsetpos`, or `rewind` discards any ungotten characters.

15.9 Unformatted Line I/O

Line oriented I/O can be performed in one of two ways—unformatted or formatted. Both forms manipulate character strings. The difference is that unformatted I/O simply reads or writes strings, whereas formatted I/O performs conversions between internal and external representations of numeric and other variables. In this section, we'll look at unformatted line I/O.

The *gets* and *puts* families operate on character strings rather than individual characters. This characteristic makes them useful in programs that deal with textual input on a line-by-line basis. The prototypes for these functions are shown below.

```
char *fgets( char *buffer, int buffer_size, FILE *stream );
char *gets( char *buffer );

int fputs( char const *buffer, FILE *stream );
int puts( char const *buffer );
```

`fgets` reads characters from the specified `stream` and copies them into the `buffer`. Reading stops after a newline character has been read and stored in the buffer. It also stops after `buffer_size - 1` characters have been stored in the buffer. Data is not lost in this case, because the next call to `fgets` will get the next characters from the stream. In either case, a NUL byte is appended to the end of whatever was stored in the buffer, thus making it a string.

If end of file is reached before any characters have been read, the buffer is unchanged and `fgets` returns a NULL pointer. Otherwise, `fgets` returns its first argument (the pointer to the buffer). The returned value is usually used only to check for end of file.

The buffer passed to `fputs` must contain a string; its characters are written to the stream. The string is expected to be NUL-terminated, which is why there isn't a buffer size argument. The string is written verbatim: if it does not contain a newline, none is written; if it contains several newlines, they are all written. Thus, whereas `fgets` tries to read one whole line, `fputs` can write a part of a line, a whole line, or several lines. If an error occurred while writing, `fputs` returns the constant EOF; otherwise it returns a non-negative value.

Program 15.3 is a function that reads lines of input from one file and writes them unchanged to another file. The constant MAX_LINE_LENGTH determines the size of the buffer, and therefore the size of the longest line that will be read. In this function the value has little significance because the resulting file will be the same whether long lines are written all at once or piece by piece. On the other hand, if the function were to count the number of lines that are copied, a too small buffer would produce an incorrect count because long lines would be read in two or more chunks. We could fix this problem by adding code to see if each chunk ended with a newline.

The correct value for the buffer size is usually a compromise that depends on the nature of the processing required. However, fgets will never cause errors by overflowing its buffer.

Note that fgets cannot read into a buffer whose size is less than two, because one space in the buffer is reserved for the NUL byte that will be added.

The gets and puts functions are almost identical to fgets and fputs. The differences allow backward compatibility. The major functional difference is that when gets reads a line of input, it *does not store* the terminating newline in the buffer. When puts writes a string, it *adds* a newline to the output after the string is written.

Another difference pertains only to gets and is obvious from the function prototypes: there is no buffer size argument. Thus gets cannot determine the length of the buffer. If a long input line is read into a short buffer, the excess characters are written in whatever memory locations follow the buffer, thus

```
/*
** Copy the standard input to the standard output, line by line.
*/
#include <stdio.h>

#define MAX_LINE_LENGTH         1024    /* longest line I can copy */

void
copylines( FILE *input, FILE *output )
{
        char    buffer[MAX_LINE_LENGTH];

        while( fgets( buffer, MAX_LINE_LENGTH, input ) != NULL )
                fputs( buffer, output );
}
```

Program 15.3 Copy lines from one file to another   copyline.c

destroying the values of one or more unrelated variables. This characteristic makes gets suitable for only the most trivial of programs, because the only way to guard against overflowing the input buffer is to declare a huge one. But no matter how large it is, there is always the possibility that the next line of input will be larger, especially when the standard input has been redirected to a file.

15.10 Formatted Line I/O

The name "formatted line I/O" is something of a misnomer, because the functions in the *scanf* and *printf* families are not limited to single lines. They can perform I/O on partial lines and multiple lines as well.

15.10.1 The scanf Family

The prototypes for the *scanf* family are shown below. The ellipsis in each prototype represents a variable-length list of pointers. The values converted from the input are stored one by one into the locations to which these arguments point.

```
int fscanf( FILE *stream, char const *format, ... );
int scanf( char const *format, ... );
int sscanf( char const *string, char const *format, ... );
```

These functions all read characters from an input source and convert them according to the codes given in the format string. The input source for fscanf is the stream given as an argument, scanf reads from the standard input, and sscanf takes input characters from the character string given as the first argument.

Input stops when the end of the format string is reached or input is read that does not match what the format string specifies. In either case, the number of input values that were converted is returned as the function value. If end of file is encountered before any input values have been converted, the function returns the constant EOF.

For these functions to work properly, the pointer arguments must be the right type for the corresponding format codes. The functions cannot verify whether their pointer arguments are the correct types, so they assume that they are and go ahead and use them. If the pointer types are incorrect, the resulting values will be garbage, and adjacent variables may be overwritten in the process.

By now the purpose of the ampersands before the arguments to the *scanf* functions should be clear. Because of C's call-by-value argument passing mechanism, the only way to identify a location as a function argument is to pass a pointer to it. A very common error is to forget the ampersand. This omission causes the *value* of the variable to be passed as the argument, which scanf (or either of the other two) interprets as if it were a pointer. When it is dereferenced, either the program aborts or data in an unexpected location is overwritten.

15.10.2 scanf Format Codes

The format string may contain any of the following:

- Whitespace characters—these match zero or more whitespace characters in the input, which are ignored.

- Format codes—these specify how the function should interpret the next input characters.

- Other characters—each time any other character appears in the format string, then the next input character must match it. If it does, the input character is discarded; if it does not, the function returns.

The format codes for the *scanf* functions all begin with a percent sign, followed by (1) an optional asterisk, (2) an optional width, (3) an optional qualifier, and (4) the format code. The asterisk causes the converted value to be discarded rather than stored. This technique is one way to skip past unneeded input. The width is given as a non-negative integer. It limits the number of input characters that will be read in order to convert this value. If a width isn't given, characters are read until the next whitespace character is found in the input. The qualifiers modify the meanings of certain format codes, and are listed in Table 15.3.

Format code	Result when used with qualifier		
	h	l	L
d, i, n	short	long	
o, u, x	unsigned short	unsigned long	
e, f, g		double	long double

Table 15.3 *scanf* qualifiers

The purpose of the qualifier is to specify the size of the argument. Omitting the qualifier when an integer argument is shorter or longer than the default integer is a common mistake. The same is true with the floating-point types. Depending on the relative sizes of these types, omitting the qualifier may result in long variables that are only half initialized or variables adjacent to short ones being overwritten.

On a machine whose default integer is the same size as a `short`, the h qualifier is not needed when converting a `short`. However, the qualifier *is* needed on a machine whose default integer size is longer than a `short`. Thus, your programs will be more portable if you use the appropriate qualifier when converting all `short` and `long` integers, and all `long double` variables.

The format code is a single character that specifies how the input characters are to be interpreted. Table 15.4 describes the codes.

Let's look at some examples that use the *scanf* functions. Once again, only the parts relevant to these functions are shown. Our first example is straightforward. It reads pairs of numbers from an input stream and does some processing on them. When end of file is reached, the loop breaks.

```
int      a, b;

while( fscanf( input, "%d %d", &a, &b ) == 2 ){
        /*
        ** Process the values a and b.
        */
}
```

This code is rather unsophisticated because any illegal characters in the input stream also break the loop. Also, because `fscanf` skips over white space, there is no way to verify whether the two values were both on the same line or on different input lines. A technique to solve this problem is shown in a later example.

The next example uses a field width.

```
nfields = fscanf( input, "%4d %4d %4d", &a, &b, &c )
```

The widths restrict each of the integer values to be four or fewer digits long. With this input,

```
1 2
```

a would become one and b would become two. c would be unchanged, and `nfields` would be two. But with this input,

```
12345 67890
```

Code	Argument	Meaning
c	char *	A single character is read and stored. Leading whitespace is *not* skipped. If a width is given, that number of characters are read and stored; *no NUL byte is appended;* the argument must point to a character array that is large enough.
i d	int *	An optionally signed integer is converted. d interprets the input as decimal; i determines the base of the value by its first characters as is done with integer literal constants.
u o x	unsigned *	An optionally signed integer is converted, but is stored as unsigned. The value is interpreted as decimal with u, octal with o, and hexadecimal with x. The code X is a synonym for x.
e f g	float *	A floating-point value is expected. It must look like a floating-point literal constant except that a decimal point is not required. E and G are synonyms for e and g.
s	char *	A sequence of nonwhitespace characters is read. The argument must point to a character array that is large enough. Input stops when whitespace is found; the string is then NUL-terminated.
[*xxx*]	char *	A sequence of characters from the given set is read. The argument must point to a character array that is large enough. Input stops when the first character that is not in the set is encountered. The string is then NUL-terminated. The code %[abc] specifies the set including a, b, and c. Beginning the list with ^ complements the set, so %[^abc] means all characters *except* a, b, and c. A right bracket may be included in the list only if it is first. It is implementation dependent whether a dash (for example, %[a-z]) specifies a range of characters.
p	void *	The input is expected to be a sequence of characters such as those produced by the %p format code of printf (see below). The conversion is performed in an implementation-dependent manner, but the result will compare equal to the value that produced the characters when printed as described above.
n	int *	The number of characters read from the input so far by this call to scanf is returned. %n conversions are not counted in the value returned by scanf. No input is consumed.
%	(none)	This code matches a single % in the input, which is discarded.

Table 15.4   *scanf* format codes

a would be 1234, b would be five, c would be 6789, and nfields would be three. The final zero would remain unread in the input.

It is difficult to maintain synchronization with line boundaries in the input when using fscanf, because it skips newlines as white space. For example, suppose that a program reads input that consists of groups of four values. These values are then processed in some way, and the next four values are

read. The simplest way to prepare input for such a program is to put each set
of four values on its own input line, making it easy to see which values form a
set. But if one of the lines contains too many or too few values, the program
becomes confused. For example, consider this input, which contains an error
in its second line:

```
1 1 1 1
2 2 2 2 2
3 3 3 3
4 4 4 4
5 5 5 5
```

If we used fscanf to read the values four at a time, the first and second sets
of values would be correct, but the third set of values would be read as 2, 3, 3,
3. Each subsequent set would also be incorrect.

```
/*
** Line-oriented input processing with sscanf
*/
#include <stdio.h>
#define BUFFER_SIZE     100      /* Longest line we'll handle */

void
function( FILE *input )
{
        int     a, b, c, d, e;
        char    buffer[ BUFFER_SIZE ];

        while( fgets( buffer, BUFFER_SIZE, input ) != NULL ){
                if( sscanf( buffer, "%d %d %d %d %d",
                    &a, &b, &c, &d, &e ) != 4 ){
                        fprintf( stderr, "Bad input skipped: %s",
                            buffer );
                        continue;
                }

                /*
                ** Process this set of input.
                */
        }
}
```

Program 15.4   Processing line-oriented input with sscanf   scanf1.c

Program 15.4 uses a more reliable approach for reading this type of input. The advantage of this method is that the input is now processed line by line. It is impossible to read a set of values that begins on one line and ends on the next. Furthermore, by trying to convert five values, input lines that have too many values are detected as well as those with too few.

A related technique is used to read line-oriented input that may be in several different formats. A line is read with `fgets` and then scanned with several `sscanf`'s, each using a different format. The format of the input line is determined by the first `sscanf` that converts the expected number of values. For instance, Program 15.5 examines the contents of a buffer that was read earlier. It extracts either one, two, or three values from a line of input and assigns default values to variables for which an input value was not given.

15.10.3 The printf Family

Functions in the *printf* family are used to create formatted output. There are three functions in this family: `fprintf`, `printf`, and `sprintf`. Their prototypes are shown below.

```
int fprintf( FILE *stream, char const *format, ... );
int printf( char const *format, ... );
int sprintf( char *buffer, char const *format, ... );
```

As you saw in Chapter 1, `printf` formats the values in its argument list according to the format codes and other characters in the `format` argument. The other members of this family work the same way. With `printf`, the resulting output goes to the standard output. With `fprintf`, any output stream can be used, and `sprintf` writes its results as a NUL-terminated string in the specified `buffer` rather than to a stream.

`sprintf` is a potential source of error. The buffer size is not an argument to `sprintf`, so output that is unexpectedly long can spill out of the end of the buffer and overwrite whatever happens to follow the buffer in memory. There are two strategies for making sure that this problem never happens. The first is to declare a very large buffer. But this solution wastes memory, and although a large buffer reduces the chance of overflow, it does not eliminate it. The second approach is to analyze the format to see how long the resulting output would be when the largest possible values are converted. For example, the largest integer on a machine with 4-byte integers is 11 characters including a sign, so the buffer should always be at least 12 characters in order to hold the value and the terminating NUL byte. There isn't a limit on the length of

```
/*
** Variable format input processing with sscanf
*/
#include <stdio.h>
#include <stdlib.h>

#define DEFAULT_A          1         /* or whatever ... */
#define DEFAULT_B          2         /* or whatever ... */

void
function( char *buffer )
{
        int     a, b, c;

        /*
        ** See if all three values are given.
        */
        if( sscanf( buffer, "%d %d %d", &a, &b, &c ) != 3 ){
                /*
                ** No, use default value for a, see if other two
                ** values are both given.
                */
                a = DEFAULT_A;
                if( sscanf( buffer, "%d %d", &b, &c ) != 2 ){
                        /*
                        ** Use default value for b too, look for
                        ** remaining value.
                        */
                        b = DEFAULT_B;
                        if( sscanf( buffer, "%d", &c ) != 1 ){
                                fprintf( stderr, "Bad input: %s",
                                    buffer );
                                exit( EXIT_FAILURE );
                        }
                }
        }
        /*
        ** Process the values a, b, and c.
        */
}
```

Program 15.5   Processing variable format input with `sscanf`   scanf2.c

strings, but the number of characters printed for a string can be restricted with an optional field in the format code.

The format codes used with the *printf* family work differently than those used with the scanf functions, so you must be careful not to intermix them. This problem is made more difficult by the fact that some of the format codes look identical without their optional fields. Unfortunately, many of the commonly used codes, such as %d, fall into this category.

Another source of error is having arguments whose types do not match the corresponding format codes. Usually the result of this error is garbage in the output, but it is possible for such a mismatch to cause the program to abort. As in the *scanf* family, these functions cannot verify that a value has the proper type for a format code, so it is up to you to make sure they match properly.

Code	Argument	Meaning
c	int	The argument is truncated to unsigned char and printed as a character.
d i	int	The argument is printed as a decimal integer. If a precision is given and the value has fewer digits, zeros are added at the front.
u o x, X	unsigned int	The argument is printed as an unsigned value in decimal (u), octal (o), or hexadecimal (x or X). x and X are identical except that abcdef are used for x conversions, and ABCDEF are used with X.
e E	double	The argument is printed in exponent form; for example, 6.023000e23 for the e code, and 6.023000E23 for the E code. The number of digits behind the decimal point is determined by the precision field; the default is six digits.
f	double	The argument is printed in conventional notation. The precision determines the number of digits behind the decimal point; the default is six.
g G	double	The argument is printed in either %f or %e (or %E, if G is given) notation, depending on its value. The %f form is used if the exponent is greater than or equal to -4 but less than the precision. Otherwise the exponent form is used.
s	char *	A string is printed.
p	void *	The value of the pointer is converted to an implementation-dependent sequence of printable characters. This code is used primarily in conjunction with the %p code in scanf.
n	int *	This code is unique in that it does not produce any output. Instead, the number of characters of output produced so far is *stored* in the corresponding argument.
%	(none)	A single % is produced in the output.

Table 15.5   *printf* format codes

15.10.4 printf Format Codes

The `format` string may contain formatting codes, which cause the next value from the argument list to be formatted in the specified manner, and other characters, which are printed verbatim. Format codes consist of a percent sign followed by (1) zero or more flag characters that modify how some conversions are performed, (2) an optional minimum field width, (3) an optional precision, (4) an optional modifier, and (5) the conversion type.

The precise meanings of the flags and other fields depend on which conversion is used. Table 15.5 describes the conversion type codes, and Table 15.6 describes the flag characters and their meanings.

The field width is a decimal integer specifying the minimum number of characters that will appear in the result. If a value has fewer characters than the field width, padding occurs to increase its length. The flags determine whether padding is done with spaces or zeros and whether it occurs on the left or the right end of the value.

For d, i, u, o, x, and X conversions, the precision specifies the minimum number of digits that will appear in the result and overrides the zero flag. If the converted value has fewer digits, leading zeros are inserted. Digits are not produced if the value zero is converted with a precision of zero. For e, E, and f conversions, the precision determines the number of digits that will appear after the decimal point. For g and G conversions, it specifies the maximum number of significant digits that will appear. When used with s conversions, the precision specifies the maximum number of characters that will be

Flag	Meaning
–	Left justify the value in its field. The default is to right justify.
0	When right justifying numeric values, the default is to use spaces to fill unused columns to the left of the value. This flag causes zeros to be used instead, and it applies to the d, i, u, o, x, X, e, E, f, g, and G codes. With the d, i, u, o, x, and X codes, the zero flag is ignored if a precision is given. The zero flag has no effect if the minus flag is also given.
+	When used with a code that formats a signed value, this forces a plus sign to appear when the value is not negative. If the value is negative, a minus sign is shown as usual. By default, plus signs are not shown.
space	Useful only for codes that convert signed values, this flag causes a space to be added to the beginning of the result when the value is not negative. Note that this flag and + are mutually exclusive; if both are given the space flag is ignored.
#	Selects an alternate form of conversion for some codes. These are described in Table 15.8.

Table 15.6   *printf* format flags

Modifier	Used With ...	Means the Argument Is ...
h	d, i, u, o, x, X	a (possibly unsigned) short integer
h	n	a pointer to a short integer
l	d, i, u, o, x, X	a (possibly unsigned) long integer
l	n	a pointer to a long integer
L	e, E, f, g, G	a long double

Table 15.7   *printf* format code modifiers

converted. The precision is given as a period followed by an optional decimal integer. If the integer is missing, a precision of zero is used.

If an asterisk is given in place of a decimal integer for the field width and/or precision, then the next argument to printf (which must be an integer) supplies the width and/or precision. Thus, either of these values may be computed rather than specified in advance.

When character or short integer values are given as arguments to printf, they are converted to integers before being passed. Sometimes the conversion can affect the output that is produced. Also, when passing a long integer as an argument in an environment where long integers occupy more memory than ordinary integers, printf must be told that the argument is a long. The modifiers, shown in Table 15.7, solve these problems by indicating the exact size of integer and floating-point arguments.

On implementations in which ints and short ints are the same length, the h modifier has no effect. Otherwise, the value to be converted will have been promoted to an (unsigned) integer when it was passed as an argument: this modifier causes it to be truncated back to its short form before the conversion takes place. With decimal conversions, the truncation is generally not

Used With ...	The # Flag ...
o	guarantees that the value produced begins with a zero.
x, X	prefixes a nonzero value with 0x (0X for the %X code).
e, E, f	ensures the result always contains a decimal point, even if no digits follow it.
g, G	does the same as for the e, E, and f codes above; in addition, trailing zeros are not removed from the fraction.

Table 15.8   Alternate forms of *printf* conversions

Format Code	String Converted		
	A	ABC	ABCDEFGH
%s	A	ABC	ABCDEFGH
%5s	¤¤¤¤A	¤¤ABC	ABCDEFGH
%.5s	A	ABC	ABCDE
%5.5s	¤¤¤¤A	¤¤ABC	ABCDE
%-5s	A¤¤¤¤	ABC¤¤	ABCDEFGH

Figure 15.1 Formatting strings with *printf*

needed. But with some octal or hexadecimal conversions, the h modifier will ensure that the proper number of digits is printed.

On implementations in which ints and long ints are the same length, the l modifier has no effect. On all other implementations, the l modifier is required, because long integers on such machines are passed in two parts on the runtime stack. If the modifier is not given, only the first part is retrieved for the conversion. Not only will this conversion produce incorrect results, but the second part of the value is then interpreted as a separate argument, disrupting the correspondence between the subsequent arguments and their format codes.

When used with several of the *printf* format codes, the # flag selects an alternate form of conversion. The details of these forms are listed in Table 15.8.

Because some implementations require the l modifier when printing long integer values and others do not, it is better to use it whenever printing longs. Then you can port the program to either type of implementation with fewer modifications.

Format Code	Number Converted			
	1	-12	12345	123456789
%d	1	-12	12345	123456789
%6d	¤¤¤¤¤1	¤¤¤-12	¤12345	123456789
%.4d	0001	-0012	12345	123456789
%6.4d	¤¤0001	¤-0012	¤12345	123456789
%-4d	1¤¤¤	-12¤	12345	123456789
%04d	0001	-012	12345	123456789
%+d	+1	-12	+12345	+123456789

Figure 15.2 Formatting integers with *printf*

Format Code	Number Converted			
	1	.01	.00012345	12345.6789
%f	1.000000	0.010000	0.000123	12345.678900
%10.2f	¤¤¤¤¤¤1.00	¤¤¤¤¤¤0.01	¤¤¤¤¤¤0.00	¤¤12345.68
%e	1.000000e+00	1.000000e-02	1.234500e-04	1.234568e+04
%.4e	1.0000e+00	1.0000e-02	1.2345e-04	1.2346e+04
%g	1	0.01	0.00012345	12345.7

Figure 15.3   Formatting floating-point values with *printf*

The abundance of codes, modifiers, qualifiers, alternate forms, and optional fields that can be used with printf can be overwhelming, but they provide great flexibility in formatting your output. Be patient, it takes time to learn them all! Here are some examples to get you started.

Figure 15.1 shows some of the possible variations in formatting of strings. Only the characters shown are printed. To avoid ambiguity, the symbol ¤ is used to denote a blank space. Figure 15.2 shows the results of formatting several integer values with various integer formats. Figure 15.3 shows some of the ways that floating-point values can be formatted. Finally, Figure 15.4 shows the results of formatting a much larger floating-point number with the same format codes as the previous figure. The apparent error in the first two outputs occurs because more significant digits are being printed than can be stored in memory.

15.11 Binary I/O

The most efficient way of writing data to a file is to write it in binary. Binary output avoids the overhead and loss of precision involved with converting numeric values to character strings. But binary data is not readable by human

Format Code	Number Converted 6.023e23
%f	602299999999999975882752.000000
%10.2f	602299999999999975882752.00
%e	6.023000e+23
%.4e	6.0230e+23
%g	6.023e+23

Figure 15.4   Formatting large floating-point values with *printf*

beings, so this technique is useful only for data that will be subsequently read by another program.

The **fread** function is used to read binary data; **fwrite** is used to write it. Their prototypes look like this:

```
size_t fread( void *buffer, size_t size, size_t count, FILE *stream );
size_t fwrite( void *buffer, size_t size, size_t count, FILE *stream );
```

buffer is a pointer to the area that holds the data. size is the number of bytes in each element of the buffer, count is the number of elements to be read or written, and of course stream is the stream with which to read or write the data.

The buffer is interpreted as an array of one or more values. The count argument specifies how many values are in the array, so to read or write a scalar, use a count of one. The functions return the number of *elements* (not bytes) actually read or written. This number may be smaller than the requested number of elements if end of file was reached on input or an error occurred on output.

Let's look at a code fragment that uses these functions.

```
struct  VALUE   {
        long    a;
        float   b;
        char    c[SIZE];
} values[ARRAY_SIZE];
...
n_values = fread( values, sizeof( struct VALUE ),
    ARRAY_SIZE, input_stream );
(process the data in the array)
fwrite( values, sizeof( struct VALUE ),
    n_values, output_stream );
```

This program reads binary data from an input file, performs some type of processing on it, and writes the result to an output file. As mentioned, this type of I/O is efficient because the bits in each value are written (or read) to (or from) the stream without any conversions. For example, suppose one of the long integer values in the array had the value 4,023,817. The bits that represent this value are 0x003d6609—these bits would be written to the stream. Binary information is not readable by human beings because the bits do not correspond to any reasonable characters. If interpreted as characters, this value is \0=f\t, which certainly does not convey the value of the number very well to us.

15.12 Flushing and Seeking Functions

There are a few additional functions that are useful when dealing with streams. The first is **fflush**, which forces the buffer for an output stream to be physically written even if it is not yet full. Its prototype is:

```
int fflush( FILE *stream );
```

This function should be called whenever it is important for buffered output to be physically written immediately. For example, calling fflush guarantees that debugging information is physically printed instead of held in the buffer until a later time.

Normally, data is written to a file *sequentially*, which means that data written later appears in the file after any data written earlier. C also supports *random access* I/O in which different locations of the file can be accessed in any order. Random access is accomplished by *seeking* to the desired position in the file before reading or writing. There are two functions that perform this operation, and their prototypes are:

```
long ftell( FILE *stream );
int fseek( FILE *stream, long offset, int from );
```

The ftell function returns the current position in the stream, that is, the offset from the beginning of the file at which the next read or write would begin. This function lets you save the current position in a file so that you can return to it later. On binary streams, the value will be the number of bytes the current position is from the beginning of the file.

On text streams, the value represents a position, but it may not accurately represent the number of characters from the beginning of the file because of the end-of-line character translations performed on text streams by some systems. However, the value returned by ftell may always be used as an offset from the beginning of the file with fseek.

fseek allows you to seek on a stream. This operation changes the position at which the next read or write will occur. The first argument is the stream to change. The second and third arguments identify the desired location in the file. Table 15.9 describes three ways that the second and third arguments can be used.

It is an error to attempt to seek before the beginning of a file. Seeking beyond the end of the file and writing extends the file. Seeking beyond the end and reading causes an end-of-file indication to be returned. On binary streams, seeks from SEEK_END may not be supported and should therefore be

If from is . . .	Then you will seek to . . .
SEEK_SET	offset bytes from the beginning of the stream; offset must be non-negative.
SEEK_CUR	offset bytes from the current location in the stream; offset may be positive or negative.
SEEK_END	offset bytes from the end of the file; offset may be positive or negative, positive values seek beyond the end of the file.

Table 15.9   fseek arguments

avoided. On text streams, the offset must be zero if from is either SEEK_CUR or SEEK_END. The offset must be a value previously returned from a call to ftell on the same stream if from is SEEK_SET.

Part of the reason for these restrictions is the end-of-line character mapping performed on text streams. Because of the mapping, the number of bytes in the text file may be different than the number of bytes the program wrote. Thus, a portable program cannot seek to a position in a text stream using the result of a computation based on the number of characters written.

There are three side effects of changing a stream's position with fseek. First, the end-of-file indicator is cleared. Second, if a character had been returned to the stream with ungetc prior to an fseek, the ungotten character is forgotten because after the seek it is no longer the next character. Finally, seeking lets you switch from reading to writing and back on streams opened for update.

Program 15.6 uses fseek to access a file of student information. The record number argument is a size_t because it doesn't make sense for it to be negative. The desired location in the file is computed by multiplying the record number and record size. This calculation works only when all records in the file are the same length. Finally, the result of fread is returned so the caller can determine whether the operation was successful.

There are three additional functions that perform these same tasks in more limited ways. Their prototypes follow.

```
void rewind( FILE *stream );
int fgetpos( FILE *stream, fpos_t *position );
int fsetpos( FILE *stream, fpos_t const *position );
```

The rewind function sets the read/write pointer back to the beginning on the indicated stream. It also clears the error indicator for the stream. The fgetpos and fsetpos functions are alternatives to ftell and fseek, respectively.

```
/*
** Reads a specific record from a file.  The arguments are the stream
** from which to read, the desired record number, and a pointer to
** the buffer into which the data should be placed.
*/
#include <stdio.h>
#include "student_info.h"

int
read_random_record( FILE *f, size_t rec_number, StudentInfo *buffer )
{
        fseek( f, (long)rec_number * sizeof( StudentInfo ),
            SEEK_SET );
        return fread( buffer, sizeof( StudentInfo ), 1, f );
}
```

Program 15.6   Random file access   rd_rand.c

The primary difference is that this pair of functions takes a pointer to a
fpos_t as an argument. fgetpos stores the current file position in this location and fsetpos sets the file position to the value.

The way a file position is represented by an fpos_t is not defined by the
standard. It may be a byte offset in the file, or it may not. Therefore, the only
safe way to use an fpos_t obtained from fgetpos is as an argument to a
subsequent fsetpos.

15.13 Changing the Buffering

The buffering performed on streams is sometimes inappropriate, so the following two functions are provided to modify it. Both functions may be called
only after the specified stream has been opened but before any other operations
have been performed on it.

```
void setbuf( FILE *stream, char *buf );
int setvbuf( FILE *stream, char *buf, int mode, size_t size );
```

setbuf installs an alternate array to be used for buffering the stream.
The array must be **BUFSIZ** (which is defined in stdio.h) characters long.
Assigning your own buffer to a stream prevents the I/O library from dynami-
cally allocating a buffer for it. If called with a NULL argument, setbuf turns

off all buffering for the stream. Characters are written to and read from the file exactly as directed by the program.[47]

It is dangerous to use an automatic array for a stream buffer. If execution leaves the block in which the array was declared before the stream is closed, the stream will continue to use the memory even after it has been allocated to other functions for other purposes.

The setvbuf function is more general. The mode argument indicates what type of buffering is desired. **_IOFBF** indicates a fully buffered stream, **_IONBF** indicates an unbuffered stream, and **_IOLBF** indicates a line buffered stream. An output stream that is line buffered is flushed each time a newline is written to the buffer.

The buf and size arguments are used to specify the buffer to use; if buf is NULL, then zero must be given for size. Generally, it is best to use an array of BUFSIZ characters for a buffer. Although using a very large buffer may increase the efficiency of the program slightly, it may also decrease the efficiency. For example, most operating systems buffer input/output operations to disk internally. Specifying a buffer that is not a multiple of the operating system's buffer size may result in extra disk operations to read or write a fraction of a block. If a larger buffer is needed, you should use a multiple of BUFSIZ. On MS-DOS machines, a buffer that matches the cluster size used for your disk may provide some improvement.

15.14 Stream Error Functions

The following functions are used to determine the state of a stream.

```
int feof( FILE *stream );
int ferror( FILE *stream );
void clearerr( FILE *stream );
```

feof returns true if the stream is currently at end of file. This condition can be cleared by performing fseek, rewind, or fsetpos on the stream. ferror reports on the error state of the stream and returns true if any read/write errors have occurred. Finally, clearerr resets the error indication for the given stream.

---

[47] In hosted runtime environments, the operating system may perform its own buffering, independent of the stream. Thus, merely calling setbuf will not allow a program to read characters from a keyboard as they are typed, because the operating system usually buffers these characters in order to implement backspace editing.

15.15 Temporary Files

Occasionally, it is convenient to use a file to hold data temporarily. When the program is finished, the file is deleted because the data it contains is no longer useful. The **tmpfile** function serves for this purpose.

```
FILE *tmpfile( void );
```

This function creates a file that is removed automatically when the file is closed or the program terminates. The file is opened with mode wb+, making it suitable for use with binary or text data.

tmpfile is not appropriate for a temporary file that must be opened with a different mode or created by one program and read by another. In these circumstances, fopen must be used, and the resulting file must be explicitly deleted using remove (see below) when it is no longer needed.

Temporary file names can be constructed with the **tmpnam** function, which has this prototype:

```
char *tmpnam( char *name );
```

If called with a NULL argument, the function returns a pointer to a static array containing the constructed file name. Otherwise, the argument is assumed to point to an array that is at least **L_tmpnam** characters long. In this case, the name is constructed in the array and the argument is returned.

Either way, the name that is constructed is guaranteed not to be the name of an existing file.[48] tmpnam generates a new unique name each time it is called up to **TMP_MAX** times.

15.16 File Manipulation Functions

There are two functions that manipulate files without performing any input/output. Their prototypes are shown below. Both functions return zero if they succeed and a nonzero value if they fail.

---

[48] Beware: The scheme used to guarantee uniqueness may fail on multiprogramming systems or systems that share a network file server. The cause of the problem is the delay between when the name is constructed and when a file of that name is created. If several programs happen to construct the same name and test for the existence of a file before any have actually created it, each program will think that it has a unique name. Creating the file as soon as the temporary name has been constructed reduces (but does not eliminate) the potential conflict.

```
int remove( char const *filename );
int rename( char const *oldname, char const *newname );
```

remove deletes the specified file. If the file is open when remove is called, the behavior is implementation dependent.

The rename function is used to change the name of a file from *oldname* to *newname*. If a file already exists with the new name, the behavior is implementation dependent. If this function fails, the file will still be accessible with its original name.

15.17 Summary

The Standard dictates the interface and operation of the functions in the standard library, which enhances program portability. An implementation may provide additional functions in its library, but may not change the required functions.

perror provides a simple method of reporting errors to the user. When a fatal error is detected, you can use exit to terminate the program.

The stdio.h header contains declarations necessary for using the I/O library functions. All I/O is a matter of moving bytes into or out of the program. The interface provided by the library for I/O is called a stream. By default, stream I/O is buffered. Binary streams are used primarily for binary data. Bytes are written to or read from a binary stream without modification. Text streams, on the other hand, are used for characters. The longest line allowed in a text stream is implementation-defined, but must be at least 254 characters long. By definition, a line is terminated by a newline character. If the host operating system uses a different convention for terminating lines, the I/O functions must translate between that form and the internal form.

A FILE is a data structure that manages the buffer and stores the I/O state for a stream. The runtime environment provides three streams to each program—the standard input, standard output, and standard error. It is common for the standard input to default to a keyboard and the other two streams to default to a display screen. A separate stream is provided for error messages so that they will be displayed in the default location even if the standard output has been redirected to another location. FOPEN_MAX is the implementation-defined limit of the number of FILEs you may have open simultaneously. The value must be at least eight. FILENAME_MAX is either the maximum length or, if there isn't a maximum length, the recommended size to use for character arrays in which filenames are stored.

To perform stream I/O on a file, it is first opened with fopen, which returns a pointer to the FILE structure assigned to the stream. This pointer must be saved in a FILE * variable. The file may then be read from and/or written to. Afterwards, the file is closed. Many of the I/O functions belong to families whose members perform essentially the same work with minor differences as to where input is obtained or output is written. The usual variants include a function that takes a stream argument, a function that works only with one of the standard streams, and a function that works with a buffer in memory rather than a stream.

Streams are opened with fopen. Its arguments are the name of the file to open and the desired mode of the stream. The mode specifies reading, writing, or appending, and also specifies whether the stream will be text or binary. freopen performs the same task, except that you can specify the stream to use. This function is most often used to reopen one of the standard streams. Always check the value returned from fopen or freopen for errors. After you have finished with a stream, you should close it with fclose.

Character-by-character I/O is performed by the *getchar* and *putchar* families of functions. The input functions fgetc and getc both take a stream argument, and getchar reads only from the standard input. The first is implemented as a function and the other two are implemented as macros. All three return a single character as an integer value. Except for performing output instead of input, the fputc, putc, and putchar functions share the properties of the corresponding input functions. ungetc is used to push an unwanted character back to a stream. The pushed character will be the first one returned by the next input operation. Changing the stream's position (seeking) causes ungotten characters to be forgotten.

Line I/O can be either formatted or unformatted. The *gets* and *puts* families perform unformatted line I/O. fgets and gets both read a line of input into a specified buffer. The former takes a stream argument and the latter works with the standard input. fgets is safer. It takes the buffer size as an argument and therefore can guarantee that a long input line will not overflow the buffer. Data is not lost—the next part of a long input line will be read by the next call to fgets. The fputs and puts functions write text to a stream. Their interfaces are analogous to the corresponding input functions. For backward compatability, gets removes the newline from the line it read, and puts writes a newline after the text from the buffer.

The *scanf* and *printf* families perform formatted I/O. There are three input functions. fscanf takes a stream argument, scanf reads from the standard input, and sscanf takes characters from a buffer in memory. The *printf* family also has three functions with similar properties. The *scanf* functions convert characters according to a format string. A list of pointer arguments indicates where the resulting values are stored. The function returns the number of values that were converted, or EOF if end of file was reached before the first conversion. The *printf* functions convert values to character form according to a format string. The values are passed as arguments.

It is more efficient to write binary data, such as integers and floating-point values, with binary I/O than with character I/O. Binary I/O reads and writes the bits in the value directly, without converting the value to characters. The result of binary output, however, is not human-readable. fread and fwrite perform binary I/O. Each takes four arguments: a pointer to a buffer, the size of one element in the buffer, the desired number of elements to read or write, and a stream.

By default, streams are sequential. However, you can perform random I/O by seeking to a different position in the file before reading or writing. The fseek function lets you specify a position in the file as an offset from the beginning of the file, the current file position, or the end of the file. ftell returns the current file position. The fsetpos and fgetpos functions are alternatives to the previous two functions. However, the only legal argument to fsetpos is a value previously returned by fgetpos on the same stream. Finally, the rewind function returns to the beginning of a file.

The buffer used for a stream can be changed by calling setbuf before any I/O has occurred on the stream. Assigning a buffer in this manner prevents one from being dynamically allocated. Passing a NULL pointer as the buffer argument disables buffering altogether. The setvbuf function is more general. With it, you can specify a buffer with a nonstandard size. You may also choose the type of buffering you desire: fully buffered, line buffered, or unbuffered.

The ferror and clearerr functions relate to the error state of a stream, that is, whether any read/write errors have occured. The first function returns the error state, and the second function resets it. The feof function returns true if the stream is currently at end of file.

The tmpfile function returns a stream that is associated with a temporary file. The file is automatically deleted after the stream is closed. The tmpname function creates a filename suitable for use as a temporary file. The name does not conflict with the names of any existing files. A file can be deleted by passing its name to the remove function. The rename function changes the name of a file. It takes two arguments, the current name of the file and the new name.

15.18 Summary of Cautions

1. Forgetting to follow debugging `printf`'s with a call to `fflush` (page 412).

2. Not checking the value returned by `fopen` (page 417).

3. Changing the file position discards any ungotten characters (page 423).

4. Specifying too small a buffer with `fgets` (page 424).

5. Input from `gets` overflowing the buffer undetected (page 424).

6. Mismatched format codes and argument pointer types with any of the *scanf* functions (page 425).

7. Forgetting to put an ampersand before each nonarray, nonpointer argument to any of the *scanf* functions (page 426).

8. Be sure to specify the proper qualifier in *scanf* format codes to convert doubles, long doubles, and short and long integers (page 427).

9. Output from `sprintf` overflowing the buffer undetected (page 430).

10. Interchanging `printf` and `scanf` format codes (page 432).

11. Mismatched format codes and argument types with any of the *printf* functions (page 432).

12. On implementations in which long integers are longer than integers, not specifying the `l` modifier when printing long integer values (page 435).

13. Be careful when using an automatic array as a stream buffer (page 441).

15.19 Summary of Programming Tips

1. Check for and report errors whenever they may occur (page 410).

2. The ability to manipulate text lines without regard for their external representation improves program portability (page 413).

3. Using *scanf* qualifiers enhances portability (page 427).

4. Portability is enhanced if you use the `l` modifier when printing long integers even if your implementation doesn't require it (page 435).

15.20 Questions

1. What happens if the value returned from `fopen` is not checked for errors?

  2. What will happen if I/O is attempted on a stream that has never been opened?

3. What will happen if a call to `fclose` fails, but the program does not check the returned value for errors?

  4. If a program is executed with its standard input redirected to come from a file, how does the program detect this fact?

5. What happens if `fgets` is called with a buffer size of one? Of two?

6. How long must the buffer be to ensure that the string produced by `sprintf` will not overflow it? Assume that your machine uses 2-byte integers.

```
sprintf( buffer, "%d %c %x", a, b, c );
```

7. How long must the buffer be to ensure that the string produced by `sprintf` will not overflow it?

```
sprintf( buffer, "%s", a );
```

8. Is the last digit printed by the `%f` format code rounded or are the unprinted digits simply truncated?

9. How can you obtain a list of all of the error messages that `perror` can print?

10. Why do `fprintf`, `fscanf`, `fputs`, and `fclose` all take a pointer to a `FILE` rather than the `FILE` structure?

11. What mode would you use to open a file that you wanted to write to, assuming (1) you do not want to lose the former contents of the file, and (2) you want to be able to write anywhere in the file?

12. Why is the `frepoen` function necessary?

13. For most programs, do you think it is worth the effort to think about whether `fgetc( stdin )` or `getchar()` would be better?

14. What does the following statement print on your system?

```
printf( "%d\n", 3.14 );
```

15. Explain how strings will be printed with the `%-6.10s` format code.

  16. When a particular value is printed with the format code `%.3f`, the result is 1.405, but when the same value is printed with the format code `%.2f`, the result is 1.40. Explain this apparent error.

15.21 Programming Exercises

★ 1. Write a program that copies the standard input to the standard output one character at a time.

◻ ★ 2. Change your solution to Exercise 1 so that it reads and writes an entire line at a time. You may assume that each line in the file will contain 80 or fewer characters (not counting the terminating newline).

★★ 3. Change your solution to Exercise 2 to remove the 80 character line length restriction. You should still process the file a line at a time, but lines longer than 80 characters may be processed a piece at a time.

★★★ 4. Change your solution to Exercise 3 to prompt for and read two filenames from the standard input. The first will be the input file, and the second will be the output file. The revised program should open both files and copy from the input file to the output file as before.

★★★ 5. Change your solution to Exercise 4 so that it looks for lines beginning with an integer. These integer values should be summed and the total should be written at the end of the output file. Other than this one change, the revised program should perform as before.

★★ 6. In Chapter 9 you wrote a function called `palindrome` that would determine whether or not a string contained a palindrome. For this problem, you are to write a function that will determine whether or not the value of an integer variable is a palindrome. For example, the value 245 is not a palindrome but 14741 is. The function should have this prototype:

```
int numeric_palindrome( int value );
```

It should return true if the value is a palindrome, otherwise false.

★★★ 7. A certain data file contains the ages of family members. The ages of the members of one family are all on the same line, and are separated by white space. For example, this data

```
45 42 22
36 35 7 3 1
22 20
```

describes three families having three, five, and two members, respectively.
    Write a program that computes the average age of each family represented in a file of this sort. It should print the average age using the `%5.2f` format, followed by a colon and the input data. You may assume that no family contains more than 10 members.

★★★★ 8. Write a program to produce a hex dump of a file. It should take a single argument from the command line, which is the name of the file to dump. If this argument is missing, the program should dump the standard input instead.

Each line of the dump should have the following format.

Columns	Contents
1–6	The current offset in the file, in hexadecimal, with leading zeros.
9–43	The hexadecimal representation of the next 16 bytes in the file. These are printed in four groups of 8 hex digits, with one space between each group.
46	An asterisk.
47–62	The character representation of the same 16 bytes in the file. If a byte is not a printable character or a space, a period is printed instead.
63	An asterisk.

All hexadecimal numbers should use uppercase A–F rather than lowercase letters.

Here are some sample lines illustrating this format.

```
000200   D405C000 82102004 91D02000 9010207F   *...... ... ... .*
000210   82102001 91D02000 0001C000 2F757372   *.. ... ...../usr*
000220   2F6C6962 2F6C642E 736F002F 6465762F   */lib/ld.so./dev/*
```

★★★ 9. The UNIX fgrep program takes a string and a series of filenames as command line arguments. It then looks through the files one by one. For each line that contains the given string, the name of the file, a colon, and the line containing the string are printed.

Write this program. The string argument comes first, and it may not contain any newline characters. The filename arguments come next. If there aren't any filenames given, the program should read the standard input. In this case, the lines printed by the program are not prefixed with a filename or colon. You may assume that the lines of text in the files will be no longer than 510 characters.

★★★★ 10. Write a program to compute checksums for files. The program is invoked as follows:

```
$ sum [ -f ] [ file . . . ]
```

The -f option is optional. I'll describe its meaning later.

Next comes an optional list of file names. If there aren't any names given, the program processes the standard input. Otherwise, the program processes each file in the order in which they are named on the command line. "Processing a file" means to compute and print the checksum for the file.

The algorithm for computing the checksum is simple. Each character in the file is added to a 16-bit, unsigned integer, and the result is the checksum value. Although simple to implement, this algorithm is not a great error detection method. Interchanging two characters in the file would not be detected as an error.

Ordinarily, the checksum is written to the standard output when the end of each file is found. If the -f option is given, the checksum is written to a file instead of the standard output. The name of the file should be `file.cks` where `file` is the input file name. This option is illegal when reading from the standard input because there isn't an input file name.

Below are a few sample runs of the program. They are valid for systems that use ASCII characters. The file `hw` contains the line "Hello World!" followed by a newline. The file `hw2` contains two such lines. None of the input contains any trailing blanks or tabs.

```
$ sum
hi
^D
219
$ sum hw
1095
$ sum -f
-f illegal when reading standard input
$ sum -f hw2
$
```

(File hw2.cks now contains 2190)

★★★★★ 11. Write a program to keep track of an inventory of parts and their value. Each part has a description that may be from 1 to 20 characters in length. When a new part is added to the inventory, it is assigned the next available part number. The first part number is 1. The program should store the quantity on hand and the total value for each part.

The program should take a single argument from the command line, which is the name of the inventory file. If the file does not exist, an empty inventory file is created. The program then prompts for transactions and processes them one by one.

The following transactions are allowed.

```
new description,quantity,cost-each
```

The new transaction enters a new part into the system. *description* is the description of the part, which may not be longer than 20 characters. *quantity* is the number of parts initially placed into inventory; it may not be negative. *cost-each* is the cost of each part. It is not an error for a new part to have the same description as an existing part. The program must compute and save the total value of these parts. The next available part number is assigned to each new part. Part numbers start at 1 and increase sequentially. The numbers of deleted parts are reused when new parts are entered.

```
buy part-number,quantity,cost-each
```

The buy transaction adds additional units to an existing part in inventory. part-number is the number of the part, quantity is the number of parts obtained (which may not be negative), and cost-each is the cost of each of the parts. The program should add the quantity and the total value of the new parts to the existing inventory.

```
sell part-number,quantity,price-each
```

The sell transaction removes units from an existing part in inventory. part-number is the number of the part, quantity is the number of parts sold (which may not be negative or larger than the quantity on hand), and price-each is the price obtained for each of the parts sold. The program should subtract this quantity from the inventory and reduce the total value for this part by the number sold. It should then compute the profit for the sale as the difference between the price obtained and the inventory value for the parts sold.

```
delete part-number
```

This transaction deletes the specified part from the inventory file.

```
print part-number
```

This transaction prints information for the specified part including the description, quantity on hand, and total value of those parts.

```
print all
```

This transaction prints information for all parts in inventory in a tabular form.

```
total
```

This transaction computes and prints the total value of all parts in inventory.

```
end
```

This transaction terminates execution of the program.

Computing the true value of an inventory when parts are obtained at different costs is complex and depends on whether the cheapest or most expensive parts are used first. The method used by this program is simple: Only the total value of each type of part is kept, and all units of one particular part are considered equal. For example, suppose 10 paper clips are initially purchased for $1.00 each. The total value of this inventory is $10.00. Later, 10 more paper clips are purchased for $1.25 each, bringing the total value of the inventory to $22.50. At this point, each paper clip is valued at $1.125. No record is kept of the individual batches even though they were purchased at different prices. When paper clips are sold, the profit is computed based on their current value as calculated above.

Here are some hints on designing the program. First, use the part number to determine where in the inventory file a part is written. The first part number is 1, so the location in the inventory file where part number 0 would go can be used to store other information. Second, you can detect deleted parts by setting their description to the empty string.

16

Standard Library

The Standard Library is a toolkit that greatly expands the power of the C programmer. Before you can use this power, however, you must become familiar with the library functions. Neglecting the library is like only learning how to use the gas pedal, steering wheel, and brake in your car but not bothering to learn about the cruise control, radio, and air conditioning. You may be able to get where you want to go, but it will be harder and won't be as much fun.

This chapter describes the library functions that have not been covered in previous chapters. The section titles include the file name that you need to #include to obtain the function prototypes.

16.1 Integer Functions

This group of functions return integer values. The functions fall into three families: arithmetic, random numbers, and string conversion.

16.1.1 Arithmetic <stdlib.h>

The library includes four integer arithmetic functions.

```
int abs( int value );
long int labs( long int value );
div_t div( int numerator, int denominator );
ldiv_t ldiv( long int numer, long int denom );
```

The abs function returns the absolute value of its argument. If the result cannot be represented as an integer, the behavior is undefined. labs does the same work for long integer values.

The `div` function divides the first argument (the numerator) by the second argument (the denominator) and produces a quotient and a remainder that are returned in a `div_t` structure. This structure contains the fields

```
int      quot;
int      rem;
```

though not necessarily in this order. If the division is not even, the quotient will be the integer of smaller magnitude that is nearest to the algebraic quotient. Note that the results of division with the / operator are not as precisely defined. When either of the operands of / are negative and the result is not exact, it is implementation defined whether the quotient is the largest integer less than or equal to the algebraic quotient or the smallest integer greater than or equal to the algebraic quotient. `ldiv` does the same work for long integer values and returns an `ldiv_t` structure.

16.1.2 Random Numbers <stdlib.h>

Random numbers are useful in programs that should not produce the same results every time they are executed, such as games and simulations. Together, the following two functions produce *pseudo-random* numbers, so called because they are computed and therefore repeatable, and thus not truly random.

```
int rand( void );
void srand( unsigned int seed );
```

`rand` returns a pseudo-random number in the range zero to RAND_MAX (which must be at least 32,767). When called repeatedly, the function returns other numbers in this range. To obtain numbers from a smaller range, first take the random number modulo the size of the desired range, then scale it by adding or subtracting an offset as needed.

To prevent the random number sequence from being the same every time the program is run, the `srand` function may be called. It initializes the random number generator with the value passed as its argument. A common technique is to use the time of day to seed the random number generator, as in this example:

```
srand( (unsigned int)time( 0 ) );
```

The `time` function is described later in this chapter.

The function in Program 16.1 uses integers to represent playing cards and uses random numbers to "shuffle" the specified number of cards in the "deck."

```
/*
** Use random numbers to shuffle the "cards" in the deck.  The second
** argument indicates the number of cards.  The first time this
** function is called, srand is called to initialize the random
** number generator.
*/
#include <stdlib.h>
#include <time.h>
#define TRUE    1
#define FALSE   0

void shuffle( int *deck, int n_cards )
{
        int     i;
        static  int     first_time = TRUE;

        /*
        ** Seed the random number generator with the current time
        ** of day if we haven't done so yet.
        */
        if( first_time ){
                first_time = FALSE;
                srand( (unsigned int)time( NULL ) );
        }

        /*
        ** "Shuffle" by interchanging random pairs of cards.
        */
        for( i = n_cards - 1; i > 0; i -= 1 ){
                int     where;
                int     temp;

                where = rand() % i;
                temp = deck[ where ];
                deck[ where ] = deck[ i ];
                deck[ i ] = temp;
        }
}
```

Program 16.1   Shuffling playing cards with random numbers   shuffle.c

16.1.3 String Conversion <stdlib.h>

The string conversion functions convert character strings to numeric values.
The simplest ones, atoi and atol, perform base 10 conversions. strtol

and `strtoul` allow you to specify the base for the conversion, and they also give you access to the remaining part of the string.

```
int atoi( char const *string );
long int atol( char const *string );
long int strtol( char const *string, char **unused, int base );
unsigned long int strtoul( char const *string, char **unused,
    int base );
```

If the first argument to any of these functions contains leading white space characters, they are skipped. The functions then convert legal characters to the indicated type of value. If there are any trailing illegal characters, they are ignored.

 `atoi` and `atol` convert characters to integer and long integer values, respectively. `strtol` converts the argument string to a `long` in the same manner as `atol`. However, `strtol` saves a pointer to the first character in the string after the converted value. If the second argument to the function is not NULL, the saved pointer is stored in the location pointed to by the second argument. The pointer allows the remainder of the string to be processed without having to guess where the conversion stopped. `strtoul` behaves in the same manner but produces an unsigned long instead.

 The third argument to both of these functions is the base with which the conversion is performed. If the base is 0, any of the forms used for writing integer literals in a program are accepted, including the forms that specify the base of the number, such as `0x2af4` and `0377`. Otherwise, the base may be a value in the range 2 through 36—the conversion is then performed with the given base. For bases 11 through 36, the characters A through Z are interpreted as digits with values 10 through 35, respectively. Lowercase characters a through z are interpreted the same as uppercase characters in this context. Thus,

```
x = strtol( "   590bear", next, 12 );
```

would return the value 9947 and store a pointer to the letter e in the variable that `next` points to. The conversion stops with b because e is not a valid digit for a base 12 number.

 If the string argument to any of these functions does not contain a legal numeric value, then 0 is returned. If the converted value cannot be represented, the value ERANGE is stored in `errno`, and one of the values in Table 16.1 is returned.

Function	Returns
strtol	LONG_MIN if the value is too large and negative, or LONG_MAX if the value is too large and positive.
strtoul	ULONG_MAX if the value is too large.

Table 16.1   Error values returned by strtol and strtoul

16.2 Floating-Point Functions

The header file math.h contains declarations for the remaining mathematical functions in the library. The return values from these functions and most of their arguments are double.

A common source of error is to omit the header file when using these functions, like this:

```
double x;
x = sqrt( 5.5 );
```

The compiler, never having seen a prototype for sqrt, mistakenly assumes that it returns an integer and erroneously converts the value to double. The resulting value is meaningless.

A *domain error* occurs if the argument to a function is not within the domain defined for that function. For example,

```
sqrt( -5.0 );
```

is a domain error because square root is undefined for negative numbers. When a domain error occurs, the function returns an error value defined by the implementation, and the value EDOM is stored in errno. A *range error* occurs if the *result* of a function is too large or too small to be represented in a double. For example,

```
exp( DBL_MAX )
```

will produce a range error because its result is too large. In this case, the function will return HUGE_VAL, a double value that is defined in math.h. If the result of a function is too small to be represented in a double, then the function will return zero instead. This case is also a range error, but it is implementation dependent whether errno is set to ERANGE in this case.

16.2.1 Trigonometry <math.h>

The usual trigonometry functions are provided.

```
double sin( double angle );
double cos( double angle );
double tan( double angle );
double asin( double value );
double acos( double value );
double atan( double value );
double atan2( double x, double y );
```

The argument to sin, cos, and tan is an angle in radians; the functions return the sine, cosine, and tangent of the angle, respectively.

The asin, acos, and atan functions return the arc sine, arc cosine, and arc tangent of their argument, respectively. A domain error will occur if the argument to asin or acos is not in the range -1 to 1. asin and atan return a value in the range $-\pi/2$ to $\pi/2$ radians, and acos returns a value in the range 0 to π radians.

The atan2 function returns the arc tangent of the expression y/x but uses the signs of both arguments to determine which quadrant the result lies within. It returns a result in the range $-\pi$ to π radians.

16.2.2 Hyperbolic <math.h>

```
double sinh( double angle );
double cosh( double angle );
double tanh( double angle );
```

These functions return the hyperbolic sine, hyperbolic cosine, and hyperbolic tangent of their argument, respectively. The argument to each is an angle in radians.

16.2.3 Logarithm and Exponent <math.h>

There are three functions that deal directly with logarithms and exponents.

```
double exp( double x );
double log( double x );
double log10( double x );
```

The exp function returns the value e raised to the power given by the argument, or e^x.

The log function returns the base e logarithm of its argument, also known as the natural logarithm. The log10 function returns the base 10 logarithm of its argument. Note that the log of a number x to an arbitrary base b may be computed like this:

$$\log_b x = \frac{\log_e x}{\log_e b}$$

A domain error occurs for both log functions if the argument is negative.

16.2.4 Floating-Point Representation <math.h>

These three functions provide a way to store floating-point values in an implementation-independent format.

```
double frexp( double value, int *exponent );
double ldexp( double fraction, int exponent );
double modf( double value, double *ipart );
```

The frexp function computes an exponent and a fraction such that $fraction \times 2^{exponent} = value$, where $0.5 \leq fraction < 1$ and *exponent* is an integer. The *exponent* is stored in the location pointed to by the second argument, and the function returns the *fraction*. The related function ldexp returns the value $fraction \times 2^{exponent}$, which is the original value. These functions are very useful when you must pass floating-point numbers among machines with incompatible floating-point formats.

The modf function breaks a floating-point value into integer and fractional parts, each having the same sign as the original value. The integer part is stored as a double in the location pointed to by the second argument, and the fractional part is returned as the function value.

16.2.5 Power <math.h>

There are two functions in this family.

```
double pow( double x, double y );
double sqrt( double x );
```

The pow function returns the value x^y. Because logarithms may be used in computing this value, a domain error occurs if x is negative and y is not an integral value.

The sqrt function returns the square root of its argument. A domain error occurs if the argument is negative.

16.2.6 Floor, Ceiling, Absolute Value, and Remainder <math.h>

The prototypes for these functions are shown below.

```
double floor( double x );
double ceil( double x );
double fabs( double x );
double fmod( double x, double y );
```

The floor function returns the largest integral value that is not greater than its argument. This value is returned as a double due to the greatly increased range of doubles over integers. The ceil function returns the smallest integral value that is not less than its argument.

fabs returns the absolute value of its argument. The fmod function returns the remainder that results when x is divided by y, and the quotient is restricted to an integral value.

16.2.7 String Conversion <stdlib.h>

These functions are similar to the integer string conversion functions except that they return floating-point values.

```
double atof( char const *string );
double strtod( char const *string, char **unused );
```

If the argument to either of these functions contains leading white space characters, they are skipped. The functions then convert legal characters to a double, ignoring any trailing illegal characters. Both functions accept all of the forms used for writing floating-point literals in a program.

strtod converts the argument string to a double in the same manner as atof. However, strtod saves a pointer to the first character in the string after the converted value. If the second argument to the function is not NULL, the saved pointer is stored in the location pointed to by the second argument. The pointer allows the remainder of the string to be processed without having to guess where the conversion stopped.

If the string argument to either of these functions does not contain a legal numeric value, then zero is returned. If the converted value is too large or small to be represented, the value ERANGE is stored in errno. HUGE_VAL is returned if the value is too large (either positive or negative), and zero is returned if it is too small.

16.3 Date and Time Functions

The library offers a large collection of functions that simplify dealing with dates and times. Their prototypes are found in time.h.

16.3.1 Processor Time <time.h>

The clock function returns the amount of processor time used by the program since it began executing.

```
clock_t clock( void );
```

Note that this value may be an approximation. If a more precise value is required, call clock at the very beginning of your main function and subtract the value obtained there from any future value returned by clock. If the implementation cannot provide the processor time, or if the time is too large to be represented in a clock_t variable, the value -1 is returned.

clock returns a number that is implementation defined; usually it is the number of times the processor's clock has ticked. To convert the value to seconds, divide it by the constant CLOCKS_PER_SEC.

On some implementations, this function may only return an approximation of the processor time used. If the host operating system is incapable of tracking processor time, it may return the amount of real time that has elapsed instead. This behavior may also occur with simple operating systems that cannot run more than one program at a time. One of the chapter exercises explores how to find out which way your system behaves.

16.3.2 Time of Day <time.h>

The time function returns the current date and time of day.

```
time_t time( time_t *returned_value );
```

If the argument is a non-NULL pointer, the time value is also stored through this pointer. If the implementation cannot provide the current date and time or if the time is too large to be represented in a time_t variable, the value -1 is returned.

The manner in which the time is encoded is not specified by the Standard, so you should not use literal constants because they may have different meanings on different implementations. A common representation is to return the number of seconds that have elapsed since an arbitrarily chosen epoch. On MS-DOS and UNIX systems, the epoch is 00:00:00 January 1, 1970.[49]

It is tempting to call time twice and subtract the values obtained to determine elapsed time, but this technique is dangerous because the Standard does not require that the resulting value represent seconds. difftime (described in the next section) should be used for this purpose.

Date and Time Conversions <time.h>

The following functions manipulate time_t values.

```
char *ctime( time_t const *time_value );
double difftime( time_t time1, time_t time2 );
```

ctime takes a pointer to a time value and returns a pointer to a string of the form

```
Sun Jul  4 04:02:48 1976\n\0
```

The spacing in this string is fixed. The day of the month always takes two positions even if the first is a space, and two digits always appear for each of the time values. The Standard doesn't mention the storage class of the memory containing the string, and many implementations use a static array for this purpose. Thus, the string will be overwritten by the next call to ctime, so you should make a copy of it if you need to save it. Note that ctime may

---

[49] On many implementations, time_t is defined as a signed, 32-bit quantity. The year 2038 should be interesting: in that year the number of seconds since 1970 will overflow a time_t variable.

actually be implemented as

```
asctime( localtime( time_value ) );
```

The `difftime` function computes the difference `time1 - time2` and converts the result to seconds; note that it returns a `double`.

The next two functions convert a `time_t` value into a `struct tm`, which allows easier access to the components of the date and time.

```
struct tm *gmtime( time_t const *time_value );
struct tm *localtime( time_t const *time_value );
```

The `gmtime` function converts the time value into Coordinated Universal Time (UTC). UTC was formerly called Greenwich Mean Time, hence the name `gmtime`. As the name implies, `localtime` converts a time value into local time. The Standard includes both of these functions but does not describe how the relationship between UTC and local time is to be implemented.

A `struct tm` contains the fields listed in Table 16.2, though not necessarily in the order in which they are listed.

The most common error made when using these values is to interpret the month incorrectly. These values are the number of months since January, so 0 represents January and 11 represents December. Although not intuitive at first, this numbering turns out to be a useful encoding for the months because it lets you use the values as subscripts to an array containing the month names.

Type & name	Range	Meaning
int tm_sec;	0 – 61	Seconds after the minute[†]
int tm_min;	0 – 59	Minutes after the hour
int tm_hour;	0 – 23	Hours after midnight
int tm_mday;	0 – 31	Day of the month
int tm_mon;	0 – 11	Months after January
int tm_year;	0 – ??	Years after 1900
int tm_wday;	0 – 6	Days after Sunday
int tm_yday;	0 – 365	Days after January 1
int tm_isdst;		Daylight Savings Time flag

[†]One must admire the thoroughness of the ANSI Standards committee that formulated the C++ standard for making allowance for the "leap seconds" that are occasionally added to the last minute of the year to adjust our time standards to the Earth's slowing rotation.

Table 16.2   Fields in a `struct tm`

The next most common error is to forget that the `tm_year` value is only the years since 1900. To compute the actual year, 1900 must be added to the value.

After you have a `struct tm`, you may either use its values directly, or you may pass it to either of these functions.

```
char *asctime( struct tm const *tm_ptr );
size_t strftime( char *string, size_t maxsize, char const *format,
    struct tm const *tm_ptr );
```

The `asctime` function converts the time represented in the argument to a string of the following form:

```
Sun Jul  4 04:02:48 1976\n\0
```

This form is the same one used by the `ctime` function, which in fact may call `asctime` to perform its work.

The `strftime` function converts a `struct tm` into a string according to a format string. This function provides tremendous flexibility in formatting dates. If the string resulting from the conversion is less than the `maxsize` argument, then the string is copied into the array that the first argument points to and `strftime` returns the length of the string. Otherwise 0 is returned and the array contents are undefined.

The format string contains ordinary characters and format codes. Ordinary characters are copied where they appear. Format codes are replaced by a date or time value. Format codes consist of a `%` character followed by a character that indicates value desired. Table 16.3 lists the format codes that are implemented. A `%` followed by any other character is undefined, which leaves individual implementations free to define additional format codes. You should avoid using them unless you are willing to sacrifice portability. The locale-specific values are determined by the current locale, as discussed later in this chapter. The `%U` and `%W` codes are identical except that the former counts the first Sunday of the year as the beginning of the first week and the latter counts the first Monday of the year as the beginning of the first week. If the time zone cannot be determined, the `%Z` code is replaced by an empty string.

Finally, the `mktime` function is used to convert a `struct tm` to a `time_t` value.

```
time_t mktime( struct tm *tm_ptr );
```

The values of `tm_wday` and `tm_yday` in the `struct tm` are ignored, and the

Code	Is Replaced By
%%	a %
%a	the day of week, using the locale's abbreviated weekday names
%A	the day of week, using the locale's full weekday names
%b	the month, using the locale's abbreviated month names
%B	the month, using the locale's full month names
%c	the date and time, using %x %X
%d	the day of month (01–31)
%H	the hour, in 24-hour clock format (00–23)
%I	the hour, in 12-hour clock format (01–12)
%j	the day number of the year (001–366)
%m	the month number (01–12)
%M	the minute (00–59)
%p	the locale's equivalent of AM or PM, whichever is appropriate
%S	the seconds (00–61)
%U	the week number of the year (00–53), starting with Sunday
%w	the day of the week; Sunday is day 0
%W	the week number of the year (00–53), starting with Monday
%x	the date, using the locale's date format
%X	the time, using the locale's time format
%y	the year within the century (00–99)
%Y	the year, including century (for example, 1984)
%Z	the time zone abbreviation

Table 16.3   `strftime` format codes

values in the other fields need not be within their usual ranges. After the conversion, the `struct tm` is then normalized, so that `tm_wday` and `tm_yday` are correct and the remaining fields are all within their usual ranges. This technique is a simple way of determining the day of the week for a particular date.

16.4 Nonlocal Jumps <setjmp.h>

The `setjmp` and `longjmp` functions provide a mechanism similar to the `goto` statement except that it is not limited in scope to one function. These functions are commonly used with deeply nested chains of function calls. If an error is detected in a lower-level function, you can return immediately to the top-level function without having to return an error flag to each intermediate function in the chain.

To use these functions, you must include the header file `setjmp.h`; their prototypes are shown below.

```
int setjmp( jmp_buf state );
void longjmp( jump_buf state, int value );
```

You declare a `jmp_buf` variable and initialize it by calling `setjmp`, which returns the value zero. `setjmp` saves program state information (for example, the current stack pointer and program counter) in the jump buffer.[50] The function in which you call `setjmp` becomes your "top-level" function.

Later, a call to `longjmp` from anywhere within the top-level function or any other function that it calls, either directly or indirectly, causes the saved state to be restored. The effect of `longjmp` is that execution immediately goes back to the top-level function by returning again from the `setjmp` function.

How can you distinguish between these two different returns from `setjmp`? When it is initially called, `setjmp` returns the value zero. When `setjmp` returns again as the result of a `longjmp`, the value that it returns is the second argument to the `longjmp` call, which must be nonzero. By checking the return value, the program can determine whether (and, in the case of multiple calls, which) `longjmp` was called.

16.4.1 Example

Program 16.2 uses `setjmp` to handle errors detected in functions that it calls without the usual logic of returning and checking for error codes. The initial call to `setjmp` establishes the point at which execution will resume after a call to `longjmp`. It returns the value zero, so the program enters the transaction processing loop. If `get_trans`, `process_trans`, or any functions called by these functions detects an error, it calls `longjmp` like this:

```
longjmp( restart, 1 );
```

Execution immediately resumes at the restart point, and `setjmp` returns with the value one.

In this example, two different types of errors are handled: fatal errors that prevent the program from continuing, and minor errors that only disrupt the transaction that was being processed. This call to `longjmp` is the latter. When `setjmp` returns one, an error message is printed and the transaction loop is entered once again. To report a fatal error, `longjmp` is called with any other value, and the program saves its data and exits.

---

[50] The address of the instruction currently being executed in the program.

```
/*
** A program to demonstrate the use of setjmp
*/
#include "trans.h"
#include <stdio.h>
#include <stdlib.h>
#include <setjmp.h>

/*
**      The variable that stores setjmp's state information.
*/
jmp_buf restart;

int
main()
{
        int     value;
        Trans   *transaction;

        /*
        ** Establish the point at which we want to resume execution
        ** after a call to longjmp.
        */
        value = setjmp( restart );

        /*
        ** Figure out what to do after a return from setjmp.
        */
        switch( value ){
        default:
                /*
                ** longjmp was called -- fatal error
                */
                fputs( "Fatal error.\n", stderr );
                break;

        case 1:
                /*
                ** longjmp was called -- minor error
                */
                fputs( "Invalid transaction.\n", stderr );
                /* FALL THROUGH and continue processing */

        case 0:
                /*
```

Program 16.2   `setjmp` and `longjmp` example

continued . . .

```
           ** Original return from setjmp: perform normal
           ** processing.
           */
           while( (transaction = get_trans()) != NULL )
                   process_trans( transaction );


     }


     /*
     ** Save data and exit the program
     */
     write_data_to_file();

     return value == 0 ? EXIT_SUCCESS : EXIT_FAILURE;

}
```

Program 16.2   setjmp and longjmp example   setjmp.c

16.4.2 When to Use Nonlocal Jumps

setjmp and longjmp are not absolutely necessary, because you can always
achieve the same result by returning an error code and checking for it in the
calling function. Returning in this manner is sometimes inconvenient, especially if the functions are already returning some value. If there is a long chain
of function calling function calling function, then each function in the chain
must check for and return the error code even if the last function called is the
only one that ever detects any errors. Using setjmp and longjmp in this
situation simplifies the intermediate functions by removing the error code logic
from them.

When the top-level function (the one that called setjmp) returns, the state
information in the jump buffer becomes invalid. Calls to longjmp after this
time are likely to fail, and the symptoms will be difficult to debug. This fact is
why longjmp can be called only by the top-level function, or by functions
called from the top-level function. Only then is the state information saved in
the jump buffer valid.

Because setjmp and longjmp implement what is effectively a goto, you
must exercise some discipline in their use. In situations like the example in
Program 16.2, these functions can contribute to cleaner, less complicated code.
However, if setjmp and longjmp are used to simulate a goto within one
function or if there are dozens of jump buffers to which execution can return,

the logic will become more difficult to understand and the program will be harder to debug and maintain, in addition to being more likely to fail. You can use `setjmp` and `longjmp`, but you should use them wisely.

16.5 Signals

Most of the actions that happen in a program are caused by the program, for example, executing various statements or requesting input. However, there are some events that the program must reach to that are not caused by the program. A common example is when the user interrupts a program. If partially computed results must be saved in order to avoid loss of data, the program must be prepared to react to this event even though there is no way to predict when it will occur.

Signals are used for this purpose. A *signal* represents an event that can occur asynchronously, that is, not synchronized with anything in the program's execution. If the program has not arranged to handle a particular signal, a default action is taken when the signal occurs. The Standard does not define what the default action is, but most implementations abort the program. Alternatively, the program can call the `signal` function to either ignore the signal or to install a *signal handler*, a function in the program to be called when a signal occurs.

16.5.1 Signal Names <signal.h>

Table 16.4 lists the signals defined by the Standard, though an implementation need not generate all of these signals and it can define additional ones if appropriate.

`SIGABRT` is the signal raised by the `abort` function to abort the program. The specific errors that will raise a `SIGFPE` signal are implementation

Signal	Meaning
SIGABRT	The program has requested abnormal termination.
SIGFPE	An arithmetic error occurred.
SIGILL	An illegal instruction was detected.
SIGSEGV	An invalid access to memory was detected.
SIGINT	An interactive attention signal was received.
SIGTERM	A request to terminate the program was received.

Table 16.4   Signals

dependent. Some common ones are arithmetic overflow or underflow and divide by zero errors. Some implementations extend this signal to provide specific information about the operation that caused the signal. Using this information may let the program react to the signal more intelligently, but reduces its portability.

The SIGILL signal indicates that the CPU tried to execute an illegal instruction. This error may be caused by incorrect compiler settings; for example, compiling a program with Intel 80386 instructions but running it on an 80286 computer. Another possible cause is an error in the execution of the program, such as calling a function using an uninitialized function pointer that has caused the CPU to attempt to execute what is actually data. SIGSEGV indicates an attempt by the program to access memory illegally. The two most common causes of this signal are attempts to access memory that is not installed on the machine or not allocated to your program by the operating system and violating boundary requirements. The latter occurs on machines that enforce boundary alignment on data. For example, if integers are required to be on an even boundary (begin at an even numbered address), an instruction that specifies an odd address to access an integer will cause a boundary violation. Uninitialized pointers are often the cause of this error.

The preceding signals are synchronous because they are all caused from within the program. Although you may not be able to predict when an arithmetic error may occur, if you run the program over and over with the same data the same error will occur at the same place every time. The last two signals, SIGINT and SIGTERM, are asynchronous. They originate from outside the program, usually by the program's user, and indicate that the user is trying to tell the program something.

SIGINT is the signal that most implementations raise when the user tries to interrupt the program. SIGTERM is an alternative signal that an implementation may use to request that the program be terminated. In systems that implement both of these signals, a common strategy is to define a signal handler for SIGINT in order to perform housekeeping and save data before exiting the program, but to *not* install a signal handler for SIGTERM so that the program can be terminated without doing this housekeeping.

16.5.2 Processing Signals <signal.h>

Usually we are concerned with handling signals that occur on their own, that is, unplanned signals. The raise function is provided to raise a signal explicitly.

```
int raise( int sig );
```

Calling this function raises the indicated signal. The program responds to the signal exactly as if it had occurred on its own. You can call this function to test signal handlers, but it can also be misused to effect a nonlocal `goto`. Avoid using it in this way.

There are three ways that a program can react when a signal occurs. The default action is defined by the implementation, often the default is to abort the program. The program can specify other behaviors for responding to signals: a signal can be ignored, or the program can install a signal handler that is called when the signal occurs. The `signal` function is used to specify the desired action.

```
void ( *signal( int sig, void ( *handler )( int ) ) )( int );
```

This prototype is daunting, so now we will unravel it. First, I'll omit the return type so we can examine the arguments:

```
signal( int sig, void ( *handler )( int ) )
```

The first argument is a signal from Table 16.4, and the second argument is the handler you want to install for that signal. The handler is a pointer to a function that takes a single integer argument and doesn't return a result. When the signal occurs, the code for the signal is passed as an argument to the handler. This argument allows one handler to process several different signals.

Now I'll omit the arguments from the prototype to make the return value apparent:

```
void ( *signal() )( int );
```

`signal` is a function that returns a pointer to another function, which takes a single integer argument and doesn't return a result. In fact, `signal` returns a pointer to the previous handler for the signal. By saving this value you can install a handler for a signal and then later return to the previous signal handler. If the call to `signal` fails, for example because of an illegal signal code, the value `SIG_ERR` is returned. This value is a macro that is defined in the header file.

There are two additional macros, `SIG_DFL` and `SIG_IGN`, that may be given as the second argument to `signal`. `SIG_DFL` reinstates the default action for the signal, and `SIG_IGN` causes the signal to be ignored.

16.5.3 Signal Handlers

When a signal occurs for which a handler has been installed, the system first reinstates the default action for the signal.[51] This change prevents an infinite loop if the signal recurs within the handler. Next the handler is called, and the signal code is passed as an argument.

The type of work the handler can perform is limited. If the signal is asynchronous, that is, it is not caused by calling the abort or raise functions, the handler should not call any library function other than signal because their results are undefined in this context. Furthermore, the handler may not access any static data except to assign a value to a static variable of type volatile sig_atomic_t. (**volatile** is described in the next section.) To be truly safe, about all that a signal handler can do is set one of these variables and then return. The rest of the program must periodically examine the variable to see if a signal has occurred.

These harsh restrictions arise from the nature of signal handling. The signal usually indicates that something went wrong. The behavior of the CPU is precisely defined in such circumstances, but the program adds a lot of context surrounding the error that may not be so well defined. For example, a signal that occurred while strcpy was executing might leave the destination string temporarily unterminated, or a signal occurring while a function was being called might leave the stack in an incomplete state. If library functions that depend on this context were called, they may fail in unexpected ways, possibly causing another signal to occur.

The access restrictions define the minimal functionality that is guaranteed to work in the signal handler. The type sig_atomic_t defines a data type that the CPU can access atomically, that is, as a single unit. For example, a 16-bit machine can access a 16-bit integer atomically but may need two operations to access a 32-bit integer. Restricting data access in the signal handler to atomic units eliminates the possibility of inconsistent results if another signal occurs in the middle of the steps that access a nonatomic variable.

The Standard states that a signal handler may terminate the program by calling exit. A handler for any signal, except SIGABRT, may also terminate the program by calling abort. However both of these are library functions, so they may not work properly when called from handlers of asynchronous signals. If you must terminate the program in this way, be aware that there is a remote chance that it may fail. If it occurs, a failure may destroy data or exhibit bizarre symptoms, but the program will eventually terminate.

---

[51] An implementation may choose to "block" the signal while the handler is being executed instead of reinstating the default action. Consult your system's documentation.

Volatile Data

A signal may occur at any time, so the values of variables that are modified by the signal handler may change at any time. Because of this, you cannot count on these variables having the same values from one program statement to the next. The volatile keyword informs the compiler of this fact, which prevents it from "optimizing" the program in a way that may change its meaning. Consider this program fragment:

```
if( value ){
        printf( "True\n" );
}
else {
        printf( "False\n" );
}
if( value ){
        printf( "True\n" );
}
else {
        printf( "False\n" );
}
```

Ordinarily, you would expect the second test to have the same result as the first. If a signal handler changes this variable, then the second test may be different. Unless the variable were declared volatile, the compiler might "optimize" the program by substituting the following code, which is ordinarily equivalent:

```
if( value ){
        printf( "True\n" );
        printf( "True\n" );
}
else {
        printf( "False\n" );
        printf( "False\n" );
}
```

Returning From a Handler

Returning from a signal handler causes the execution of the program to resume from the point where the signal occurred. An exception to this rule is SIGFPE. Because the computation cannot be completed, the effect of returning from this signal is undefined.

If you wish to catch future signals of the type that occurred, be sure to call `signal` to reinstall the handler before returning from the handler. Otherwise, only the first signal will be caught. The next signal will be processed with the default action.

Because of the differences in how various computers react to unanticipated errors, the specification of the signal mechanism is somewhat loose. For example, implementations need not use any or all of the signals defined, and the default action for a signal may or may not be reinstated before calling its handler. On the other hand, the severe limitations imposed on signal handling functions reflects the intersection of the restrictions imposed by different hardware and software environments.

The result of these restrictions and implementation dependencies is that programs that handle signals are less portable than those that do not. Using signals only where necessary and not violating the rules in signal handling functions (even though it may appear to work on one machine) help minimize the portability problems inherent in this type of program.

16.6 Printing Variable Argument Lists <stdarg.h>

The functions in this group are used when variable argument lists must be printed. *Note:* They require inclusion of both the `stdio.h` and `stdarg.h` header files.

```
int vprintf( char const *format, va_list arg );
int vfprintf( FILE *stream, char const *format, va_list arg );
int vsprintf( char *buffer, char const *format, va_list arg );
```

These functions are equivalent to their standard counterparts except that a variable argument list is used (see Chapter 7 for details on variable argument lists). `arg` must be initialized using `va_start` before the functions are called, and none of these functions call `va_end`.

16.7 Execution Environment

These functions communicate with or affect the program's execution environment.

16.7.1 Terminating Execution *<stdlib.h>*

These three functions relate to normal and abnormal program termination.

```
void abort( void )
void atexit( void (func)( void ) );
void exit( int status );
```

abort is called to terminate the execution of a program abnormally. Because the function raises the SIGABRT signal to accomplish this result, the program can install a signal handler to perform any desired action prior to (or instead of) aborting.

atexit registers functions as *exit functions*. Exit functions are called when the program is about to terminate normally, either because exit was called or because the main function has returned. An exit function may not take any arguments.

exit, which was described in Chapter 15, is called to terminate the program normally. If the initial invocation of the main function returns a value, the effect is the same as if exit had been called with that value as its argument.

When exit is called, all of the exit functions registered with atexit are called in the reverse order that they were registered. Then, the buffers are flushed for all streams that need it, and all open files are closed. Files created with tmpfile are removed. The exit status is then returned to the host environment and the program ceases to execute.

Because execution ceases, the exit function never returns to its caller. However, if one of the functions registered with atexit makes another call to exit, the effect is undefined. This error may result in an infinite loop, possibly stopping when there isn't any more memory for the stack.

16.7.2 Assertions *<assert.h>*

An *assertion* is a declaration of something that should be true. ANSI C implements an **assert** macro that is useful when debugging programs. Its prototype is shown below.[52]

---

[52] Because it is a macro rather than a function, assert doesn't actually have a prototype. However, the prototype shown illustrates how assert is used.

```
void assert( int expression );
```

When executed, the macro tests the expression argument. If it is false (zero), then a diagnostic message is printed to the standard error and the program terminates. The format of this message is implementation defined, but it will include the expression and the name of the source file and the line number of the assertion. If the expression is true (nonzero), nothing is printed.

This macro provides a convenient way to check for things that ought to be true. For example, a function that is called with a pointer argument that must not be NULL could verify the value with an assertion:

```
assert( value != NULL );
```

If the function is mistakenly called with a NULL argument, the program will print a message that looks something like this:

```
Assertion failed: value != NULL, file list.c, line 274
```

Using assertions in this way makes debugging easier because the program stops as soon as an error is detected. Furthermore, the message indicates exactly where the symptom appeared. Without an assertion, the program may continue to run and fail later, making it harder to debug.

Note that assert is only appropriate for verifying expressions that must be true. You cannot use it to check for conditions that you are trying to handle, such as detecting illegal input and asking the user for another value, because it terminates the program.

When the program is thoroughly tested, you can eliminate the assertions by defining the name **NDEBUG** when compiling the program.[53] You can use the -DNDEBUG compiler command line option or add

```
#define NDEBUG
```

to the source file prior to where assert.h is included. With NDEBUG defined, the preprocessor discards the assertions, thus eliminating their overhead without having to physically delete them from the source code.

---

[53] Any value may be used; all that matters is whether NDEBUG is defined or not.

16.7.3 The Environment <stdlib.h>

The *environment* is an implementation-defined list of name/value pairs maintained by the operating system. The getenv function searches this list for a specific name and, if found, returns a pointer to its value. The program must not modify the returned string. If the name is not found, a NULL pointer is returned instead.

```
char *getenv( char const *name );
```

Note that the standard does not define a corresponding putenv function. Some implementations provide one anyway, but you should avoid using it if portability is an issue.

16.7.4 Executing System Commands <stdlib.h>

The system function passes its string argument to the host environment so that it can be executed as a command by the system's command processor.

```
void system( char const *command );
```

The exact manner in which this task is performed is implementation dependent, as is the value returned by system. However, system may be called with a NULL argument to inquire whether a command processor actually exists. In this case, system returns a nonzero value if a command processor is available, otherwise it returns zero.

16.8 Sorting and Searching <stdlib.h>

The qsort function sorts data in an array into ascending order. Because it is typeless, you can use qsort to sort any type of data, as long as the elements of the array are fixed size.

```
void qsort( void *base, size_t n_elements, size_t el_size,
      int (*compare)( void const *, void const * ) );
```

The first argument points to the array to be sorted, the second indicates how many elements are in the array, and the third is the size (in characters) of each element. The fourth argument is a pointer to a function that compares elements of the type being sorted. qsort calls this function to compare the

```
/*
** Demonstrates sorting an array of structures with qsort
*/
#include <stdlib.h>
#include <string.h>

typedef struct {
        char    key[ 10 ];      /* the sort key for the array */
        int     other_data;     /* data associated with the key */
} Record;

/*
** Comparison function: compares only the key value.
*/
int r_compare( void const *a, void const *b ){
        return strcmp( ((Record *)a)->key, ((Record *)b)->key );
}

int
main()
{
        Record  array[ 50 ];

        /*
        ** Code that fills the array with 50 elements.
        */

        qsort( array, 50, sizeof( Record ), r_compare );

        /*
        ** Array is now sorted by the key field of the structures.
        */

        return EXIT_SUCCESS;
}
```

Program 16.3 Sorting an array with `qsort`   qsort.c

data in the array when sorting it. By passing a pointer to an appropriate comparison function, you can use `qsort` to sort an array of any type of values.

The comparison function takes two arguments, which are pointers to two values to be compared. The function should return an integer less than, equal to, or greater than zero according to whether the first value is less than, equal to, or greater than the second, respectively.

Because of the typeless nature of this function, the arguments are declared as void *. Casts must be used in the comparison function to convert them to pointers of the proper type. Program 16.3 illustrates how an array of structures containing a key value and some additional data would be sorted.

The bsearch function performs a binary search to locate a specific element in a sorted array. The result is undefined if the array is not sorted.

```
void *bsearch( void const *key, void const *base, size_t n_elements,
     size_t el_size, int (*compare)( void const *, void const * ) );
```

The first argument points to the value you want to find, the second points to the array to be searched, the third indicates the number of elements in the array, and the fourth is the size (in characters) of each element. The final argument is a pointer to a comparison function as we described for qsort. bsearch returns a pointer to the desired array element. If the desired value does not exist, NULL is returned.

Note that the key argument must be the same type of value as the array elements. If the array contains structures that have a key field and some other data, you must create an entire structure and fill in the key field. The other fields can be left empty, because the comparison function will examine only the key field. This use of bsearch is illustrated in Program 16.4.

```
/*
** Demonstrates searching an array of structures with bsearch
*/
#include <stdlib.h>
#include <string.h>

typedef struct {
        char    key[ 10 ];      /* the sort key for the array */
        int     other_data;     /* data associated with the key */
} Record;

/*
** Comparison function: compares only the key value.
*/
int r_compare( void const *a, void const *b ){
        return strcmp( ((Record *)a)->key, ((Record *)b)->key );
}
```

Program 16.4   Searching an array with bsearch

continued . . .

```
int
main()
{
        Record   array[ 50 ];
        Record   key;
        Record   *ans;

        /*
        ** Code that fills the array with 50 elements and sorts it
        */

        /*
        ** Create a key record (only the key field filled in with the
        ** value we want to locate) and search the array.
        */
        strcpy( key.key, "value" );
        ans = bsearch( &key, array, 50, sizeof( Record ),
            r_compare );

        /*
        ** ans now points to the array element whose key field
        ** matches the value, or NULL if none matched.
        */

        return EXIT_SUCCESS;
}
```

Program 16.4   Searching an array with `bsearch`   bsearch.c

16.9 Locales

In an effort to make C more useful worldwide, the Standard defines a *locale*, which is a particular set of parameters for things that vary from country to country. The default is the `"C"` locale, and other locales may be defined by the implementation. Changing the locale may affect how other library functions work. The effects of changing the locale are described at the end of this section.

The `setlocale` function, whose prototype is shown below, is used to change either the entire locale or a portion of it.

```
char *setlocale( int category, char const *locale );
```

The `category` argument specifies which portion of the locale to change. The permissible values are listed in Table 16.5.

If the second argument to `setlocale` is `NULL`, the function returns a pointer to the name of the current locale for the given category. This value may be saved and used in a subsequent call to `setlocale` to restore a previous locale. If the second argument is not `NULL`, it specifies the name of the new locale to use. If the call is successful, the function returns the name of the new locale, otherwise `NULL` is returned and the locale is not affected.

16.9.1 Numeric and Monetary Formatting <locale.h>

The rules for formatting numeric and monetary values differ from place to place in the world. For example, a number that would be written 1,234.56 in the United States would be written 1.234,56 in many European countries. The `localeconv` function obtains the information needed to properly format both nonmonetary and monetary values according to the current locale. Note that this function does not actually perform the formatting; it simply provides information about how it should be done.

```
struct lconv *localeconv( void );
```

The `lconv` structure contains two types of parameters: characters and character pointers. The character parameters have nonnegative values. If a character parameter is `CHAR_MAX`, then that value is not available (or not used) in the current locale. A pointer to an empty string indicates the same thing for the character pointer parameters.

Value	Changes
LC_ALL	The entire locale.
LC_COLLATE	The collating sequence, which affects the behavior of the `strcoll` and `strxfrm` functions (see below).
LC_CTYPE	The character type classifications used by the functions defined in `ctype.h`.
LC_MONETARY	The characters to be used when formatting monetary values.
LC_NUMERIC	The characters to be used when formatting nonmonetary values. Also changes the decimal point character used by the formatted input/output functions and string conversion functions.
LC_TIME	The behavior of the `strftime` function.

Table 16.5 `setlocale` categories

Field and Type	Meaning
char *decimal_point	The character to use as a decimal point. This value will never be an empty string.
char *thousands_sep	The character used to separate groups of digits that appear to the left of the decimal point.
char *grouping	Specifies how many digits are in each digit group to the left of the decimal point.

Table 16.6   Parameters for formatting nonmonetary numeric values

Numeric Formatting

The parameters listed in Table 16.6 are used when formatting numeric quantities that are not monetary. The grouping string is interpreted as follows. The first value in the string specifies how many digits appear in the first group to the left of the decimal point. The next value in the string corresponds to the next group to the left, and so forth. Two values have special significance: CHAR_MAX indicates that the remaining digits are not broken into groups, and 0 indicates that the preceding value applies to all remaining groups in the number.

Typical North American formatting is indicated with the parameters

```
decimal_point="."
thousands_sep=","
grouping="\3"
```

The grouping string contains a three followed by a zero (the terminating NUL byte).[54] These values mean that the first group to the left of the decimal point will contain three digits, and all the remaining groups will also contain three digits. The value 1234567.89 would appear as 1,234,567.89 when formatted according to these parameters.

Here is another example.

```
grouping="\4\3"
thousands_sep="-"
```

These values express the rules for formatting telephone numbers in North America. The value 2125551234 would be formatted as 212-555-1234 according to these parameters.

---

[54] Note that this number is a binary three, not the character three!

Monetary Formatting

The rules for formatting monetary values are much more complex due to the many different ways of indicating positive and negative values, positioning the currency symbol relative to the value, and so forth. In addition, the rules change when formatting a monetary value for international publication. We begin with the parameters used when formatting local (not international) monetary quantities, shown in Table 16.7.

When formatting monetary values for international use, the string int_curr_symbol is used instead of currency_symbol, and the character int_frac_digits is used instead of frac_digits. International currency

Field and Type	Meaning
char *currency_symbol	The local currency symbol.
char *mon_decimal_point	The decimal point character.
char *mon_thousands_sep	The character used to separate digit groups that appear to the left of the decimal point.
char *mon_grouping	Specifies the number of digits in each group appearing to the left of the decimal point.
char *positive_sign	The string used to indicate a nonnegative amount.
char *negative_sign	The string used to indicate a negative amount.
char frac_digits	The number of digits appearing to the right of the decimal point.
char p_cs_precedes	1 if the currency_symbol precedes a nonnegative value; 0 if it follows.
char n_cs_precedes	1 if the currency_symbol precedes a negative value; 0 if it follows.
char p_sep_by_space	1 if the currency_symbol is separated by a space from a nonnegative value; else 0.
char n_sep_by_space	1 if the currency_symbol is separated by a space from a negative value; else 0.
char p_sign_posn	Indicates where the positive_sign appears in a nonnegative value. The following values are allowed: 0 Parentheses surround the currency symbol and value. 1 The sign precedes the currency symbol and value. 2 The sign follows the currency symbol and value. 3 The sign immediately precedes the currency symbol. 4 The sign immediately follows the currency symbol.
char n_sign_posn	Indicates where the negative_sign appears in a negative value. The values used for p_sign_posn are also used here.

Table 16.7   Parameters for formatting local monetary values

symbols are formed in accordance with the ISO 4217:1987 standard. The first three characters of this string are the alphabetic international currency symbol, and the fourth character is used to separate the symbol from the value.

The following values will format monetary values in a style acceptable in the United States.

```
currency_symbol="$"        p_cs_precedes='\1'
mon_decimal_point="."      n_cs_precedes='\1'
mon_thousands_sep=","      p_sep_by_space='\0'
mon_grouping="\3"          n_sep_by_space='\0'
positive_sign=""           p_sign_posn='\1'
negative_sign="CR"         n_sign_posn='\2'
frac_digits='\2'
```

Using these parameters, the values 1234567890 and -1234567890 would appear as $1,234,567,890.00 and $1,234,567,890.00CR respectively.

Setting n_sign_posn='\0' causes the negative value above to appear as ($1,234,567,890.00).

16.9.2 Strings and Locales <string.h>

The collating sequence of a machine's character set is fixed, yet the locale provides a way to specify alternate sequences. When a collating sequence other than the default must be used, the following two functions are provided.

```
int strcoll( char const *s1, char const *s2 );
size_t strxfrm( char *s1, char const *s2, size_t size );
```

The strcoll function compares the two strings as specified by the LC_COLLATE category of the current locale. It returns a value less than, equal to, or greater than zero according to whether the first string is less than, equal to, or greater than the second string.

Note that this comparison may require considerably more computation than strcmp because of the need to obey a collating sequence that is not native to the machine. strxfrm is provided to reduce the computation required when strings must be compared repeatedly in this manner. It converts its second argument, interpreted in the current locale, into another string that is not dependent on the locale. Although the contents of the converted string are indeterminate, strcmp gives the same result comparing two strings converted in this manner as strcoll produces comparing the original strings.

16.9.3 Effects of Changing the Locale

Changing the locale has some effects in addition to those previously described.

1.   A locale may add characters to (but may not change the meanings of existing characters of) the character set used when the program is executing. For example, many European languages make use of extended character sets that include accents, currency symbols, and other special characters.

2.   The direction of printing may change. Specifically, the locale determines where a character should be printed in relation to the previous character that was printed.

3.   The *printf* and *scanf* families of functions use the decimal point character defined by the current locale.

4.   The `isalpha`, `islower`, `isspace`, and `isupper` functions may include more characters than previously described if the locale extends the execution character set.

5.   The collating sequence of the execution character set may change. This is the sequence used by `strcoll` to compare strings to each other.

6.   Many aspects of the date and time format produced by `strftime` are specific to the locale, as previously described.

16.10 Summary

The standard library includes many useful functions. The first group of functions return integer results. `abs` and `labs` return the absolute value of their arguments. The `div` and `ldiv` functions perform integer division. Unlike the `/` operator, the value of the quotient is well defined when one of the arguments is negative. The `rand` function returns a pseudo-random number. Calling `srand` allows you to start at arbitrary points in the sequence of pseudo-random values. The `atoi` and `atol` functions convert a string to an integer value. The `strtol` and `strtoul` functions perform the same conversion, but give you more control.

Most of the next group of functions take `double` arguments and return `double` results. The usual trigonometry functions, `sin`, `cos`, `tan`, `asin`, `acos`, `atan`, and `atan2`, are provided. The first three take a single argument, an angle in radians, and return the sine, cosine, and tangent of the angle, respectively. The second three return the arc sine, arc cosine, and arc tangent of their argument, respectively. The last function computes arc tangent from an x and y value. The hyperbolic sine, cosine, and tangent are computed by sinh, cosh, and tanh, respectively. The exp function returns the value e raised to the power of the argument. The log function returns the natural logarithm of its argument, and log10 returns the base 10 logarithm.

The frexp and ldexp functions are useful for constructing machine-independent representations of floating point numbers. frexp computes a representation for a given value, and ldexp interprets a representation to recover the original value. The modf function breaks a floating-point value into integer and fractional parts. The pow function raises its first argument to the power specified by its second argument. sqrt returns the square root of its argument. floor returns the largest integer not greater than its argument, and ceil returns the smallest integer not less than its argument. fabs returns the absolute value of its argument. fmod takes two arguments, and returns the remainder that results from an integer division of the second argument into the first. Finally, the atof and strtod convert strings to floating-point values. The latter function provides more control over the conversion.

The next group of functions deal with dates and times. clock returns the amount of processor time used by a program since it began executing. The time function returns the current date and time of day as a time_t value. The ctime function converts a time_t value into a human-readable representation of the date and time. difftime computes the difference in seconds between two time_t values. gmtime and localtime convert a time_t value to a struct tm containing all of the components of the date and time. The former function uses Universal Coordinated Time and the latter uses local time. The asctime and strftime functions convert a struct tm to a human-readable representation of the date and time. The latter function provides great control over the format of the result. Finally, mktime normalizes the values in a struct tm and converts them to a time_t value.

Nonlocal jumps are provided by setjmp and longjmp. setjmp is called to save processor state information in a jmp_buf variable. Then, a subsequent call to longjmp restores the saved processor state. longjmp may not be called after the function that called setjmp returns.

Signals represent unexpected events that may occur during the execution of a program, such as a user interrupt or an arithmetic error. The default action when a signal occurs is implementation defined, though terminating the program is common. You may change the default action by defining a signal handler and installing it with the signal function. The type of work that you may perform in a signal handler is severely restricted because the program may be in an inconsistent state after the signal occurs. Volatile data may change its value, apparently all by itself. For example, a variable that is changed in a signal handler should be declared volatile. The raise function causes the signal indicated by its argument to occur.

The vprintf, vfprintf, and vsprintf functions perform the same work as the *printf* family of functions, except that the values to be printed are passed as a variable argument list. The abort function aborts the program by raising the SIGABRT signal. The atexit function registers exit functions, which are called before the program exits. The assert macro is used to terminate the program when an expression that should be true is actually false. When debugging is completed, defining the NDEBUG symbol eliminates the assertions without deleting them from the source code. getenv retrieves values from the operating system environment. system takes a string as an argument, and uses the local command processor to execute the string as a command.

The qsort function sorts an array of values into ascending order, and the bsearch function performs a binary search to locate a value in a sorted array. Both of these funtions are typeless—they work on arrays of any type of data.

A locale is a set of parameters that tailor the behavior of C programs to countries around the world. The setlocale function is used to change the entire locale or parts of it. The locale includes parameters that define how numeric formatting should be performed. The types of values described include nonmonetary, local monetary, and international monetary values. The locale does not perform any formatting, it simply provides the specifications for the formatting. A locale can specify a collating sequence that is different from the machine's default sequence. In this case, strxcoll is used to compare strings according to the current collating sequence. The value that it returns is analogous to that returned by strcmp. The strxfrm function converts a string in the current collating sequence to a string in the default collating sequence. Strings converted in this manner can be compared with strcmp; the result of the comparison will be the same as the result of comparing the original strings with strxcoll.

16.11 Summary of Cautions

1. Not including the math.h header file can make the math functions produce incorrect results (page 457).

2. The clock function may only be an approximation of processor time (page 461).

3. The value returned by time is not necessarily seconds (page 462).

4. The month in a struct tm is *not* a number in the range 1–12 (page 463).

5. The year in a `struct tm` is the number of years since 1900 (page 464).

6. `longjmp` may not be used to return to a function that is no longer active (page 468).

7. Calling `exit` or `abort` from the handler of an asynchronous signal is not safe (page 472).

8. You must reinstall a signal handler each time the signal occurs (page 474).

9. Avoid multiple calls to `exit` (page 475).

16.12 Summary of Programming Tips

1. Misusing `setjmp` and `longjmp` leads to spaghetti code (page 468).

2. Handling signals makes programs less portable (page 474).

3. Using assertions simplifies debugging (page 476).

16.13 Questions

  1. What does the following function call return?

```
strtol( "12345", NULL, -5 );
```

2. If the "random" numbers produced by the `rand` function are not truly random, are they really any good?

  3. What is the result of the following program on your system?

```
#include <stdlib.h>

int
main()
{
        int     i;

        for( i = 0; i < 100; i += 1 )
                printf( "%d\n", rand() % 2 );
}
```

4. How would you write a program to determine whether the `clock` function on your system measures the cpu time used or elapsed time?

  5. The following code fragment attempts to print the current time in military format. What is wrong with it?

```
#include <time.h>
struct tm *tm;
time_t now;
...
now = time();
tm = localtime( now );
printf( "%d:%02d:%02d %d/%02d/%02d\n",
      tm->tm_hour, tm->tm_min, tm->tm_sec,
      tm->tm_mon, tm->tm_mday, tm->tm_year );
```

6. What is wrong with the following program? What happens when it is executed on your system?

```
#include <stdlib.h>
#include <setjmp.h>

jmp_buf jbuf;

void
set_buffer()
{
        setjmp( jbuf );
}

int
main( int ac, char **av )
{
        int     a = atoi( av[ 1 ] );
        int     b = atoi( av[ 2 ] );

        set_buffer();
        printf( "%d plus %d equals %d\n",
            a, b, a + b );
        longjmp( jbuf, 1 );
        printf( "After longjmp\n" );
        return EXIT_SUCCESS;
}
```

7. Write a program that will determine whether an integer division by zero or a floating-point division by zero results in a SIGFPE signal. How do you explain the results?

8. The comparison function used by qsort should return a negative value if the first argument is less than the second, and a positive value if the first argument is greater than the second. Would it make any difference in qsort's behavior if the comparison function returned the opposite values instead?

16.14 Programming Exercises

* 1. A popular joke among computer people is to say, "My age is 29, but I'm not telling you the base of that number!" If the base is 16, the person is really 41 years old. Write a program that takes an age as a command line argument and computes the smallest radix (base) in the range 2 through 36 for which the age appears to be a number less than or equal to 29. For example, if the user enters 41, the program should say to use base 16 because decimal 41 is 29 in base 16.

✍ ** 2. Write a function that simulates the throwing of a six-sided die by returning a random integer in the range 1 through 6. Be sure that each of the values is equally likely to appear. The first time the function is called, it should seed the random number generator with the time of day.

** 3. Write a program that tells the current time of day as a three-year-old child would (for example, the big hand is on the 6 and the little hand is on the 12).

** 4. Write a program that takes three integers as command line arguments and interprets them as a month (1–12), a day (1–31), and a year (0–?). It should then print the day of the week on which the specified date fell (or will fall). For what range of years is it accurate?

** 5. Winter weather reports often give the "wind chill," which measures how cold a particular temperature and wind speed feel. For example, if it is -5° Celsius (23° Fahrenheit) with a wind of 10 meters per second (22.37 mph), the wind chill temperature is -22.3° Celsius (-8.2° Fahrenheit).

   Write a function with the following prototype to compute the wind chill.

   ```
   double wind_chill( double temp, double velocity );
   ```

   temp is the air temperature in degrees Celsius, and velocity is the wind speed in meters per second. The function returns the wind chill temperature, which is also in degrees Celsius.

   Wind chill is computed using this formula:

   $$Windchill = \frac{(A + B\sqrt{V} + CV)\Delta t}{A + B\sqrt{X} + CX}$$

   For a given air temperature and wind velocity, it gives the temperature that produces the same cooling effect with a 4 mph wind (the wind chill standard). V is the wind velocity in meters per second. Δt is 33 – temp, the difference between neutral skin temperature of 33° Celsius and the air temperature. The constants are $A=10.45$, $B=10$, $C=-1$, and $X=1.78816$, which is 4 mph converted to meters per second.

★★ 6. The formula for determining the monthly payment for a mortgage is

$$P = \frac{AI}{1 - (1 + I)^{-N}}$$

where A is the amount of the loan, I is the interest rate per period (as a decimal, not a percentage), and N is the number of periods over which the loan will be repaid. For example, a $100,000 loan repaid over 20 years at 8% interest has a monthly payment of $836.44 (20 years is 240 payment periods, and the interest per payment period is 0.66667).

Write the function, prototyped below, to compute the loan payment.

```
double payment( double amount, double interest,
    int years );
```

`years` specifies the duration of the loan, `amount` is the amount of the loan, and `interest` is the annual interest rate expressed as a percentage (for example, 12%). The function should compute and return the monthly payment for the loan, rounded to the nearest penny.

★★★ 7. Well-designed random number generators return values that appear to be random, yet over time are uniform. Numbers derived from the random values should also have these properties. For example, a poorly designed random number generator might return values that appear random but in fact alternate between even and odd numbers. If these seemingly random values are taken modulo two (to simulate the results of flipping a coin, for instance), the result is an alternating sequence of zeros and ones. A different flaw would be a generator that returned only odd values. Taking these values modulo two would result in a continuous sequence of ones. Neither of these sequences can be used because they are not random enough.

Write a program to test the random number generator on your system. You should generate 10,000 random numbers and perform two types of tests. The first is a frequency test. Take each random number modulo two, and count how many times the result is zero and one. Do the same for modulo three through ten. The results will not be precisely uniform, but there should not be any large peaks or valleys in the frequencies.

The second test checks for cyclic frequency. Take each random number and the preceding one modulo two. Use these remainders as the subscripts of a two-dimensional array and increment the specified location. Repeat for modulo three through ten. Once again, the results will not be exactly even, but they should be approximately uniform.

Modify your program so that you can provide different values to seed the random number generator, and run tests with several different seeds. How good is your random number generator?

★★★ 8. A certain data file contains the ages of family members. The ages of the members of one family are all on the same line, separated by white space. For example, this data

```
45 42 22
36 35 7 3 1
22 20
```

describes three families having three, five, and two members, respectively.

Write a program that computes the average age of each family represented in a file of this sort. It should print the average age using the %5.2f format, followed by a colon and the input data. This problem is identical to one from the previous chapter but without the limitation on how many members a family can have! You may, however, assume that the input lines will not exceed 512 characters each.

★★★ 9. What are the odds of 2 students in a class of 30 sharing the same birthday? How big would a group of people have to be for the odds of any 2 of them sharing a birthday to be 50%?

Write a program to determine these answers. Get 30 random numbers and take them modulo 365 to represent days of the year (ignore leap years). Then check to see if any of the numbers match. Repeat this test 10,000 times to get an estimate for the odds.

To answer the second question, modify the program so that it will accept the group size as a command line argument. Seed the random number generator with the time of day, and run the program several times to get an idea of how accurate the odds estimate is.

★★★★ 10. An *insertion sort* is performed by adding values to an array one by one. The first value is simply stored at the beginning of the array. Each subsequent value is added by finding its proper position in the array, moving existing values as needed to make room for it, and then inserting it.

Write a function called insertion_sort that performs this task. Its prototype should be the same as qsort. *Hint:* Consider the array that you get as having a sorted part on the left and an unsorted part on the right. Initially the sorted part will be empty. As your function inserts each value, the boundary between the sorted and unsorted parts moves to accommodate the insertion. When all elements have been inserted, the unsorted part is now empty and the array is sorted.

17

Classic Abstract Data Types

There are several abstract data types (ADTs) whose properties make them so useful that they are indispensable components of a C programmer's toolkit: the list, stack, queue, and tree. Linked lists were discussed in Chapter 12; this chapter covers the remaining ADTs.

The first part of the chapter describes the properties and basic implementations of these structures. The chapter ends by discussing how to improve the flexibility of their implementations and the resulting safety compromises.

17.1 Memory Allocation

There is one decision that must be made for all ADTs—how to obtain the memory that stores the values. There are three choices: a static array, a dynamically allocated array, and a dynamically allocated linked structure.

The static array imposes a fixed size on the structure. Moreover, this size must be determined at compile time. However, it is the simplest technique and least prone to error.

Using a dynamic array lets you wait until runtime to decide how big to make the array. It also lets you dynamically resize the array when needed by allocating a new, larger array, copying the values from the original array to the new one, and then deleting the original array. In deciding whether or not to use a dynamic array, you must weigh the increased complexity against the flexibility of an ADT without a fixed, predetermined size limit.

Finally, linked structures offer the greatest flexibility. Each element is individually allocated when needed, so there isn't any maximum size restriction other than the memory available on the machine. However, a linked structure consumes extra memory for the links, and traversing a linked structure to access a specific element is not as efficient as accessing a value in an array.

17.2 Stacks

The *stack* is a data structure characterized by its *Last-In First-Out* or *LIFO* behavior. Partygoers are well acquainted with stacks: the host's driveway is a stack of cars. The last car parked is the first one that must be removed, and the first car that was parked cannot be moved until all the others are gone.

17.2.1 Stack Interface

The basic stack operations are usually called *push* and *pop*. Push adds a new value to the top of the stack, and pop removes the topmost value and returns it. Access is provided only to the top value on the stack.

In the traditional stack interface, the only way to access the top element is to remove it. An alternative interface for the stack has three basic operations: *push*, *pop*, and *top*. Push operates as described above, but pop simply removes the top element—its value is not returned. Top returns the value of the top element without removing it from the stack.

The traditional `pop` function has a side effect: it changes the state of the stack. It is also the only way to access the top element of the stack. Having a `top` function lets you repeatedly access the value on the top of the stack without having to save it in a local variable. This capability is another example of the benefits of designing functions without side effects.

We need two additional functions to use the stack. An empty stack cannot be popped, so we need a function to tell us if the stack is empty. A stack implemented with a maximum size limit should have a function that tells us whether the stack is full.

17.2.2 Implementing a Stack

The stack is one of the easiest ADTs to implement. The basic approach is to store the values into successive locations in an array as they are pushed. You must keep track of the subscript of the value that was most recently pushed. To pop the stack you simply decrement this value. The header file in Program 17.1 describes the nontraditional interface for a stack module.

Note that the interface contains only the information that a client needs to use the stack; specifically, it does not reveal how the stack is implemented. In fact, with a minor modification that we discuss later, this same header file can be used with all three implementation techniques. Defining the interface in this manner is good practice because it prevents the client from making assumptions that depend on a particular implementation.

```
/*
** Interface for a stack module
*/

#define STACK_TYPE      int      /* Type of value on the stack */

/*
** push
**      Pushes a new value on the stack.  The argument is the value
**      to be pushed.
*/
void    push( STACK_TYPE value );

/*
** pop
**      Pops a value off of the stack, discarding it.
*/
void    pop( void );

/*
** top
**      Returns the topmost value on the stack without changing the
**      stack.
*/
STACK_TYPE top( void );

/*
** is_empty
**      Returns TRUE if the stack is empty, else FALSE.
*/
int     is_empty( void );

/*
** is_full
**      Returns TRUE if the stack is full, else FALSE.
*/
int     is_full( void );
```

Program 17.1   Stack interface   stack.h

An interesting feature of this interface is its declaration of the type of value to
be stored on the stack. The client would modify this declaration to suit his
needs before compiling the stack module.

An Arrayed Stack

Our first implementation, in Program 17.2, uses a static array. The size of the stack is given in a #define, which must be set by the client before the module is compiled. This restriction is relaxed in the stack implementations discussed later.

Everything that is not part of the external interface is declared static to prevent the client from accessing the values in any way other than through the defined interface.

```
/*
** A stack implemented with a static array.  The array size can
** be adjusted only by changing the #define and recompiling
** the module.
*/
#include "stack.h"
#include <assert.h>

#define STACK_SIZE        100       /* Max # of values on the stack */

/*
**      The array that holds the values on the stack, and a pointer
**      to the topmost value on the stack.
*/
static   STACK_TYPE       stack[ STACK_SIZE ];
static   int              top_element = -1;

/*
**      push
*/
void
push( STACK_TYPE value )
{
        assert( !is_full() );
        top_element += 1;
        stack[ top_element ] = value;

}

/*
**      pop
*/
```

Program 17.2   Stack implemented with a static array   *continued . . .*

```
void
pop( void )
{
        assert( !is_empty() );
        top_element -= 1;
}


/*
**      top
*/
STACK_TYPE top( void )
{
        assert( !is_empty() );
        return stack[ top_element ];
}


/*
**      is_empty
*/
int
is_empty( void )
{
        return top_element == -1;
}


/*
**      is_full
*/
int
is_full( void )
{
        return top_element == STACK_SIZE - 1;
}
```

Program 17.2   Stack implemented with a static array   a_stack.c

The variable top_element holds the subscript of the value at the top of the stack. It is initialized to −1 to indicate that the stack is empty. By incrementing this variable in push before storing the new value, top_element always contains the subscript of the topmost value. If it were initialized to 0, top_element would be keeping track of the next available space in the array. This approach works but is slightly less efficient because a subtraction is required in order to access the top element.

A traditional pop function, written with straightforward code, would look like this:

```
STACK_TYPE
pop( void )
{
        STACK_TYPE temp;

        assert( !is_empty() );
        temp = stack[ top_element ];
        top_element -= 1;
        return temp;

}
```

The ordering of these operations is important. top_element is decremented *after* the value is copied from the array, in contrast to push, where it is incremented *before* copying the value into the array. We can make the pop function more efficient by eliminating the temporary variable and the copying that goes with it:

```
        assert( !is_empty() );
        return stack[ top_element-- ];
```

pop need not erase values from the stack—simply decrementing the top pointer is enough because the old value can no longer be accessed by the client.

A noteworthy feature of this stack module is its use of assert to guard against illegal operations, such as popping a stack that is already empty or pushing another value on a stack that is full. The assertions call the is_full and is_empty functions rather than testing top_element themselves. This approach makes it easier to change the implementation should you decide later to detect empty and full differently.

Assertions are appropriate for errors that the client cannot recover from. But if the client wants to be sure that the program doesn't abort, the program must check whether there is space on the stack before attempting to push a new value. Therefore the assertions must only check things that the client can also check.

A Dynamically Arrayed Stack

The next implementation uses a dynamic array, but first we need to add two new functions in the interface:

```
/*
** create_stack
**      Create the stack.  The argument specifies
**      how many elements the stack can hold.
**      NOTE: this does not apply to the static
**      array version of the stack.
*/
void    create_stack( size_t size );

/*
** destroy_stack
**      Destroy the stack.  This frees the memory
**      used by the stack.  NOTE: this does not
**      apply to the static array stack either.
*/
void    destroy_stack( void );
```

The first function creates the stack with whatever size the user passes as an argument. The second deletes the stack, and is needed to avoid memory leaks.

These declarations may be added to stack.h even though the previous stack implementation does not define either function. Note that there is no danger of a client mistakenly calling either of these functions for a statically arrayed stack because they do not exist in that module.

A better approach is to implement the unneeded functions in the array module as stubs that do nothing. The interfaces for the two implementations will then be identical, thus making it easier to switch from one implementation to another.

Interestingly, using a dynamically allocated array does not change the implementation much (see Program 17.3). The array has been replaced by a pointer, and the stack_size variable has been introduced to remember the size of the stack. The default initialization will make both of these zero.

The create_stack function first checks that the stack was not already created. It then allocates the requested amount of memory and verifies that the allocation was successful. After destroy_stack frees the memory, it sets the size and pointer variables back to zero so that another stack can be created later.

The only changes to the rest of the module are the comparison to the stack_size variable rather than the STACK_SIZE constant in is_full and the addition of an assertion to both is_full and is_empty. The assertion prevents any of the stack functions from being called before the stack has been created. The other stack functions don't need the new assertion because they all call one of these two functions.

```
/*
** A stack implemented with a dynamically allocated array.
** The array size is given when create is called, which must
** happen before any other stack operations are attempted.
*/
#include "stack.h"
#include <stdio.h>
#include <stdlib.h>
#include <malloc.h>
#include <assert.h>


/*
**        The array that holds the values on the stack, and a pointer
**        to the topmost value on the stack.
*/
static   STACK_TYPE      *stack;
static   size_t          stack_size;
static   int             top_element = -1;

/*
**        create_stack
*/
void
create_stack( size_t size )
{
        assert( stack_size == 0 );
        stack_size = size;
        stack = malloc( stack_size * sizeof( STACK_TYPE ) );
        assert( stack != NULL );
}


/*
**        destroy_stack
*/
void
destroy_stack( void )
{
        assert( stack_size > 0 );
        stack_size = 0;
        free( stack );
        stack = NULL;
}


/*
**        push
```

Program 17.3   Stack implemented with a dynamic array   *continued . . .*

```
*/
void
push( STACK_TYPE value )
{
        assert( !is_full() );
        top_element += 1;
        stack[ top_element ] = value;
}

/*
**      pop
*/
void
pop( void )
{
        assert( !is_empty() );
        top_element -= 1;
}

/*
**      top
*/
STACK_TYPE top( void )
{
        assert( !is_empty() );
        return stack[ top_element ];
}

/*
**      is_empty
*/
int
is_empty( void )
{
        assert( stack_size > 0 );
        return top_element == -1;
}

/*
**      is_full
*/
int
is_full( void )
{
        assert( stack_size > 0 );
```

Program 17.3   Stack implemented with a dynamic array

continued . . .

```
        return top_element == stack_size - 1;
}
```

Program 17.3   Stack implemented with a dynamic array   d_stack.c

Using `assert` to check the success of a memory allocation can lead to unexpected program aborts in environments where memory is limited. An alternative strategy would be to return a value from `create_stack` indicating whether or not it was successful. In the event of a failure, the client program could try again with a smaller size.

A Linked Stack

Because only the top element on a stack is accessible, a singly linked list works well for a linked stack. Pushing a value on the stack is accomplished by adding the new value at the start of the list. Popping the stack removes the first value from the list. The value at the head of the list is always easily accessible.

In the implementation shown in Program 17.4, there isn't any need for a `create_stack` function, but `destroy_stack` can be implemented to empty the stack. Because the memory to hold the values is dynamically allocated, it must be freed to avoid memory leaks.

```
/*
** A stack implemented with a linked list.  This stack has no size
** limit.
*/
#include "stack.h"
#include <stdio.h>
#include <stdlib.h>
#include <malloc.h>
#include <assert.h>

#define FALSE 0
```

Program 17.4   Stack implemented with a linked list   *continued . . .*

```
/*
**      Define a structure to hold one value.  The link field will
**      point to the next value on the stack.
*/
typedef struct STACK_NODE {
        STACK_TYPE      value;
        struct STACK_NODE *next;
} StackNode;

/*
**      A pointer to the topmost node on the stack.
*/
static  StackNode       *stack;

/*
**      create_stack
*/
void
create_stack( size_t size )
{
}

/*
**      destroy_stack
*/
void
destroy_stack( void )
{
        while( !is_empty() )
                pop();
}

/*
**      push
*/
void
push( STACK_TYPE value )
{
        StackNode       *new_node;

        new_node = malloc( sizeof( StackNode ) );
        assert( new_node != NULL );
        new_node->value = value;
        new_node->next = stack;
        stack = new_node;
```

Program 17.4   Stack implemented with a linked list   *continued . . .*

```
}

/*
**      pop
*/
void
pop( void )
{
        StackNode       *first_node;

        assert( !is_empty() );
        first_node = stack;
        stack = first_node->next;
        free( first_node );
}

/*
**      top
*/
STACK_TYPE top( void )
{
        assert( !is_empty() );
        return stack->value;
}

/*
**      is_empty
*/
int
is_empty( void )
{
        return stack == NULL;
}

/*
**      is_full
*/
int
is_full( void )
{
        return FALSE;
}
```

Program 17.4   Stack implemented with a linked list   l_stack.c

The structure is needed to bundle a value and a pointer together, and the stack variable is now a pointer to one of these structures. The stack is empty when this pointer is NULL, as it is initially.

The destroy_stack function pops values until the stack is empty. Again, notice that existing is_empty and pop functions are called rather than repeating the needed code.

create_stack is an empty function, and because this stack cannot fill up, is_full always returns false.

17.3 Queues

A *queue* has a different ordering than a stack: queues are *First-In, First-Out* or *FIFO* structures. Waiting lines are usually queues. The person that arrived first is at the head of the line, and new arrivals join the line at its end.

17.3.1 Queue Interface

Unlike stacks, there aren't generally accepted names for the queue functions that perform insertion and removal of values, so we will use insert and delete. Also, there is not complete agreement on whether insertions occur at the front of the queue or at the rear. In principle it doesn't make any difference what you call the end of the line where insertions occur, but inserting at the rear and removing from the front of the queue may be easier to remember because this method more accurately describes our human experiences with waiting lines.

```
/*
** Interface for a queue module
*/

#include <stdlib.h>

#define QUEUE_TYPE        int      /* Type of value in the queue */

/*
** create_queue
**          Creates a queue.  The argument indicates the maximum number
```

Program 17.5   Queue interface   *continued . . .*

```
**        of values that the queue will hold.  NOTE: this applies only
**        to the dynamically allocated array implementation.
*/
void    create_queue( size_t size );


/*
** destroy_queue
**        Destroys a queue.  NOTE: this applies only to the linked and
**        dynamically allocated array implementations.
*/
void    destroy_queue( void );


/*
** insert
**        Adds a new value on the queue.  The argument is the value
**        to be inserted.
*/
void    insert( QUEUE_TYPE value );


/*
** delete
**        Removes a value from the queue, discarding it.
*/
void    delete( void );


/*
** first
**        Returns the first value on the queue without changing the
**        queue itself.
*/
QUEUE_TYPE first( void );


/*
** is_empty
**        Returns TRUE if the queue is empty, else FALSE
*/
int     is_empty( void );


/*
** is_full
**        Returns TRUE if the queue is full, else FALSE
*/
int     is_full( void );
```

Program 17.5   Queue interface   queue.h

In the traditional interface, `delete` removes the value from the front of the queue and returns it. In the alternate interface, `delete` takes the value out of the queue but does not return it; the `first` function returns the first value in the queue without removing it.

The header file in Program 17.5 defines the alternate interface. It includes prototypes for the `create_queue` and `destroy_queue` functions needed by the linked and dynamic implementations.

17.3.2 Implementing a Queue

Queues are more difficult to implement than stacks. Two pointers are needed—one for the front of the line and one for the rear. Also, arrays are not as well suited to queues as they are to stacks because of the way queues use memory.

A stack is always rooted at one end of the array. A queue, however, uses different elements of the array as values are inserted and removed. Consider a queue implemented as an array of five values. Here is how it will look after the values 10, 20, 30, 40, and 50 have been inserted.

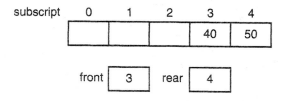

After three removals, it looks like this:

subscript	0	1	2	3	4
				40	50

front | 3 | rear | 4 |

The array is not full, but there isn't any room at its end to insert new values.

One solution to this problem is to move the remaining elements back toward the beginning of the array when a value is removed. The copying overhead makes this approach impractical, especially for large queues.

A better alternative is to have the rear of the queue "wrap around" to the front of the array so that new values can be stored in the space made available by earlier removals. This method is often called a *circular array*. The following diagram illustrates this concept.

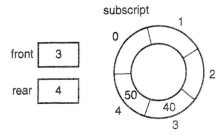

Inserting another value gives this result:

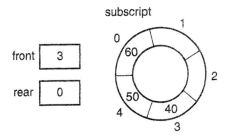

The circular array is easy to implement—when the rear subscript moves off the end of the array, set it back to zero, as is done in the following code.

```
rear += 1;
if( rear >= QUEUE_SIZE )
        rear = 0;
```

The following approach has the same result.

```
rear = ( rear + 1 ) % QUEUE_SIZE;
```

The same technique must be applied when incrementing `front`.

The circular array introduces a problem of its own, though. It is more complex to determine whether a circular array is full or empty. Suppose the queue were full, as this one is:

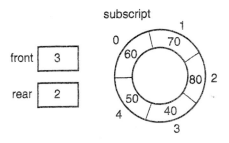

Note the values of front and rear: three and two, respectively. If four values are removed from the queue, front will be incremented four times, giving this configuration:

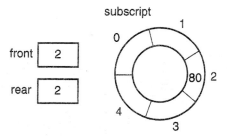

When the last value is removed, the queue looks like this:

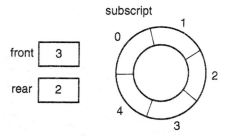

The problem is that the values of front and rear are now the same as they were when the queue was full. Any comparison of them that is true when the queue is empty will also be true when it is full, so we cannot test for an empty queue by comparing front and rear.

There are two ways to solve this problem. The first is to introduce a new variable that counts how many values are in the queue. It is incremented with each insertion and decremented with each removal. Testing this variable to determine whether the queue is empty or full is easy.

The second approach is to redefine the meaning of full. If one element in the array is always left unused, then when the queue is "full" the front and rear values will be different than when the queue is empty. By not allowing the array to become completely full, the problem is avoided.

One minor question remains: What values should front and rear have when the queue is empty? When the queue has one value in it, we want front and rear to both point to the value. An insertion increments rear, so in order for rear to point to the value after the first insertion, rear must be one less than front when the queue is empty. Fortunately, this state is also the result of removing the last value from the queue, so removing the last value is not a special case.

The queue is empty when

```
( rear + 1 ) % QUEUE_SIZE == front
```

Because we must stop inserting values just before `front` and `rear` reach this relationship, the queue must be called "full" when

```
( rear + 2 ) % QUEUE_SIZE == front
```

An Arrayed Queue

Program 17.6 implements a queue with a static array. It uses the "don't completely fill the array" technique of distinguishing between an empty and a full queue.

```
/*
** A queue implemented with a static array.  The array size can
** be adjusted only by changing the #define and recompiling
** the module.
*/
#include "queue.h"
#include <stdio.h>
#include <assert.h>

#define QUEUE_SIZE      100     /* Max # of values on the queue */
#define ARRAY_SIZE      ( QUEUE_SIZE + 1 )      /* Size of array */

/*
**      The array that holds the values on the queue, and pointers
**      to the front and rear of the queue.
*/
static  QUEUE_TYPE      queue[ ARRAY_SIZE ];
static  size_t          front = 1;
static  size_t          rear = 0;

/*
**      insert
*/
void
insert( QUEUE_TYPE value )
```

Program 17.6   Queue implemented with a static array   *continued . . .*

```
{
        assert( !is_full() );
        rear = ( rear + 1 ) % ARRAY_SIZE;
        queue[ rear ] = value;
}

/*
**      delete
*/
void
delete( void )
{
        assert( !is_empty() );
        front = ( front + 1 ) % ARRAY_SIZE;
}

/*
**      first
*/
QUEUE_TYPE first( void )
{
        assert( !is_empty() );
        return queue[ front ];
}

/*
**      is_empty
*/
int
is_empty( void )
{
        return ( rear + 1 ) % ARRAY_SIZE == front;
}

/*
**      is_full
*/
int
is_full( void )
{
        return ( rear + 2 ) % ARRAY_SIZE == front;
}
```

Program 17.6   Queue implemented with a static array   a_queue.c

The QUEUE_SIZE constant is set to the maximum number of values that the client wants on the queue. Because this implementation never fills the queue, ARRAY_SIZE is defined as one more than QUEUE_SIZE. The functions are straightforward implementations of the techniques we discussed.

We could have used any values to initialize front and rear as long as rear is one less than front. These particular values leave the first element of the array unused until the first time rear wraps around, but so what?

Dynamically Arrayed and Linked Queues

The modifications needed to dynamically allocate the array for a queue are analogous to those needed for a stack. Consequently, its implementation is left to the exercises.

The linked queue is simpler in some respects than its arrayed cousins. It doesn't use an array, so the problems of the circular array disappear. Testing for empty is simply a matter of seeing if the list is empty. The test for full always returns false. This implementation is also left as an exercise.

17.4 Trees

A complete description of all the varieties of trees is beyond the scope of this book. However, the techniques for implementing trees are illustrated quite nicely by describing one very useful variety: the binary search tree.

A *tree* is a structure that is either empty or has a value and zero or more *children*, each of which is also a tree. This recursive definition implies correctly that there isn't an inherent limit to the height of a tree. A *binary tree* is a specialized form of tree in which each node has at most two children, named *left* and *right*. A *binary search tree* has one additional property: The value in each node is greater than all of the values in its left subtree and less than all of the values in its right subtree. Note that this definition precludes having duplicate values in the tree. These properties make binary search trees an excellent tool for quickly locating data using a key. Figure 17.1 is an example of a binary search tree. Each node in the tree has exactly one parent (the node above it), and zero, one, or two children (the nodes directly beneath it). The only exception is the topmost node, called the *root* of the tree, which doesn't have a parent. The nodes without children are called *leaf* nodes or *leaves*. Trees are drawn with the root at the top and the leaves at the bottom.[55]

---

[55] Note that trees in nature, with their roots at the bottom and their leaves on top, are actually upside down.

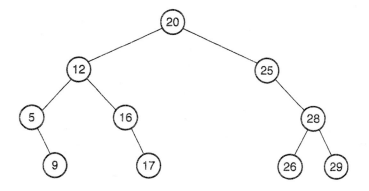

Figure 17.1   Binary search tree

17.4.1 Insertions into a Binary Search Tree

When a new value is to be added to a binary search tree, it must be put in the proper position so that the search tree property is maintained. Fortunately, this task is simple. The basic algorithm works like this:

> *If the tree is empty:*
>   *Insert the new value as the root node*
> *Otherwise:*
>   *If the new value is less than the current node's value:*
>   *Insert the new value in the left subtree of the current node*
>   *Otherwise:*
>   *Insert the new value in the right subtree of the current node.*

The recursive expression of this algorithm is a direct consequence of the recursive definition of the tree.

To insert 15 into the tree in Figure 17.1, compare 15 with 20. It is less so the value is inserted into the left subtree. This subtree's root is 12, so the process is repeated with this node: compare 15 with 12. This time 15 is greater, so we insert 15 into 12's right subtree. We now compare 15 with 16. It is less, so we insert 15 into the left subtree of node 16. But this subtree is empty, so the node containing 15 becomes the root of the new left subtree of node 16.

Because the recursion occurs at the end of the algorithm (tail recursion), it is more efficient to implement the algorithm iteratively.

17.4.2 Deletions from a Binary Search Tree

Removing a value from a tree is more difficult than removing a value from a stack or a queue. Deleting a node from the middle of a tree disconnects its subtrees from the rest of the tree—we must reconnect them or they will be lost.

There are three cases that we must handle: deleting nodes with no children, with one child, and with two children. The first situation is easy. Deleting a leaf node doesn't disconnect any subtrees, so there is nothing to reconnect. Deleting a node with only one child is almost as easy: the parent of the deleted node inherits the child. This solution prevents that subtree from being disconnected, yet preserves the ordering of the binary search tree.

The last case is more difficult. If a node has two children, its parent cannot inherit both of them. One strategy is to not delete the node at all. Instead, the largest value in the node's left subtree is deleted and that value replaces the one that was originally to have been deleted. The deletion functions are implemented as exercises.

17.4.3 Searching a Binary Search Tree

Because of the ordering imposed on a binary search tree, searching the tree for a particular value is easy. Here is the algorithm:

> If the tree is empty:
>   The value is not in the tree
> Otherwise:
>   If the root contains the value:
>   The value is found
>   Otherwise:
>   If the value is less than the root:
>   Search the left subtree
>   Otherwise:
>   Search the right subtree

The recursion in this algorithm is also tail recursion, so an iterative implementation is preferred.

What do you do when the value is found? It depends on the client's needs. Sometimes, all that is required is to check for membership. In this case, returning a true/false status is adequate. If the data is a structure that is identified by a key field, the client will want to access the non-key members of the structure that was located, which requires returning a pointer to the structure.

17.4.4 Tree Traversals

Trees do not limit you to accessing only one value as do stacks and queues. Thus trees have another basic operation—the traversal. When you examine all of the nodes in a tree, you are *traversing* the tree. There are several different orders in which the nodes may be traversed, the most common being *pre-order*, *in-order*, *post-order*, and *breadth-first*. All traversals start at the root of the tree or at the node which is the root of whatever subtree you wish to traverse.

A pre-order traversal examines the value in the node and then recursively traverses the left and right subtrees. For example, a pre-order traversal of the tree

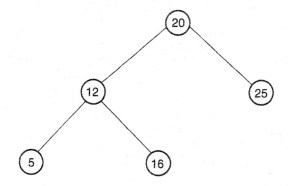

would begin by processing the value 20. We then traverse the left subtree:

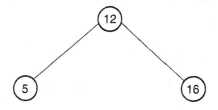

After processing the value 12, we would traverse its left subtree

and process the value 5. Its left and right subtrees are empty, so we have now completed this subtree.

Having finished the left subtree of node 12, we continue with its right subtree and process the value 16. Both of its subtrees are also empty, which means we have completed the subtree whose root is 16 and the subtree whose root is 12.

Having finished the left subtree of 20, the next step is to process its right subtree:

Processing the value 25 completes the traversal.

For a larger example, consider the binary search tree in Figure 17.1 If each node's value is printed when the node was examined, the output of a pre-order traversal would be: 20, 12, 5, 9, 16, 17, 25, 28, 26, 29.

An in-order traversal first traverses the left subtree, then examines the value in the node, and traverses the right subtree last. An in-order traversal of the tree in Fgure 17.1 would examine the nodes in this order: 5, 9, 12, 16, 17, 20, 25, 26, 28, 29.

A post-order traversal traverses the left and right subtrees first and examines the node's value last. A post-order traversal of the same tree would examine the nodes in this order: 9, 5, 17, 16, 12, 26, 29, 28, 25, 20.

Finally, a breadth-first traversal examines the nodes of the tree level by level. First the root is processed, then its children, then all of its grandchildren, and so forth. Traversing the sample tree in this manner would examine the nodes in this order: 20, 12, 25, 5, 16, 28, 9, 17, 26, 29. Although the first three traversals are easily implemented as recursive functions, the breadth-first traversal is an iterative algorithm that uses a queue. The exercises describe it in more detail.

17.4.5 Binary Search Tree Interface

The interface in Program 17.7 prototypes the function for inserting values into a binary search tree. It also includes a find function to find a specific value in the tree, which returns a pointer to the value that was found. Only one traversal function is defined, because the interfaces for the remaining ones differ in name only.

17.4.6 Implementing a Binary Search Tree

Although linked tree implementations are by far the most common, it is possible to store a binary search tree in an array. Of course, the fixed length of the array limits the number of elements that can be added to the tree, but if you

```
/*
** Interface for a binary search tree module
*/

#define TREE_TYPE          int      /* Type of value in the tree */

/*
** insert
**       Add a new value to the tree.  The argument is the value
**       to be added and must not already exist in the tree.
*/
void    insert( TREE_TYPE value );

/*
** find
**       Searches for a specific value, which is passed as the first
**       argument.
*/
TREE_TYPE *find( TREE_TYPE value );

/*
** pre_order_traverse
**       Does a pre-order traversal of the tree.  The argument is a
**       pointer to a callback function that will be called for
**       each node in the tree, with the value passed as an argument.
*/
void    pre_order_traverse( void (*callback)( TREE_TYPE value ) );
```

Program 17.7   Binary search tree interface   tree.h

use dynamic allocation you can create a larger space and copy the values into it when the original array overflows.

An Arrayed, Binary Search Tree

The key to representing a tree in an array is to use subscripts to locate parents and children of a particular value. The rules are easy:

> *The parent of node N is node $N/2$.*
> *The left child of node N is node $2N$.*
> *The right child of node N is node $2N + 1$.*

The formula for the parent works because the integer division operator truncates any fractional part.

Alas, there is a minor problem. These rules assume that the root of the tree is node one, but C arrays begin with subscript zero. The easiest solution is to simply ignore the first element of the array. If the elements are so large that this approach would waste too much space, then you can use these alternate rules for zero-based array subscripts instead:

> *The parent of node* N *is node* $(N + 1) / 2 - 1$.
> *The left child of node* N *is node* $2N + 1$.
> *The right child of node* N *is node* $2N + 2$.

Program 17.8 is a binary search tree implemented with a static array. There are several points of interest in this implementation. It uses the simpler rules for determining children so the array is declared one larger than the advertised size and its first element is ignored. Functions are defined to compute the left and right children of a node. Even though the computation is simple, the function names make the code that use them much clearer. These functions also simplify the task of modifying the module to use the alternate set of rules.

This implementation uses the value zero to indicate a node that is not being used. If zero is a legitimate data value, a different value must be chosen and the array elements must be initialized dynamically. Another technique is to have a companion array of boolean values to indicate which nodes are in use.

A problem with an arrayed tree is that the space in the array is often not used effectively. Space is wasted because new values must be inserted at specific places in the tree and cannot just be put wherever there happens to be space.

To illustrate, suppose an array of 100 elements is used to hold a tree. If the values 1, 2, 3, 4, 5, 6, and 7 are inserted in that order, they will be stored in locations 1, 2, 4, 8, 16, 32, and 64, respectively. But now the value 8 cannot be inserted because the right child of 7 would be stored in location 128, and the array is not that large. Whether or not this problem actually happens depends entirely on the order in which the values are inserted. If the same values were inserted in this order, 4, 2, 1, 3, 6, 5, and 7, they would occupy locations 1 through 7 of the array, and the value 8 could be inserted without difficulty.

With a dynamically allocated array, we can reallocate the array when more space is needed. This technique is not a very good solution to the problem of an unbalanced tree, though, because each new insertion requires the array size to be doubled, and the space available for dynamic memory allocation will soon be exhausted. A better solution is to use a linked binary tree rather than an array.

```
/*
** A binary search tree implemented with a static array.  The
** array size can be adjusted only by changing the #define and
** recompiling the module.
*/
#include "tree.h"
#include <assert.h>
#include <stdio.h>

#define TREE_SIZE        100      /* Max # of values in the tree */
#define ARRAY_SIZE       ( TREE_SIZE + 1 )

/*
**       The array that holds the values in the tree.
*/
static  TREE_TYPE        tree[ ARRAY_SIZE ];

/*
** left_child
**       Compute the subscript of the left child of a node.
*/
static int
left_child( int current )
{
        return current * 2;
}

/*
** right_child
**       Compute the subscript of the right child of a node.
*/
static int
right_child( int current )
{
        return current * 2 + 1;
}

/*
** insert
*/
void
insert( TREE_TYPE value )
{
        int      current;
```

Program 17.8   Binary search tree implemented with a static array   *continued . . .*

```
        /*
        ** Ensure the value is nonzero, because zero indicates an
        ** unused node.
        */
        assert( value != 0 );

        /*
        ** Start with the root node.
        */
        current = 1;

        /*
        ** Go to the proper subtree until we reach a leaf.
        */
        while( tree[ current ] != 0 ){
                /*
                ** Go to the left or right subtree, as appropriate.
                ** (And make sure we don't have a duplicate value!)
                */
                if( value < tree[ current ] )
                        current = left_child( current );
                else {
                        assert( value != tree[ current ] );
                        current = right_child( current );
                }
                assert( current < ARRAY_SIZE );
        }

        tree[ current ] = value;
}

/*
** find
*/
TREE_TYPE *
find( TREE_TYPE value )
{
        int     current;

        /*
        ** Start with the root node.  Until we find the value,
        ** go to the proper subtree.
        */
        current = 1;
```

Program 17.8   Binary search tree implemented with a static array   *continued . . .*

```
        while( current < ARRAY_SIZE && tree[ current ] != value ){
                /*
                ** Go to the left or right subtree, as appropriate.
                */
                if( value < tree[ current ] )
                        current = left_child( current );
                else
                        current = right_child( current );
        }

        if( current < ARRAY_SIZE )
                return tree + current;
        else
                return 0;
}


/*
** do_pre_order_traverse
**      Do one level of a pre-order traverse.  This helper function
**      is needed to save the information of which node we're
**      currently processing; this is not a part of the client's
**      interface.
*/
static void
do_pre_order_traverse( int current,
    void (*callback)( TREE_TYPE value ) )
{
        if( current < ARRAY_SIZE && tree[ current ] != 0 ){
                callback( tree[ current ] );
                do_pre_order_traverse( left_child( current ),
                    callback );
                do_pre_order_traverse( right_child( current ),
                    callback );
        }
}


/*
** pre_order_traverse
*/
void
pre_order_traverse( void (*callback)( TREE_TYPE value ) )
{
        do_pre_order_traverse( 1, callback );
}
```

Program 17.8 Binary search tree implemented with a static array   a_tree.c

A Linked Binary Search Tree

The linked implementation eliminates the problem of unused array space by dynamically allocating memory to hold each new value and linking these structures together into a tree. Thus, there isn't any unused memory.

Program 17.9 is the linked implementation. Compare it with the arrayed tree implementation in Program 17.8. Because each node in the tree must point to its left and right children, a structure is used to hold the value and the two pointers. The array is replaced by a pointer to the root of the tree. This pointer is initially NULL, indicating that the tree is empty.

The insert function uses two pointers.[56] The first is used to examine nodes in the tree to find the proper place to insert the new value. The second is a pointer to whatever link points to the node currently being examined. When a leaf is reached, this pointer is the one that must be changed to insert the new node. The function walks down the tree, going left or right according to how the new value compares with the current node's value, until a leaf is reached. Then a new node is created and linked into the tree. This iterative algorithm inserts the first node in the tree properly without a special case.

Variations on the Tree Interface

As it is shown, the find function really only checks for membership. Returning a pointer to the value that was found isn't too useful because the caller already knows the value: it was passed as an argument!

Suppose the values contained in the tree are in fact structures that contain a key value and some data. Now we can modify the find function to be much more useful. Locating a particular node by its key and then returning a pointer to the structure gives the client something he didn't previously have—the data that is associated with the key. However, to achieve this result find must somehow compare only the key portion of the value in each node. The solution is to write a function that makes this comparison and pass find a pointer to the function like we did with qsort.

Sometimes the client may want to traverse the tree himself, for example, to count the number of children belonging to each node. Both the TreeNode structure and the pointer to the root node of the tree must be made public for the client to traverse the tree. The safest way of providing the root pointer is through a function, thus preventing the client from changing the root pointer himself and losing the tree.

---

[56] We used the same technique in Chapter 12 in the function that inserted values into an ordered, singly linked list. If you look at the path that is followed from the root of the tree to the leaf where the insertion will occur, you will see that it is essentially a singly linked list.

```
/*
** A binary search tree implemented by linking dynamically allocated
** structures.
*/
#include "tree.h"
#include <assert.h>
#include <stdio.h>
#include <malloc.h>

/*
**      The TreeNode structure holds the value and pointers for one
**      tree node.
*/
typedef struct TREE_NODE {
        TREE_TYPE         value;
        struct TREE_NODE *left;
        struct TREE_NODE *right;
} TreeNode;

/*
**      The pointer to the root node in the tree.
*/
static  TreeNode        *tree;

/*
**      insert
*/
void
insert( TREE_TYPE value )
{
        TreeNode        *current;
        TreeNode        **link;

        /*
        ** Start with the root node.
        */
        link = &tree;

        /*
        ** As long as we keep finding values, go to the proper
        ** subtree.
        */
        while( (current = *link) != NULL ){
                /*
                ** Go to the left or right subtree, as appropriate.
```

Program 17.9 Linked binary search tree

continued . . .

```
                        ** (And make sure we don't have a duplicate value!)
                        */
                        if( value < current->value )
                                link = &current->left;
                        else {
                                assert( value != current->value );
                                link = &current->right;
                        }
                }

                /*
                ** Allocate a new node; make the proper link field point
                ** to it.
                */
                current = malloc( sizeof( TreeNode ) );
                assert( current != NULL );
                current->value = value;
                current->left = NULL;
                current->right = NULL;
                *link = current;
        }

/*
**      find
*/
TREE_TYPE *
find( TREE_TYPE value )
{
        TreeNode        *current;

        /*
        ** Start with the root node.  Until we find the value,
        ** go to the proper subtree.
        */
        current = tree;

        while( current != NULL && current->value != value ){
                /*
                ** Go to the left or right subtree, as appropriate.
                */
                if( value < current->value )
                        current = current->left;
                else
                        current = current->right;
        }
```

Program 17.9 Linked binary search tree *continued . . .*

```
        if( current != NULL )
                return &current->value;
        else
                return NULL;
}


/*
** do_pre_order_traverse
**      Do one level of a pre-order traverse.  This helper function
**      is needed to save the information of which node we're
**      currently processing; this is not a part of the
**      client's interface.
*/
static void
do_pre_order_traverse( TreeNode *current,
    void (*callback)( TREE_TYPE value ) )
{
        if( current != NULL ){
                callback( current->value );
                do_pre_order_traverse( current->left, callback );
                do_pre_order_traverse( current->right, callback );
        }
}


/*
**      pre_order_traverse
*/
void
pre_order_traverse( void (*callback)( TREE_TYPE value ) )
{
        do_pre_order_traverse( tree, callback );
}
```

Program 17.9   Linked binary search tree   l_tree.c

It is often helpful for each tree node to have a pointer to its parent node. The client can use the parent pointer to move both up and down in the tree. The find function in this more public tree could then return a pointer to the tree node rather than the value, which would allow the client to use that pointer as the beginning of other traversals.

One final improvement is a destroy_tree function to free all of the memory that was allocated for the tree. The implementation of this function is left as an exercise.

17.5 Improvements in Implementation

The implementations in this chapter illustrate how the different ADTs work, but they are inadequate in several respects for use in real programs. This section identifies these problems and suggests how to solve them. We use the arrayed stack as an example, but the techniques described apply to the other ADTs as well.

17.5.1 Having More Than One Stack

The main problem with the implementations so far is that they encapsulate the memory used to hold the structure as well as the functions that manipulate it. Thus a program cannot have more than one stack!

This limitation is easily solved by removing the declarations of the array and `top_element` from the stack implementation module and putting them in the client's code instead. They are then accessed by the stack functions through arguments, so the functions are no longer tied to one array. The client can create any number of arrays and manipulate them as stacks by calling the stack functions.

The danger with this approach is the loss of encapsulation. If the client has the data, he can access it directly. Illegal accesses, for example adding a new value to the array in the wrong place or adding a value without adjusting `top_element`, can result in lost or illegal data or may cause the stack functions to fail.

A related problem is ensuring that the client passes the correct stack and `top_element` arguments to each stack function that is called. If these arguments are mixed up, the result is garbage. We can reduce the likelihood of this happening by bundling the stack array and its `top_element` value together in a structure.

There wasn't any danger of either problem occurring when the stack module contained the data. The exercises describe a modification that lets the stack module manage more than one stack.

17.5.2 Having More Than One Type

Even if the previous problem is solved, the type of values stored on the stack is fixed at compile time by the type in the `stack.h` header file. If you need a stack of integers and a stack of floats, you're out of luck.

The simplistic way of solving this problem is to write a separate copy of the stack functions to deal with each different data type. This approach does the job but involves a lot of duplicated code, which makes maintenance more difficult.

A more elegant approach is to implement the entire stack module as a #define that takes the desired type as a parameter. This definition is then used to create the routines for each type that is required. For this solution to work, though, we must find a way to make the names of the functions generated for different types unique so that they don't conflict with each other. You must also be careful to create only one set of routines for each type no matter how many stacks of that type you need. An example of this approach is presented in Section 17.5.4.

A third approach is to make the stack typeless by having it store void * values. To store integers and other data that takes the same amount of space as a pointer, casts are used to convert the desired type to void * in the argument to push and to convert the value returned by top back to the desired type. To work with larger data, such as structures, pointers to the data are stored on the stack.

The problem with this approach is the loss of type checking. There is no way to verify that the value passed to push is the correct type for the stack being used. If an integer is accidentally pushed on a stack that contains pointers, the result is almost sure to be disaster.

Making the tree module typeless is a little more difficult because the tree functions must compare values in the tree nodes. However, we can pass a pointer to a comparison function written by the client as an argument to each tree function. Again, the result of passing the wrong pointer is disaster.

17.5.3 Name Clashes

Both the stack and queue modules have is_full and is_empty functions, and both the queue and tree modules have an insert function. If you wanted to add a delete function to the tree module, it would conflict with the one already in the queue module.

To coexist in one program, the names of all of these functions must be unique. However, there is strong motivation to retain the "standard" names associated with each data structure whenever possible. The solution is to compromise: choose a naming convention that is tolerable and stick with it. For example, is_queue_empty and is_stack_empty solve the problem. Their disadvantage is that the longer names are not as convenient to use, yet they do not convey any additional information.

17.5.4 Standard Libraries of ADTs

Computer science is not an old discipline, but we have certainly been at it long enough to learn everything there is to know about the behavior of stacks and queues. Then why does everyone write their own stack and queue functions? Why aren't these ADTs part of the standard library?

It is because of the three problems just discussed. The name clashes are solved easily enough, but the lack of type safety and the dangers that come from giving the client direct access to the data make it infeasible to write a library of functions that implement a stack in a general, yet safe way.

Solving this problem requires *genericity*, the ability to write a set of functions in which the types of the data have not yet been decided. This set of functions is then *instantiated*, or created, with each different type that is needed. C does not provide this capability, but we can use the #define mechanism to approximate it.

Program 17.10a contains a #define whose body is the entire implementation of an arrayed stack. The arguments to the #define are the type of value to be stored, a suffix, and the array size to use. The suffix is appended to each of the names defined by the implementation to avoid name clashes.

Program 17.10b uses the declaration in Program 17.10a to create two stacks, one that holds up to ten integers and another that holds up to five floats. When each #define is expanded, a new set of stack routines is created to manipulate the proper type of data. However, if two stacks of integers were needed, two sets of identical functions would be created.

We solve this problem by rewriting Program 17.10a as three separate macros: one to declare the interface, one to create the functions that manipulate the data, and one to create the data. When the first stack of integers is needed, all three macros are used. Additional stacks of integers are created by repeatedly invoking the last macro. The interface to the stack must also be changed. The functions must take an additional argument that specifies the stack to manipulate. These modifications are the subject of a programming exercise.

This technique makes it possible to create a library of generic abstract data types. However, the added flexiblity comes with a price. The user has several new responsibilities. He or she must now:

1. decide on a naming convention to avoid name clashes among stacks of different types,

2. be sure to create exactly one set of stack routines for each different type,

3. be sure to use the proper name (for example, push_int versus push_float) when accessing a stack,

```
/*
** GENERIC implementation of a stack with a static array.  The array
** size is given as one of the arguments when the stack is
** instantiated.
*/
#include <assert.h>

#define GENERIC_STACK( STACK_TYPE, SUFFIX, STACK_SIZE )              \
                                                                     \
        static  STACK_TYPE      stack##SUFFIX[ STACK_SIZE ];         \
        static  int             top_element##SUFFIX = -1;            \
                                                                     \
        int                                                          \
        is_empty##SUFFIX( void )                                     \
        {                                                            \
                return top_element##SUFFIX == -1;                    \
        }                                                            \
                                                                     \
        int                                                          \
        is_full##SUFFIX( void )                                      \
        {                                                            \
                return top_element##SUFFIX == STACK_SIZE - 1;        \
        }                                                            \
                                                                     \
        void                                                         \
        push##SUFFIX( STACK_TYPE value )                             \
        {                                                            \
                assert( !is_full##SUFFIX() );                        \
                top_element##SUFFIX += 1;                            \
                stack##SUFFIX[ top_element##SUFFIX ] = value;        \
        }                                                            \
                                                                     \
        void                                                         \
        pop##SUFFIX( void )                                          \
        {                                                            \
                assert( !is_empty##SUFFIX() );                       \
                top_element##SUFFIX -= 1;                            \
        }                                                            \
                                                                     \
        STACK_TYPE top##SUFFIX( void )                               \
        {                                                            \
                assert( !is_empty##SUFFIX() );                       \
                return stack##SUFFIX[ top_element##SUFFIX ];         \
        }
```

Program 17.10a   Generic arrayed stack   g_stack.h

```
/*
** A client that uses the generic stack module to create two stacks
** holding different types of data.
*/
#include <stdlib.h>
#include <stdio.h>
#include "g_stack.h"

/*
**          Create two stacks, one of integers and one of floats.
*/
GENERIC_STACK( int, _int, 10 )
GENERIC_STACK( float, _float, 5 )

int
main()
{
        /*
        ** Push several values on each stack.
        */
        push_int( 5 );
        push_int( 22 );
        push_int( 15 );
        push_float( 25.3 );
        push_float( -40.5 );

        /*
        ** Empty the integer stack and print the values.
        */
        while( !is_empty_int() ){
                printf( "Popping %d\n", top_int() );
                pop_int();
        }

        /*
        ** Empty the float stack and print the values.
        */
        while( !is_empty_float() ){
                printf( "Popping %f\n", top_float() );
                pop_float();
        }

        return EXIT_SUCCESS;
}
```

Program 17.10b   Using the generic arrayed stack   g_client.c

4.   be sure to pass the proper stack data structure to the functions.

It is not surprising that genericity is hard to implement in C, because the language was designed long before the notion was described. Genericity is one of the problems addressed more completely by Object-Oriented languages.

17.6 Summary

There are three techniques for obtaining memory for ADTs: a static array, a dynamically allocated array, and a dynamically allocated linked structure. The static array imposes a predetermined, fixed size on the structure. The size of a dynamic array can be computed at run time, and the array can be reallocated if needed. A linked structure doesn't impose any limit on the maximum number of values.

A stack is a last-in, first-out structure. Its interface provides functions to push a new value on the stack and pop a value off the stack. An alternate interface adds a third function which returns the top value on the stack without popping it. A stack is easily implemented with an array by using a variable, initialized to -1, to remember the subscript of the top element. To push a new value on the stack, the variable is incremented and the value is then stored in the array. When popping a value, the variable is decremented after accessing the value in the array. Two additional functions are required to use a dynamically allocated stack. One creates the stack to a specified size, and the other destroys it. A singly linked list also works well for implementing a stack. Values are pushed by inserting them at the beginning of the list, and the stack is popped by removing the first element.

A queue is a first-in, first-out structure. Its interface provides functions to insert a new value and to delete an existing value. Because of the ordering a queue imposes on its elements, a circular array is a more appropriate implemention than an ordinary array. When a variable used as a subscript for a circular array is incremented past the end of the array, its value wraps around to zero. To determine when the array is full, you may use a variable that counts the number of inserted values. To use the front and rear pointers of the queue to detect this condition, there must always be at least one empty element in the array.

A binary search tree (BST) is a structure that is either empty or has a value and up to two children, called left and right, which are also BSTs. The value in a node of a BST is greater than all the values contained in its left subtree, and less than all the values in its right subtree. Because of this ordering, it is very efficient to search for a value in a BST—if a node does not contain the desired value, you can always tell which of its subtrees to examine. To insert a value into a BST, you first search for it. If the value is not found, insert it at the location where the search failed. When removing a value from a BST, care must be taken not to disconnect its subtrees from the tree. A tree is traversed by processing all of its nodes in some order. There are four common orderings. A pre-order traversal processes the node, and then traverses its left and right subtrees. An in-order traversal traverses the left subtree, processes the node, and then traverses the right subtree. A post-order traversal traverses the left and right subtrees, and then processes the node. A breadth-first traversal processes the nodes left to right on each level from the root down to the leaves. An array can be used to implement a BST, but will waste a lot of memory if the tree is unbalanced. A linked BST avoids this waste.

There are three problems associated with straightforward implementations of these ADTs. First, they only allow you to have one stack, queue, or tree. This problem is solved by separating the allocation of the structure from the functions that manipulate it, however the resulting loss of encapsulation increases the chances of errors. The second problem is the inability to declare stacks, queues, or trees of different types. Creating a separate copy of the ADT functions for each type makes maintaining the code more difficult. A better approach is to implement the code with a #define which is then expanded with each required type, though you must choose a naming convention carefully. Another approach is to make the ADT typeless by casting the values to be stored to void *. A drawback of this strategy is the loss of type checking. The third problem is avoiding name clashes among the different ADTs and among the versions of a single ADT that handle different types of data. Generic implementations of the ADTs can be created, though they require the user to accept more responsibility for their correct use.

17.7 Summary of Cautions

1. Using assertions to check for memory allocations is dangerous (page 502).

2. The calculations for an arrayed binary tree assume that the array subscripts begin at one (page 518).

3. Encapsulating the data in the module that services it prevents the client from accessing the data incorrectly (page 526).

4. There is no type checking with typeless functions, so be careful to pass the correct type of data (page 527).

17.8 Summary of Programming Tips

1. Avoiding functions with side effects makes the program easier to understand (page 494).

2. The interface for a module should not divulge details of the implementation (page 494).

3. Parameterizing the data type makes it easier to change (page 495).

4. Only the advertised interface for a module should be public (page 496).

5. Use assertions to guard against illegal operations (page 498).

6. Making different implementations adhere to a common interface makes modules more interchangeable (page 499).

7. Reuse existing code rather than rewriting it (page 505).

8. Iteration is more efficient than tail recursion (page 513).

17.9 Questions

1. Suppose you have a program that reads a series of names but must print them in the opposite order. What ADT is most appropriate for this task?

2. Which ADT would be most appropriate for organizing the milk on a supermarket shelf? Consider what happens both when customers buy milk and when the supermarket gets a new shipment of milk.

3. In the traditional interface for a stack, the pop function returns the value that it removed from the stack. Would it be possible to provide both interfaces in one module?

4. Would the stack module be significantly more powerful if it had an empty function that removed all values from the stack?

5. The variable top_element is incremented *before* storing the value in push but is decremented *after* returning the value in pop. What would happen if the order of these operations was reversed?

6. What would happen if all of the assertions were removed from the stack module that uses a static array?

7. In the linked implementation of a stack, why does the destroy_stack function pop each of the values on the stack one by one?

8. The pop function in the linked stack implementation declares a local variable called first_node. Can this variable be omitted?

9. When a circular array is full, the `front` and `rear` values have the same relationship to one another as they do when the array is empty. However, full and empty are different states. Conceptually, how can this situation happen?

10. Which solution is better for solving the problem of detecting a full circular array: (1) always leaving one array element unused, or (2) a separate variable to count the number of values in the array?

11. Write the statements that compute the number of values on a queue from the values of `front` and `rear`.

12. Which is better suited for the storage of a queue, a singly linked list or a doubly linked list?

13. Draw the tree that would result from inserting the following values, in this order, into a binary search tree: 20, 15, 18, 32, 5, 91, -4, 76, 33, 41, 34, 21, 90.

14. Inserting values into a binary search tree in either ascending or descending order produces a tree that is unbalanced. What is the efficiency of searching such a tree for a value?

15. In what order would the nodes of the following tree be processed using a preorder traversal? An in-order traversal? A post-order traversal? A breadth-first traversal?

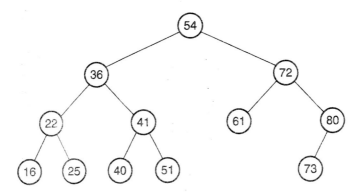

16. Rewrite the `do_pre_order_traversal` function to perform an in-order tree traversal.

17. Rewrite the `do_pre_order_traversal` function to perform a post-order tree traversal.

18. Which traversal of a binary search tree will visit the nodes in ascending order of their values? Which will visit the nodes in descending order?

19. The `destroy_tree` function deletes a tree by freeing all of the memory

allocated for the nodes in the tree, which means that all of the tree nodes must be processed in a particular order. What type of traversal would be most appropriate for this task?

17.10 Programming Exercises

★ 1. Add a `resize_stack` function to the dynamically allocated stack module. The function takes one argument: the new size for the stack.

★★ 2. Convert the queue module to use dynamic array allocation and add a `resize_queue` function (similar to the one described in Programming Exercise 1) to it.

⌂ ★★★ 3. Convert the queue module to use linked list allocation.

★★★ 4. The stack, queue, and tree modules would be more useful if they could handle more than one stack, queue, or tree. Change the dynamically arrayed stack module so that it can manage up to ten separate stacks. You will have to change the interfaces to the stack functions to accept another argument—the index of the desired stack.

★★ 5. Write a function to count the number of nodes in a binary search tree. You may use whichever implementation you prefer.

⌂ ★★★ 6. Write a function to do a breadth-first traversal of the arrayed binary search tree. Use the following algorithm:

> *Add the root node to a queue.*
> *While the queue is not empty:*
> *Remove the first node from the queue and process it.*
> *Add all of the node's children to the queue.*

★★★★ 7. Write a function to check whether a binary tree is in fact a binary search tree. You may use whichever implementation you prefer.

★★★★★ 8. Write a function for the arrayed tree module that deletes a value from the tree. If the value to be deleted is not found in the tree, the function may abort the program.

★★ 9. Write a `destroy_tree` function for the linked implementation of the binary search tree. The function should free all of the memory used in the tree.

★★★★★ 10. Write a function for the linked tree module that deletes a value from the tree. If the value to be deleted is not found in the tree, the function may abort the program.

★★★★ 11. Rewrite the #define in Program 17.10a as three separate #defines.

    a.   one to declare the stack interface

    b.   one to create the implementation

    c.   one to create the data for a stack

You must change the interface for the stack to pass the stack data as an explicit argument. (It will be more convenient to package the stack data into a structure.) These modifications will let a single set of stack functions manipulate any stack of the corresponding type.

18

Runtime Environment

In this chapter, we will examine the assembly language code produced by one specific compiler for one specific computer in order to learn several interesting things about the runtime environment for this implementation. Among the questions that will be answered are, "What are the limits of my runtime environment?" and "How do I get C and assembly language programs to work together?"

18.1 Determining the Runtime Environment

Your compiler or environment is sure to be different than the one we look at here, so you will need to perform experiments like these yourself in order to find out how things work on your machine.

The first step is obtaining an assembly language listing from your compiler. On UNIX systems, the -s compiler option causes the compiler to write the assembly language for each source file in a file whose name has the .s suffix. The Borland compilers also support this option, though they use the .asm suffix. Consult the documentation for specific details of other systems.

You will also need to read the assembly language code for your machine. It is not necessary to be a skillful assembly language programmer, but you will need a basic understanding of what each instruction is doing and how to interpret addressing modes. A manual describing your computer's instruction set is an excellent reference for this task.

Assembly language is not taught in this chapter because that is not the point of this book. Your assembly language is likely to differ from this one anyway. Nevertheless, if you compile the test program, the explanations of my machine's assembly language may help you decipher yours, because both assembly programs implement the same source code.

```
/*
** Program to determine the C runtime environment.
*/

/*
** Static initialization
*/
int     static_variable = 5;

void
f()
{
        register int    i1, i2, i3, i4, i5,
                        i6, i7, i8, i9, i10;
        register char   *c1, *c2, *c3, *c4, *c5,
                        *c6, *c7, *c8, *c9, *c10;
        extern  int     a_very_long_name_to_see_how_long_they_can_be;
        double  dbl;
        int     func_ret_int();
        double  func_ret_double();
        char    *func_ret_char_ptr();

        /*
        ** Maximum number of register variables.
        */
        i1 = 1; i2 = 2; i3 = 3; i4 = 4; i5 = 5;
        i6 = 6; i7 = 7; i8 = 8; i9 = 9; i10 = 10;
        c1 = (char *)110; c2 = (char *)120;
        c3 = (char *)130; c4 = (char *)140;
        c5 = (char *)150; c6 = (char *)160;
        c7 = (char *)170; c8 = (char *)180;
        c9 = (char *)190; c10 = (char *)200;

        /*
        ** External names
        */
        a_very_long_name_to_see_how_long_they_can_be = 1;

        /*
        ** Function calling/returning protocol, stack frame
        */
        i2 = func_ret_int( 10, i1, i10 );
        dbl = func_ret_double();
        c1 = func_ret_char_ptr( c1 );
}
```

Program 18.1   Test program

continued . . .

```
int
func_ret_int( int a, int b, register int c )
{
        int     d;

        d = b - 6;
        return a + b + c;
}

double
func_ret_double()
{
        return 3.14;
}

char *
func_ret_char_ptr( char *cp )
{
        return cp + 1;
}
```

Program 18.1   Test program   runtime.c

18.1.1 Test Program

So let's look at Program 18.1, the test program. It contains various pieces of code whose implementations are of interest. The program doesn't accomplish anything useful, but it doesn't have to—all that we want to do is to look at the assembly code the compiler produces for it. If there are other aspects of your runtime environment you wish to investigate, modify the program to include examples of them.

The assembly code in Program 18.2 was produced for a computer using a microprocessor from the Motorola 68000 family. I have edited this code to make it more clear and to remove irrelevant declarations.

This is a long program. Like most compiler output, it contains no comments to help the reader. But don't let it intimidate you! I'll explain most of it line by line in a series of examples that show a fragment of C code followed by the assembly code produced from it. The complete listing is given only as a reference so you can see how all of the little pieces in the examples fit together.

```
        .data
        .even
        .globl  _static_variable
_static_variable:
        .long   5
        .text

        .globl  _f
_f:     link    a6,#-88
        moveml  #0x3cfc,sp@
        moveq   #1,d7
        moveq   #2,d6
        moveq   #3,d5
        moveq   #4,d4
        moveq   #5,d3
        moveq   #6,d2
        movl    #7,a6@(-4)
        movl    #8,a6@(-8)
        movl    #9,a6@(-12)
        movl    #10,a6@(-16)
        movl    #110,a5
        movl    #120,a4
        movl    #130,a3
        movl    #140,a2
        movl    #150,a6@(-20)
        movl    #160,a6@(-24)
        movl    #170,a6@(-28)
        movl    #180,a6@(-32)
        movl    #190,a6@(-36)
        movl    #200,a6@(-40)
        movl    #1,_a_very_long_name_to_see_how_long_they_can_be
        movl    a6@(-16),sp@-
        movl    d7,sp@-
        pea     10
        jbsr    _func_ret_int
        lea     sp@(12),sp
        movl    d0,d6
        jbsr    _func_ret_double
        movl    d0,a6@(-48)
        movl    d1,a6@(-44)
        pea     a5@
        jbsr    _func_ret_char_ptr
        addqw   #4,sp
        movl    d0,a5
        moveml  a6@(-88),#0x3cfc
```

Program 18.2   Assembly language code for test program   *continued . . .*

```
            unlk    a6
            rts

            .globl  _func_ret_int
_func_ret_int:
            link    a6,#-8
            moveml  #0x80,sp@
            movl    a6@(16),d7
            movl    a6@(12),d0
            subql   #6,d0
            movl    d0,a6@(-4)
            movl    a6@(8),d0
            addl    a6@(12),d0
            addl    d7,d0
            moveml  a6@(-8),#0x80
            unlk    a6
            rts

            .globl  _func_ret_double
_func_ret_double:
            link    a6,#0
            moveml  #0,sp@
            movl    L2000000,d0
            movl    L2000000+4,d1
            unlk    a6
            rts
L2000000:           .long   0x40091eb8,0x51eb851f

            .globl  _func_ret_char_ptr
_func_ret_char_ptr:
            link    a6,#0
            moveml  #0,sp@
            movl    a6@(8),d0
            addql   #1,d0
            unlk    a6
            rts
```

Program 18.2   Assembly language code for test program   runtime.s

18.1.2 Static Variables and Initialization

The first thing the test program did was to declare and initialize a variable in static memory.

```
/*
** Static initialization
*/
int      static_variable = 5;
```

```
        .data
        .even
        .globl _static_variable
_static_variable:
        .long    5
```

The assembly code begins with directives to enter the data section of the program and make sure that the variable begins at an even address. The boundary alignment is a requirement of the 68000. Then the variable name is declared global. Notice that the name begins with an underscore. Many (but not all) C implementations add an underscore to the beginning of external names declared in the C code to prevent these names from conflicting with names used in various library routines. Finally, space is created for the variable, and it is initialized with the proper value.

18.1.3 The Stack Frame

The function f begins next. There are three parts to a function: the *prologue*, the *body*, and the *epilogue*. The prologue of a function does the work needed to start up a function, such as reserving memory on the stack for local variables. The epilogue takes care of cleaning up the stack just before the function returns. The body of the function, of course, is where the useful work is performed.

```
void
f()
{
        register int    i1, i2, i3, i4, i5,
                        i6, i7, i8, i9, i10;
        register char   *c1, *c2, *c3, *c4, *c5,
                        *c6, *c7, *c8, *c9, *c10;
        extern   int    a_very_long_name_to_see_...
        double  dbl;
        int     func_ret_int( );
        double  func_ret_double();
        char    *func_ret_char_ptr( );
```

```
        .text
```

```
            .globl   _f
_f:         link     a6,#-88
            moveml   #0x3cfc,sp@
```

These instructions begin with a directive to enter the code (text) segment of the program, followed by a global declaration for the function name. Note once again the underscore added to the front of the name. The first executable instruction begins to construct the *stack frame* for this function. The stack frame is the area on the stack that the function will use for storage of variables and other values. The link instruction will be explained in detail later; all that is important now is that it reserves 88 bytes of space on the stack for storage of local variables and other values.

The last instruction in this sequence writes copies of the values in selected registers to the stack. The 68000 has eight registers for manipulating data, called d0 through d7, and eight more registers for manipulating addresses, called a0 through a7. The value 0x3cfc indicates that registers d2 through d7 and a2 through a5 are to be stored; these are the "other values" mentioned earlier. It will become clear shortly why these particular registers were saved.

The local variable declarations and function prototypes don't produce any assembly code. Had any local variables been initialized in its declaration, instructions would appear here to perform the assignment.

18.1.4 Register Variables

The body of the function comes next. The purpose of this part of the test program is to determine how many variables can be stored in registers. It declares a lot of register variables and initializes each of them with a different value. The assembly code answers the question by showing where each value was stored.

```
/*
** Maximum number of register variables.
*/
i1 = 1; i2 = 2; i3 = 3; i4 = 4; i5 = 5;
i6 = 6; i7 = 7; i8 = 8; i9 = 9; i10 = 10;
c1 = (char *)110; c2 = (char *)120;
c3 = (char *)130; c4 = (char *)140;
c5 = (char *)150; c6 = (char *)160;
c7 = (char *)170; c8 = (char *)180;
c9 = (char *)190; c10 = (char *)200;
```

```
moveq   #1,d7
```

```
moveq    #2,d6
moveq    #3,d5
moveq    #4,d4
moveq    #5,d3
moveq    #6,d2
movl     #7,a6@(-4)
movl     #8,a6@(-8)
movl     #9,a6@(-12)
movl     #10,a6@(-16)
movl     #110,a5
movl     #120,a4
movl     #130,a3
movl     #140,a2
movl     #150,a6@(-20)
movl     #160,a6@(-24)
movl     #170,a6@(-28)
movl     #180,a6@(-32)
movl     #190,a6@(-36)
movl     #200,a6@(-40)
```

The integer variables are initialized first. Notice that the values 1 through 6 are put in data registers, but 7 through 10 are put somewhere else. This code shows that up to 6 integer values may be kept in the data registers. What about data types other than integer? Some implementations will not put char variables in registers. On some machines doubles are too long to fit in a register, and other machines have special registers that are used for floating-point values. It is easy to modify the test program to discover these details.

The next several instructions initialize the pointer variables. The first 4 values go to registers, and the remaining ones are put somewhere else. Thus, this compiler allows up to 4 pointer variables to be in registers. What about other types of pointers? Again, further experimentation is needed. On many machines, though, the size of a pointer is the same no matter what it is pointing at, so you may find that any type of pointer can be stored in a register.

Where are the other variables put? The addressing mode used performs indirection and indexing. This combination works much like a subscript on an array. Register a6 is called the *frame pointer* and points to a "reference" location within the stack frame. All values in the stack frame are accessed by means of offsets from this reference location; a6@(-28) specifies an offset of -28. Notice that the offsets begin with -4 and grow by four each time. Integers and pointers on this machine occupy 4 bytes of memory each. With these offsets, you can make a map showing exactly where each variable appears on the stack relative to the frame pointer, a6.

Having seen that registers d2-d7 and a2-a5 are being used to hold register variables, it now becomes clear why those registers were saved in the function prologue. A function must save the values in any register that it intends to use for register variables so that the original values can be restored before returning to the calling function, thus preserving *its* register variables.

One last thing about register variables: Why were registers d0-d1, a0-a1, and a6-a7 not used for register variables? On this machine, a6 is used as the frame pointer and a7 is the stack pointer. (This assembly language gives it the alias sp.) A later example will show that d0 and d1 are used in returning values from functions, so they can't be used for register variables.

But there is no apparent use of a0 or a1 in this code. The obvious conclusion is that they have some purpose, but the test program did not contain any code of that type. Further experimentation is needed to answer this question.

18.1.5 Length of External Identifiers

The next test tries to determine the maximum allowable length of external identifiers. This test seems easy enough: declare and use a variable with a long name and see what happens.

```
/*
** External names
*/
a_very_long_name_to_see_how_long_they_can_be = 1;
```

```
movl    #1,a_very_long_name_to_see_how_long_they_can_be
```

It appears from this code that there isn't a limit on the length of names. More precisely, this name is within whatever limit there is. To find the limit, keep making the name longer and longer until it is truncated in the assembly program.

In fact, this test is not adequate. The final limit on external names is imposed by the linker, which may happily read long names but ignore all but the first several characters. The Standard requires external names to be significant in at least their first six characters (though differences in the case of letters might be lost). To test what the linker does, simply link the program and examine the resulting load map or name list.

18.1.6 Determining the Stack Frame Layout

The runtime stack holds data needed for each function to run, including its automatic variables and return addresses. The next few tests will determine two related things: the organization of the stack frame and the protocol for calling and returning from functions. The results show how to interface C and assembly language programs.

Passing Function Arguments

This example begins the call to a function.

```
/*
** Function calling/returning protocol, stack frame
*/
i2 = func_ret_int( 10, i1, i10 );
```

```
movl    a6@(-16),sp@-
movl    d7,sp@-
pea     10
jbsr    _func_ret_int
```

The first three instructions push the arguments to the function on the stack. The first argument that is pushed is the one stored at a6@(-16): the offsets examined earlier show that this value is the variable i10. d7 is pushed next; it contains the variable i1. The last argument is pushed differently than the others. The pea instruction simply pushes its operand on the stack, which is an efficient way to push a literal constant. Why are the arguments being pushed on the stack in the opposite order from how they appeared in the argument list? The answer will become clear shortly.

These instructions begin to create the stack frame belonging to the function that is about to be called. By tracing the instructions and keeping track of their effects, we can construct a complete picture of the stack frame. This

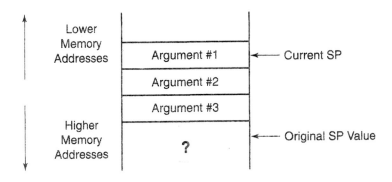

Figure 18.1   Stack frame after pushing the arguments

picture provides information that is helpful if you need to trace the execution of a C program at the assembly language level. Figure 18.1 shows what has been built so far. The diagram shows lower memory addresses at the top and higher memory addresses at the bottom. The stack grows toward lower memory addresses (upward) as values are pushed on it. The stack contents below the original stack pointer are unknown, so it is shown as a question mark.

The next instruction is a "jump subroutine:" it pushes the return address on the stack and branches to the beginning of _func_ret_int. The return address is used by the called function when it is finished to go back to where it was called. The stack now looks like Figure 18.2.

Function Prologue

Execution continues with the prologue of the called function:

```
int
func_ret_int( int a, int b, register int c )
{
        int     d;
```

```
        .globl  _func_ret_int
_func_ret_int:
        link    a6,#-8
        moveml  #0x80,sp@
        movl    a6@(16),d7
```

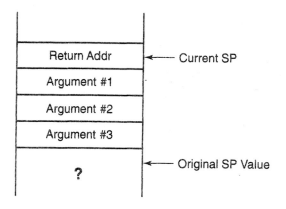

Figure 18.2   Stack frame after the jump subroutine instruction

The prologue is similar to the one examined earlier; the instructions must be examined in more detail to complete the map of the stack frame. The link instruction has several steps. First, the contents of a6 are pushed on the stack. Second, the current value in the stack pointer is copied into a6. Figure 18.3 illustrates this result.

Finally, the link instruction subtracts 8 from the stack pointer. As before, this creates the space that will hold the local variables and saved register values. The next instruction saves a single register into the stack frame; the operand 0x80 designates register d7. The register is stored at the top of the stack, which indicates that the top portion of the stack frame is where register values are saved; the remaining part of the stack frame must be where local variables are stored. Figure 18.4 shows what we know so far about the stack frame.

The last task the prologue performs is to copy a value from the stack into d7. The function declares the third argument to be a register variable, and the third argument is 16 bytes down from the frame pointer. On this machine, register arguments are passed on the stack normally and copied into a register in the function prologue. This additional instruction is overhead—if there aren't enough instructions in the function that use the argument, there won't be enough savings in speed or space to offset the overhead of copying the argument into a register.

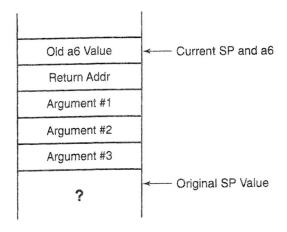

Figure 18.3   Stack frame during the link instruction

Argument Ordering on the Stack

We can now deduce why the arguments are pushed on the stack in reverse order. The called function accesses the arguments using offsets from the frame pointer. When the arguments are pushed in reverse order, the *first* argument is on *top* of the pile and its offset from the frame pointer is a constant. In fact, the offset from the frame pointer to *any* argument will be a constant value that is independent of how many arguments were pushed.

What would happen if the arguments were pushed in the opposite order? Then the offset to the first argument would depend on how many were pushed. The compiler could compute this value except for one problem—the actual number of arguments passed might be different from the number of parameters that the function expects. In this situation, the offsets would be incorrect, and when the function tried to access an argument it would not get the one it wanted.

How are extra arguments handled in the reverse-order scheme? The diagram of the stack frame shows that any extra arguments that were passed would appear below the first ones; the distance from the frame pointer to the first argument would be unchanged. Therefore, the function would access the first three arguments properly and simply ignore the extras.

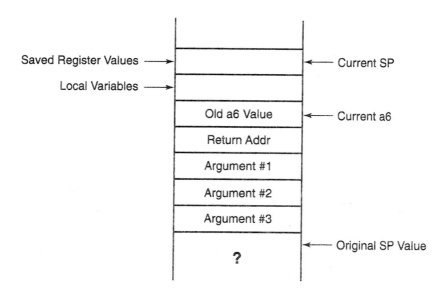

Figure 18.4   Stack frame after the `link` instruction

If the function somehow knew that there were extra arguments, on this machine it could access their values by taking the address of the last argument and incrementing this pointer. But it is better to use the stdarg.h macros, which provide a portable interface for accessing variable arguments.

Final Stack Frame Layout

The map of the stack frame *for this compiler* is now complete, and is shown in Figure 18.5.

Let's continue looking at the function:

```
d = b - 6;
return a + b + c;
}
```

```
movl    a6@(12),d0
subql   #6,d0
movl    d0,a6@(-4)
movl    a6@(8),d0
```

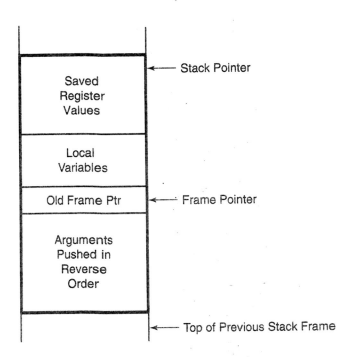

Figure 18.5   Stack frame layout

```
addl     a6@(12),d0
addl     d7,d0
moveml   a6@(-8),#0x80
unlk     a6
rts
```

The stack frame map makes it easy to determine that the first `movl` instruction copies the second argument into `d0`. The next instruction subtracts 6 from this value, and the third stores the result in the local variable `d`. `d0` is used as a "scratchpad" or temporary location for computations; this is one of the reasons it cannot be used to hold register variables.

The next three instructions evaluate the expression in the `return` statement. This value is the one we want to return to the calling function. But the result is just left in `d0`; remember this detail for later.

Function Epilogue

This function's epilogue begins with the `moveml` instruction, which restores the previously saved register value(s). Then the `unlk` (*unlink*) instruction copies the value in `a6` into the stack pointer and loads `a6` with its former value, which is popped off of the stack in the process. The effect of this action is to delete the portion of the stack frame above the return address. Finally, the `rts` instruction returns from the function by popping the return address off the stack into the program counter.

Execution now resumes in the calling program. Notice that the stack is not entirely cleaned up yet.

```
i2 = func_ret_int( 10, i1, i10 );
```

```
lea      sp@(12),sp
movl     d0,d6
```

The first instruction executed after we've returned to the calling program adds 12 to the stack pointer. The addition effectively pops the argument values off of the stack, which is now in exactly the same state that it was in before the function call began.

It is interesting that the *called* function does not remove its entire stack frame from the stack: the arguments are left for the *calling* program to remove. The reason, once again, has to do with variable argument lists. The calling function pushes the arguments on the stack, so it is the only one who knows for sure how many arguments there are. Hence, only the calling function can safely remove them.

Return Values

The epilogue did not touch d0, so it still contains the value returned by the function. The second instruction executed after returning from the function copies d0 into d6, which is the variable (i2) to which the result is assigned.

With this compiler, then, a function returns a value by leaving it in d0; the calling function gets the value from d0 after the function has returned. This protocol is the other reason that d0 is not used to hold register variables.

The next function called returns a double.

```
dbl = func_ret_double();
c1 = func_ret_char_ptr( c1 );
```

```
jbsr     _func_ret_double
movl     d0,a6@(-48)
movl     d1,a6@(-44)

pea      a5@
jbsr     _func_ret_char_ptr
addqw    #4,sp
movl     d0,a5
```

This function doesn't have any arguments, so nothing is pushed on the stack. After it returns, both d0 and d1 are stored. On this machine, doubles are 8 bytes long, too big to fit in one register. Therefore, both d0 and d1 are needed to return one of these values.

The last function call illustrates how pointer values are returned from functions: they are also passed back through d0. A different compiler might pass pointer values back through a0 or some other register. The remaining instructions in the program are the prologue for this function.

18.1.7 Expression Side Effects

In Chapter 4 I mentioned that if an expression such as

```
y + 3;
```

appeared in a program, it would be evaluated but would not affect the program because its result was not saved. A footnote then explained that it actually *could* affect the execution of the program in a subtle way.

Consider Program 18.3, which is supposed to return the value of a + b. The function computes a result but doesn't return anything because the expression was erroneously omitted from the return statement. But with this compiler, the function actually works! d0 is used to compute x, and because this

```
/*
** A function that works on some machines despite a major error.
*/
int
erroneous( int a, int b )
{
        int     x;

        /*
        ** Compute the answer, and return it
        */
        x = a + b;
        return;
}
```

Program 18.3   A function that accidentally returns the proper value   no-ret.c

expression is the last one evaluated, d0 still contains the result when the function has finished. Quite accidentally, the function returns the proper value to the calling program.

Now suppose we inserted the expression

```
a + 3;
```

before the return statement. This new computation would change d0. Even though the result of the expression is not stored in any variable, it has affected the execution of the program by changing the value that is returned by this function.

A similar problem can be caused by debugging statements. If you add the statement

```
printf( "Function returns the value %d\n", x );
```

before the return statement, the function no longer returns the correct value. Remove the debugging statement and it starts working again. It is extremely frustrating when your debugging statements change the behavior of the program!

These effects are all made possible by the original error—the omission of the expression from the return statement. This scenario may sound unlikely, but it occurred surprisingly often with old C compilers because they would not warn the programmer of a function that was supposed to return a value but did not.

18.2 Interfacing With Assembly Language

This experiment has shown everything needed to write assembly language programs that can call or be called by C programs. The relevant results for *this* environment are summarized below—*your environment surely differs in one or more ways!*

First, the name of the assembly program must follow the rules for external identifiers. On this system, it must begin with an underscore.

Second, the assembly program must follow the proper protocol for function calls and returns. There are two cases: calling a C function from an assembly language program and calling an assembly language function from a C program. To call C from assembly language:

1. If registers d0, d1, a0, or a1 contain important values, they must be saved before calling the C function, because the C function will not preserve them.

2. Any arguments to the function must be pushed on the stack in reverse order.

3. The function must be called with a "jump subroutine" type of instruction that pushes the return address on the stack.

4. When the C function returns, the assembly program must remove any arguments from the stack.

5. If a return value was expected, it will be in d0 (if the value is a double, the other half of it will be in d1).

6. Any registers that were saved before the call may now be restored.

To write an assembly program that is called from C:

1. Save any registers (other than d0, d1, a0, and a1) that you wish to modify.

2. Argument values are obtained from the stack where the calling C function pushed them.

3. If the function should return a value, it is left in d0 (in which case d0 *must not* be saved and restored).

4. Before returning, the function must remove anything it put on the stack.

It is not necessary to build a complete C-style stack frame in your assembly program. All you need to do to call a C function is to push the arguments in the right manner and clean them up when the function returns. In an assembly program called by a C function, you must access the arguments from where the C function put them.

Before you can actually write assembly functions, you will need to know the assembly language for your machine. The cursory knowledge that allowed us to figure out what an existing assembly program does is not enough for writing new programs.

Programs 18.4 and 18.5 are two examples that call assembly functions from C functions and vice versa. They are useful illustrations even though they are specific to this environment. The first example is an assembly language program that returns the sum of three integer arguments. The function does not bother completing the stack frame; it just computes the sum and returns. We would call this function from a C function in this manner:

```
sum = sum_three_values( 25, 14, -6 );
```

The next example shows a fragment of an assembly language program which has three values to print. It calls printf to do the job.

18.3 Runtime Efficiency

When is a program "too big?" On older computers, when the program grew larger than the amount of main memory, it simply would not run, thus it was "too big." Even on modern machines, a program that must be stored in *ROM* must be small enough to fit into the available memory.[57]

```
| Sum three integer arguments and return the
| total.

        .text

        .globl  _sum_three_values
_sum_three_values:
        movl    sp@(4),d0       |Get 1st arg,
        addl    sp@(8),d0       |add 2nd arg,
        addl    sp@(12),d0      |add last arg.
        rts                     |Return.
```

Program 18.4   Assembly language program that sums three integers   sum.s

---

[57] Read Only Memory (ROM) is memory that cannot be changed. It is often used to hold programs in computers dedicated to controlling some device.

```
| Need to print the three values x, y, and z.
|
        movl      z,sp@-          | Push args on the
        movl      y,sp@-          | stack in reverse
        movl      x,sp@-          | order: format, x,
        movl      #format,sp@-    | y, and z.
        jbsr      _printf         | Now call printf
        addl      #16,sp          | Clean up stack
        \&...
        .data
format: .ascii    "x = %d, y = %d, and z = %d"
        .byte     012, 0          | Newline and null
        .even
x:      .long     25
y:      .long     45
z:      .long     50
```

Program 18.5   Assembly language program that calls `printf`   printf.s

But many modern computer systems make this boundary less obvious than it once was by providing *virtual memory*. Virtual memory is implemented by the operating system, which brings the active parts of the program into memory when needed and copies inactive parts to disk, thus allowing the system to run larger programs. But the larger the program the more copying is required. So rather than being unable to run the program at all, we get a gradual reduction in performance as the program grows larger. So when is the program too big? When it runs too slowly.

The issue of execution speed is obviously related to its size. The slower the program executes, the more uncomfortable it will be to use it. It is hard to identify the point at which a program is suddenly "too slow" unless it must respond to some physical events over which it has no control. For example, a program to operate a CD player is clearly too slow if it cannot process the data as fast as it comes off of the CD.

18.3.1 Improving Efficiency

Modern optimizing compilers do a very good job of producing efficient object code from a C program. Therefore, spending time trying to make your code more efficient by making small changes to it is usually not very productive.

If a program is too large or too slow, selecting a more efficient algorithm or data structure is a much more effective way to improve the performance than playing with individual variables to see if declaring them `register` helps or not. This fact does not give you license to be sloppy in your coding, however, because poor code always makes things worse.

If a program is too large, it is easy to imagine where you might look for ways to make it smaller: the largest functions and data structures. But if a program is too slow, where do you even start to look to improve its speed? The answer is to *profile* the program, which simply means to measure how much time is spent executing each of its parts. The portions of the program that take the longest are obvious candidates for optimization. Making the most heavily used parts of the program faster is an effective use of your time.

Most UNIX systems come with profiling tools, and such tools are available for many other systems as well. Figure 18.6 is a portion of the output from one such tool. It shows the number of times each function was called and the number of seconds that were spent in that function during one execution of a particular program. The total execution time was 32.95 seconds. There are three interesting points we can learn from this list.

1. Some of the most often used functions are library functions. In this example, `malloc` and `free` head the list. You cannot change how they are implemented, but if the program was redesigned so that it did not dynamically allocate memory or did so less often, its speed could be improved by up to 25%.

2. Some functions used a lot of time because they were called a lot. Even though each individual call was quick, there were a lot of them. `_nextch_from_chrlst` is an example. Each call to this function used only about 4.3 microseconds. Because it is so short, it is unlikely that you could improve this function very much. But it is worth looking at simply because it is called so often. A few judicious `register` declarations might make a significant difference.

3. Some functions were not called often, but each call took a long time. For example, the function `_lookup_macro` averaged over 265 microseconds per call. Finding a faster algorithm to perform this task could make the program up to 7¾% faster.[58]

As a last resort, you could recode individual functions in assembly language.

---

[58] Actually there is a fourth point to be learned. `malloc` was called 20,833 times more often than `free`, so some memory has leaked!

```
Seconds   # Calls   Function Name
-------   -------   --------------------
   4.94    293426   malloc
   3.21    272593   free
   2.85    658973   _nextch_from_chrlst
   2.82    272593   _insert
   2.69    791309   _check_traverse
   2.57      9664   _lookup_macro
   1.35    372915   _append_to_chrlst
   1.23    254501   _interpolate
   1.10    302714   _next_input_char
   1.09    285031   _input_filter
   0.91    197235   demote
   0.90    272419   putfreehdr
   0.82    285031   _nextchar
   0.79      7620   _lookup_number_register
   0.77     63946   _new_character
   0.65    292822   allocate
   0.57    272594   _getfreehdr
   0.51     34374   _next_text_char
   0.46    151006   _duplicate_char
   0.41      6473   _expression
   0.37      8843   _sub_expression
   0.35     23774   _skip_white_space
   0.34    203535   _copy_interpolate
   0.32     10984   _copy_function
   0.31    133032   _duplicate_ascii_char
   0.31       604   _process_filled_text
   0.31     52627   _next_ascii_char
```

Figure 18.6   Sample profiling information

The smaller the function, the easier it is to recode. The benefit may also be greater, because the fixed overhead of the C prologue and epilogue consume a greater percentage of the execution time of small functions. Recoding larger functions in assembly language is more difficult and is therefore a less productive use of your time.

Often the profile will not tell you anything that you don't already know, but sometimes the results can be quite unexpected. The advantage of profiling is that you can be sure you are spending your time on the areas in the program that can benefit most from improvement.

18.4 Summary

Some of the tasks we've examined on this machine are accomplished in the same way in many other environments as well. For example, most environments construct some kind of stack frame in which functions store their data. The details of the frame might vary, but the basic idea is quite common.

Other tasks are likely to be different from one environment to the next. Some computers have specific hardware to keep track of function arguments, so they may be handled differently than we have seen. Other machines might pass function values back differently.

In fact, different compilers can produce very different code for the same machine. Another compiler for our test machine was able to use anywhere from 9 to 14 register variables, depending on other circumstances. Different compilers may have different stack frame conventions or use incompatible techniques for calling and returning from functions. Therefore you cannot, in general, use different compilers to compile different pieces of one program.

The best way to improve the efficiency of a program is to select better algorithms for it. The next best way to improve the execution speed is to profile the program to see where it is spending most of its time. Concentrating your optimization efforts on these portions of the program will give you the best results.

Learning about your machine's runtime environment is both useful and dangerous—useful because the knowledge you gain lets you do things you would not otherwise be able to do; dangerous because anything that depends on this knowledge is likely to impair the portability of your program. These days, with computers becoming obsolete before they reach the store shelves, the possibility of moving from one machine to another is very real, which is a strong motivation to produce portable code.

18.5 Summary of Cautions

1. The linker, not the compiler, determines the maximum length of external identifiers (page 545).
2. You cannot link programs produced by different compilers (page 559).

18.6 Summary of Programming Tips

1. Use `stdarg` to implement variable argument lists (page 550).

2. Improving the algorithm is more effective than optimizing the code (page 557).

3. Using techniques specific to one environment makes the program nonportable (page 559).

18.7 Questions

1. What does the stack frame look like for your environment?

2. What is the longest external identifier that is significant on your system?

3. How many variables will your environment store in registers? Does it make any distinction between pointer and nonpointer values?

4. How are arguments passed to functions in your environment? How are values returned from functions?

⊸ 5. If a function declares one or more of its arguments to be register variables on the machine examined in this chapter, the arguments to the function are pushed on the stack as usual and then copied into the right registers in the function prologue. It would be more efficient to pass those arguments through the registers directly. Could this argument passing technique be implemented, and if so, how could it be done?

⊸ 6. In the environment discussed, the calling function is responsible for removing the arguments that it pushed on the stack. Is it possible for the called function to perform this task instead? If not, what is required to make it possible?

7. If assembly language programs are more efficient than C programs, why not write everything in assembly language?

18.8 Programming Exercises

★ 1. Write an assembly language function for your system that takes three integer arguments and returns their sum.

★ 2. Write an assembly language program that creates three integer values and calls `printf` to print them out.

⊸ ★★ 3. Suppose the `stdarg.h` file was accidentally deleted from your system. Write a set of `stdarg` macros as described in Chapter 7.

Appendix

Selected Problem Solutions

This appendix gives solutions for selected questions and programming exercises from the chapters. In the case of programming exercises, there are often many correct solutions in addition to the ones given here.

Chapter 1 Questions

1-2. The declaration needs to be written only once, which makes it easier to maintain if modifications are needed later. Also, writing it only once eliminates the chance that additional copies are written differently from each other.

1-5. `scanf( "%d %d %s", &quantity, &price, department );`

1-8. When an array is passed as a function argument, the function has no way of knowing its size. Therefore, `gets` has no way to prevent a very long input line from overflowing the `input` array. The `fgets` function, which requires that the array size be passed as an argument, does not have this problem.

Chapter 1 Programming Exercises

1-2. By reading the input character by character rather than line by line, the line length limit is avoided. The solution would be more readable if it defined symbols TRUE and FALSE, but this technique has not yet been discussed.

```
/*
** Copy the standard input to the standard output, and number the
** output lines.
*/

#include <stdio.h>
#include <stdlib.h>
```

Solution 1.2

continued . . .

```
int
main()
{
        int     ch;
        int     line;
        int     at_beginning;

        line = 0;
        at_beginning = 1;
        /*
        ** Read characters and process them one by one.
        */
        while( (ch = getchar()) != EOF ){
                /*
                ** If we're at the beginning of a line, print the
                ** line number.
                */
                if( at_beginning == 1 ){
                        at_beginning = 0;
                        line += 1;
                        printf( "%d ", line );
                }

                /*
                ** Print the character, and check for end of line.
                */
                putchar( ch );
                if( ch == '\n' )
                        at_beginning = 1;
        }

        return EXIT_SUCCESS;
}
```

Solution 1.2   number.c

1-5. We can still break the loop when the output line is full, but otherwise the loop
must continue. We must also check how many characters are copied in each
range to prevent a NUL byte from being copied into the output buffer too early.
Here is a modification that does the job.

```
/*
** Process a line of input by concatenating the characters from
```

Solution 1.5   *continued* . . .

```
** the indicated columns.  The output line is then NUL terminated.
*/
void
rearrange( char *output, char const *input,
    int const n_columns, int const columns[] )
{
        int     col;            /* subscript for columns array */
        int     output_col;     /* output column counter */
        int     len;            /* length of input line */

        len = strlen( input );
        output_col = 0;

        /*
        ** Process each pair of column numbers.
        */
        for( col = 0; col < n_columns; col += 2 ){
                int     nchars = columns[col + 1] - columns[col] + 1;

                /*
                ** If the input line isn't this long, skip the range.
                */
                if( columns[col] >= len )
                        continue;

                /*
                ** If the output array is full, we're done.
                */
                if( output_col == MAX_INPUT - 1 )
                        break;

                /*
                ** If there isn't room in the output array, only copy
                ** what will fit.
                */
                if( output_col + nchars > MAX_INPUT - 1 )
                        nchars = MAX_INPUT - output_col - 1;

                /*
                ** See how many characters the input line has in this
                ** range.  If it is less than nchars, adjust nchars.
                */
                if( columns[col] + nchars - 1 >= len )
                        nchars = len - columns[col];
```

Solution 1.5   *continued . . .*

```
                /*
                ** Copy the relevant data.
                */
                strncpy( output + output_col, input + columns[col],
                    nchars );
                output_col += nchars;
        }

    output[output_col] = '\0';
}
```

Solution 1.5   rearran2.c

Chapter 2 Questions

2-4.   The character equivalences given assume that the implementation uses ASCII.

\40   = 32 = the space character.

\100 = 64 = '@'

\x40 = 64 = '@'

\x100   is twelve bits (though the first three are zeros). On most machines this number is too big to be stored in a character, so the result is implementation dependent.

\0123   consists of two characters: '\012' and '3'. The resulting value is implementation dependent.

\x0123 is too big to fit into a character. The resulting value is implementation dependent.

2-7.   Both. True: The language doesn't impose any rules regarding what a program ought to look like, except for preprocessor directives. False: Programs written without style are difficult or impossible to maintain, so how the program looks is extremely important for all but the most trivial of programs.

2-8.   Both programs are missing the closing brace to the `while` loop, however, it is easier to see in the second program than in the first. This example illustrates the value of indenting the statements in a function.

2-11.   When a header is changed, every file that includes it must be recompiled.

If This File Is Changed	These Must Be Recompiled
list.c	list.c
list.h	list.c, table.c, main.c
table.h	table.c, main.c

The Borland C/C++ compiler's Windows Integrated Development Environment looks for these relationships among the files and automatically compiles only those that are needed. UNIX systems have a tool called make that performs the same job, though with this tool you must construct a "makefile" that describes the relationships among the files.

Chapter 2 Programming Exercises

2-2. The program is easy to implement with a counter. However, it is not as trivial as it first seems. Try testing your solution with this input: }{

```
/*
** Check the pairing of braces in a C program.
*/

#include <stdio.h>
#include <stdlib.h>

int
main()
{
        int     ch;
        int     braces;

        braces = 0;

        /*
        ** Read the program character by character.
        */
        while( (ch = getchar()) != EOF ){
                /*
                ** Opening braces are always legal.
                */
                if( ch == '{' )
                        braces += 1;

                /*
                ** A closing brace is legal only if matched to an
                ** opening brace.
                */
                if( ch == '}' )
                        if( braces == 0 )
                                printf( "Extra closing brace!\n" );
                        else
```

Solution 2.2

continued . . .

```
                        braces -= 1;
    }

    /*
    ** No more input: make sure there aren't any opening braces
    ** that were not matched.
    */
    if( braces > 0 )
            printf( "%d unmatched opening brace(s)!\n", braces );

    return EXIT_SUCCESS;

}
```

Solution 2.2   braces.c

Chapter 3 Questions

3-3. Declare integer variables that must be a particular size with names like `int8`, `int16`, `int32`. For integers that you want to be the default size, use names like `defint8`, `defint16`, and `defint32` depending on the largest value they must hold. Then create a file called `int_sizes.h` for each machine containing `typedef`'s that select the best integer size for each of your names. On a typical 32-bit machine this file would contain:

```
typedef signed char      int8;
typedef short int        int16;
typedef int              int32;
typedef int              defint8;
typedef int              defint16;
typedef int              defint32;
```

On a typical machine with 16-bit integers, the file would contain:

```
typedef signed char      int8;
typedef int              int16;
typedef long int         int32;
typedef int              defint8;
typedef int              defint16;
typedef long int         defint32;
```

`#define`'s could also be used.

3-7. The variable `jar` is an enumerated type, but its value is actually an integer. However, the `printf` format code `%s` is used to print strings, not integers. Consequently, the output cannot be determined.

Had the format code been %d, then the output would have been

```
32
48
```

3-10. No. In any given number of bits n, there are only 2^n distinct combinations of the bit values. The only thing that changes between a signed and an unsigned value is how half of those values are interpreted. In a signed number, they are negative; in an unsigned number, they are the larger positive values.

3-11. The float has a greater range than the int, but it cannot have more distinct values without using more bits. The logic in the previous answer implies that they hold the same number of distinct values, but for most floating-point systems this answer is wrong. There are usually lots of representations for zero, and by using unnormalized fractions, lots of representations for other values as well. Thus the number of distinct values is less than that of an int.

3-21. Yes, it is possible, but you should not count on it. It is also quite possible that they will not, even if there were no intervening function calls. On some architectures, a hardware interrupt will push machine state information on the stack, which could destroy the variables.

Chapter 4 Questions

4-1. It is legal, but it doesn't affect the program's state. None of the operators involved have any side effects and the result that is computed is not assigned to any variable.

4-4. Use the empty statement.

```
if( condition )
         ;
else {
        statements
}
```

Equivalently, you can invert the condition to omit the empty then clause.

```
if( ! ( condition ) ){
        statements
}
```

4-9. There are no break statements, so both messages are printed for each even number.

```
odd
```

```
even
odd
odd
even
odd
```

4-12. It is easier to start with the most special case and work your way back to the more general cases.

```
if( year % 400 == 0 )
        leap_year = 1;
else if( year % 100 == 0 )
        leap_year = 0;
else if( year % 4 == 0 )
        leap_year = 1;
else
        leap_year = 0;
```

Chapter 4 Programming Exercises

4-1. Floating-point variables must be used, and the program should check for negative inputs.

```
/*
** Compute the square root of a number.
*/

#include <stdio.h>
#include <stdlib.h>

int
main()
{
        float    new_guess;
        float    last_guess;
        float    number;

        /*
        ** Prompt for and read the data, then check it.
        */
        printf( "Enter a number: " );
        scanf( "%f", &number );
        if( number < 0 ){
                printf( "Cannot compute the square root of a "
```

Solution 4.1

continued . . .

```
                        "negative number!\n" );
                return EXIT_FAILURE;
        }

        /*
        ** Compute approximations to the square root until they
        ** don't change any more.
        */
        new_guess = 1;
        do {
                last_guess = new_guess;
                new_guess = ( last_guess + number / last_guess ) / 2;
                printf( "%.15e\n", new_guess );
        } while( new_guess != last_guess );

        /*
        ** Print results.
        */
        printf( "Square root of %g is %g\n", number, new_guess );

        return EXIT_SUCCESS;
}
```

Solution 4.1   sqrt.c

4-4. The assignment of src to dst could be embedded within the if statement.

```
/*
** Copy exactly N characters from the string in src to the dst
** array (padding with NULs if needed).
*/
void
copy_n( char dst[], char src[], int n )
{
        int     dst_index, src_index;

        src_index = 0;

        for( dst_index = 0; dst_index < n; dst_index += 1 ){
                dst[dst_index] = src[src_index];
                if( src[src_index] != 0 )
                        src_index += 1;
        }
}
```

Solution 4.4   copy_n.c

Chapter 5 Questions

5-2. Trick question. The obvious answer is -10 (2 - 3 * 4), but in fact it is implementation dependent. The multiplication must be completed before the addition, but there isn't a rule that determines the order in which the function calls are done. Thus, the answer could be any of the following:

```
-10   ( 2 - 3 * 4 ) or ( 2 - 4 * 3 )
 -5   ( 3 - 2 * 4 ) or ( 3 - 4 * 2 )
 -2   ( 4 - 2 * 3 ) or ( 4 - 3 * 2 )
```

5-4. No, they each do precisely the same work. If you want to get picky, the `if` version might possibly be a tad longer because it has two instructions to store into `i`. However, only one of them will be executed, so there isn't any difference in speed.

5-6. The `()` operator doesn't have any side effects, but the function being called might.

Operator	Side Effect
++, --	In both prefix and postfix forms, these operators modify the L-value on which they operate.
=	And all of the other assignment operators: they all modify the L-value given as the left operand.

Chapter 5 Programming Exercises

5-1. The preferred way of converting case is with the `tolower` library function, like this:

```
/*
** Copy the standard input to the standard output, converting
** all uppercase characters to lowercase. Note: This depends
** on the fact that tolower returns its argument unchanged if
** the argument is not an uppercase letter.
*/
#include <stdio.h>
#include <ctype.h>

int
main( void )
{
        int     ch;
```

Solution 5.1a continued . . .

```
        while( (ch = getchar()) != EOF )
                putchar( tolower( ch ) );
}
```

Solution 5.1a   uc_lc.c

But we haven't discussed this function yet, so here is another approach:

```
/*
** Copy the standard input to the standard output, converting
** all uppercase characters to lowercase.
*/
#include <stdio.h>

int
main( void )
{
        int     ch;

        while( (ch = getchar()) != EOF ){
                if( ch >= 'A' && ch <= 'Z' )
                        ch += 'a' - 'A';
                putchar( ch );
        }
}
```

Solution 5.1b   uc_lc_b.c

The second program works fine on systems that use ASCII characters. But on systems with character sets in which the uppercase alphabetic characters are not contiguous, such as EBCDIC, it violates the specification by converting non-characters, which is why the library functions are preferred.

5-3.   Portability is achieved by not hard-coding a bit count. This solution uses a single bit shifted through an unsigned integer to control the loop that constructs the answer.

```
/*
** Reverse the order of the bits in an unsigned integer value.
*/

unsigned int
reverse_bits( unsigned int value )
```

Solution 5.3   *continued . . .*

```
{
        unsigned int    answer;
        unsigned int    i;

        answer = 0;

        /*
        ** Keep going as long as i is nonzero.  This makes the loop
        ** independent of the machine's word size, hence portable.
        */
        for( i = 1; i != 0; i <<= 1 ){
                /*
                ** Shift the old answer to make room for the next
                ** bit; then OR in a 1 if the value's last bit is
                ** set; then shift the value to its next bit.
                */
                answer <<= 1;
                if( value & 1 )
                        answer |= 1;
                value >>= 1;
        }

        return answer;
}
```

Solution 5.3   reverse.c

Chapter 6 Questions

6-1. The machine doesn't make this determination. The compiler creates the appropriate instructions based on the declared type of the value, and the machine blindly executes the instructions.

6-4. It is dangerous. First, the result of dereferencing a NULL pointer is implementation specific, so programs should not do it. Allowing a program to continue after such an access is unfortunate, because of the strong possibility that the program is not operating correctly.

6-6. Two things are wrong. By dereferencing the incremented value of the pointer, the first element in the array is not zeroed. In addition, the pointer is dereferenced after it has moved past the end of the array. This sets some other memory location to zero.

Note that pi was declared immediately after the array. If the compiler happened to put it in memory immediately after the array, the result is disaster. When the pointer moves past the end of the array, the last location to be set to zero will be the one holding the pointer. The pointer (now zero) will still be less than &array[ARRAY_SIZE], so the loop will continue to execute. The pointer is incremented before being dereferenced, so the next value to get zapped will be the one stored at location four (assuming four-byte integers). If the hardware does not catch this error and terminate the program, the loop will continue merrily on its way through memory, wiping out values as it goes. When the array is reached once more, the process begins again, making a rather subtle infinite loop.

Chapter 6 Programming Exercises

6-3. The key to this algorithm is to stop when the pointers meet or cross one another; otherwise, the characters will be reversed twice, with no net effect.

```c
/*
** Reverse the string contained in the argument.
*/

void
reverse_string( char *str )
{
        char    *last_char;

        /*
        ** Set last_char to point to the last character in the
        ** string.
        */
        for( last_char = str; *last_char != '\0'; last_char++ )
                ;

        last_char--;

        /*
        ** Interchange the characters that str and last_char point
        ** to, advance str and move last_char back one, and keep
        ** doing this until the two pointers meet or cross.
        */
        while( str < last_char ){
                char    temp;

                temp = *str;
                *str++ = *last_char;
                *last_char-- = temp;
        }
}
```

Solution 6.3   rev_str.c

Chapter 7 Questions

7-1.   Have the stub print out a message when it is called, perhaps printing the values it was given as arguments.

7-7.   The function assumes that it will be called with an array of exactly ten elements. If called with a larger array, it ignores the remaining elements. If called with a shorter array, it accesses values outside of the array.

7-8.   There must be some goal at which the recursion or the iteration stops, and each recursive call and each iteration of the loop must make some progress toward this goal.

Chapter 7 Programming Exercises

7-1.   The Hermite polynomials are used in physics and statistics. They are also used in programming texts as exercises in recursion.

```c
/*
** Compute the value of a Hermite polynomial
**
**      Inputs:
**              n, x: identifying values
**
**      Output:
**              value of polynomial (return value)
*/

int
hermite( int n, int x )
{
        /*
        ** Do special cases where no recursion is required.
        */
        if( n <= 0 )
                return 1;
        if( n == 1 )
                return 2 * x;

        /*
        ** Otherwise, recursively compute value.
        */
        return 2 * x * hermite( n - 1, x ) -
            2 * ( n - 1 ) * hermite( n - 2, x );
}
```

Solution 7.1   hermite.c

7-3.   This should be written iteratively, not recursively.

```
/*
** Convert a string of digits to an integer.
*/

int
ascii_to_integer( char *string )
{
        int     value;
        int     digit;

        value = 0;

        /*
        ** Convert digits of the string one by one.
        */
        while( *string >= '0' && *string <= '9' ){
                value *= 10;
                value += *string - '0';
        }

        /*
        ** Error check: if we stopped because of a nondigit, set the
        ** result to zero.
        */
        if( *string != '\0' )
                value = 0;

        return value;
}
```

Solution 7.3   atoi.c

Chapter 8 Questions

8-1.   The answers for two of the expressions cannot be determined because we don't
       know where the compiler chose to store ip.

ints	100	ip	112
ints[4]	50	ip[4]	80
ints + 4	116	ip + 4	128
*ints + 4	14	*ip + 4;	44
*(ints + 4)	50	*(ip + 4)	80
ints[-2]	illegal	ip[-2]	20
&ints	100	&ip	can't tell

&ints[4]	116	&ip[4]	128
&ints + 4	116	&ip + 4	can't tell
&ints[-2]	illegal	&ip[-2]	104

8-5. It is often true that 80% of a program's run time is spent executing 20% of its code. The efficiency of statements in the other 80% of the code is not significant, so the use of pointers is not justified by the gain in efficiency.

8-8. In the first assignment, the compiler thinks a is a pointer variable, so it will get the pointer value stored there, add 12 (3 scaled by the size of an integer), and then apply indirection to the result. But a is actually where the array of characters begins, so the value obtained as the "pointer" will be the concatenated values of the first four characters in the array. The value 12 is added to it, and the indirection interprets the result as an address. It either fetches the contents of some random location in memory, or it causes the program to abort with some sort of addressing fault.

In the second assignment, the compiler thinks b is the name of an array, so it adds 12 (the scaled result of 3) to the address where b is stored, and the indirection obtains the value found there. In fact, b is a pointer variable, so the value fetched from three words further in memory is from some other, random variable. This question illustrates that pointers and arrays, while related, are definitely not the same.

8-12. When performing any operation that accesses the elements in the order in which they appear in memory. For example, initializing an array, reading or writing more than one element of an array, and flattening an array by incrementing a pointer to access its underlying memory all qualify.

8-17. The first parameter is a scalar, so the function gets a copy of the value. Changes made to the copy do not affect the original argument, so the const keyword is not what prevents the original argument from being modified.

The second parameter is actually a pointer to an integer. The pointer is a copy and can be modified without affecting the original argument, but the function could conceivably use indirection on the pointer to modify one of the caller's values. The const keyword prevents this modification.

Chapter 8 Programming Exercises

8-2. Because the table is fairly short, a series of if statements could be used; we use a loop instead, as that works both for short and long tables. The table (similar to those shown in the tax instruction booklet) shows many values more than once in order to make the instructions more clear. The solution given does not store these redundant values. Note that the data are declared static to prevent client programs from accessing it directly. The program would be better if the data were stored in structures rather than arrays, but we haven't learned about structures yet.

```
/*
** Compute the 1995 U.S. federal income tax for a single taxpayer.
*/

#include <float.h>

static  double  income_limits[]
        = { 0,    23350,   56550,    117950,  256500,       DBL_MAX };
static  float   base_tax[]
        = { 0,    3502.5, 12798.5, 31832.5, 81710.5 };
static  float   percentage[]
        = { .15, .28,      .31,      .36,      .396 };

double
single_tax( double income )
{
        int     category;

        /*
        ** Find the correct income category.  The DBL_MAX added to
        ** the end of this list guarantees that the loop will not
        ** go too far.
        */
        for( category = 1;
            income >= income_limits[ category ];
            category += 1 )
                ;
        category -= 1;

        /*
        ** Compute the tax.
        */
        return base_tax[ category ] + percentage[ category ] *
            ( income - income_limits[ category ] );
}
```

Solution 8.2   sing_tax.c

8-5. Considering the work it does, the program is quite compact. Because it is independent of the matrix size, subscripts cannot be used in the function—this program is a good exercise in using pointers. However, it is technically illegal because it flattens the arrays.

```
/*
** Multiply two matrices together.
*/

void
matrix_multiply( int *m1, int *m2, register int *r,
    int x, int y, int z )
{
        register int    *m1p;
        register int    *m2p;
        register int    k;
        int      row;
        int      column;


        /*
        ** The outer two loops go through the solution matrix element
        ** by element.  Because this is done in storage order, we
        ** can access these elements using indirection on r.
        */
        for( row = 0; row < x; row += 1 ){
                for( column = 0; column < z; column += 1 ){
                        /*
                        ** Compute one value in the result.  This is
                        ** done by getting pointers to the proper
                        ** elements in m1 and m2, and then advancing
                        ** them as we go through the loop.
                        */
                        m1p = m1 + row * y;
                        m2p = m2 + column;
                        *r = 0;

                        for( k = 0; k < y; k += 1 ){
                                *r += *m1p * *m2p;
                                m1p += 1;
                                m2p += z;
                        }

                        /*
                        ** Advance r to point to the next element.
                        */
                        r++;
                }
        }
}
```

Solution 8.5   matmult.c

Chapter 9 Questions

9-1. This question is arguable (though I do have a conclusion). The efficiency of manipulating character arrays and the flexibility in their access are advantages of the existing state of affairs. Disadvantages include the possibility of error: overflowing an array, using a subscript to access beyond the end of a string, the inability to resize an array holding a string, and so forth.

My conclusion is drawn from modern, object-oriented technologies. String classes invariably include complete error checking, dynamic memory allocation for the string contents, and other such safeguards. These features all exact a penalty in efficiency. But it doesn't make any difference how efficient a program is if it does not work, and modern software projects tend to be much larger than those common when C was designed.

Therefore, while the lack of an explicit string type was probably seen as an advantage years ago, the dangers inherent in this approach justify the implementation of advanced, comprehensive string classes in more modern languages. The same advantages can be achieved by C programmers willing to use strings with discipline.

9-4. Use one of the memory library functions:

```
memcpy( y, x, 50 );
```

The important thing is to not use any of the `str---` functions, because they would stop at the first NUL byte. It is more complicated to write your own loop, and only rarely is it more efficient to do so.

9-8. If the buffer contains a string, `memchr` will look in memory starting at the beginning of `buffer` for the first byte that contains the value zero and will return a pointer to that byte. Subtracting `buffer` from this pointer gives the length of the string stored in the buffer. `strlen` does exactly the same thing, although the value returned by `strlen` will be unsigned (`size_t`) and the result of the pointer subtraction will be signed (`ptrdiff_t`).

However, if the data in the buffer is not NUL-terminated, `memchr` will return the NULL pointer. Subtracting `buffer` from this value yields a meaningless result. `strlen`, on the other hand, continues looking past the end of the array until it finally finds a NUL byte.

Although the same result could be obtained by using `strlen`, in general it is not possible to search for the NUL byte with the string functions because that value terminates the string. If this byte is the one you want to locate, use the memory functions instead.

Chapter 9 Programming Exercises

9-2. It is unfortunate that the standard library does not include this function!

```
/*
** Safe string length.  Returns the length of a string that
** is possibly not NUL-terminated.  'size' is the length of the
** buffer in which this string is stored.
*/

#include <string.h>
#include <stddef.h>

size_t
my_strnlen( char const *string, int size )
{
        register size_t length;

        for( length = 0; length < size; length += 1 )
                if( *string++ == '\0' )
                        break;

        return length;
}
```

Solution 9.2   mstrnlen.c

9-6. There are two approaches to this problem. First, the simple but inefficient approach.

```
/*
** String copy that returns a pointer to the end
** of the destination argument.  (Version 1)
*/

#include <string.h>

char *
my_strcpy_end( char *dst, char const *src )
{
        strcpy( dst, src );

        return dst + strlen( dst );
}
```

Solution 9.2a   mstrcpe1.c

The problem with this solution is that the final call to `strlen` consumes at least as much time as we might expect to save on a subsequent concatenation.

The second approach avoids the library routines. The `register` declarations are an attempt to improve the efficiency of the function.

```
/*
** String copy that returns a pointer to the end
** of the destination argument, without using any
** of the library string routines.  (Version 2)
*/

#include <string.h>

char *
my_strcpy_end( register char *dst, register char const *src )
{
        while( ( *dst++ = *src++ ) != '\0' )
                ;

        return dst - 1;
}
```

Solution 9.2b   mstrcpe2.c

The problem with this second solution is that it does not exploit the added efficiency of machines that implement special string handling instructions.

9-11. The buffer array is 101 bytes long to hold 100 bytes of input plus a terminating NUL byte. `strtok` is used to extract the words one by one.

```
/*
** Count the number of times the word "the" appears in the standard
** input.  Case is important, and the words in the input are
** separated from each other by one or more white space characters.
*/

#include <stdio.h>
#include <string.h>
#include <stdlib.h>

char    const   whitespace[] = " \n\r\f\t\v";

int
main()
```

Solution 9.11   *continued . . .*

```
{
        char    buffer[101];
        int     count;

        count = 0;

        /*
        ** Read lines until EOF is found.
        */
        while( gets( buffer ) ){
                char    *word;

                /*
                ** Extract words from the buffer one by one
                ** until there are no more.
                */
                for( word = strtok( buffer, whitespace );
                    word != NULL;
                    word = strtok( NULL, whitespace ) ){
                            if( strcmp( word, "the" ) == 0 )
                                    count += 1;

                }

        }

        printf( "%d\n", count );

        return EXIT_SUCCESS;

}
```

Solution 9.11   the.c

9-15.   Although not stated in the specification, the function checks both arguments to
        ensure that they are not NULL. The file stdio.h is included for the definition
        of NULL. If this test passes, we can only assume that the input string is prop-
        erly terminated.

```
/*
** Convert the digit string 'src' to dollars-and-cents form and store
** it in 'dst'.
*/

#include <stdio.h>

void
```

Solution 9.15   *continued . . .*

```
dollars( register char *dst, register char const *src )
{
        int     len;

        if( dst == NULL || src == NULL )
                return;

        *dst++ = '$';
        len = strlen( src );

        /*
        ** If digit string is long enough, copy the digits that will
        ** be on the left of the decimal point, putting in commas
        ** where appropriate.  If the string is shorter than 3
        ** digits, force a '0' into dst ahead of the '.' .
        */
        if( len >= 3 ){
                int     i;

                for( i = len - 2; i > 0; ){
                        *dst++ = *src++;
                        if( --i > 0 && i % 3 == 0 )
                                *dst++ = ',';
                }
        } else
                *dst++ = '0';

        /*
        ** Store the decimal point, and then store the remaining
        ** digits from 'src'.  If 'src' had fewer than two digits,
        ** force in '0's instead.  Then NUL terminate 'dst'.
        */
        *dst++ = '.';
        *dst++ = len < 2 ? '0' : *src++;
        *dst++ = len < 1 ? '0' : *src;
        *dst = 0;
}
```

Solution 9.15   dollars.c

Chapter 10 Questions

10-2.   A structure is a scalar. Like any other scalar, when the name of a structure is
        used as an R-value in an expression it refers to the values stored in the struc-
        ture. When used as an L-value, the name refers to the place in which the
        structure is stored. When an array name is used as an R-value in an

expression, however, its value is a pointer to the first element in the array. Because its value is a constant pointer, an array name cannot be used as an L-value.

10-7.   One answer cannot be determined because we don't know where the compiler chose to store np.

Expression	Value
nodes	200
nodes.a	illegal
nodes[3].a	12
nodes[3].c	200
nodes[3].c->a	5
*nodes	{5, nodes+3, NULL}
*nodes.a	illegal
(*nodes).a	5
nodes->a	5
nodes[3].b->b	248
*nodes[3].b->b	{18, nodes+12, nodes+1 }
&nodes	200
&nodes[3].a	236
&nodes[3].c	244
&nodes[3].c->a	200
&nodes->a	200
np	224
np->a	22
np->c->c->a	15
npp	216
npp->a	illegal
*npp	248
**npp	{18, nodes+2, nodes+1}
*npp->a	illegal
(*npp)->a	18
&np	don't know
&np->a	224
&np->c->c->a	212

10-11.   x should be declared an integer (or an unsigned integer), and masking and shifting are used to store the proper values. Translating each statement individually gives this code:

```
x &= 0x0fff;
x |= ( aaa & 0xf ) << 12;
x &= 0xf00f;
x |= ( bbb & 0xff ) << 4;
x &= 0xfff1;
x |= ( ccc & 0x7 ) << 1;
x &= 0xfffe;
```

```
x |= ( dddd & 0x1 );
```

If all you care about is the final result, the following code is more efficient:

```
x = ( aaa & 0xf ) << 12 | \
    ( bbb & 0xff ) << 4 | \
    ( ccc & 0x7 ) << 1 | \
    ( ddd & 0x1 );
```

Here is another approach:

```
x = aaa & 0xf;
x <<= 8;
x |= bbb & 0xff;
x <<= 3;
x |= ccc & 0x7;
x <<= 1;
x |= ddd & 1;
```

Chapter 10 Programming Exercises

10-1. The problem doesn't explicitly require it, but the correct approach is to declare a structure for a phone number, and then use this structure for three members in the billing information structure.

```
/*
** Structure for long distance telephone billing record.
*/
struct PHONE_NUMBER {
        short   area;
        short   exchange;
        short   station;
};

struct LONG_DISTANCE_BILL {
        short   month;
        short   day;
        short   year;
        int     time;
        struct  PHONE_NUMBER    called;
        struct  PHONE_NUMBER    calling;
        struct  PHONE_NUMBER    billed;
};
```

Solution 10.2a   phone1.h

Another approach is to have an array of PHONE_NUMBERs like this:

```
/*
** Structure for long distance telephone billing record.
*/
enum    PN_TYPE { CALLED, CALLING, BILLED };

struct LONG_DISTANCE_BILL {
        short    month;
        short    day;
        short    year;
        int      time;
        struct   PHONE_NUMBER    numbers[3];
};
```

Solution 10.2b   phone2.h

Chapter 11 Questions

11-3. If the input is contained in a file, it must have been put there by some other program, an editor for example. If this is the case, the maximum line length supported by the editor program makes a logical choice for your input buffer size.

11-4. The primary advantage is that the memory will be automatically freed when the function that allocated it returns. This property occurs because of how stacks work, and it guarantees that there will be no memory leaks. But this behavior is also a disadvantage. Because the allocated memory disappears when the function returns, it cannot be used for data that are passed back to the calling program.

11-5. a.   The literal constant 2 is used as the size of an integer. This value will work on machines with two-byte integers, but on machines with four-byte integers only half the needed memory will be allocated. sizeof should be used instead.

b.   The value returned from malloc is not checked. If memory runs out, it will be NULL.

c.   Adjusting the pointer back to change the subscript range will probably work, but it violates the Standard by going off the left end of the array.

d.   Having adjusted the pointer so that the subscript of the first element is one, the for loop then mistakenly starts at zero. On many systems this error will destroy information used by malloc to keep track of the heap, often causing the program to crash.

e. The input values are not checked to see if they are in the proper range before incrementing the array. Illegal input values can also cause the program to crash in interesting ways.

f. If the array is to be returned, it must not be `free`'d.

Chapter 11 Programming Exercises

11-2. This function allocates an array, and reallocates it as necessary using a fixed increment. The increment DELTA can be tuned to balance efficiency against wasted memory.

```
/*
** Read an EOF-terminated list of integers from the standard input
** and return a dynamically allocated array containing the values.
** The first element of the array contains a count of the number
** of values it contains.
*/

#include <stdio.h>
#include <malloc.h>

#define DELTA          100

int *
readints()
{
        int     *array;
        int     size;
        int     count;
        int     value;

        /*
        ** Get the initial array, large enough to hold DELTA values.
        */
        size = DELTA;
        array = malloc( ( size + 1 ) * sizeof( int ) );
        if( array == NULL )
                return NULL;

        /*
        ** Get values from the standard input.
        */
        count = 0;
        while( scanf( "%d", &value ) == 1 ){
```

Solution 11.2

continued . . .

```
            /*
            ** Make the array bigger if needed, then store
            ** the value.
            */
            count += 1;
            if( count > size ){
                    size += DELTA;
                    array = realloc( array,
                          ( size + 1 ) * sizeof( int ) );
                    if( array == NULL )
                            return NULL;

            }
            array[ count ] = value;
    }


    /*
    ** Resize the array to the exact size, then store the count
    ** and return the array.  This never makes the array bigger
    ** and so should never fail.  (Check it anyway!)
    */
    if( count < size ){
            array = realloc( array,
                ( count + 1 ) * sizeof( int ) );
            if( array == NULL )
                    return NULL;

    }
    array[ 0 ] = count;
    return array;

}
```

Solution 11.2   readints.c

Chapter 12 Questions

12-2. Compared to sll_insert, which doesn't have any special case code, the
       header node technique has only disadvantages. Paradoxically, the technique,
       which is claimed to eliminate the special case of an empty list, actually intro-
       duces code to handle special cases. When the list is created, the dummy node
       must be added. Other functions that manipulate the list must always skip over
       the dummy node. Finally, the dummy node wastes memory.

12-4. If the root node were dynamically allocated, the objective could be achieved by
       not allocating the complete node:

```
Node    *root;
root = malloc( sizeof(Node) - sizeof(ValueType) );
```

A safer approach is to declare a structure that contains just the pointers. The root is one of these structures, and each node includes one of them. The interesting aspect about this approach is the mutual dependence of the structures; each contains fields of the other type. The mutual dependence leads to a chicken-and-egg problem in their declaration: Which one is declared first? The problem is solved only with an incomplete declaration of one of the structure tags.

```
struct  DLL_NODE;

struct  DLL_POINTERS    {
        struct DLL_NODE *fwd;
        struct DLL_NODE *bwd;
};

struct  DLL_NODE        {
        struct DLL_POINTERS     pointers;
        int     value;
};
```

12-7. It is much more efficient to search the alternate structure than one list containing all the words. For example, to find a word that begins with the letter "b" it is no longer necessary to traverse past each of the nodes containing words that begin with "a." If the words began with all 26 letters of the alphabet with equal frequency, the search time would be improved by a factor of nearly 26. The actual improvement will be somewhat less than that.

Chapter 12 Programming Exercises

12-1. This function is simple, though it is specific to the type of node for which it is declared—you must know the internal structure of the node. The next chapter discusses techniques to solve this problem.

```
/*
** Count the number of nodes on a singly linked list.
*/

#include "singly_linked_list_node.h"
#include <stdio.h>

int
sll_count_nodes( struct NODE *first )
{
```

Solution 12.1

continued . . .

```
int      count;

for( count = 0; first != NULL; first = first->link ){
        count += 1;
}

return count;
}
```

Solution 12.1
sll_cnt.c

If called with a pointer to a node somewhere in the middle of a list, this function will count the number of nodes in the rest of the list.

12-5. First, the answer to the question: taking a pointer to the node we wish to remove makes the function independent of the type of data stored in the list, so by including different header files for different lists, the same code can be used with any type of values. On the other hand, if we don't already know which node contains the value to be deleted, we'll have to search for it first.

```
/*
** Remove a specified node from a singly linked list.  The first
** argument points to the root pointer for the list, and the second
** points to the node to be removed. TRUE is returned if it can be
** removed, otherwise FALSE is returned.
*/

#include <stdlib.h>
#include <stdio.h>
#include <assert.h>
#include "singly_linked_list_node.h"

#define FALSE   0
#define TRUE    1

int
sll_remove( struct NODE **linkp, struct NODE *delete )
{
        register Node   *current;

        assert( delete != NULL );

        /*
        ** Look for the indicated node.
```

Solution 12.5
continued . . .

```
*/
while( ( current = *linkp ) != NULL && current != delete )
        linkp = &current->link;

if( current == delete ){
        *linkp = current->link;
        free( current );
        return TRUE;
}
else
        return FALSE;
}
```

Solution 12.5   sll_remv.c

Note that having this function free the deleted node limits its use to lists of
dynamically allocated nodes. Another option would be to leave it to the caller
to delete the node if the function returns true. Of course memory leaks will
result if the caller doesn't delete nodes that were dynamically allocated.

A question for discussion: Why is the assert required in this function?

Chapter 13 Questions

13-1. a. VIII, b. III, c. X, d. XI, e. IV, f. IX, g. XVI, h. VII, i. VI, j. XIX,
      k. XXI, l. XXIII, m. XXV

13-4. Depending on your environment, it might help to declare the argument trans
      as a register variable. The benefit of putting pointers in registers is consider-
      able on some machines. Second, declare a local variable to hold the value
      trans->product, like this:

```
register Product *the_product;

the_product = trans->product;
the_product->orders += 1;
the_product->quantity_on_hand -= trans->quantity;
the_product->supplier->reorder_quantity
    += trans->quantity;
if( the_product->export_restricted ){
    . . .
}
```

This expression is used over and over and need not be recomputed each time.
Some compilers will do both of these things for you automatically but some
won't.

13-7.   The sole advantage is so obvious that it may be hard to think of, and it is the reason the function was written in the first place—this function makes it easier to process the command line arguments. Everything else about this function is a disadvantage. You can only process the arguments in the manner supported by the function. Because it is not part of the Standard, using getopt reduces the portability of your program.

13-11.   First, some implementations put string literals into memory that cannot be modified. Attempting to overwrite such a literal will terminate the program. Second, some implementations will only store one copy of string literals that are used more than once in a program. Modifying one of these literals will change the value of all of them, making debugging difficult. For example, the statement

```
printf( "Hello\n" );
```

will actually print Bye! if the statement

```
strcpy( "Hello\n", "Bye!\n" );
```

were executed first.

Chapter 13 Programming Exercises

13-1.   This problem was given in Chapter 9 but without the restriction about if statements. The intent of the restriction is to get you to think about alternative implementations. The function is_not_print, which negates the result of isprint, avoids the need for a special case in the main loop. To improve this program, rewrite it with an array of structures, where each element holds the function pointer, label, and count for one category.

```
/*
** Compute the percentage of characters read from the standard
** input that are in each of several character categories.
*/
#include <stdlib.h>
#include <stdio.h>
#include <ctype.h>

/*
**      Define a function to compute whether a character is not
**      printable; this eliminates a special case for this
**      category in the code below.
*/
```

Solution 13.1   <continued>continued . . .</continued>

```
int is_not_print( int ch )
{
        return !isprint( ch );
}

/*
**      Jump table of classification functions for each category.
*/
static  int     (*test_func[])( int ) = {
        iscntrl,
        isspace,
        isdigit,
        islower,
        isupper,
        ispunct,
        is_not_print
};
#define N_CATEGORIES    \
          ( sizeof( test_func ) / sizeof( test_func[ 0 ] ) )

/*
**      The name of each of the character categories.
*/
char    *label[] = {
        "control",
        "whitespace",
        "digit",
        "lower case",
        "upper case",
        "punctuation",
        "non-printable"
};

/*
**      Number of characters seen in each category so far, and
**      total # of characters.
*/
int     count[ N_CATEGORIES ];
int     total;

main()
{
        int     ch;
        int     category;
```

Solution 13.1

continued . . .

```
/*
** Read and process each character
*/
while( (ch = getchar()) != EOF ){
        total += 1;

        /*
        ** Call each of the test functions with this
        ** character; if true, increment the associated
        ** counter.
        */
        for( category = 0; category < N_CATEGORIES;
             category += 1 ){
                  if( test_func[ category ]( ch ) )
                          count[ category ] += 1;

        }

}

/*
** Print the results.
*/
if( total == 0 ){
        printf( "No characters in the input!\n" );
}
else {
        for( category = 0; category < N_CATEGORIES;
             category += 1 ){
                printf( "%3.0f%% %s characters\n",
                        count[ category ] * 100.0 / total,
                        label[ category ] );

        }

}

        return EXIT_SUCCESS;

}
```

Solution 13.1   char_cat.c

Chapter 14 Questions

14-1. The file name and current line might be handy when printed in error messages,
      particularly in the early stages of debugging. In fact, the assert macro uses
      them for this purpose. __DATE__ and __TIME__ might be used to compile
      version information into a program. Finally, __STDC__ might be used with
      conditional compilation to select between ANSI and pre-ANSI constructs in
      source code that must be processed by both types of compilers.

14-6.   It is impossible to determine from the code that was given. If process is implemented as a macro and evaluates its argument more than once, the side effect of incrementing the subscript will likely cause the result to be incorrect.

14-7.   There are several things wrong with this code, some of which are rather subtle. The major problem is that the macro *depends on* its argument having the side effect of incrementing the array subscript. This dependency is very dangerous, and is made worse by the fact that the name of the macro doesn't indicate what it is really doing (which is the second problem). Suppose the loop is later rewritten like this:

```
for( i = 0; i < SIZE; i += 1 )
        sum += SUM( array[ i ] );
```

Though it looks equivalent, the program now fails. The final problem: Because the macro always accesses two elements in the array, the program fails if SIZE is an odd value.

Chapter 14 Programming Exercises

14-1.   The only tricky thing about this problem is the fact that both options may be selected. This possibility rules out the use of #elif to help determine if neither one was defined.

```
/*
** Print the indicated ledger in whichever style(s) is
** indicated by the symbols that are defined.
*/

void
print_ledger( int x )
{
#ifdef   OPTION_LONG
#        define  OK       1
         print_ledger_long( x );
#endif

#ifdef   OPTION_DETAILED
#        define  OK       1
         print_ledger_detailed( x );
#endif

#ifndef  OK
         print_ledger_default( x );
```

Solution 14.1

continued . . .

```
#endif
}
```

Solution 14.1   prt_ldgr.c

Chapter 15 Questions

15-1. If the open failed for any reason, the value returned will be NULL. When this value is passed to any subsequent I/O function, that function will fail. It depends on the implementation whether or not the program will abort. If it doesn't, then the I/O operation may have modified the contents of some unpredictable locations in memory.

15-2. It will fail because the FILE structure you are trying to use has never been initialized properly. The contents of unpredictable memory locations may be changed in the attempt.

15-4. Different operating systems provide various mechanisms to detect redirection, but usually the program does not need to know whether its input is coming from a file or from a keyboard. The operating system takes care of handling most of the device-independent aspects of input operations, and the library I/O functions take care of the rest. For most applications, the program can read the standard input in the same way no matter where the input is actually coming from.

15-16. If the value is 1.4049, the %.3f code will cause the trailing 4 to be rounded to a 5, but with the %.2f code the trailing 0 is not rounded up because the first digit that is truncated is a 4.

Chapter 15 Programming Exercises

15-2. The assumption that the input lines are restricted in length simplifies matters greatly. If gets is used, the buffer must be at least 81 bytes to hold 80 characters of data plus the terminating null. If fgets is used, it must be at least 82 bytes long because the newline is also stored.

```
/*
** Copy standard input to standard output, one line
** at a time.  Lines must be 80 data bytes or shorter.
*/

#include <stdio.h>

#define BUFSIZE 81        /* 80 data bytes + the null byte */
```

Solution 15.2   *continued . . .*

```
main()
{
        char     buf[BUFSIZE];

        while( gets( buf ) != NULL )
                puts( buf );

        return EXIT_SUCCESS;
}
```

Solution 15.2   prog2.c

15-9. The restriction that the string cannot contain newlines means that the program can read data from the file a line at a time. There is no need to try to match strings that cross line boundaries. This restriction means that strstr can be used for searching the lines. The restriction on the length of the input lines simplifies the solution. The length limitation could be removed with a dynamically allocated buffer that is lengthened when an input line is found that does not completely fit. The majority of the program deals with getting the filenames and opening files.

```
/*
** Find and print all of the lines in the named files that
** contain the given string.
**
**       Usage:
**                fgrep string file [ file ... ]
*/

#include <stdio.h>
#include <string.h>
#include <stdlib.h>

#define BUFFER_SIZE      512

void
search( char *filename, FILE *stream, char *string )
{
        char     buffer[ BUFFER_SIZE ];

        while( fgets( buffer, BUFFER_SIZE, stream ) != NULL ){
                if( strstr( buffer, string ) != NULL ){
```

Solution 15.9   continued . . .

```
                                if( filename != NULL )
                                        printf( "%s:", filename );
                                fputs( buffer, stdout );
                        }
                }
}

int
main( int ac, char **av )
{
        char    *string;

        if( ac <= 1 ){
                fprintf( stderr, "Usage: fgrep string file ...\n" );
                exit( EXIT_FAILURE );
        }

        /*
        ** Get the string.
        */
        string = *++av;

        /*
        ** Process the files.
        */
        if( ac <= 2 )
                search( NULL, stdin, string );
        else {
                while( *++av != NULL ){
                        FILE    *stream;

                        stream = fopen( *av, "r" );
                        if( stream == NULL )
                                perror( *av );
                        else {
                                search( *av, stream, string );
                                fclose( stream );
                        }
                }
        }

        return EXIT_SUCCESS;
}
```

Solution 15.9   fgrep.c

Chapter 16 Questions

16-1. This situation is not defined by the Standard, so you have to try it and see. But even if it appears to have some useful result, *don't use it!* Your code won't be portable.

16-3. It will depend on the quality of the random number generator supplied with your compiler. Ideally, a random series of zeros and ones is produced. Some random number generators are not that good and produce an alternating series of zeros and ones—not very random looking. If your implementation is one of these, you may find that the high order bits are more random than the low order bits.

16-5. First, a NULL pointer must be passed to time. Nothing is passed here, so the compiler should complain that the call does not match the prototype. Second, a pointer to the time value must be passed to localtime, which the compiler should also catch. Third, the month is a number in the range 0–11, but it is being printed as is in the date portion of the output. One should be added to the month before printing. Fourth, the year will print strangely when the year 2000 arrives.

Chapter 16 Programming Exercises

16-2. Except for the "equally likely" requirement, this problem is trivial. Here is an example. Ordinarily you would just take the random number modulo 6, giving a value from 0 to 5, add 1 to this value and return it. But if the largest value returned by the random generator is 32,767, the values are not all equally likely. The values from 0 to 32,765 will return equal numbers of 0's, 1's 2's, and so forth. But the last two values, 32,766 and 32,767, will produce 0 and 1 respectively, giving each of them a greater likelihood of occurring (5462/32768 instead of 5461/32768). The difference is minute only because we want such a small range of answers. If the function were trying to generate a random number in the range 1 to 30,000, then the first 2,768 values would be twice as likely to occur as any of the others. The loop eliminates this error by generating another random value should either of these last two values occur.

```
/*
** Simulate the throwing of a six-sided die by returning a
** random number in the range one through six.
*/
#include <stdlib.h>
#include <stdio.h>
```

Solution 16.2

continued . . .

```
/*
**      Compute the largest number returned by the random number
**      generator that will produce a six as the value of the die.
*/
#define MAX_OK_RAND      \
            (int)( ( ( (long)RAND_MAX + 1 ) / 6 ) * 6 - 1 )


int
throw_die( void ){
        static  int     is_seeded = 0;
        int     value;

        if( !is_seeded ){
                is_seeded = 1;
                srand( (unsigned int)time( NULL ) );
        }

        do {
                value = rand();
        } while( value > MAX_OK_RAND );

        return value % 6 + 1;
}
```

Solution 16.2   die.c

16-7. This program is essentially a throwaway. The inelegant solution is more than
adequate for the task.

```
/*
** Test the randomness of the values produced by rand.
*/

#include <stdlib.h>
#include <stdio.h>

/*
**      Arrays to count the relative frequency of various numbers.
*/
int     frequency2[2];
int     frequency3[3];
int     frequency4[4];
int     frequency5[5];
int     frequency6[6];
```

Solution 16.7   *continued . . .*

```
int      frequency7[7];
int      frequency8[8];
int      frequency9[9];
int      frequency10[10];

/*
**       Arrays to count the cyclic frequency of various numbers.
*/
int      cycle2[2][2];
int      cycle3[3][3];
int      cycle4[4][4];
int      cycle5[5][5];
int      cycle6[6][6];
int      cycle7[7][7];
int      cycle8[8][8];
int      cycle9[9][9];
int      cycle10[10][10];


/*
**       Macro to count both the frequency and cyclic frequency for
**       a specific number.
*/
#define CHECK( number, f_table, c_table )                           \
                 remainder = x % number;                            \
                 f_table[ remainder ] += 1;                         \
                 c_table[ remainder ][ last_x % number ] += 1

/*
**       Macro to print a frequency table.
*/
#define PRINT_F( number, f_table )                                  \
        printf( "\nFrequency of random numbers modulo %d\n\t",    \
            number );                                               \
        for( i = 0; i < number; i += 1 )                            \
                printf( " %5d", f_table[ i ] );                     \
        printf( "\n" )


/*
**       Macro to print a cyclic frequency table.
*/
#define PRINT_C( number, c_table )                                  \
        printf( "\nCyclic frequency of random numbers modulo %d\n", \
            number );                                               \
        for( i = 0; i < number; i += 1 ){                           \
```

Solution 16.7

continued . . .

```
                    printf( "\t" );                                      \
                    for( j = 0; j < number; j += 1 )                     \
                            printf( " %5d", c_table[ i ][ j ] );         \
                    printf( "\n" );                                      \
        }


int
main( int ac, char **av )
{
        int     i;
        int     j;
        int     x;
        int     last_x;
        int     remainder;

        /*
        ** If a seed was given, seed the generator.
        */
        if( ac > 1 )
                srand( atoi( av[ 1 ] ) );


        last_x = rand();


        /*
        ** Run the tests.
        */
        for( i = 0; i < 10000; i += 1 ){
                x = rand();
                CHECK( 2, frequency2, cycle2 );
                CHECK( 3, frequency3, cycle3 );
                CHECK( 4, frequency4, cycle4 );
                CHECK( 5, frequency5, cycle5 );
                CHECK( 6, frequency6, cycle6 );
                CHECK( 7, frequency7, cycle7 );
                CHECK( 8, frequency8, cycle8 );
                CHECK( 9, frequency9, cycle9 );
                CHECK( 10, frequency10, cycle10 );
                last_x = x;
        }


        /*
        ** Print the results.
        */
        PRINT_F( 2, frequency2 );
```

Solution 16.7

continued . . .

```
PRINT_F( 3, frequency3 );
PRINT_F( 4, frequency4 );
PRINT_F( 5, frequency5 );
PRINT_F( 6, frequency6 );
PRINT_F( 7, frequency7 );
PRINT_F( 8, frequency8 );
PRINT_F( 9, frequency9 );
PRINT_F( 10, frequency10 );

PRINT_C( 2, cycle2 );
PRINT_C( 3, cycle3 );
PRINT_C( 4, cycle4 );
PRINT_C( 5, cycle5 );
PRINT_C( 6, cycle6 );
PRINT_C( 7, cycle7 );
PRINT_C( 8, cycle8 );
PRINT_C( 9, cycle9 );
PRINT_C( 10, cycle10 );

return EXIT_SUCCESS;
}
```

Solution 16.7   testrand.c

Chapter 17 Questions

17-3.   The traditional and the alternate interface can easily coexist. `top` returns the
        value on the top of the stack without removing it, and `pop` removes the value
        and returns it. The client who wants the traditional behavior uses `pop` in the
        traditional manner. The alternate interface is obtained by calling `top` and
        ignoring the value that `pop` returns.

17-7.   Because each was allocated individually using `malloc`, popping them one by
        one ensures that each is freed. The code to free them already exists in `pop`, so
        calling it is better than duplicating the code.

17-9.   Consider that an array of five elements can be in six distinct states: it may be
        empty, or it may contain one, two, three, four, or five values. But `front` and
        `rear` must always refer to one of the five elements in the array. So for any
        given value of `front`, there are only five distinct states for `rear`: it can be
        equal to `front`, `front + 1`, `front + 2`, `front + 3`, or `front + 4`
        (remember that `front + 5` is really `front` because of the wraparound). It is
        not possible to represent six distinct states with variables that can only attain
        five distinct states.

17-12. Assuming you had a pointer to the rear of the list, a singly linked list would be fine. The queue is never traversed backwards, so the extra link of a doubly linked list has no advantage.

17-18. An in-order traversal does ascending order. There isn't a predefined traversal that gives descending order, though modifying the in-order traversal to visit the right subtree before the left subtree would do the job.

Chapter 17 Programming Exercises

17-3. This conversion is similar to the linked stack, but when the last value is removed, the `rear` pointer must also be set NULL.

```
/*
** A queue implemented with a linked list.  This queue has no size
** limit.
*/
#include "queue.h"
#include <stdio.h>
#include <assert.h>

/*
**      Define a structure to hold one value.  The link field will
**      point to the next value on the queue.
*/
typedef struct QUEUE_NODE {
        QUEUE_TYPE      value;
        struct QUEUE_NODE *next;
} QueueNode;

/*
**      Pointers to the first and the last nodes on the queue.
*/
static  QueueNode       *front;
static  QueueNode       *rear;

/*
**      destroy_queue
*/
void
destroy_queue( void )
{
        while( !is_empty() )
                delete();
}
```

Solution 17.3

continued . . .

```
/*
**        insert
*/
void
insert( QUEUE_TYPE value )
{
        QueueNode        *new_node;

        /*
        ** Allocate a new node, and fill in its fields.
        */
        new_node = (QueueNode *)malloc( sizeof( QueueNode ) );
        assert( new_node != NULL );
        new_node->value = value;
        new_node->next = NULL;

        /*
        ** Insert it at the end of the queue.
        */
        if( rear == NULL ){
                front = new_node;
        }
        else {
                rear->next = new_node;
        }
        rear = new_node;
}

/*
**        delete
*/
void
delete( void )
{
        QueueNode        *next_node;

        /*
        ** Remove a node from the front of the queue.  If this is the
        ** last node, set rear to NULL too.
        */
        assert( !is_empty() );
        next_node = front->next;
        free( front );
        front = next_node;
```

Solution 17.3

continued . . .

```
            if( front == NULL )
                    rear = NULL;
}


/*
**      first
*/
QUEUE_TYPE first( void )
{
        assert( !is_empty() );
        return front->value;
}

/*
**      is_empty
*/
int
is_empty( void )
{
        return front == NULL;
}

/*
**      is_full
*/
int
is_full( void )
{
        return 0;
}
```

Solution 17.3   l_queue.c

17-6. If the queue module is used, the name clashes will have to be resolved.

```
/*
** Do a breadth_first_traversal of an arrayed binary search tree.
*/
void
breadth_first_traversal( void (*callback)( TREE_TYPE value ) )
{
        int     current;
        int     child;
```

Solution 17.6   *continued . . .*

```
/*
** Insert the root node into the queue.
*/
queue_insert( 1 );

/*
** While the queue is not empty...
*/
while( !is_queue_empty() ){
        /*
        ** Take the first value off the queue and process it
        */
        current = queue_first();
        queue_delete();
        callback( tree[ current ] );

        /*
        ** Add the children of the node to the queue.
        */
        child = left_child( current );
        if( child < ARRAY_SIZE && tree[ child ] != 0 )
                queue_insert( child );
        child = left_child( current );
        if( child < ARRAY_SIZE && tree[ child ] != 0 )
                queue_insert( child );
    }
}
```

Solution 17.6   breadth.c

Chapter 18 Questions

18-5. This idea sounds great, but it cannot be implemented. The `register` keyword
       is optional in the function's prototype, so there isn't a reliable way that the
       calling function can tell which (if any) arguments are so declared.

18-6. No, it is not possible; only the calling function knows how many arguments
       were actually pushed on the stack. If an argument count were pushed, how-
       ever, then the called function could remove the arguments. It would first have
       pop the return address and save it, though.

Chapter 18 Programming Exercises

18-3. The answer actually depends on the specific environment, but here is a solution
       for the environment that was discussed in this chapter. The user must provide
       the actual type of the argument after it undergoes the standard type conver-
       sions, just as with the real `stdarg.h` macros.

```
/*
** Replacement for the library stdarg.h macros.
*/

/*
** va_list
**      Define the type for a variable that will  hold a pointer to
**      the variable portion of the argument list.  char * is used
**      because arithmetic on them is not scaled.
*/
typedef char    *va_list;

/*
** va_start
**      A macro to initialize a va_list variable to point to the
**      first of the variable arguments on the stack.
*/
#define va_start(arg_ptr,arg)  arg_ptr = (char *)&arg + sizeof( arg )

/*
** va_arg
**      A macro that returns the value of the next variable argument
**      on the stack; it also increments arg_ptr to the next
**      argument.
*/
#define va_arg(arg_ptr,type)    *((type *)arg_ptr)++

/*
** va_end
**      Called after the last access to variable arguments; nothing
**      needs to be done in this environment.
*/
#define va_end(arg_ptr)
```

Solution 18.3   mystdarg.h

Index